FLORIDORO

THE OTHER VOICE IN EARLY MODERN EUROPE

A Series Edited by Margaret L. King and Albert Rabil Jr.

RECENT BOOKS IN THE SERIES

Moderata Fonte (Modesta Pozzo)

FLORIDORO

A Chivalric Romance

෨ඁ

Edited with an Introduction by Valeria Finucci
Translated by Julia Kisacky
Annotated by Valeria Finucci and Julia Kisacky

THE UNIVERSITY OF CHICAGO PRESS
Chicago & London

Moderata Fonte (Modesta Pozzo), 1555–1592

Valeria Finucci is professor of Italian Studies at Duke University. Among her publications is Giulia Bigolina's *Urania: A Romance*, published in the Other Voice in Early Modern Europe series by the University of Chicago Press.

Julia Kisacky is senior lecturer in Italian at Baylor University. She is the author of *Magic in Boiardo and Ariosto*.

The University of Chicago Press, Chicago 60637
The University of Chicago Press, Ltd., London
© 2006 by The University of Chicago
All rights reserved. Published 2006
Printed in the United States of America

15 14 13 12 11 10 09 08 07 06   1 2 3 4 5

ISBN-13: 978-0-226-25677-1 (cloth)
ISBN-13: 978-0-226-25678-8 (paper)
ISBN-10: 0-226-25677-4 (cloth)
ISBN-10: 0-226-25678-2 (paper)

Publication of this volume was supported in part by a subvention from Baylor University College of Arts and Sciences.

Library of Congress Cataloging-in-Publication

Fonte, Moderata, 1555–1592.
[Floridoro. English]
Floridoro : a chivalric romance / Moderata Fonte (Modesta Pozzo) ; introduction by Valeria Finucci ; translated by Julia Kisacky ; annotated by Valeria Finucci and Julia Kisacky.
p.   cm. — (The other voice in early modern Europe)
Includes bibliographical references and index.
ISBN 0-226-25677-4 (cloth : alk. paper) — ISBN 0-226-25678-2 (pbk. : alk. paper)
I. Finucci, Valeria. II. Kisacky, Julia, 1965– III. Title. IV. Series.
PQ4623.F36F5613   2006
851'.4—dc22
2006011167

To Paola Finucci, Jeanne Kisacky, and sisterhood

CONTENTS

ACKNOWLEDGMENTS

The making of this edition has been a thoroughly collaborative project, and we are indebted to many friends and institutions for the support they have provided. Our first debt of gratitude is to Albert Rabil and Margaret L. King, the editors of this series, who encouraged the project and saw it through. We also would like to thank our anonymous reader for his/her sharp comments and further bibliographical advice, and Randy Petilos at the University of Chicago Press for his wit, solicitude, and savoir faire.

I (JK) started to be interested in Moderata Fonte during an NEH 2001 Summer Institute, titled "A Literature of Their Own? Women Writing— Venice, London, Paris—1550–1700." This institute, ably directed by Al Rabil with the invaluable assistance of his wife, Janet, introduced me to a number of colleagues with similar interests and was both an intense educational experience and a rare pleasure. I am immensely grateful to my sister Jeanne Kisacky for her comments on the draft from a scholarly, nonspecialist viewpoint. I have learned a great deal during the process of writing this translation and would like to thank Gloria Allaire, Francesca D'Alessandro Behr, Heidi Hornik-Parsons, Liz Horodowich, William Jensen, Thomas F. Madden, John M. Najemy, Eric Rust, Janet Sheets, John Thorburn, and Amy Vail for their collegial assistance. Lastly, I would also like to thank my department chair, Manuel Ortuño, and the College of Arts and Sciences of Baylor University for giving me a teaching reduction in spring 2004, which enabled me to move the project along more rapidly.

I (VF) jumped at the opportunity to see *Floridoro* in translation after I had worked on it for its publication in a modern Italian edition in 1995 and seen the genre of romances of chivalry written by women take a life of its own since. I would like to express my gratitude again to Lina Bolzoni and Mario Saccenti for encouraging me to pursue my interest in Fonte more than ten years ago, and more recently to Naomi Yavneh and Naomi Miller for keeping me focused, and Eleonora Carinci for her enthusiasm. Charles Ross and John Watkins invited me to share an earlier version of the introduction with a scholarly crowd at the Newberry Library and I would like to thank them for their comments. My own institution, Duke University, provided me with a research fund to travel to Venice.

When we started this project we hardly knew each other, but working at it together has been such a smooth, mutually enjoyable experience that we should perhaps do it again.

Valeria Finucci
Julia Kisacky

THE OTHER VOICE IN EARLY MODERN EUROPE: INTRODUCTION TO THE SERIES

Margaret L. King and Albert Rabil Jr.

THE OLD VOICE AND THE OTHER VOICE

In western Europe and the United States, women are nearing equality in the professions, in business, and in politics. Most enjoy access to education, reproductive rights, and autonomy in financial affairs. Issues vital to women are on the public agenda: equal pay, child care, domestic abuse, breast cancer research, and curricular revision with an eye to the inclusion of women.

These recent achievements have their origins in things women (and some male supporters) said for the first time about six hundred years ago. Theirs is the "other voice," in contradistinction to the "first voice," the voice of the educated men who created Western culture. Coincident with a general reshaping of European culture in the period 1300–1700 (called the Renaissance or early modern period), questions of female equality and opportunity were raised that still resound and are still unresolved.

The other voice emerged against the backdrop of a three-thousand-year history of the derogation of women rooted in the civilizations related to Western culture: Hebrew, Greek, Roman, and Christian. Negative attitudes toward women inherited from these traditions pervaded the intellectual, medical, legal, religious, and social systems that developed during the European Middle Ages.

The following pages describe the traditional, overwhelmingly male views of women's nature inherited by early modern Europeans and the new tradition that the "other voice" called into being to begin to challenge reigning assumptions. This review should serve as a framework for understanding the texts published in the series the Other Voice in Early Modern Europe. Introductions specific to each text and author follow this essay in all the volumes of the series.

TRADITIONAL VIEWS OF WOMEN, 500 B.C.E.–1500 C.E.

Embedded in the philosophical and medical theories of the ancient Greeks were perceptions of the female as inferior to the male in both mind and body. Similarly, the structure of civil legislation inherited from the ancient Romans was biased against women, and the views on women developed by Christian thinkers out of the Hebrew Bible and the Christian New Testament were negative and disabling. Literary works composed in the vernacular of ordinary people, and widely recited or read, conveyed these negative assumptions. The social networks within which most women lived—those of the family and the institutions of the Roman Catholic Church—were shaped by this negative tradition and sharply limited the areas in which women might act in and upon the world.

GREEK PHILOSOPHY AND FEMALE NATURE. Greek biology assumed that women were inferior to men and defined them as merely childbearers and housekeepers. This view was authoritatively expressed in the works of the philosopher Aristotle.

Aristotle thought in dualities. He considered action superior to inaction, form (the inner design or structure of any object) superior to matter, completion to incompletion, possession to deprivation. In each of these dualities, he associated the male principle with the superior quality and the female with the inferior. "The male principle in nature," he argued, "is associated with active, formative and perfected characteristics, while the female is passive, material and deprived, desiring the male in order to become complete."[1] Men are always identified with virile qualities, such as judgment, courage, and stamina, and women with their opposites—irrationality, cowardice, and weakness.

The masculine principle was considered superior even in the womb. The man's semen, Aristotle believed, created the form of a new human creature, while the female body contributed only matter. (The existence of the ovum, and with it the other facts of human embryology, was not established until the seventeenth century.) Although the later Greek physician Galen believed there was a female component in generation, contributed by "female semen," the followers of both Aristotle and Galen saw the male role in human generation as more active and more important.

In the Aristotelian view, the male principle sought always to reproduce

---

1. Aristotle, *Physics* 1.9.192a20–24, in *The Complete Works of Aristotle*, ed. Jonathan Barnes, rev. Oxford trans., 2 vols. (Princeton, 1984), 1:328.

itself. The creation of a female was always a mistake, therefore, resulting from an imperfect act of generation. Every female born was considered a "defective" or "mutilated" male (as Aristotle's terminology has variously been translated), a "monstrosity" of nature.[2]

For Greek theorists, the biology of males and females was the key to their psychology. The female was softer and more docile, more apt to be despondent, querulous, and deceitful. Being incomplete, moreover, she craved sexual fulfillment in intercourse with a male. The male was intellectual, active, and in control of his passions.

These psychological polarities derived from the theory that the universe consisted of four elements (earth, fire, air, and water), expressed in human bodies as four "humors" (black bile, yellow bile, blood, and phlegm) considered, respectively, dry, hot, damp, and cold and corresponding to mental states ("melancholic," "choleric," "sanguine," "phlegmatic"). In this scheme the male, sharing the principles of earth and fire, was dry and hot; the female, sharing the principles of air and water, was cold and damp.

Female psychology was further affected by her dominant organ, the uterus (womb), *hystera* in Greek. The passions generated by the womb made women lustful, deceitful, talkative, irrational, indeed—when these affects were in excess—"hysterical."

Aristotle's biology also had social and political consequences. If the male principle was superior and the female inferior, then in the household, as in the state, men should rule and women must be subordinate. That hierarchy did not rule out the companionship of husband and wife, whose cooperation was necessary for the welfare of children and the preservation of property. Such mutuality supported male preeminence.

Aristotle's teacher Plato suggested a different possibility: that men and women might possess the same virtues. The setting for this proposal is the imaginary and ideal Republic that Plato sketches in a dialogue of that name. Here, for a privileged elite capable of leading wisely, all distinctions of class and wealth dissolve, as, consequently, do those of gender. Without households or property, as Plato constructs his ideal society, there is no need for the subordination of women. Women may therefore be educated to the same level as men to assume leadership. Plato's Republic remained imaginary, however. In real societies, the subordination of women remained the norm and the prescription.

The views of women inherited from the Greek philosophical tradition became the basis for medieval thought. In the thirteenth century, the su-

2. Aristotle, *Generation of Animals* 2.3.737a27–28, in *The Complete Works*, 1: 1144.

preme Scholastic philosopher Thomas Aquinas, among others, still echoed Aristotle's views of human reproduction, of male and female personalities, and of the preeminent male role in the social hierarchy.

ROMAN LAW AND THE FEMALE CONDITION. Roman law, like Greek philosophy, underlay medieval thought and shaped medieval society. The ancient belief that adult property-owning men should administer households and make decisions affecting the community at large is the very fulcrum of Roman law.

About 450 B.C.E., during Rome's republican era, the community's customary law was recorded (legendarily) on twelve tablets erected in the city's central forum. It was later elaborated by professional jurists whose activity increased in the imperial era, when much new legislation was passed, especially on issues affecting family and inheritance. This growing, changing body of laws was eventually codified in the *Corpus of Civil Law* under the direction of the emperor Justinian, generations after the empire ceased to be ruled from Rome. That *Corpus*, read and commented on by medieval scholars from the eleventh century on, inspired the legal systems of most of the cities and kingdoms of Europe.

Laws regarding dowries, divorce, and inheritance pertain primarily to women. Since those laws aimed to maintain and preserve property, the women concerned were those from the property-owning minority. Their subordination to male family members points to the even greater subordination of lower-class and slave women, about whom the laws speak little.

In the early republic, the *paterfamilias*, or "father of the family," possessed *patria potestas*, "paternal power." The term *pater*, "father," in both these cases does not necessarily mean biological father but denotes the head of a household. The father was the person who owned the household's property and, indeed, its human members. The *paterfamilias* had absolute power—including the power, rarely exercised, of life or death—over his wife, his children, and his slaves, as much as his cattle.

Male children could be "emancipated," an act that granted legal autonomy and the right to own property. Those over fourteen could be emancipated by a special grant from the father or automatically by their father's death. But females could never be emancipated; instead, they passed from the authority of their father to that of a husband or, if widowed or orphaned while still unmarried, to a guardian or tutor.

Marriage in its traditional form placed the woman under her husband's authority, or *manus*. He could divorce her on grounds of adultery, drinking wine, or stealing from the household, but she could not divorce him. She could neither possess property in her own right nor bequeath any to her children upon her death. When her husband died, the household property passed not to her but to his male heirs. And when her father died, she had no claim to any family inheritance, which was directed to her brothers or more remote male relatives. The effect of these laws was to exclude women from civil society, itself based on property ownership.

In the later republican and imperial periods, these rules were significantly modified. Women rarely married according to the traditional form. The practice of "free" marriage allowed a woman to remain under her father's authority, to possess property given her by her father (most frequently the "dowry," recoverable from the husband's household on his death), and to inherit from her father. She could also bequeath property to her own children and divorce her husband, just as he could divorce her.

Despite this greater freedom, women still suffered enormous disability under Roman law. Heirs could belong only to the father's side, never the mother's. Moreover, although she could bequeath her property to her children, she could not establish a line of succession in doing so. A woman was "the beginning and end of her own family," said the jurist Ulpian. Moreover, women could play no public role. They could not hold public office, represent anyone in a legal case, or even witness a will. Women had only a private existence and no public personality.

The dowry system, the guardian, women's limited ability to transmit wealth, and total political disability are all features of Roman law adopted by the medieval communities of western Europe, although modified according to local customary laws..

CHRISTIAN DOCTINE AND WOMEN'S PLACE. The Hebrew Bible and the Christian New Testament authorized later writers to limit women to the realm of the family and to burden them with the guilt of original sin. The passages most fruitful for this purpose were the creation narratives in Genesis and sentences from the Epistles defining women's role within the Christian family and community.

Each of the first two chapters of Genesis contains a creation narrative. In the first "God created man in his own image, in the image of God he created him; male and female he created them" (Gn 1:27). In the second, God created Eve from Adam's rib (2:21–23). Christian theologians relied principally on Genesis 2 for their understanding of the relation between man and woman, interpreting the creation of Eve from Adam as proof of her subordination to him.

The creation story in Genesis 2 leads to that of the temptations in Genesis 3: of Eve by the wily serpent and of Adam by Eve. As read by Christian theologians from Tertullian to Thomas Aquinas, the narrative made Eve responsible for the Fall and its consequences. She instigated the act; she deceived her husband; she suffered the greater punishment. Her disobedience made it necessary for Jesus to be incarnated and to die on the cross. From the pulpit, moralists and preachers for centuries conveyed to women the guilt that they bore for original sin.

The Epistles offered advice to early Christians on building communities of the faithful. Among the matters to be regulated was the place of women. Paul offered views favorable to women in Galatians 3:28: "There is neither Jew nor Greek, there is neither slave nor free, there is neither male nor female; for you are all one in Christ Jesus." Paul also referred to women as his coworkers and placed them on a par with himself and his male coworkers (Phlm 4:2–3; Rom 16:1–3; 1 Cor 16:19). Elsewhere, Paul limited women's possibilities: "But I want you to understand that the head of every man is Christ; the head of a woman is her husband, and the head of Christ is God" (1 Cor 11:3).

Biblical passages by later writers (although attributed to Paul) enjoined women to forgo jewels, expensive clothes, and elaborate coiffures; and they forbade women to "teach or have authority over men," telling them to "learn in silence with all submissiveness" as is proper for one responsible for sin, consoling them, however, with the thought that they will be saved through childbearing (1 Tm 2:9–15). Other texts among the later Epistles defined women as the weaker sex and emphasized their subordination to their husbands (1 Pt 3:7; Col 3:18; Eph 5:22–23).

These passages from the New Testament became the arsenal employed by theologians of the early church to transmit negative attitudes toward women to medieval Christian culture—above all, Tertullian (*On the Apparel of Women*), Jerome (*Against Jovinian*), and Augustine (*The Literal Meaning of Genesis*).

THE IMAGE OF WOMEN IN MEDIEVAL LITERATURE. The philosophical, legal, and religious traditions born in antiquity formed the basis of the medieval intellectual synthesis wrought by trained thinkers, mostly clerics, writing in Latin and based largely in universities. The vernacular literary tradition that developed alongside the learned tradition also spoke about female nature and women's roles. Medieval stories, poems, and epics also portrayed women negatively—as lustful and deceitful—while praising good housekeepers and loyal wives as replicas of the Virgin Mary or the female saints and martyrs.

There is an exception in the movement of "courtly love" that evolved in southern France from the twelfth century. Courtly love was the erotic love between a nobleman and noblewoman, the latter usually superior in social rank. It was always adulterous. From the conventions of courtly love derive modern Western notions of romantic love. The tradition has had an impact disproportionate to its size, for it affected only a tiny elite, and very few women. The exaltation of the female lover probably does not reflect a higher evaluation of women or a step toward their sexual liberation. More likely it gives expression to the social and sexual tensions besetting the knightly class at a specific historical juncture.

The literary fashion of courtly love was on the wane by the thirteenth century, when the widely read *Romance of the Rose* was composed in French by two authors of significantly different dispositions. Guillaume de Lorris composed the initial four thousand verses about 1235, and Jean de Meun added about seventeen thousand verses—more than four times the original—about 1265.

The fragment composed by Guillaume de Lorris stands squarely in the tradition of courtly love. Here the poet, in a dream, is admitted into a walled garden where he finds a magic fountain in which a rosebush is reflected. He longs to pick one rose, but the thorns prevent his doing so, even as he is wounded by arrows from the god of love, whose commands he agrees to obey. The rest of this part of the poem recounts the poet's unsuccessful efforts to pluck the rose.

The longer part of the *Romance* by Jean de Meun also describes a dream. But here allegorical characters give long didactic speeches, providing a social satire on a variety of themes, some pertaining to women. Love is an anxious and tormented state, the poem explains: women are greedy and manipulative, marriage is miserable, beautiful women are lustful, ugly ones cease to please, and a chaste woman is as rare as a black swan.

Shortly after Jean de Meun completed *The Romance of the Rose*, Mathéolus penned his *Lamentations*, a long Latin diatribe against marriage translated into French about a century later. The *Lamentations* sum up medieval attitudes toward women and provoked the important response by Christine de Pizan in her *Book of the City of Ladies*.

In 1355, Giovanni Boccaccio wrote *Il Corbaccio*, another antifeminist manifesto, although ironically by an author whose other works pioneered new directions in Renaissance thought. The former husband of his lover appears to Boccaccio, condemning his unmoderated lust and detailing the defects of women. Boccaccio concedes at the end "how much men naturally surpass women in nobility" and is cured of his desires.[3]

---

3. Giovanni Boccaccio, *The Corbaccio, or The Labyrinth of Love*, trans. and ed. Anthony K. Cassell, rev. ed. (Binghamton, N.Y., 1993), 71.

WOMEN'S ROLES: THE FAMILY. The negative perceptions of women expressed in the intellectual tradition are also implicit in the actual roles that women played in European society. Assigned to subordinate positions in the household and the church, they were barred from significant participation in public life.

Medieval European households, like those in antiquity and in non-Western civilizations, were headed by males. It was the male serf (or peasant), feudal lord, town merchant, or citizen who was polled or taxed or succeeded to an inheritance or had any acknowledged public role, although his wife or widow could stand as a temporary surrogate. From about 1100, the position of property-holding males was further enhanced: inheritance was confined to the male, or agnate, line—with depressing consequences for women.

A wife never fully belonged to her husband's family, nor was she a daughter to her father's family. She left her father's house young to marry whomever her parents chose. Her dowry was managed by her husband, and at her death it normally passed to her children by him.

A married woman's life was occupied nearly constantly with cycles of pregnancy, childbearing, and lactation. Women bore children through all the years of their fertility, and many died in childbirth. They were also responsible for raising young children up to six or seven. In the propertied classes that responsibility was shared, since it was common for a wet nurse to take over breast-feeding and for servants to perform other chores.

Women trained their daughters in the household duties appropriate to their status, nearly always tasks associated with textiles: spinning, weaving, sewing, embroidering. Their sons were sent out of the house as apprentices or students, or their training was assumed by fathers in later childhood and adolescence. On the death of her husband, a woman's children became the responsibility of his family. She generally did not take "his" children with her to a new marriage or back to her father's house, except sometimes in the artisan classes.

Women also worked. Rural peasants performed farm chores, merchant wives often practiced their husbands' trades, the unmarried daughters of the urban poor worked as servants or prostitutes. All wives produced or embellished textiles and did the housekeeping, while wealthy ones managed servants. These labors were unpaid or poorly paid but often contributed substantially to family wealth.

WOMEN'S ROLES: THE CHURCH. Membership in a household, whether a father's or a husband's, meant for women a lifelong subordination to others. In western Europe, the Roman Catholic Church offered an alternative to the career of wife and mother. A woman could enter a convent, parallel in function to the monasteries for men that evolved in the early Christian centuries.

In the convent, a woman pledged herself to a celibate life, lived according to strict community rules, and worshiped daily. Often the convent offered training in Latin, allowing some women to become considerable scholars and authors as well as scribes, artists, and musicians. For women who chose the conventual life, the benefits could be enormous, but for numerous others placed in convents by paternal choice, the life could be restrictive and burdensome.

The conventual life declined as an alternative for women as the modern age approached. Reformed monastic institutions resisted responsibility for related female orders. The church increasingly restricted female institutional life by insisting on closer male supervision.

Women often sought other options. Some joined the communities of laywomen that sprang up spontaneously in the thirteenth century in the urban zones of western Europe, especially in Flanders and Italy. Some joined the heretical movements that flourished in late medieval Christendom, whose anticlerical and often antifamily positions particularly appealed to women. In these communities, some women were acclaimed as "holy women" or "saints," whereas others often were condemned as frauds or heretics.

In all, although the options offered to women by the church were sometimes less than satisfactory, they were sometimes richly rewarding. After 1520, the convent remained an option only in Roman Catholic territories. Protestantism engendered an ideal of marriage as a heroic endeavor and appeared to place husband and wife on a more equal footing. Sermons and treatises, however, still called for female subordination and obedience.

THE OTHER VOICE, 1300–1700

When the modern era opened, European culture was so firmly structured by a framework of negative attitudes toward women that to dismantle it was a monumental labor. The process began as part of a larger cultural movement that entailed the critical reexamination of ideas inherited from the ancient and medieval past. The humanists launched that critical reexamination.

THE HUMANIST FOUNDATION. Originating in Italy in the fourteenth century, humanism quickly became the dominant intellectual movement in Europe. Spreading in the sixteenth century from Italy to the rest of Europe, it fueled the literary, scientific, and philosophical movements of the era and laid the basis for the eighteenth-century Enlightenment.

Humanists regarded the Scholastic philosophy of medieval universities as out of touch with the realities of urban life. They found in the rhetorical discourse of classical Rome a language adapted to civic life and public speech. They learned to read, speak, and write classical Latin and, eventually, classical Greek. They founded schools to teach others to do so, establishing the pattern for elementary and secondary education for the next three hundred years.

In the service of complex government bureaucracies, humanists employed their skills to write eloquent letters, deliver public orations, and formulate public policy. They developed new scripts for copying manuscripts and used the new printing press to disseminate texts, for which they created methods of critical editing.

Humanism was a movement led by males who accepted the evaluation of women in ancient texts and generally shared the misogynist perceptions of their culture. (Female humanists, as we will see, did not.) Yet humanism also opened the door to a reevaluation of the nature and capacity of women. By calling authors, texts, and ideas into question, it made possible the fundamental rereading of the whole intellectual tradition that was required in order to free women from cultural prejudice and social subordination.

A DIFFERENT CITY. The other voice first appeared when, after so many centuries, the accumulation of misogynist concepts evoked a response from a capable female defender: Christine de Pizan (1365–1431). Introducing her *Book of the City of Ladies* (1405), she described how she was affected by reading Mathéolus's *Lamentations:* "Just the sight of this book . . . made me wonder how it happened that so many different men . . . are so inclined to express both in speaking and in their treatises and writings so many wicked insults about women and their behavior."[4] These statements impelled her to detest herself "and the entire feminine sex, as though we were monstrosities in nature."[5]

The rest of *The Book of the City of Ladies* presents a justification of the female sex and a vision of an ideal community of women. A pioneer, she has received the message of female inferiority and rejected it. From the fourteenth to the seventeenth century, a huge body of literature accumulated that responded to the dominant tradition.

The result was a literary explosion consisting of works by both men and women, in Latin and in the vernaculars: works enumerating the achieve-

---

4. Christine de Pizan, *The Book of the City of Ladies,* trans. Earl Jeffrey Richards, foreword by Marina Warner (New York, 1982), 1.1.1, pp. 3–4.

5. Ibid., 1.1.1–2, p. 5.

ments of notable women; works rebutting the main accusations made against women; works arguing for the equal education of men and women; works defining and redefining women's proper role in the family, at court, in public; works describing women's lives and experiences. Recent monographs and articles have begun to hint at the great range of this movement, involving probably several thousand titles. The protofeminism of these "other voices" constitutes a significant fraction of the literary product of the early modern era.

THE CATALOGS. About 1365, the same Boccaccio whose *Corbaccio* rehearses the usual charges against female nature wrote another work, *Concerning Famous Women*. A humanist treatise drawing on classical texts, it praised 106 notable women: ninety-eight of them from pagan Greek and Roman antiquity, one (Eve) from the Bible, and seven from the medieval religious and cultural tradition; his book helped make all readers aware of a sex normally condemned or forgotten. Boccaccio's outlook nevertheless was unfriendly to women, for it singled out for praise those women who possessed the traditional virtues of chastity, silence, and obedience. Women who were active in the public realm—for example, rulers and warriors—were depicted as usually being lascivious and as suffering terrible punishments for entering the masculine sphere. Women were his subject, but Boccaccio's standard remained male.

Christine de Pizan's *Book of the City of Ladies* contains a second catalog, one responding specifically to Boccaccio's. Whereas Boccaccio portrays female virtue as exceptional, she depicts it as universal. Many women in history were leaders, or remained chaste despite the lascivious approaches of men, or were visionaries and brave martyrs.

The work of Boccaccio inspired a series of catalogs of illustrious women of the biblical, classical, Christian, and local pasts, among them Filippo da Bergamo's *Of Illustrious Women*, Pierre de Brantôme's *Lives of Illustrious Women*, Pierre Le Moyne's *Gallerie of Heroic Women*, and Pietro Paolo de Ribera's *Immortal Triumphs and Heroic Enterprises of 845 Women*. Whatever their embedded prejudices, these works drove home to the public the possibility of female excellence.

THE DEBATE. At the same time, many questions remained: Could a woman be virtuous? Could she perform noteworthy deeds? Was she even, strictly speaking, of the same human species as men? These questions were debated over four centuries, in French, German, Italian, Spanish, and English, by authors male and female, among Catholics, Protestants, and Jews, in ponderous volumes and breezy pamphlets. The whole literary genre has been called the *querelle des femmes,* the "woman question."

The opening volley of this battle occurred in the first years of the fifteenth century, in a literary debate sparked by Christine de Pizan. She exchanged letters critical of Jean de Meun's contribution to *The Romance of the Rose* with two French royal secretaries, Jean de Montreuil and Gontier Col. When the matter became public, Jean Gerson, one of Europe's leading theologians, supported de Pizan's arguments against de Meun, for the moment silencing the opposition.

The debate resurfaced repeatedly over the next two hundred years. *The Triumph of Women* (1438) by Juan Rodríguez de la Camara (or Juan Rodríguez del Padron) struck a new note by presenting arguments for the superiority of women to men. *The Champion of Women* (1440–42) by Martin Le Franc addresses once again the negative views of women presented in *The Romance of the Rose* and offers counterevidence of female virtue and achievement.

A cameo of the debate on women is included in *The Courtier,* one of the most widely read books of the era, published by the Italian Baldassare Castiglione in 1528 and immediately translated into other European vernaculars. *The Courtier* depicts a series of evenings at the court of the duke of Urbino in which many men and some women of the highest social stratum amuse themselves by discussing a range of literary and social issues. The "woman question" is a pervasive theme throughout, and the third of its four books is devoted entirely to that issue.

In a verbal duel, Gasparo Pallavicino and Giuliano de' Medici present the main claims of the two traditions. Gasparo argues the innate inferiority of women and their inclination to vice. Only in bearing children do they profit the world. Giuliano counters that women share the same spiritual and mental capacities as men and may excel in wisdom and action. Men and women are of the same essence: just as no stone can be more perfectly a stone than another, so no human being can be more perfectly human than others, whether male or female. It was an astonishing assertion, boldly made to an audience as large as all Europe.

THE TREATISES. Humanism provided the materials for a positive counterconcept to the misogyny embedded in Scholastic philosophy and law and inherited from the Greek, Roman, and Christian pasts. A series of humanist treatises on marriage and family, on education and deportment, and on the nature of women helped construct these new perspectives.

The works by Francesco Barbaro and Leon Battista Alberti—*On Marriage* (1415) and *On the Family* (1434–37)—far from defending female equality, reasserted women's responsibility for rearing children and managing the housekeeping while being obedient, chaste, and silent. Nevertheless, they served the cause of reexamining the issue of women's nature by placing domestic issues at the center of scholarly concern and reopening the pertinent classical texts. In addition, Barbaro emphasized the companionate nature of marriage and the importance of a wife's spiritual and mental qualities for the well-being of the family.

These themes reappear in later humanist works on marriage and the education of women by Juan Luis Vives and Erasmus. Both were moderately sympathetic to the condition of women without reaching beyond the usual masculine prescriptions for female behavior.

An outlook more favorable to women characterizes the nearly uknown work *In Praise of Women* (ca. 1487) by the Italian humanist Bartolommeo Goggio. In addition to providing a catalog of illustrious women, Goggio argued that male and female are the same in essence, but that women (reworking the Adam and Eve narrative from quite a new angle) are actually superior. In the same vein, the Italian humanist Mario Equicola asserted the spiritual equality of men and women in *On Women* (1501). In 1525, Galeazzo Flavio Capra (or Capella) published his work *On the Excellence and Dignity of Women.* This humanist tradition of treatises defending the worthiness of women culminates in the work of Henricus Cornelius Agrippa *On the Nobility and Preeminence of the Female Sex.* No work by a male humanist more succinctly or explicitly presents the case for female dignity.

THE WITCH BOOKS. While humanists grappled with the issues pertaining to women and family, other learned men turned their attention to what they perceived as a very great problem: witches. Witch-hunting manuals, explorations of the witch phenomenon, and even defenses of witches are not at first glance pertinent to the tradition of the other voice. But they do relate in this way: most accused witches were women. The hostility aroused by supposed witch activity is comparable to the hostility aroused by women. The evil deeds the victims of the hunt were charged with were exaggerations of the vices to which, many believed, all women were prone.

The connection between the witch accusation and the hatred of women is explicit in the notorious witch-hunting manual *The Hammer of Witches* (1486) by two Dominican inquisitors, Heinrich Krämer and Jacob Sprenger. Here the inconstancy, deceitfulness, and lustfulness traditionally associated with women are depicted in exaggerated form as the core features of witch behavior. These traits inclined women to make a bargain with the devil—sealed by sexual intercourse—by which they acquired unholy powers. Such bizarre claims, far from being rejected by rational men, were broadcast by intellectuals. The German Ulrich Molitur, the Frenchman Nicolas Rémy, and the Italian Stefano Guazzo all coolly informed the public of sinister orgies and midnight pacts with the devil. The celebrated French jurist, historian, and political philosopher Jean Bodin argued that because women were especially prone to diabolism, regular legal procedures could properly be suspended in order to try those accused of this "exceptional crime."

A few experts such as the physician Johann Weyer, a student of Agrippa's, raised their voices in protest. In 1563, he explained the witch phenomenon thus, without discarding belief in diabolism: the devil deluded foolish old women afflicted by melancholia, causing them to believe they had magical powers. Weyer's rational skepticism, which had good credibility in the community of the learned, worked to revise the conventional views of women and witchcraft.

WOMEN'S WORKS. To the many categories of works produced on the question of women's worth must be added nearly all works written by women. A woman writing was in herself a statement of women's claim to dignity.

Only a few women wrote anything before the dawn of the modern era, for three reasons. First, they rarely received the education that would enable them to write. Second, they were not admitted to the public roles—as administrator, bureaucrat, lawyer or notary, or university professor—in which they might gain knowledge of the kinds of things the literate public thought worth writing about. Third, the culture imposed silence on women, considering speaking out a form of unchastity. Given these conditions, it is remarkable that any women wrote. Those who did before the fourteenth century were almost always nuns or religious women whose isolation made their pronouncements more acceptable.

From the fourteenth century on, the volume of women's writings rose. Women continued to write devotional literature, although not always as cloistered nuns. They also wrote diaries, often intended as keepsakes for their children; books of advice to their sons and daughters; letters to family members and friends; and family memoirs, in a few cases elaborate enough to be considered histories.

A few women wrote works directly concerning the "woman question," and some of these, such as the humanists Isotta Nogarola, Cassandra Fedele, Laura Cereta, and Olympia Morata, were highly trained. A few were professional writers, living by the income of their pens; the very first among them was Christine de Pizan, noteworthy in this context as in so many others. In addition to *The Book of the City of Ladies* and her critiques of *The Romance of the Rose*, she wrote *The Treasure of the City of Ladies* (a guide to social decorum for women), an advice book for her son, much courtly verse, and a full-scale history of the reign of King Charles V of France.

WOMEN PATRONS. Women who did not themselves write but encouraged others to do so boosted the development of an alternative tradition. Highly placed women patrons supported authors, artists, musicians, poets, and learned men. Such patrons, drawn mostly from the Italian elites and the courts of northern Europe, figure disproportionately as the dedicatees of the important works of early feminism.

For a start, it might be noted that the catalogs of Boccaccio and Alvaro de Luna were dedicated to the Florentine noblewoman Andrea Acciaiuoli and to Doña María, first wife of King Juan II of Castile, while the French translation of Boccaccio's work was commissioned by Anne of Brittany, wife of King Charles VIII of France. The humanist treatises of Goggio, Equicola, Vives, and Agrippa were dedicated, respectively, to Eleanora of Aragon, wife of Ercole I d'Este, duke of Ferrara; to Margherita Cantelma of Mantua; to Catherine of Aragon, wife of King Henry VIII of England; and to Margaret, Duchess of Austria and regent of the Netherlands. As late as 1696, Mary Astell's *Serious Proposal to the Ladies, for the Advancement of Their True and Greatest Interest* was dedicated to Princess Anne of Denmark.

These authors presumed that their efforts would be welcome to female patrons, or they may have written at the bidding of those patrons. Silent themselves, perhaps even unresponsive, these loftily placed women helped shape the tradition of the other voice.

THE ISSUES. The literary forms and patterns in which the tradition of the other voice presented itself have now been sketched. It remains to highlight the major issues around which this tradition crystallizes. In brief, there are four problems to which our authors return again and again, in plays and catalogs, in verse and letters, in treatises and dialogues, in every language: the problem of chastity, the problem of power, the problem of speech, and the problem of knowledge. Of these the greatest, preconditioning the others, is the problem of chastity.

THE PROBLEM OF CHASTITY. In traditional European culture, as in those of antiquity and others around the globe, chastity was perceived as woman's quintessential virtue—in contrast to courage, or generosity, or leadership, or rationality, seen as virtues characteristic of men. Opponents of women charged them with insatiable lust. Women themselves and their defenders—without disputing the validity of the standard—responded that women were capable of chastity.

The requirement of chastity kept women at home, silenced them, isolated them, left them in ignorance. It was the source of all other impediments. Why was it so important to the society of men, of whom chastity was not required, and who more often than not considered it their right to violate the chastity of any woman they encountered?

Female chastity ensured the continuity of the male-headed household. If a man's wife was not chaste, he could not be sure of the legitimacy of his offspring. If they were not his and they acquired his property, it was not his household, but some other man's, that had endured. If his daughter was not chaste, she could not be transferred to another man's household as his wife, and he was dishonored.

The whole system of the integrity of the household and the transmission of property was bound up in female chastity. Such a requirement pertained only to property-owning classes, of course. Poor women could not expect to maintain their chastity, least of all if they were in contact with high-status men to whom all women but those of their own household were prey.

In Catholic Europe, the requirement of chastity was further buttressed by moral and religious imperatives. Original sin was inextricably linked with the sexual act. Virginity was seen as heroic virtue, far more impressive than, say, the avoidance of idleness or greed. Monasticism, the cultural institution that dominated medieval Europe for centuries, was grounded in the renunciation of the flesh. The Catholic reform of the eleventh century imposed a similar standard on all the clergy and a heightened awareness of sexual requirements on all the laity. Although men were asked to be chaste, female unchastity was much worse: it led to the devil, as Eve had led mankind to sin.

To such requirements, women and their defenders protested their innocence. Furthermore, following the example of holy women who had escaped the requirements of family and sought the religious life, some women began to conceive of female communities as alternatives both to family and to the cloister. Christine de Pizan's city of ladies was such a community. Moderata Fonte and Mary Astell envisioned others. The luxurious salons of the French *précieuses* of the seventeenth century, or the comfortable English drawing rooms of the next, may have been born of the same impulse. Here women not only might escape, if briefly, the subordinate position that life in the family entailed but might also make claims to power, exercise their capacity for speech, and display their knowledge.

THE PROBLEM OF POWER. Women were excluded from power: the whole cultural tradition insisted on it. Only men were citizens, only men bore arms, only men could be chiefs or lords or kings. There were exceptions that did not disprove the rule, when wives or widows or mothers took the place of men, awaiting their return or the maturation of a male heir. A woman who attempted to rule in her own right was perceived as an anomaly, a monster, at once a deformed woman and an insufficient male, sexually confused and consequently unsafe.

The association of such images with women who held or sought power explains some otherwise odd features of early modern culture. Queen Elizabeth I of England, one of the few women to hold full regal authority in European history, played with such male/female images—positive ones, of course—in representing herself to her subjects. She was a prince, and manly, even though she was female. She was also (she claimed) virginal, a condition absolutely essential if she was to avoid the attacks of her opponents. Catherine de' Medici, who ruled France as widow and regent for her sons, also adopted such imagery in defining her position. She chose as one symbol the figure of Artemisia, an androgynous ancient warrior-heroine who combined a female persona with masculine powers.

Power in a woman, without such sexual imagery, seems to have been indigestible by the culture. A rare note was struck by the Englishman Sir Thomas Elyot in his *Defence of Good Women* (1540), justifying both women's participation in civic life and their prowess in arms. The old tune was sung by the Scots reformer John Knox in his *First Blast of the Trumpet against the Monstrous Regiment of Women* (1558); for him rule by women, defects in nature, was a hideous contradiction in terms.

The confused sexuality of the imagery of female potency was not reserved for rulers. Any woman who excelled was likely to be called an Amazon, recalling the self-mutilated warrior women of antiquity who repudiated all men, gave up their sons, and raised only their daughters. She was often said to have "exceeded her sex" or to have possessed "masculine virtue"—as the very fact of conspicuous excellence conferred masculinity even on the female subject. The catalogs of notable women often showed those female heroes dressed in armor, armed to the teeth, like men. Amazonian heroines romp through the epics of the age—Ariosto's *Orlando Furioso* (1532) and Spenser's *Faerie Queene* (1590–1609). Excellence in a woman was perceived as a claim for power, and power was reserved for the masculine realm. A woman who possessed either one was masculinized and lost title to her own female identity.

THE PROBLEM OF SPEECH. Just as power had a sexual dimension when it was claimed by women, so did speech. A good woman spoke little. Excessive speech was an indication of unchastity. By speech, women seduced men. Eve had lured Adam into sin by her speech. Accused witches were commonly accused of having spoken abusively, or irrationally, or simply too much. As enlightened a figure as Francesco Barbaro insisted on silence in a woman, which he linked to her perfect unanimity with her husband's will and her unblemished virtue (her chastity). Another Italian humanist, Leonardo Bruni, in advising a noblewoman on her studies, barred her not from speech but from public speaking. That was reserved for men.

Related to the problem of speech was that of costume—another, if silent, form of self-expression. Assigned the task of pleasing men as their primary occupation, elite women often tended toward elaborate costume, hairdressing, and the use of cosmetics. Clergy and secular moralists alike condemned these practices. The appropriate function of costume and adornment was to announce the status of a woman's husband or father. Any further indulgence in adornment was akin to unchastity.

THE PROBLEM OF KNOWLEDGE. When the Italian noblewoman Isotta Nogarola had begun to attain a reputation as a humanist, she was accused of incest—a telling instance of the association of learning in women with unchastity. That chilling association inclined any woman who was educated to deny that she was or to make exaggerated claims of heroic chastity.

If educated women were pursued with suspicions of sexual misconduct, women seeking an education faced an even more daunting obstacle: the assumption that women were by nature incapable of learning, that reasoning was a particularly masculine ability. Just as they proclaimed their chastity, women and their defenders insisted on their capacity for learning. The major work by a male writer on female education—that by Juan Luis Vives, *On the Education of a Christian Woman* (1523)—granted female capacity for intellection but still argued that a woman's whole education was to be shaped around the requirement of chastity and a future within the household. Female writers of the following generations—Marie de Gournay in France, Anna Maria van Schurman in Holland, and Mary Astell in England—began to envision other possibilities.

The pioneers of female education were the Italian women humanists who managed to attain a literacy in Latin and a knowledge of classical and Christian literature equivalent to that of prominent men. Their works implicitly and explicitly raise questions about women's social roles, defining problems that beset women attempting to break out of the cultural limits that had bound them. Like Christine de Pizan, who achieved an advanced education through her father's tutoring and her own devices, their bold questioning makes clear the importance of training. Only when women were educated to the same standard as male leaders would they be able to raise that other voice and insist on their dignity as human beings morally, intellectually, and legally equal to men.

THE OTHER VOICE. The other voice, a voice of protest, was mostly female, but it was also male. It spoke in the vernaculars and in Latin, in treatises and dialogues, in plays and poetry, in letters and diaries, and in pamphlets. It battered at the wall of prejudice that encircled women and raised a banner announcing its claims. The female was equal (or even superior) to the male in essential nature—moral, spiritual, and intellectual. Women were capable of higher education, of holding positions of power and influence in the public realm, and of speaking and writing persuasively. The last bastion of masculine supremacy, centered on the notions of a woman's primary domestic responsibility and the requirement of female chastity, was not as yet assaulted—although visions of productive female communities as alternatives to the family indicated an awareness of the problem.

During the period 1300–1700, the other voice remained only a voice, and one only dimly heard. It did not result—yet—in an alteration of social patterns. Indeed, to this day they have not entirely been altered. Yet the call for justice issued as long as six centuries ago by those writing in the tradition of the other voice must be recognized as the source and origin of the mature feminist tradition and of the realignment of social institutions accomplished in the modern age.

We thank the volume editors in this series, who responded with many suggestions to an earlier draft of this introduction, making it a collaborative enterprise. Many of their suggestions and criticisms have resulted in revisions of this introduction, although we remain responsible for the final product.

PROJECTED TITLES IN THE SERIES

Isabella Andreini, *Mirtilla*, edited and translated by Laura Stortoni

Tullia d'Aragona, *Complete Poems and Letters*, edited and translated by Julia Hairston

Tullia d'Aragona, *The Wretch, Otherwise Known as Guerrino*, edited and translated by Julia Hairston and John McLucas

Francesco Barbaro et al., *On Marriage and the Family*, edited and translated by Margaret L. King

Francesco Buoninsegni and Arcangela Tarabotti, *Menippean Satire: "Against Feminine Extravagance" and "Antisatire,"* edited and translated by Elissa Weaver

Rosalba Carriera, *Letters, Diaries, and Art*, edited and translated by Catherine M. Sama

Madame du Chatelet, *Selected Works*, edited by Judith Zinsser

Vittoria Colonna, Chiara Matraini, and Lucrezia Marinella, *Marian Writings*, edited and translated by Susan Haskins

Princess Elizabeth of Bohemia, *Correspondence with Descartes*, edited and translated by Lisa Shapiro

Isabella d'Este, *Selected Letters*, edited and translated by Deanna Shemek

Fairy-Tales by Seventeenth-Century French Women Writers, edited and translated by Lewis Seifert and Domna C. Stanton

Moderata Fonte and Lucrezia Marinella, *Religious Narratives*, edited and translated by Virginia Cox

Catharina Regina von Greiffenberg, *Meditations on the Life of Christ*, edited and translated by Lynne Tatlock

In Praise of Women: Italian Fifteenth-Century Defenses of Women, edited and translated by Daniel Bornstein

Lucrezia Marinella, *L'Enrico, or Byzantium Conquered*, edited and translated by Virginia Cox

Lucrezia Marinella, *Happy Arcadia*, edited and translated by Susan Haskins and Letizia Panizza

Chiara Matraini, *Selected Poetry and Prose*, edited and translated by Elaine MacLachlan

Alessandro Piccolomini, *Rethinking Marriage in Sixteenth-Century Italy*, edited and translated by Letizia Panizza

Christine de Pizan, *Debate over the "Romance of the Rose,"* edited and translated by David F. Hult

Christine de Pizan, *Life of Charles V*, edited and translated by Nadia Margolis

Christine de Pizan, *The Long Road of Learning*, edited and translated by Andrea Tarnowski

Oliva Sabuco, *The New Philosophy: True Medicine*, edited and translated by Gianna Pomata

Gabrielle Suchon, *"On Philosophy" and "On Morality,"* edited and translated by Domna Stanton with Rebecca Wilkin

Sara Copio Sullam, *Sara Copio Sullam: Jewish Poet and Intellectual in Early Seventeenth-Century Venice*, edited and translated by Don Harrán

Arcangela Tarabotti, *Convent Life as Inferno: A Report*, introduction and notes by Francesca Medioli, translated by Letizia Panizza

Laura Terracina, *Works*, edited and translated by Michael Sherberg

MODERATA FONTE AND THE GENRE OF
WOMEN'S CHIVALRIC ROMANCES

THE OTHER VOICE

In a sonnet included in the 1581 text of Moderata Fonte's *Floridoro* (original title: *Tredici canti del Floridoro*), the Venetian historian Nicolò Doglioni reflects that it is common in poetry that "an expert lover sings about love or that a soldier waxes on arms, a sailor on winds, an architect on buildings, and a pilgrim on different people and customs." But it is nothing short of the marvelous, Doglioni adds, that an inexpert young virgin (*verginella*) enclosed within constricting walls sings perfectly of all of the above to the amazement of those around her and of nature itself.[1] Doglioni is not alone in expressing his wonder. In the following decades and centuries many readers, including, regretfully, literary historians, not only did not know the extent of women's engagement in poetic matters but were even less aware that women had proven their mettle with, as Moderata Fonte puts it, "the glorious deeds and the sweet affections of illustrious knights and ladies," that is, with the genre of chivalric romances.[2] Writing fifty years earlier, Ludovico Ariosto had made a similar conjunction of knights and ladies, love

---

1. "Che d'amor canti il ben esperto amante,/D'armi il soldato, il marinar de venti,/L'architetto di fabriche, e di genti/Varie e d'usanze il peregrino errante,/Maraviglia non '. . . /Ma che tu non esperta verginella,/Stando rinchiusa in fra l'anguste mura/Di tutto ciò perfettamente canti/Non pur stupisce il mondo, e la natura." Nicolò Doglioni, "Alla Sig. Moderata Fonte," in Moderata Fonte, *Tredici canti del Floridoro* (Venice: Stamparia de' Rampazetti, 1581).

2. *Floridoro* 1.2. Hereafter canto and octave will be given directly in the text. Throughout this essay I shall draw from my "Moderata Fonte e il romanzo cavalleresco al femminile," which constituted the introduction to my Italian edition of *Tredici canti del Floridoro* (Modena: Mucchi, 1995), ix–xxxix. I shall also draw from my "When the Mirror Lies: Sisterhood Reconsidered in Moderata Fonte's *Thirteen Cantos of Floridoro*," in *Sibling Relations and Gender in the Early Modern World*, ed. Naomi Miller and Naomi Yavneh (Aldershot: Ashgate, 2006), 116–28.

and arms at the start of his *Orlando furioso* (1532) the sine qua non of the genre.[3]

Until a few years ago there was indeed no mention in anthologies of any woman's having penned a chivalric and epic romance in the early modern period. More perplexingly, if women were mentioned, their authorship was occasionally put in question. Their voices, however, have not been lost. Recovered no more than ten years ago, the tradition of female-authored epic romances in Italian is attracting much attention these days, so much so that many of this genre's exemplars in *ottava rima* are being republished in modern critical editions and will soon appear in English translation as well in the "Other Voice" series.[4] The extent to which there is another voice, and a gendered one at that, and what this voice says in the context of a genre like the chivalric romance in which imitation is a necessary, almost indispensable tool, will be the subject of my inquiry.

BIOGRAPHY

Moderata Fonte was born as Modesta Pozzo in Venice on June 15, 1555, the day of Saint Modestus, hence the name, according to her uncle and hagiographer, Giovanni Nicolò Doglioni.[5] Her family belonged to the upper

3. "I sing of knights and ladies, of love and arms, of courtly chivalry, of courageous deeds." Ludovico Ariosto, *Orlando furioso* (Milan: Garzanti, 1974), 1.1.

4. As far as I know, I was the first to reconstruct this tradition (see below for names)—and mention all the women writers who seem to have written in the genre—in "La scrittura epico-cavalleresca al femminile: Moderata Fonte e *Tredici canti del Floridoro*," *Annali d'Italianistica* 12 (1994): 203–31. I then included the list in the introductory chapter of my edition of Fonte's *Floridoro*, x–xii. To come up with the roster of works and names of authors, I consulted Marina Beer, "Appendice II," in *Romanzi di cavalleria: Il Furioso e il romanzo italiano del primo Cinquecento* (Rome: Bulzoni, 1987), 327–89; Antonio Belloni, "Il fallimento dell'ideale eroico," in his *Il Seicento* (Milan: Vallardi, 1929), 181–238; Alessandro Cutolo, *I romanzi cavallereschi in prosa e in rima del Fondo Castiglioni presso la Biblioteca Braidense di Milano* (Milan: Hoepli, 1944); Giuseppina Fumagalli, *La fortuna dell'Orlando Furioso in Italia nel sec. XVI* (Ferrara: Zuffi, 1912); Gaetano Melzi, *Bibliografia dei romanzi e dei poemi cavallereschi d'Italia*, in *Storia ed analisi dei romanzi di cavalleria*, ed. Giulio Ferrario, vol. 4 (Milan: Ferrario, 1829); Leopoldo Ferri, *Biblioteca italiana* (Padua: Crescini, 1812); Gaetano Melzi and Gian Paolo Tosi, *Bibliografia dei romanzi di cavalleria in versi e in prosa italiani* (Milan: Daelli, 1865); and appendix 3 in *Nel cerchio della luna: Figure di donna in alcuni testi del XVI secolo*, ed. Marina Zancan (Venice: Marsilio, 1983), 254–64. In the succeeding ten years the field has become quite lively, and I am delighted to acknowledge in the notes below publications on the writers I first mentioned in that essay. See also Virginia Cox, "Women as Readers and Writers of Chivalric Poetry in Early Modern Italy," in *Sguardi sull'Italia*, ed. Gino Bedani et al. (Exeter: Society for Italian Studies, 1997), 134–45.

5. See "Vita della Sig.ra Modesta Pozzo de' Zorzi, nominata Moderata Fonte, descritta da Gio. Nicolò Doglioni, l'anno MDXCIII," which is included in the first edition of Fonte's *Il merito delle donne . . . in due giornate. Ove chiaramente si scuopre quanto siano elle degne e più perfette de gli uomini* (Ven-

middle class of *cittadini originari,* and her father, Hieronimo, was a lawyer.[6] Modesta had a slightly older brother, Leonardo, born in 1553. Both children were orphaned in quick succession of mother and father at a very tender age (Modesta was only a toddler) and were subsequently raised by the maternal grandmother, Cecilia de' Mazzi, and her second husband, Prospero Saraceni. As was customary for the times, Modesta was sent to a convent to learn reading and writing and only at nine returned to the Saraceni household, where her relatives, "recognizing this natural talent on her part, set about stimulating her gift for poetry by constantly suggesting new subjects for her to write about and keeping her supplied with books to read and study, as far as she was able."[7] Since it was not customary for girls at the time, even those with an educated family background, to have their own private tutors, Modesta learned by pestering her brother about his lessons and by sharing his homework assignments. She seemed to profit greatly from that experience and was soon able to read and write in Latin.[8]

Upon marrying Saraceni's daughter, a young lady very close in age to Modesta, Doglioni, a man of letters of some renown and a notary, allowed the orphan to come to live in his household.[9] Modesta was thus able to

---

ice: Imberti, 1600), but may have circulated independently. A translation as "Life of Moderata Fonte" is in Moderata Fonte, *The Worth of Women,* ed. and trans. Virginia Cox (Chicago: University of Chicago Press, 1997), 31–40.

6. Hieronimo (or Girolamo) got a degree from the University of Bologna "in astonishingly short time and with flying colors" and became "an advocate of civil cases" in Venice. See Doglioni, "Life of Moderata Fonte," 33.

7. Ibid., 34.

8. Ibid., 35. On the paucity of education provided for women at the time, see Vittorio Baldo, *Alunni, maestri e scuole in Venezia alla fine del XVI secolo* (Como: New Press, 1977); and Paul Grendler, *Schooling in Renaissance Italy: Literacy and Learning, 1300–1600* (Baltimore: Johns Hopkins University Press, 1989). On the education of young girls *(putte)* in convents in the early modern period, see Gabriella Zarri, "Le istituzioni dell'educazione femminile," in her *Recinti: Donne, clausura e matrimonio nella prima età moderna* (Bologna: Il Mulino, 2000), 173–78. On the political uses of convents, see Jutta Sperling, *Convents and the Body Politic in Late Renaissance Venice* (Chicago: University of Chicago Press, 1999).

9. Among other things, Doglioni (1548–1629) published a treatise on the Gregorian reform of the calendar, perhaps the earliest piece on the subject, entitled *L'anno dove si ha perfetto, et pieno raguaglio, di quanto può ciascun desiderare, sì d'intorno alle cose del mondo celeste, et elementare, come d'intorno a quelle de' tempi et del calendario* (Venice: Rampazetto, 1587). He also published two books on the history of Venice, *Historia venetiana scritta brevemente da Gio. Nicolo Doglioni, delle cose successe dalla prima fondation di Venetia sino all'anno di Christo 1597* (Venice: Zenaro, 1598); and another, under the pen name of Leonico Goldioni, written to bring up to date Francesco Sansovino's authoritative description of Venice, titled *Le cose maravigliose dell'inclita città di Venetia, riformate, accommodate e grandemente ampliate da Leonico Goldioni* (Venice: Imberti, 1603; rpt., Naples: Liquori, 2003). Demonstrating encyclopedic knowledge, Doglioni wrote in addition a catalogue of the most important events in the world, *Compendio historico universale di tutte le cose notabili già successe nel Mondo dal principio*

further her education and became a sort of *enfant prodige* in Venice. She lived with the Doglionis until she married on February 15, 1583. This was quite late for a woman at the time and was perhaps the result of problems in retrieving the paternal and maternal inheritance in order to come up with a dowry commensurate to her rank.[10] Her husband, Filippo Zorzi (or de' Zorzi), belonged, like her, to the Venetian *cittadini originari* and worked as a lawyer in the city's water management ministry with the title of *provveditore alle acque*.[11] His job consisted in supervising the waterways of the lagoon and the mines of the *Serenissima* on the mainland. He was also an occasional poet and published a short ecological treatise on air.[12] The couple had four children, two daughters, Cecilia and an unnamed one who may have died at birth, and two sons, Pietro and Hieronimo, of whom only the first reached adulthood. Zorzi must have been an open-minded man, for soon after the wedding he gave his wife full control over the dowry she had brought in marriage.[13] Modesta died in giving birth to her fourth child on November 2,

---

della sua creatione fino all'anno di Christo 1594 (Venice: Zenaro, 1594; rpt. 1601,1605, 1622); and *L'Ungheria, spiegata da Gio. Nicolo Doglioni* (Venice: Zenaro, 1595). Some of Doglioni's intellectual interests are echoed in Fonte's *Worth of Women*, especially in book 2, and in the recreation of the myth of Venice in *Floridoro* 12–13.

10. We know that there must have been some inheritance-related problems between Modesta and her brother, because Doglioni refers to them. See below as I return more fully to the subject in the context of *Floridoro*. The date of marriage comes from a document penned by her husband, now in Archivio di Stato di Venezia (hereafter ASV), Notarile. Atti 7852, 629v–630v. See also Cox, in Fonte, *Worth of Women*, 37 n. 19.

11. The wife herself mentions him in her writing: "Signor Filippo Giorgi, who is also advocate fiscal for that most honored institution, the Officio dell'Acque, and whose diligence, loyalty, and efficiency are much appreciated by our most respected Senate." In *Worth of Women*, 197.

12. A sonnet by Zorzi to his wife appears in one of Fonte's publications, *La Resurretione*. See below. He published *Dell'aria e sue qualità* (Venice: Rampazetto, 1596). Filippo died on June 26, 1598. See ASV, Provveditori alla Sanità, Necrologie, reg. 827, 196r.

13. In ASV, Notarile. Atti 7852, 629v–630v. Dowries were women's property. The husband was given the wife's dowry to administer, and he could use it to earn a profit or as an annuity, but could not sell it or alienate it. Dowries lasted a wife's lifetime, so the husband was bound to return it to her family upon her death or separation. Scholarship on the dowry and inheritance system in Venice and the Veneto region is becoming abundant. See Anna Bellavitis, "Patrimoni e matrimoni a Venezia nel Cinquecento," in *Le ricchezze delle donne. Diritti patrimoniali e poteri familiari in Italia (XIII–XIX secc.)*, ed. Giulia Calvi and Isabelle Chabot (Turin: Rosenberg and Sellier, 1998), 149–60; Stanley Chojnacki, *Women and Men in Renaissance Venice: Twelve Essays on Patrician Society* (Baltimore: Johns Hopkins University Press, 2000); and "Getting Back the Dowry: Venice 1350–1530," in *Time, Space, and Women's Lives in Early Modern Europe*, ed. Anne Jacobson Schutte, Thomas Kuehn, and Silvana Seidel Menchi (Kirksville, MO: Truman State University Press, 2001); and Donald Queller and Thomas Madden, "Father of the Bride: Fathers, Daughters, and Dowries in Late Medieval and Early Renaissance Venice," *Renaissance Quarterly* 46 (1993): 685–711. For additional bibliography, see notes below in this introduction.

1592, and was buried at the church of the Frari in Venice.[14] She left a tax form, penned most probably by her and dated August 21, 1582, as well as a will, her second, compiled during one pregnancy, as many women did at the time, which registers a set of instructions regarding her property.[15]

WORKS

Modesta Pozzo entered the literary world under the pen name of Moderata Fonte. Many writers at the time, including her uncle Doglioni, had a nom de plume for literary purposes, especially when becoming members of literary academies. But this was not particularly common for women, who in any case were rarely members of academies at the time. Modesta's choice of a pseudonym shows a surprising creativity. In her fictitious name, the figuratively modest well (Modesta Pozzo) of the patronymic is turned into a mid-sized fountain (Moderata Fonte), that is, a spring of life, a source of knowledge, and a stream of learning. As the young writer explains in a letter dated November 17, 1580, and sent to Francesco I de' Medici, grand duke of Tuscany, she chose the pseudonym when she sent her first work, *Floridoro*, to print, "since my own true name I have not judged it well to expose to public censure, being a young marriageable woman and, according to the custom of the city, obligated in many respects."[16] On December 26, 1581, the young Fonte was called to recite a religious drama in front of the Doge, a benevolent paternalistic tradition that upper-class families used to publicly display their daughters' "extraordinary" accomplishments.[17] She published

14. The death certificate, which specifies that she was thirty-six and lived in the parish of San Basso in Venice, is in ASV, Provveditori alla Sanità, Necrologie, r. 824, f. 129, year 1592. On Fonte's death during parturition, see Naomi Yavneh, "Lying-in and Dying: Moderata Fonte's Death in Childbirth and the Maternal Body in Renaissance Venice," *Rinascimento* 43 (2003): 177–203.

15. The tax form is in ASV, Dieci Savi alle Decime di Rialto, b. 157 bis, n. 751. The will is dated July 11, 1585. See ASV, Notarile. Atti 1192, n. 467.

16. "sotto imaginato nome di Moderata Fonte, poi che 'l mio vero, et proprio non hò giudicato esser bene di esponer alla publica censura, essendo giovane da marito, et secondo l'uso della città obligata à molti rispetti." The letter, most probably in her own hands, is in Archivio di Stato di Firenze, Mediceo del Principato, Carteggio universale, f. 741, cc. 97 and 126. It is now printed in Eleonora Carinci, "Una lettera autografa inedita di Moderata Fonte (al granduca di Toscana Francesco I)," *Critica del testo* 5, no. 3 (2002): 678–79.

17. Valeria Miani, for example (1560?–post 1611), a playwright in Padua, who wrote a pastoral (which had some success) and, remarkably, a tragedy, was called at sixteen too to recite an oration for Princess Maria's passage through that city on her way to Portugal. Miani's *Celinda* is being presently edited for this series by Valeria Finucci. Another child prodigy is Issicratea Monte, who also delivered orations in the 1570s in Padua at sixteen or so. She died young. Fathers occasionally sponsored their bright daughters' talents to the point of changing their own lives to accommodate them. A case in point is that of Annibal Guasco, who, having recognized

it as *Le feste*.[18] Next, Fonte sent to press two religious compositions, both in verse, one on the passion, which came out in 1582, and the other on the resurrection of Christ, a long pious poem (*poema sacro*) of 142 octaves, published in 1592 after a hiatus of ten years during which she did not bring out a single work.[19] Then, eight years after her death, came the publication for which she is most known today, *The Worth of Women* (*Il merito delle donne*), which, according to her uncle, was completed just the day before she died. The manuscript was printed in Venice only eight years later, in 1600, thanks to the goodwill of her children, Cecilia and Pietro, who added a preface and two sonnets to their mother's work.[20] Although the publication of *The Worth of Women* did not exactly put Fonte's name on everybody's lips, she was still mentioned appreciatively as an important Venetian writer in Doglioni's survey, *Le cose maravigliose dell'inclità città di Venetia*, a few years later.[21]

The Worth of Women is an argumentative, at times hilarious text on the position of women in early modern society, specifically the Venetian society of the late sixteenth century. Published as a response to a misogynist treatise by Giuseppe Passi, *The Defects of Women* (*I donneschi difetti*), although written independently of it a few years earlier, Fonte's work is quite different from Lucrezia Marinella's equally polemical *The Nobility and Excellence of Women*, a text specifically commissioned for that purpose and published in that very year.[22] Rather than arguing for the nobility of women, a subject often used

---

the prodigious intellectual talents of his young daughter, Lavinia, chose to educate her fully by hiring numerous tutors and even by changing cities to further her development. See Annibal Guasco, *Discourse to Lady Lavinia His Daughter* (1586), ed. and trans. Peggy Osborn (Chicago: University of Chicago Press, 2003), 49–51.

18. *Le Feste. Rappresentazione avanti il Serenissimo Prencipe di Venetia Nicolò Da Ponte, il giorno di Santo Stefano 1581* (Venice: Guerra, 1581). According to Doglioni, Fonte wrote many other *rappresentazioni* that were later published anonymously. See "Life of Moderata Fonte," 36.

19. Moderata Fonte, *La Passione di Christo, descritta in ottava rima* (Venice: Guerra, 1582), and *La Resurrettione di Giesu Christo, Nostro Signore, che segue alla Santissima Passione, descritta in ottava rima* (Venice: Imberti, 1592). Fonte also wrote occasional poetry. See Stephen Kolsky, "Per la carriera poetica di Moderata Fonte: Alcuni documenti poco conosciuti," *Esperienze letterarie* 24 (1999): 3–17.

20. Fonte's book was more or less forgotten for a few centuries until it was published in a modern critical edition by Adriana Chemello (Venice: Eidos, 1988), following a partial reprint nine years earlier by Ginevra Conti Odorisio in *Donna e società nel Seicento* (Rome: Bulzoni, 1979), 159–96. In English, see Fonte, *Worth of Women*. The book is now also available in French as *Le Mérite des femmes*, ed. Frédérique Verrier (Paris: Éditions Rue d'Ulm, 2002); and in German as *Das Verdienst der Frauen*, ed. Daniela Hacke (Munich: C. H. Beck, 2001).

21. See Doglioni, *Le cose maravigliose dell'inclita città di Venetia*, 187.

22. Giuseppe Passi, *I donneschi difetti* (Venice: Somasco, 1599); Lucrezia Marinella, *La nobiltà et l'eccellenza delle donne, co' diffetti e mancamenti de gli huomini* (Venice: Ciotti, 1601); now available in English in this series as *The Nobility and Excellence of Women and the Defects and Vices of Men*, ed. and trans. Anne Dunhill (Chicago: University of Chicago Press, 1999). On the controversy, see also Stephen Kolsky, "Moderata Fonte, Lucrezia Marinella, Giuseppe Passi: An Early Seventeenth-

by male authors when writing benevolently of this sex, Fonte concentrates in her book on women's natural worth. Women, she writes, are part of the natural system, just like men, and thus they too have a place—and not an inferior one—in the social order. Men's feeling that the other sex is secondary to them is the result of "an abuse that has been introduced into the world and that men have then, over time, gradually translated into law and custom," Fonte writes, "and it has become so entrenched that they claim (and even actually believe) that the status they have gained through their bullying is theirs by right."[23]

Using a dialogue among seven women—characterized as either married, unmarried, or widowed, the usual categories reserved to them at the time—Fonte sets up lively arguments and counterarguments centering on the reasons why women have been historically oppressed, culturally marginalized, and intellectually dismissed. Since there is no man present at the conversation, which takes place in a woman's palazzo in Venice, the exchange is uninhibited and can touch on a variety of female issues, such as marriage, dowries, relationships, and on women's sometimes friendly and sometimes adversarial relationship with the men in their family—brothers, husbands, fathers, and sons.

The emphasis is on the limitations that society places on women and on the weaknesses of the very men who supervise their female counterparts.

Century Feminist Controversy," *Modern Language Review* 96 (2001): 973–89, and more generally, Letizia Panizza, "Polemical Prose Writing, 1500–1650," in *A History of Women's Writing in Italy*, ed. Letizia Panizza and Sharon Wood (Cambridge: Cambridge University Press, 2000), 65–78.

23. Fonte, *Worth of Women*, 61. Work on Fonte's *Worth of Women* is now in full swing. Here is a selected list: Adriana Chemello, "La donna, il modello, l'immaginario: Moderata Fonte e Lucrezia Marinella," in Zancan, *Nel cerchio della luna*, 95–160; Adriana Chemello, "Gioco e dissimulazione in Moderata Fonte," in Moderata Fonte, *Il merito delle donne*, ed. Adriana Chemello, ix–lxiii; Beatrice Collina, "Moderata Fonte e *Il merito delle donne*," *Annali d'Italianistica* 7 (1989): 142–64; Paola Malpezzi-Price, *Moderata Fonte: Women and Life in Sixteenth-Century Venice* (London: Associated University Presses, 2003), and "A Woman's Discourse in the Italian Renaissance: Moderata Fonte's *Il merito delle donne*," *Annali d'Italianistica* 7 (1989): 165–81; Virginia Cox, "Moderata Fonte and *The Worth of Women*," in Fonte, *Worth of Women*, 1–23; Stephen Kolsky, "Wells of Knowledge: Moderata Fonte's *Il merito delle donne*," *Italianist* 13 (1993): 57–96; Bodo Guthmüller, "'Non taceremo più a lungo.' Sul dialogo in *Il merito delle donne* di Moderata Fonte," *Filologia e critica* 17 (1992): 258–79; Patricia Labalme, "Venetian Women on Women: The Early Modern Feminists," *Studi Veneziani* 5 (1981): 81–109; Satya Datta, "La presenza di una coscienza femminista nella Venezia dei primi secoli dell'età moderna," *Studi Veneziani* 32 (1996): 105–37; Margaret Rosenthal, "Venetian Women Writers and Their Discontents," in *Sexuality and Gender in Early Modern Europe: Institutions, Texts, Images*, ed. James Grantham Turner (Cambridge: Cambridge University Press, 1993), 107–32; and Constance Jordan, "Renaissance Women Defending Women: Arguments against Patriarchy," in *Italian Women Writers from the Renaissance to the Present: Revising the Canon*, ed. Maria Ornella Marotti (University Park: Pennsylvania State University Press, 1996), 55–67. There is now even a theatrical production of *The Worth of Women* by Daria Martelli, *Moderata Fonte e Il merito delle donne* (Venice: Centro Internazionale della Grafica, 1993).

Why are women unjustly treated when they too—alongside men—are made in the image of God? a discussant asks. Why have women found themselves bereft of any possibility of having the kind of life that their family's wealth and status can assure them just because their fathers forgot to provide for them in their will or because brothers carelessly used the dotal money to further their business transactions? No matter how pacifying the attitude of some of the ladies in the gathering, the general understanding is that men are not worth their current highly regarded place in society: they squander the family patrimony, are prone to violent deeds, and are naturally suspicious. Even sons, in fact, forget the goodness of their upbringing and turn against their mothers—some of the women complain—if it is convenient for them to do so.

The reader is repeatedly offered the chance to sympathize with women's plight and to understand that only male jealousy limits and castigates this sex. The point had already been made by the Paduan writer Giulia Bigolina in her prose fiction *Urania*, written forty years earlier and containing the first treatise ever penned in Italian on women's worth, so far as is now known. But here the number of pages dedicated to the subject, coupled with a tone that is at times sarcastic, at others matter-of-fact, even demotic, but always engaging, makes the logic of the argument inescapable.[24]

The tone changes in book 2 as the women present an encyclopedic view of the world in which they live. As they touch on issues as far ranging as geography, politics, history, art, medicine, cosmology, and literature, the seven female discussants make clear that they too share in the knowledge of the world around them. *The Worth of Women* ends on a weak note, perhaps because the environment these women were sure to rejoin as soon as they left the comfort of the estate in which they had spent two days in total freedom could not be changed after all. Thus the final assertion that being married is not so bad for women, all things considered, sounds hollow and somewhat betrays the revolutionary assessment of women's place in society carefully laid out in the conversations of the previous hours.

FLORIDORO: STRUCTURE

Floridoro is a chivalric romance made up of thirteen cantos of various lengths for a total of 1,050 rhymed octaves. We do not know when Fonte began to write it, but she had a swift poetic vein, according to her uncle: "She

---

24. Giulia Bigolina, *Urania,* ed. Valeria Finucci (Rome: Bulzoni, 2002); and in English translation, *Urania, a Romance,* ed. and trans. Valeria Finucci (Chicago: University of Chicago Press, 2005). Written in the early 1550s, Bigolina's work was left unedited and was unknown until its recent publication.

wrote poetry so quickly that it seemed almost incredible."[25] The book is dedicated to Francesco de' Medici, who had just married (1579) the Venetian Bianca Capello, "honor of her sex and of her time," as Fonte states in the text (12.7).[26] The timing of the publication, when many writers in Venice were celebrating Capello's fortune, may explain why *Floridoro* was sent to press incomplete. In the letter to the grand duke that accompanies the gift of her book, Fonte writes that she was convinced to publish by people of learning she trusted, and that she had already made an outline of all the remaining cantos, which she planned to complete, if her pleasing and gracious labors ("gratiose mie fatiche") were successful upon publication: "And if it turns out somewhat pleasing to the world and especially to your Most Serene Highness, since the work is already totally plotted, and will reach better than fifty cantos, I will force myself with all my strength to reduce it to its perfection."[27] Whether Fonte was disheartened by Francesco de' Medici's lack of praise of her poetic output and thus stopped writing, whether she lost interest in the project or lacked time to complete it, is anybody's guess. There exists no sequel to the first thirteen cantos of *Floridoro*, although we know from her uncle that she wrote more sections than those she chose to send to press.[28]

Fonte gives the contemporary union of Florence and Venice through the marriage of a Medici and a Capello a mythic source by developing two story lines. They are dealt with contemporaneously as much as possible

---

25. Doglioni continues: "The *Floridoro*, too, and all the other things, she wrote in the same manner, for, as a woman, she had to attend to womanly tasks like sewing, and she did not wish to neglect these labors because of the false notion, so widespread in our city today, that women should excel in nothing but the running of the household." In "Life of Moderata Fonte," 39.

26. The Medici genealogy up to Francesco is retraced in canto 3 of *Floridoro*. Bianca Capello was a woman whose claim to noble origins was uncertain but whose charm and beauty skyrocketed her to the top rung of power when she married the grand duke of Tuscany, her second husband. The grand duke had daughters from his previous union, but not sons. Capello tried desperately to have a child to assure her line of succession, to the point of faking a pregnancy and claiming that she had indeed given birth to a son. The boy, who could have been the offspring of a lady-in-waiting, subsequently was marginalized, made to live somewhat in obscurity as a Knight of Malta, and not allowed to marry. See Maria Bellonci, "Il figlio inventato," in *Segni sul muro* (Milan: Mondadori, 1988), 47. At the time Fonte wrote of Capello's hereditary line in *Floridoro*'s cantos 12 and 13, this "plot" had not been unmasked. See also Maria Luisa Mariotti Masi, *Una veneziana alla corte dei Medici* (Milan: Mursia, 1986).

27. "La qual cosa, se conoscerò esser di qualche gusto al Mondo, et specialm[en]te, alla v[ostra] Ser[enissim]a Alt[ezz]a (essendo già totalm[en]te ordita l'opera, che arriverà à meglio di cinquanta canti) mi sforzerò con tutte le forze mie di ridurla alla sua perfettione." Carinci, "Una lettera autografa," 679.

28. "During her stay in my household," Doglioni recounts, "she wrote the *Floridoro* (not just the cantos that appeared in the public edition, but others that have not yet been published)." "Life of Moderata Fonte," 36. These cantos may have constituted a continuation of *Floridoro*, but they could just as well be stories found wanting and left out of the original 1581 edition.

within the text: one line, agnatic, follows the knight Floridoro, while the other, cognatic, concentrates on a female knight of equal strength and valor, Risamante. From the stock of Floridoro, who in due time will marry the Greek princess Celsidea, will come the founders of the city of Venice, while the descendants of Risamante's daughter, Salarisa, will become the Medici. Throughout Fonte shows that women writers, like their male counterparts, have no problem in using narratives of aggression, fraternal strife, and paternal backstabbing to make their heroes central to the ideologies of state formation, patriliny, and birthright that are not only crucial to plots of chivalric romances (and perhaps one main reason for their success) but also, more prosaically, indispensable to secure a prince's sponsorship and recognition.[29]

No matter the title, the main character of this romance of chivalry is, however, not Floridoro, who enters the narrative quite late (he would have presumably been given more weight had the book not been rushed to press),[30] but Risamante, whose adventures start and conclude *Floridoro*, and who is present in almost every canto.[31] Fonte gives Risamante an identical twin sister, Biondaura, and engages both throughout in a fierce political and military battle for the possession of the kingdom of Armenia, which was capriciously, if perhaps understandably, left by their father at his deathbed only to one daughter, Biondaura.

Described as opposite in their personalities—Risamante is a woman warrior with strength and determination, while Biondaura epitomizes the damsel-in-distress type for whom every knight will prove his mettle—the two sisters are so indistinguishable in beauty as to be consistently misrecognized for one another. In short, they are the two faces of womanhood identifiable in the poetry and culture of all times: one is the masculine, aggressive, overbearing subject, and the other is the pliant, though often unavailable, object of male desire. One is feared and the other is loved, and yet both look so much alike that even their closest allies cannot detect a difference.

In the most successful chivalric romances that constitute the tradition, the trajectories these women are made to pursue can be easily detailed. The

---

29. In his *Orlando furioso* (1532), for one, Ludovico Ariosto had famously celebrated the lineage of the Este, the ruling family of Ferrara, through the heroics of their ancestors, Bradamante and Ruggiero.

30. Floridoro enters at canto 5.45–48 and is also present in 7.6–45, 8.51–69, 9.6–37, 10.58–95, and 11.5–77.

31. In this sense *Floridoro* is "the epopee of feminism," as Emilio Zanette sardonically puts it, growling at Fonte's "sloppiness." See his "Bianca Capello e la sua poetessa," *Nuova Antologia* 88 (1953): 455–68. Zanette's assessment of *Floridoro* is overall negative ("opera sciatta e scialba," 465).

strong woman is given a dynastic marriage, if she has conducted herself properly, as in the case of Ariosto's Bradamante, or a career as an unmarried sister, if she has been chaste but too strong willed, as in the case of Marfisa.[32] When too different or too castrating, she is killed off, as with Torquato Tasso's Clorinda in the influential epic *Gerusalemme Liberata* (*Jerusalem Delivered*), published the same year as *Floridoro*.[33] The feminine woman, on the other hand, gets the husband she wants after a few seemingly salacious encounters—the case of Angelica in the *Furioso* and most probably of Armida in Tasso.[34] A woman writer has obviously some problems following this construction. Fonte's Biondaura is, like Angelica, for example, the woman-as-other, a projection of men's desires, personally unavailable but ready for consumption as a fetish, a Galatea for any aspiring Pygmalion. Yet Fonte gives Queen Biondaura agency without making her appear castrating. She also does not make her function as an exchangeable commodity—a woman for a reign—since she presents her as promising little to any man taking up her defense.[35]

Likewise, Risamante is engaged in quests, like Ariosto's Bradamante and Marfisa, like indeed all heroes of romances. But whereas Bradamante's major quest is to reunite with and eventually marry her beloved Ruggiero, the main quest for Risamante is the armed recovery of her inheritance (of which more later). This is coupled with her rectification of women's problems along the way. So Risamante is asked by the knight Nicobaldo, a loving husband who

32. For such a career in Bradamante, see Valeria Finucci, "Un-dressing the Warrior/Re-dressing the Woman: The Education of Bradamante," in *The Lady Vanishes: Subjectivity and Representation in Castiglione and Ariosto* (Stanford: Stanford University Press, 1992), 227–53. For the case of Marfisa, see Thomas Roche, "Ariosto's Marfisa or Camilla Domesticated," *Modern Language Notes* 103 (1988): 113–33.

33. On the narrative necessity for Clorinda to be put six feet under, see Valeria Finucci, "Performing Maternity: Female Imagination, Paternal Erasure, and Monstrous Birth in Tasso's *Gerusalemme liberata*," in *The Manly Masquerade: Masculinity, Paternity, and Castration in the Italian Renaissance* (Durham: Duke University Press, 2003), 119–57.

34. For the case of Angelica, see Valeria Finucci, "The Narcissistic Woman: Angelica and the Mystique of Femininity," in *The Lady Vanishes*, 107–44; for the case of Armida, see Jo Ann Cavallo, "Tasso's Armida and the Victory of Romance," in *Renaissance Transactions: Ariosto and Tasso*, ed. Valeria Finucci (Durham: Duke University Press, 1999), 77–111. More generally on women in chivalric romances, see Maggie Günsberg, "'Donna liberata'? The Portrayal of Women in the Italian Renaissance Epic," *Italianist* 7 (1987): 7–35.

35. Nor is Biondaura changed into an Armida, who in Tasso from a temptress becomes a passive emblem of female humility. This, in Yavneh's eloquent assessment, "grants her a teleology which transforms the threatening figure of errant sexuality into a Marian emblem of humility and chastity, the 'passive vessel' exalted precisely by her willing submission to God's Word." See her "The Ambiguity of Beauty in Tasso and Petrarch," in Turner, *Sexuality and Gender in Early Modern Europe*, 134.

professes an undying love for his hard-won wife, Lucimena—one of the few
occasions in literary texts where wives are treated as lovingly as virgin be-
loveds—to rescue his wife, kidnapped by a witch. Risamante also frees the
queen of Phrygia, who lives in a cave in harmonious isolation with her strik-
ingly handsome son to avoid her husband's vengeance, following her be-
trayal of the marital ties during his long absence from home. But Risamante's
main purpose is not to get married, although this, we are told, will happen
in due time. Fonte even forgets to give a proper name to the knight whom
she will marry; the child she will engender from this union, moreover, is
not a boy—the heir we would expect, given that the Medici stock will issue
from this infant—but a daughter, whose name, Salarisa, echoes that of her
mother Risamante. This is the opposite of Ariosto's choice in the *Furioso*,
where the son of Bradamante and Ruggiero, the founder of the Este family
in Ferrara, is to be named Ruggierino, a name that reflects, diminutively but
with precision, only his father's legacy.

Other characters pop in and out in *Floridoro*, according to a system that
Ariosto made popular, in which the readers' attention is kept high by aptly
interweaving narrative lines and by creating dilations.[36] Fonte limits herself
usually to two shifts in each canto. The book has also many independent
strands that are left incomplete but are quite readable and enjoyable as they
stand. There is, for example, the story of the cross-dressed Odoria and the
knight Risardo, who meet haphazardly but fall in love and marry during
their journey to the temple of Delphi. Their tale promises to become a
major one, but we know no more. There is the narrative of the widowed
queen of Dacia, who is ominously betrayed by the knight Amandriano but
saves herself and her reputation through the unexpected help of the wizard
Celidante. We do not know what happens to her afterward. There is the
thwarted adventure of the dwarf in love with the sunny Raggidora for whom
he comes from the depths of Africa, and whom he lovingly protects from
court intrigue. Here too we are left wondering about a possible resolution.
Most interestingly, there is the unfinished story of Circetta on the island of
Ithaca, whose magic, learned from her mother, Circe, has nothing lugubri-
ous about it, tempered as it is by a sense of justice coming to her from her
father, Ulysses.

Knights such as Risardo, Floridoro, Filardo, Silano, and the neuras-
thenic Acreonte move all over the Mediterranean, with the side adventures
that their journeys provide, in order to joust in Greece and have a chance to

---

36. On this technique, perfected by Ariosto but later used by many writers of complex ro-
mances, see Daniel Javitch, "*Cantus Interruptus* in the *Orlando furioso*," *MLN* 95 (1980): 66–80.

be crowned victor by the Greek princess Celsidea, King Cleardo's beautiful and only daughter. But whereas in most chivalric romances woman's beauty brings confusion and a challenge to authority, Celsidea conveys order.[37] The winner of the official joust in Athens will get neither her hand nor her body, but a simple crown (10.86). That is, woman remains the outward reason for the tournament of champions in *Floridoro*, but not its reward. Knights are shown as competing with one another for reasons that have to do with their own sense of pride and power, but whereas in men's narrative the winner gets the woman as his prize,[38] in women's narrative women do not get exchanged in games in which they have nothing to say, although they can gladly accept the role of cultural icons and ceremoniously crown the champion at the end.

It is remarkable that the beauty of Princess Celsidea—sufficient, we are told, for so many knights to start a long and perilous journey by land and sea—is indeed marginal, since Fonte, in first introducing Celsidea, concentrates not on her physical endowment but on her wits and chaste ways and on her father's delight in making her sit next to him while he is conducting official business:

> [a girl] who surpassed in esteem and acclaim all other beautiful
>   women,
> a girl endowed as well with excellent wits,
> for an unworthy spirit cannot reign in a beautiful body.
>
> This girl's gracious, noble appearance
> (she was called Celsidea)
> and her habits were so lovely and pious
> that she seemed not a mortal woman but a goddess,
> such that her fame overshadowed that of all other women
> throughout the world, nor did people speak of anything else.
> And while every man talks and reasons of her,
> every other woman loses the claim of being beautiful.
>
> For his pleasure the king was accustomed by day
> to seat this maiden by his side. (1.7–9)

---

37. To give an example of a disorderly woman, when Angelica in the *Furioso* runs away in canto 1, both Orlando and Rinaldo, the two key paladins of King Charlemagne, leave their military duties behind to pursue her, thus causing disarray in the Christian camp.

38. At the very start of Matteo Maria Boiardo's *Orlando Innamorato*, for example, Angelica is made to promise to the warrior who wins the joust: "if you can unhorse Uberto, / My body will be your reward" (bk. 1, 1.28).

Surprisingly, Celsidea's beauty pales in comparison to the handsomeness of the youthful knight Floridoro. He too first appears next to his father, and his blond hair, exquisite clothes, milky skin, and ruby complexion make for a striking entrance. Everybody indeed seems to think of him as a beautiful maiden with whom to fall in love, had he not a masculine pitch of voice:

> The expression of his comely face was so agreeable,
> so lovely the splendor of his beautiful, golden hair,
> and his appearance was so divine,
> that every heart, even a harsh one, was inclined to love him.

> With his shrewd father came the noble son,
> in delightful and lovely clothing.
> Love laughed in his tranquil brow;
> rather he appeared Love's very image.
> His splendid white and vermilion complexion
> made every eye eager to contemplate him.
> Every part of him, except his speech,
> appeared that of an illustrious and beautiful girl. (5.45–46)

Following Renaissance iconography, we have been accustomed to see woman as the object of erotic curiosity, her features euphemistically analyzed in the process of figurative dismembering through evocative remembering that informed so much Petrarchist written, oral, musical, and aesthetic representation at the time.[39] Men, on the other hand, have been usually represented as subjects of inquiry and therefore as active, a priori heterosexual, and historically identifiable individuals. This does not seem to be the case here, and the reason might very well be that Fonte was unwilling, or even perhaps unable, to stick to such a mythopoetic conceit and portray a man both sensitive and masculine. As presented, Floridoro (also called Biancador when he has to assume a fake identity, a name that again goes against type, since white [*bianco*] is a color often reserved to young women in narrative) is the least menacing knight coming to the doors of Athens. Fonte's subtle erotic register

---

39. And indeed Celsidea too gets a description along those lines from a helmsman who has briefly seen her (4.13–16). The literature on the subject is vast. See Nancy Vickers, "Diana Described: Scattered Woman and Scattered Rhyme," in *Writing and Sexual Difference*, ed. Elizabeth Adel (Chicago: University of Chicago Press, 1982); and "The Body Re-Membered: Petrarchan Lyrics and the Strategies of Description," in *Mimesis: From Mirror to Method, Augustine to Descartes*, ed. John Lyons and Stephen Nichols (Hanover: University Press of New England, 1982), 100–109; Amedeo Quondam, *Il naso di Laura. Lingua e poesia lirica nella tradizione del classicismo* (Modena: Panini, 1991); Mary Rogers, "The Decorum of Women's Beauty: Trissino, Firenzuola, Luigini and the Representation of Women in Sixteenth Century Painting," *Renaissance Studies* 2 (1988): 47–88; and Elizabeth Cropper, "On Beautiful Women, Parmigianino, *Petrarchismo*, and the Vernacular Style," *Art Bulletin* 58 (1976): 374–94.

in representing him moves along the lines used to characterize, say, the male beloved in Michelangelo's sonnets rather than Ariosto's fiercely hyperactive knight, Rodomonte. Unexpectedly, Floridoro is referred to as a "damigel" (7.14)—a word subtly conveying the image of a young man dressed affectedly or, as in this case, expressing a subtly eroticized femininity—by the more manly constructed Filardo, his best friend and confidant, sidekick of his adventures, and steady rescuer in times of need. Filardo, Fonte writes, was

> a dear companion of his . . .
> . . . .
> who loved him with a sincere and holy love,
> . . . .
> with whom he held in common laughter and weeping,
> good and ill, the sad state and the glad. (7.13)

Given Floridoro's upbringing in Filardo's family after he lost his own mother, we could take Fonte at her word and see nothing carnal in this male/male relationship. But then how much closer than today must have been men's bonds in the Renaissance, given the scene below in which an acquiescent Floridoro in a state of petrified paralysis cries over his love for Celsidea, and a solicitous Filardo consoles him by delicately drying his eyes!

> Floridoro streams a whirlpool
> of weeping over his delicate cheeks.
> Filardo comforts him, and dries his beautiful
> eyes [*gli occhi belli*] with a linen cloth [*col lin gli asciuga*], and
>   implores him to speak. (8.65)

Petrarch's original iconic image of a self-absorbed Laura doing the same ("asciugandosi gli occhi col bel velo") in a context that enhances her desirability in the most famous canzone of his entire collection keeps its sensual appeal here and its delicate focus on the tactile, but is stunningly regendered.[40]

To be sure, Fonte does not take out the erotic element from her narrative, nor does she shy away from the Ariostan (and later Tassean) characterization of the erotic quest as a deviant narrative moment ("differimento," in Sergio Zatti's characterization).[41] Risardo, for example, switches his quest because of beautiful Odoria, and Floridoro is fully engaged in the largely platonic pursuit of Celsidea. But whereas in male chivalric romances the hero chasing love over other dynastic or simply manly concerns is feminized

---

40. Francesco Petrarca, canzone 126, "Chiare, fresche e dolci acque," in *Petrarch's Lyric Poems*, ed. Robert Durling (Cambridge: Harvard University Press, 1976).

41. See Sergio Zatti, *L'uniforme cristiano e il multiforme pagano. Saggio sulla Gerusalemme liberata* (Milan: Il Saggiatore, 1983).

by his single-mindedness (let us recall the thorough feminization of Orlando in the *Furioso* and of the unreformed Rinaldo in *Jerusalem Delivered*), feminization in *Floridoro* comes from a repeated characterization of men as either inconstant or, the case here, as sullen and melancholic. There was of course a budding tradition of gender trespassing in the early sixteenth century, as shown in the many cross-dressed female adolescents of court theater, such as Santilla in Bibbiena's *La Calandria* and Lelia in Gl'Intronati's *The Deceived*. This curiosity was matched in art, especially in Rome, Venice, and Lombardy, by a visible regendering of Leonardo's female portraits into androgynous boys. As the vernacular lyric became figurally entangled with classical mythological representations of Eros in the Renaissance, Petrarchan erotics started to be reoriented. According to Stephen J. Campbell, this became possible because "the Petrarchan dyad of lover-beloved is actually a triad: the third protagonist of Petrarch's *Rime sparse* is the ambiguously benign and demonic figure of Amor himself." [42] Such seems to be the case in Fonte too, as the two early lengthy quotes show, in which an eroticized Amor presides over the marriage-bound pair of Floridoro and Celsidea. Under Love's auspices, the immature sensuousness of the melancholic Floridoro will be redeemed, the author anticipates, by the chastity-inspiring—and attentive but emotionally aloof—Diana-like Celsidea.

THE EPIC ROMANCE IN THE HANDS OF WOMEN WRITERS

Chivalric romances were the most popular Renaissance literary genre, and books such as Matteo Maria Boiardo's *Orlando Innamorato* (1494) and Ariosto's *Orlando furioso*, the effective founders of the genre, were the first best-sellers ever in Italian literature, with sales in the sixteenth century handily surpassing those of the Bible. The *Innamorato* had an initial printing of 228, but the *Furioso* was printed right away in an edition of 2,000, and the book went through 120 editions in the years between 1540 and 1580. [43] The popularity of Ariosto's text went far beyond sales, as this romance was sung in squares, put to music, quoted in court gatherings, memorized almost in its entirety,

42. Stephen J. Campbell, "Eros in the Flesh: Petrarchan Desire, the Embodied Eros, and Male Beauty in Italian Art, 1500–1540," *Journal of Medieval and Early Modern Studies* 35, no. 3 (2005): 629–62. See also Jodi Cranston, "Desire and Gravitas in Bindo's Portraits," in *Raphael, Cellini, and a Renaissance Banker: The Patronage of Bindo Altoviti*, ed. Alan Chong, Donatella Pegazzano, Dimitrios Zikos, exhibition catalogue (Boston: Isabella Stewart Gardner Museum, 2003). More generally on the issue of eroticized representations of masculinity and male beauty, see Valeria Finucci, *Manly Masquerade*, chaps. 4, 5 and 6.

43. See Daniel Javitch, *Proclaiming a Classic: The Canonization of the Orlando Furioso* (Princeton: Princeton University Press, 1991), 10. According to Beer, the *Innamorato* had 1,250 copies circulating eleven years later. See her *Romanzi di cavalleria*, 207–65.

cherished by "country lasses and crude shepherdesses," and even taught in school because parents asked for it, against the judgment of an array of well-meaning if out-of-touch educators.[44] To make the book more affordable and sell more easily, editors printed it in two columns and in a popular semi-gothic style.[45] The *Furioso* also spawned numberless sequels and prequels; it led to successful translations of other classical works, such as Ovid's *Metamorphoses*, into the vernacular Italian *ottava rima*; and it spilled into the theater as the plays sponsored by the local courts started to experiment with cross-dressed characters echoing the cross-dressed female warriors crowding the romances of chivalry.[46] The *Furioso* motivated closer readings of classical epics, such as Virgil's *Aeneid*, a task already started by Dante in the vernacular in the *Divine Comedy* and continued by Petrarch in Latin with *Africa*, but now in full swing, as appropriate epic genealogies were created by poets in the service of any local prince.

To write romances of chivalry was the passion of any writer who could hold a pen in his hand, we are told, and even faith was spurred by this new fashion, as writers, following post-Tridentine dicta, started to pen religious epic poems on lives of saints, all dutifully written in ottava rima.[47] Prostitutes too were recommended at least to pretend to read the *Furioso*, together with Petrarch and Boccaccio, after they had finished their housework. They were also told to put these books in prominent places in their household to show their good taste, as the prostitute Nanna counsels her

---

44. As Giuseppe Malatesta wrote in *Della nuova poesia* (Verona: Sebastiano delle Donne, 1589), "If you frequent the courts, if you walk along the streets, or through the squares, if you find yourself in salons, if you enter academies, you never hear anything but Ariosto being read or recited. Indeed, why do I say courts and academies when in private homes, in country houses, even in hovels and huts one also finds the *Furioso* continually recited? Leaving aside that there is not a school, a study, or an academy where this wonderful poem is not held dear, I am speaking as well of uneducated country lasses and crude shepherdesses" (138–39); trans. in Javitch, *Proclaiming a Classic*, 14. See also Paul Grendler, "Form and Function in Italian Renaissance Popular Books," *Renaissance Quarterly* 46 (1993): 451–85, and "What Zuanne Read in School: Vernacular Texts in Sixteenth-Century Venetian Schools," *Sixteenth Century Journal* 13, no. 1 (1982): 41–54.

45. See Enrica Pace, "Aspetti tipografico-editoriali di un 'best-seller' del secolo XVI: l'*Orlando furioso*," *Schifanoia* 3 (1987): 103–14; Paul Grendler, "Chivalric Romances in the Italian Renaissance," *Medieval and Renaissance History* 10 (1988): 59–102; and in general Brian Richardson, *Printing, Writers, and Readers in Renaissance Italy* (Cambridge: Cambridge University Press, 1999).

46. On the exhilarating fortune of the *Furioso*, see Giuseppina Fumagalli, *La fortuna dell'Orlando Furioso*.

47. I mentioned earlier the two religious epic poems that Fonte wrote; but many writers, male and female, published similar works in the period. To limit myself to the more or less contemporary output by women writers, I should mention Lucrezia Marinella's *La colomba sacra* (Venice: Ciotti, 1595) and *La vita di Maria vergine, imperatrice dell'universo* (Venice: Barezzo, 1610); and Maddalena Salvetti Acciaioli, *Davide perseguitato* (Florence: Caneo, 1611).

student of whoredom, Pippa, in Pietro Aretino's *Ragionamenti*.[48] Parents loved
to name their daughters after Ariosto's two women warriors, Bradamante
and Marfisa.[49] The first actresses ever allowed on stage in Italy—Vincenza
Armani, Vittoria Piissimi, and Flaminia Romana—promoted their careers
with deft interpretations of episodes of the *Furioso* centered on Bradamante
and Marfisa. In fact, Flaminia was dubbed a "true Marfisa" and would arrive
in cities where her theatrical performances were to take place cross-dressed
as such.[50] In dance, Margherita Gonzaga's *Balletto delle donne* (1585) in Mantua
had women fighters (*guerriere combattenti*) modeled after the strong women
of verse romances.[51] Three real women, "so manly in vivaciousness and
spirit" like the women warriors of romances, the local historian Ugurgieri
Azzolini tells us, strengthened Siena besieged by imperial troops by lead-
ing a multitude of courageous women to fortify the city with trenches and
ramparts.[52]

Many authors felt, however, that it was too dangerous for women to read
"all those lascivious books, all those romances and many errant knights."[53]
Books of chivalry circulated in convents even after the establishment of the
Index of Forbidden Books.[54] Worried religious educators, such as the bishop of
Verona, Sebastiano Pisani, recommended mother superiors to check thor-
oughly in nuns' cells and confiscate all books of chivalry, novellas, or po-

---

48. Pietro Aretino, *Ragionamenti*, ed. Romualdo Marrone (Rome: Newton, 1993), day 1, 147.
Aretino's advice must have been popular in the society of Venetian prostitutes, since the cour-
tesan Isabella Bellocchio had the *Furioso* prominently displayed in her house, as we know from
the documents of her trial for heresy. See Margaret Rosenthal, *The Honest Courtesan: Veronica
Franco, Citizen and Writer in Sixteenth-Century Venice* (Chicago: University of Chicago Press, 1992),
330–31.

49. For example, at the Este court in Ferrara the noblewoman Marfisa d'Este was a celebrated
patroness of arts.

50. See Eric Nicholson, "Romance as Role Model: Early Female Performances of *Orlando furioso*
and *Gerusalemme liberata*," in *Renaissance Transactions: Ariosto and Tasso*, ed. Valeria Finucci (Durham:
Duke University Press, 1999), 246–47.

51. See Nina Treadwell, "'Simil combattimento fatto da Dame': The Musico-Theatrical En-
tertainments of Margherita Gonzaga's *Balletto delle donne* and the Female Warrior in Ferrarese
Cultural History," in *Gender, Sexuality and Early Music*, ed. Todd Borgerding (New York: Rout-
ledge, 2002), 32.

52. See Isidoro Ugurgieri Azzolini, *Le pompe sanesi, o' vero Relazione delli huomini, e donne illustri di
Siena e suo Stato* (Pistoia: Fortunati, 1649), 2 : 406 ff.

53. I cite from Lodovico Dolce, *Dialogo della institution delle donne* (Venice: Giolito, 1945), 19r
(my translation).

54. "Tengono et legono libri vani, come Furioso, Petrarca, Bochacio." Gabriella Zarri, "Mon-
asteri femminili e città (secoli XV e XVIII)," in *Storia d'Italia, Annali IX: La chiesa e il potere politico
dal medioevo all'età contemporanea*, ed. Giorgio Chittolini and Giovanni Miccoli (Turin: Einaudi,
1986), 394.

etry hidden in armoires or under their beds.[55] In the city of Lucca, in the very decade in which *Floridoro* was published, an Order for Nuns circulated ("Ordine per monache," 1585) that forbade the reading of all romances, novellas, comedies, sonnets, songs, letters, and whatever contained sensual or explicit words.[56] A family interested in educating its children in a Christian way "should not have in their home love books or books of tales," Silvio Antoniano wrote, "comedies and romances and similar work, because there is no usefulness in them, they can cause problems, and they can be secret and pernicious teachers of grave sins."[57] A woman who read epic poetry had a doubtful reputation, the angry parents of Fabriano Fabriani argued in 1547 in making the case for having their son apprehended by the guards and put in prison because he had married, against their better judgment, Angelica Sangiorgio, known for enjoying readings of the *Furioso*.[58] Visiting Naples in 1632, the French writer Jean-Jacques Bouchard marveled at the popularity of the *libri di cavalleria*, and complained that there were bookstores full of no other merchandise than these books rented out at specific charges per day.[59]

It is no wonder then that women writers started to write in the genre, no matter how seemingly masculine was a narrative that required battles of epic proportion and heroic deeds of fully armored giants. The models these women had were essentially two: Ariosto and his followers, like Lodovico Dolce and Bernardo Tasso, including Ariosto's predecessor, Boiardo, with their digressive narratives of meandering adventures—and these constitute what we would call the romances of chivalry proper—and Torquato Tasso,

55. Sebastiano Pisani, *Ordini et decreti per le monache della città e diocese di Verona pubblicati et stampati di ordine dell'Illustrissimo et reverendissimo Sebastiano Pisani di Verona* (Verona: Battista Merlo, 1667), 68. On Renaissance women as readers and owners of books and for a list of books owned by Venetian women, see Tiziana Plebani, "Nascita e caratteristiche del pubblico di lettrici tra medioevo e età moderna," in *Donna, disciplina, creanza cristiana dal XV al XVII secolo*, ed. Gabriella Zarri (Rome: Edizioni di Storia e Letteratura, 1996), 23–44.

56. "Sono proibiti alle monache tutti li libri di romanzi, novelle, commedie, sonetti, canzoni, lettere et ogn'altra scrittura che contenga materia, concetti, e parole sensuali et secolaresche." Gian Ludovico Masetti Zannini, *Motivi storici della educazione femminile* (Naples: D'Auria, 1982), 339.

57. Silvio Antoniano, *Tre libri dell'educazione Christiana*, c. 89B, in Masetti Zannini, *Motivi storici della educazione femminile*, 242 (my translation).

58. The case, registered in the Cancelleria vecchia, Matrimoni 1 of the Archivio Arcivescovile of Bologna, 1547, is cited by Lucia Ferrante, "Marriage and Women's Subjectivity in a Patrilineal System: The Case of Early Modern Bologna," in *Gender, Kinship, Power: A Comparative and Interdisciplinary History*, ed. Mary Jo Maynes at al. (New York: Routledge, 1996), 124.

59. "Il y a des boutiques qui ne font autre merchandise que de louer de ces romans à tant par jour, et vous ne voyez autre chose en la rue des librairies que cet écriteau: *Qui si locano libri di Cavalleria*." *Journal II. Voyage dans le royaume de Naples. Voyage dans la campagne de Rome*, ed. Emanuele Kanceff (Turin: Giappichelli, 1976), 267.

who with *Jerusalem Delivered*, which came out the same year as *Floridoro*, set out to construct an epic, Christian narrative in which the forces of good and evil were presented in dichotomized, occasionally dogmatic ways. The two forms of narrative, and the individual merit of these two major authors in founding a genre that was peculiarly and thoroughly "Italian," produced a lively literary *querelle* in which for the first time fruitful discussion took place regarding what constitutes a well-defined literary genre and how one should write within its parameters.[60] This of course made writing epic and chivalric romances even more fashionable. At first glance one would guess that a narrative à la Ariosto was rewarding and liberating for women writers, given the range of possibilities that women in the *Furioso* had to assert their individuality, but the pull of an ordered, less sexualized female engagement and of a linear development à la Tasso also had its appeal; hence the varied production of the time.

The first woman to publish in Italy what could arguably be said to constitute a chivalric romance was Laura Terracina, whose *Discorso sopra il principio di tutti i canti dell'Orlando furioso* was printed thirteen times after the original 1551 edition in Venice. To call Terracina's output a chivalric romance is to stretch the limits of the genre, for there is no original plot and no independent story line in this text. But Terracina's method is intriguing: by using the first line of each Ariostan canto to develop her argument, she is able to comment from a woman's point of view on the social danger of male lust. She also responds forcefully to attacks on women's honor.[61] Hence, we surmise, her popularity in the classroom, where the text was liked for its allegorized and moralized readings of episodes in the *Furioso*, especially because, I hasten to add, many teachers were not aware that the author was a woman. Thus Ascanius Fontana comments that he employs "il Terracina" for those students who want to read works in ottava rima, and Alexius Salto likes "il Terracina" for the use of allegory.[62]

The second female-authored chivalric romance published in Italy, *Il Meschino detto il Guerrino*, by Tullia d'Aragona, came out a few years after the author's death and enjoyed two editions (1560 and 1594). This chivalric

60. This *querelle*, with writers pro and con compiling authoritative defenses of their points of view, has been reconstructed by Daniel Javitch in *Proclaiming a Classic*.

61. Laura Terracina, *Discorso sopra il principio di tutti i canti dell' Orlando furioso* (Venice: Giolito, 1550). On Terracina, see Deanna Shemek, "Getting a Word in Edgewise: Laura Terracina's *Discorsi* on the *Orlando furioso*," in her *Ladies Errant: Wayward Women and Social Order in Early Modern Italy* (Durham: Duke University Press, 1998), 126–57; and Cox, "Women as Readers and Writers of Chivalric Poetry," 136.

62. "il Terracina che fa [l'allegoria] sopra tutti i primi canti del *Furioso*." In Baldo, *Alunni, maestri e scuole*, 73.

romance in thirty-six cantos comes from the Spanish tradition, d'Aragona writes, which she chose because she wanted to offer something "most chaste, all pure, all Christian, and in which there is no example, no word, nor anything else that cannot be read at any hour by any respectable and holy man, and by any woman—be she married, virgin, widow, or nun."[63] To offer something that pure requires a thorough moralizing of Ariosto, and as a result we do not even find women warriors in d'Aragona's narrative. Likewise, moments of female transgression are very much circumscribed.

A more lively chivalric romance is Margherita Sarrocchi's *Scanderbeide*, published in Rome in 1606, first in nine cantos and then in a definitive version of twenty-three cantos in 1623. This work concentrates on the Albanian national hero, Giorgio Castriota, who fought against the Turks by forming a league of princes, with aid from Venice, Naples, and Rome. Here the model Sarrocchi had in mind is not Ariosto, but Tasso, given the more heroic and celebratory needs of her hero fighting the Ottomans.[64] Lucrezia Marinella's *L'Enrico overo Bisantio acquistato* also moves along Tasso's epic lines; it was published in Venice in 1635. The work is in twenty-seven cantos and highlights the epic accomplishments of the fearless Venetian hero Enrico Dandolo during the Fourth Crusade, in which Constantinople was taken and sacked.[65] Then in 1640 in Florence Barbara Albizzi-Tagliamochi published *Ascanio errante*, based ostensibly on Virgil's epic of which it takes one of the strands, and boasting a poetic verve and felicitous characterization that make it quite readable.[66]

---

63. Tullia d'Aragona, "To the Readers," in *Il Meschino, altramente detto il Guerrino* (Venice: Sessa, 1560), n.p.. The translation is mine. Although d'Aragona writes that her model was Amadis de Gaule, there was a more recent and closer Italian example in Francesco da Barberino's *Guerin Meschino* (1473) that she most probably followed. For doubts on d'Aragona's authorship, see Virginia Cox, "Fiction, 1560–1650," in Panizza and Wood, *History of Women's Writing in Italy*, 58–60. See also Gloria Allaire, "Tullia d'Aragona's *Il Meschino altramante detto il Guerino* as Key to a Reappraisal of Her Work," *Quaderni d'Italianistica* 16, no. 1 (1995): 33–50.

64. Giorgio Castriota was called Iskender Bey by the Ottomans, a name corrupted into Scanderbeg, thus the title of Sarrocchi's epic. On Sarrocchi, see Masetti Zannini, *Motivi storici della educazione femminile*, 39–44; and Serena Pezzini, "Ideologia della conquista, ideologia dell'accoglienza: La *Scanderbeide* di Margherita Sarrocchi (1623)," *MLN* 120 (2005): 190–222. For an English translation of the *Scanderbeide*, see *Scanderbeide: The Heroic Deeds of George Scanderbeg, King of Epirus*, trans. Rinaldina Russell (Chicago: University of Chicago Press, 2006).

65. Lucrezia Marinella, *Enrico ovvero Bisanzio acquistato* (Venice: Imberti, 1635). On *Enrico*, see Christine Ristaino, "The Epic Woman: *L'Enrico ovvero Bisanzio acquistato*," in "Lucrezia Marinella's Oeuvre: Between Tradition and Innovation" (Ph.D. diss., University of North Carolina–Chapel Hill, 2003), 118–62. The work was reprinted twice in the nineteenth century, in 1844 and 1854. An English translation by Maria Galli Stampino is under way for the Other Voice series.

66. On Albizzi-Tagliamochi, see Leopoldo Ferri, *Biblioteca femminile italiana* (Padua: Crescini, 1812).

FLORIDORO AND THE GENDERING
OF ROMANCES OF CHIVALRY

Discounting the two earlier examples of chivalric romance by Laura Ter-
racina and Tullia d'Aragona, which, given the format of the former and the
overt imitation of the latter, could not significantly diverge from the authors
being imitated, Fonte's *Floridoro* represents the first sustained effort on the
part of a woman writer to pen a Renaissance epic romance on the model of
Ariosto and Boiardo. The task was not easy. It is not so much that women
did not know how to write of jousts, for example, since books on the subject
were popular and easily available.⁶⁷ Nor was it too difficult for women to dig
into classical sources, since many classics had been vigorously translated
into Italian throughout the century. Women writers were not put off by rep-
resentations of scenes of hunting either, since falconry, shooting, and races
were popular weekly, if not daily, events.⁶⁸ The problem was rather the no-
ticeable lack of successful female models offered by the available printed lit-
erature. Women in fiction were hardly real, often either too good or too bad.
Fonte declares almost right away that there was, however, a wider range of
feminine facets unrepresented in literature that needed to be accounted for,
since women could do all things men did when the circumstances of their
upbringing were equal, whether on the battlefield or the writing table. She
significantly puts the two activities together in the same octave in *Floridoro*:

> Women in every age were by nature
> endowed with great judgment and spirit,
> nor are they born less apt than men to demonstrate
> (with study and care) their wisdom and valor.
> And why, if their bodily form is the same,
> if their substances are not varied,
> if they have the same food and speech, must they
> have then different courage and wisdom?
>
> Always one has seen and sees (provided that a
> woman wanted to devote thought to it)

---

67. On books of duels, see Francesco Erspamer, *La biblioteca di Don Ferrante: Duello e onore nella
cultura del Cinquecento* (Rome: Bulzoni, 1982), 181–200. Although traditionally women have not
been associated with armed combat, there were cases in which they fought men with lance
or sword. See, for example, Sabba Castiglione, *Ricordi o vero ammaestramenti* (Venice: Lorenzini,
1562), c. 112b. Women also joined the Crusades not just as wives or paramours but as combat-
ants. See James Brundage, "The Crusader's Wife: A Canonistic Quandary," *Studia Gratiana* 12
(1967): 625–41.

68. Women too occasionally took part in hunting trips. Fonte herself has a noblewoman, Luci-
mena, who got lost while hunting for pleasure one day with her husband Nicobaldo (6.50).

more than one woman succeed in the military,
and take away the esteem and acclaim from many men.
Just so in letters and in every
endeavor that men undertake and pursue,
women have achieved and achieve such good results
that they have no cause at all to envy men. (4.1–2)

Limitations for Fonte, in short, come not from women's nature but from patriarchal culture. Fathers have simply not cared to educate their daughters, nor have they taught them, say, how to fight, as they have their sons, on the assumption that it was not worth their effort or that it would do their daughters no good, even on the marriage market:

If when a daughter is born the father
set her with his son to equivalent tasks,
she would not be in lofty and fair deeds
inferior or unequal to her brother,
whether he placed her among the armed squads
with himself, or set her to learn some liberal art.
But because she is raised in other pursuits,
for her education she is held in low regard. (4.4)

Since *Floridoro* was not completed, we do not know whether any of the women's goals in this poem will be thoroughly accomplished. Fonte repeatedly makes clear that her ladies, no matter their country or rank, are kept in a social and family structure that imprisons them and from which they long to escape.[69] Even within the patriarchal household, *Floridoro's* women are never safe. Fonte rewrites, for example, one of the most classical epic episodes—that of the inseparable male couple engaged in a nighttime expedition with heroic connotations—into a nocturnal sortie to rape the well-guarded princess Celsidea. The couple Diomedes and Ulysses in Homer's *Iliad*, Euryalus and Nisus in Virgil's *Aeneid*, Opleo and Timante in Statius's *Thebaid*, and Cloridano and Medoro in the *Furioso* are justly famous because they show *pietas*, a well-developed bent for heroic behavior, and an undying faith in the other that prompts them to sacrifice their lives for the higher cause of service to the king, as well as friendship. But in *Floridoro* Acreonte convinces his brother, also his best friend, to leave the king's table surreptitiously at night for the purpose of climbing up to the bedroom of his host's daughter. Celsidea's rape is avoided when Floridoro appears, deus ex machina, to save her. An armed encounter follows and one knight dies in

69. For more on the point, see Stephen Kolsky, "Moderata Fonte's *Tredici canti del Floridoro*: Women in a Man's Genre," *Rivista di studi italiani* 17 (1999): 176.

the dark night, as in many rewritings of the story, but Fonte turns the topos around when she savagely has the would-be rapist killed by his own brother, even if by mistake.

Another example, among a number available, of the specificity of Fonte's project regarding women can be found in the figure of Circetta. In the writer's hands, the goal of the temptress Circetta, who is, against type, a virgin in *Floridoro*, strangely enough is not to bewitch men but to escape the fate that makes her the prisoner of an island where she is supposed to bewitch. The diminutive Circetta is first introduced while performing the magic task of transforming a man into a tree (5.24), thus echoing a similar transformation of, among others, the knight Astolfo by Alcina in the *Furioso*, after she has fulfilled her sexual desires and has become weary of his love. But Circetta is introduced as "the most sweet virgin" (5.37) and is made to blush when the knight Silano compliments her:

> The lady lowers her honest and chaste eyes
> at that speech which is by no means unwelcome to her,
> and adorns her face with the beautiful color
> that the rose reveals in the morning sun. (5.39)

Circetta will not be in charge of a program of seduction, for Fonte hints at a destiny that is the exact opposite of the stereotype that we would expect her to embody: she will be seduced rather than a seducer, and also, it seems, deceived and abandoned, just like her mother. Circetta is made to argue cogently for a reformist reading of her mother's fame and legacy: Circe, "the beautiful and virtuous fay" (8.12), as she announces, used magical arts not for the purposes for which she was rendered famous in literature but out of self-defense:

> "And be silent, you who say unjustly
> that she transformed his companions into beasts,
> for she never, if not forced,
> caused displeasure to whoever turned to offend her." (8.13)[70]

---

70. Circetta's characterization recalls that of Ariosto's seer, Melissa. The alluring and dangerous (literally castrating) Circe is present in many chivalric romances. In Matteo Maria Boiardo's *Orlando Innamorato*, Circella, blinded by her love for Ulisse, drinks her own magical potion and turns into a deer. See *Orlando Innamorato*, trans. Charles Ross (Berkeley: University of California Press, 1989), 1.6.52. For a history of the myth, see Judith Yarnall, *Transformations of Circe: The History of an Enchantress* (Urbana: University of Illinois Press, 1994). For a more in-depth look at the characterization of Circetta, see Valeria Finucci, "Moderata Fonte e il romanzo cavalleresco al femminile," xxxiv–xxxv; Malpezzi-Price, "The Enchantress or the Rewriting of the Myth of Circe," in *Moderata Fonte*, 113–21; Cox, "Women as Readers and Writers of Chivalric Poetry," 142–43; and Julia Kisacky, "The Perils of Power: Government in Moderata Fonte's *Floridoro*," paper presented at the AAIS meeting, Chapel Hill, NC, April 2005.

The kind of magic Circetta espouses is naturalistic: she wants to control nature (for example, she has in mind the creation of a magic mountain on Ithaca), not to control men. By making the figure of the witch devoid of maliciousness (a project that Fonte explores a second time with a similar witch's agenda turned positive in the story of Lucimena), and by taking away from Circetta any suspicion of sexuality, the author shows that the Circe stereotype is a fantasy created by men for men. The actively sexual woman, let us remember, was invented to provide an outlet for male curiosity and homosocial gratifications as well as to indulge voyeuristic desires on the part of male readers. But since the sexually active and desiring woman was perceived as dangerous because she had the power to subvert the male/dominant and woman/passive relationship, it was customary in narrative to have her abandoned by the hero when he, having gratified his sexual urges, could conveniently move to greener pastures. The sexually active woman was subsequently also degraded by making her no longer function as an object of desire—Alcina in Ariosto is shown, for example, as toothless, senile, and with scarce, disheveled hair after the knight Ruggiero has unmasked her "false" charms. It goes without saying that women writers have problems in identifying with this pathetic narrative of female loss, well aware that their representation as devilish and predatory human beings hardly fits the sense of their gender identity in culture. Fonte was not alone in this rewriting. In the female-authored chivalric romance published next, chronologically speaking, Marinella's *Enrico*, the Circe-cast Erina goes one step further, and from sisterly and virginal, like Fonte's Circetta, she becomes a contemplative type bent on doing only good.[71]

If marrying is no longer the overriding quest of women in narrative, if lust is described as unappealing to them, and if the use of guile is not in their agenda, what else is there for women writers to flesh out for their female characters when engaged in a program of epic imitation? I would argue that there is one issue in which women have just as much invested as men, an issue that it would pay to investigate: power—that is, how to get it, how to share it, how to will it. That power has often been presented as a male privilege, and that women writers had (and often still have) problems in linking power—with the complementary questions of rights, lineage, and inheritance—to any female character, go without saying. That Fonte ingeniously tried to see how this topic could be worked in *Floridoro*, years before she returned aggressively to the subject in *The Worth of Women*, is the subject of the final part of this introduction.

---

71. For this reading see Cox, "Women as Readers and Writers of Chivalric Poetry," 142–43. In Sarrocchi's *Scanderbeide* enchanting witches are absent. See Pezzini, "Ideologia della conquista," 218.

As was customary in epic romances and comedies, Fonte highlights is-
sues of power through the use of siblings. But rather than using twin boys or
fraternal twins of opposite sex, as in the case of Ruggiero and Clorinda and
of Bradamante and Ricciardetto in the *Furioso*, of Lidio and Santilla in Bibbi-
ena's *Calandria*, and of Lelia and Fabrizio in Gl'Intronati's *The Deceived*, Fonte
puts a pair of female twins at the core of her narrative.[72] From the beginning,
as I mentioned earlier, she gives the woman warrior Risamante the quest to
recover the inheritance that she is due as the daughter of the king of Arme-
nia, a goal that she can achieve only by fighting her identical twin, Biond-
aura, the reign's sole heir. The recovery of a patrilineally oriented kinship
and patrimony on the part of Risamante, rather than marriage, constitutes
in many ways the backbone of *Floridoro*. Fonte follows closely her female
knight's efforts to get a kingdom the way men in romances of chivalry do,
and this was indeed the only issue that she resolved before sending *Floridoro*
to press. What she left to the readers to figure out was whether Risamante
would share the territory she had just gained with her twin or whether she
would break all sisterly ties and punish her. In a previous study I suggested
that Fonte's inability, or unwillingness, fully to unravel this episode with
perhaps a few more octaves had a twofold origin. One was biographical, in
that she married soon after *Floridoro* suddenly came out, and we know that
she published no more for a decade. The other was authorial, in that she felt
perhaps unable to negotiate the formulaic closure—with the "good" hero
killing the "bad" hero (in our case, Risamante killing the defender of her sis-
ter, King Cloridabello) and becoming the ruler of the state—that had made
the genre so successful.[73] Such was, for one, the ending of Virgil's *Aeneid*,
the text against which all Italian writers of epics had to measure themselves.

I would like to return to the issue of authorial lack of closure from
another angle and suggest that Fonte's impasse may have come from the
fact that it was psychologically impossible for her to choose a twin over her
identical other or, in patriarchal terms, to pick one offspring over another,
even though this was customarily done in society. When all differences be-

---

72. The structure of twinning is very much present in classical literature too, as in Plautus's
Menaechmi. For the fantasies that this mirroring construction engenders, see Giulio Ferroni, "Il
sistema comico della gemellarità," in his *Il testo e la scena: Saggi sul teatro del Cinquecento* (Rome: Bul-
zoni, 1980), 65–84; and Valeria Finucci, "Androgynous Doubling and Hermaphroditic Anxiet-
ies: Bibbiena's *La calandria*," in *Manly Masquerade*, 189–223.

73. See Finucci, "Moderata Fonte e il romanzo cavalleresco al femminile," xxxii, xxxviii. Like-
wise, although Marinella has two women warriors fighting each other in her epic, the Byzantine
Meandra and the Venetian Claudia, both eventually succumb in the match and share the "honor
of the victory" (24.48). On Marinella, see Ristaino, "Lucrezia Marinella's Oeuvre."

tween the two sisters have been dismantled and the time has come to present Biondaura to the readers (she has been the subject of conversation or the object of a voyeuristic gaze through a portrait, but has always been physically absent), the narrative line seems suddenly to lose momentum and Fonte opts out, as if the enemy twins had become one and the mirror had ceased to function as a go-between.

Fonte begins the chronicle of her twins early in *Floridoro* by differentiating them through naming as soon as they are born: Biondaura's name echoes the evasive, ethereal, and light-diffusing Petrarchan woman; and Risamante gets a name that de-dramatizes the implications of her narrative cross-dressing by hinting at a possible sunny, playful disposition. They are identical in everything, Fonte adds, apart from their outward gendered characteristics: one is soft and delicate like a woman and the other goes around the world armed like a warrior (2.30). Sometime after their birth the twins are separated by a benevolent father figure, a wizard named Celidante, who kidnaps Risamante, knowing that she is predestined to leave a mark in the world and wanting to educate her for the task.[74] In due time the father chooses to believe that Risamante is lost for good, and at his death he leaves the kingdom to his only remaining daughter "and did not even name the other" (2.35).

Risamante is apprised of her noble origins only seventeen years later. Newly conscious of her rights, she reads paternal negligence, rather than paternal might, in the king's decision. Thus, in phallic disrespect for his Law, she asks her sister for half of her inheritance. They are born of the same father, she argues, and therefore have equal rights, in addition to equal features (2.33). Biondaura rejects this request and responds that her land is hers by right. Thus, in "just rage," Risamante wages a war against her.

To be sure, the issue of which twin should have the right to the father's property is a complex one. Who is born first when both are born almost at once? Was the one born first generated first as well? More generally, how do women inherit? At the time of Fonte's writing, the legal system in place throughout Italy with municipal variations (*ius proprium*) was slowly moving

---

74. With this plot twist Fonte overtly imitates both Boiardo and Ariosto. The twins Ruggiero and Marfisa, Boiardo writes in a narrative that Ariosto reprises, lost their mother and father and were raised by the vavasour and necromancer Atalante on an isolated mountain. Knowing the boy's destiny, Atalante then made sure that he learned proper military skills, just as Celidante will do for Risamante in *Floridoro*. See *Orlando Innamorato*, bk. 1, 1.73–75. The twins are always separated in those narratives. The figure of Celidante is modeled upon that of Atlante in *Orlando furioso* (and Atalante in the *Innamorato*), but with a difference in the gender of the person to be protected: a man, Ruggiero, in the case of Ariosto's wizard, and a woman, Risamante, in the case of Fonte. Both protagonists are twins, both lost their parents early in life, and both will get their due—a kingdom—at the end.

from a method called *in fraterna*, in which all brothers shared equally in the father's patrimony, to one based on primogeniture, which meant that younger sons could not inherit as wealth started to concentrate on the firstborn male of the *casato*. Women had access to the father's estate only through dowries, which they could not claim legally, however, although it was often understood that dowries were indispensable to the honor of the family, and thus they were provided if at all possible, even if debts had to be incurred. When there was no son to inherit the father's property, daughters would inherit, at least in Venice, in equal parts, while in Florence an indirect, even collateral, male line took precedence over daughters for property devolution in order to keep the family name alive.[75] Maternal inheritance, if there was any, was divided equally among males and females when there was no will. All in all, daughters were not treated equally among themselves, and by the end of the sixteenth century, just as cadet brothers were given a living allowance (*vitalizio*) and sent to the military or the church, so only one or two daugh-

---

75. For the need to give a dowry to guarantee the honor of the family, see Queller and Madden, "Father of the Bride," 704. Roman law (*ius commune*), which was the law of the country, allowed inheritance rights for women, even when they had a dowry, but municipalities could—and did—enact their own restrictions. For the juridical place of women in early modern society, the dowry system, and the dotal size in Venice and the Veneto region at the time, see Bellavitis, "Patrimoni e matrimoni a Venezia nel Cinquecento"; Chojnacki, *Women and Men in Renaissance Venice*; James Grubb, *Provincial Families of the Renaissance: Private and Public Life in the Veneto* (Baltimore: Johns Hopkins University Press, 1996); Joanne Ferraro, *Marriage Wars in Late Renaissance Venice* (New York: Oxford University Press, 2001); and Alison Smith, "Gender, Ownership, and Domestic Space: Inventories and Family Archives in Renaissance Verona," *Renaissance Studies* 8 (1998): 375–91.

In Florence rules were more restrictive for women regarding not only property, including the ability to will their own, but also inheritance rights. Women there were also restricted in their capacity to sign documents and had to use a *procuratore* (*mundualdus*) for most transactions. For the Tuscan case, see Thomas Kuehn, *Law, Family, and Women: Toward a Legal Anthropology of Renaissance Italy* (Chicago: University of Chicago Press, 1991); Anthony Molho, "Deception and Marriage Strategy in Renaissance Florence: The Case of Women's Age," *Renaissance Quarterly* 41 (1988): 193–217; and Christiane Klapisch-Zuber, *Women, Family, and Ritual in Renaissance Italy* (Chicago: University of Chicago Press, 1985). For Naples and the south, see Maria Antonietta Visceglia, *Il bisogno d'eternità: I comportamenti aristocratici a Napoli in età moderna* (Naples: Guida, 1988). More generally, see Gianna Pomata, "Family and Gender," in *Early Modern Italy: 1550–1796*, ed. John Marino (New York: Oxford University Press, 2002), 69–86; Mario Bellomo, *La condizione giuridica della donna in Italia* (Turin: Einaudi, 1970); Marzio Barbagli, *Sotto lo stesso tetto: Mutamenti della famiglia in Italia dal XV al XX secolo* (Bologna: Il Mulino, 1984); and Dean Trevor and K. J. P Lowe, eds., *Marriage in Italy: 1300–1650* (Cambridge: Cambridge University Press, 1998). On forced marriage and the possibility for women to recur to the law to rescind it, see Daniela Hacke, "'Non lo volevo per marito in modo alcuno': Forced Marriages, Generation Conflicts, and the Limits of Patriarchal Power in Early Modern Venice, c. 1580–1680," in Schutte, Kuehn, and Menchi, *Time, Space, and Women's Lives in Early Modern Europe*, 203–21.

ters were allowed to marry and the others were allocated, unwillingly if not coercively, to the convent. Of those who married, the first, the last, or the most physically attractive was customarily given the highest dowry in order to attract a promising husband. Since even convents required money to take in unmarried and unmarriageable daughters, women of all classes considered a dowry indispensable to their survival. They also saw the dowry as a precise indicator of their place in society. A daughter with no property, Fonte vehemently asserts, has almost no choice other than to become a prostitute.[76]

In reading through *Floridoro* one senses that there is something personal in Fonte's emphasis that fathers ought to guarantee the sustenance of their nubile family dependents and that provisions should be made for them in due time.[77] I have already mentioned Doglioni's remarks that Fonte had to engage in a legal battle to win her right to a congruent amount of her father's assets. Following *favor agnationis*, a father's assets would usually go to an older brother. If the parents died intestate, however (and such could have been the case here), the money would go to both, but this often required going to court.[78] Indeed, in *The Worth of Women* Fonte mentions the case of sisters who had received from their father "a share in his estate . . . but who then find themselves imprisoned in the home like slaves to their brothers, who deprive them of their rights and seize their portion for themselves, in defiance of all justice."[79] She remembers her heartache directly in *Floridoro*:

---

76. Lucrezia, one of the interlocutors, was disinherited by her father and thus knows the problem firsthand. See also Virginia Cox, "The Single Self: Feminist Thought and the Marriage Market in Early Modern Venice," *Renaissance Quarterly* 47 (1995): 513–81.

77. Women soon started to sign over any property claim to their agnatic family with an official renunciation once they were granted a dowry. According to Gianna Pomata, after 1560, 70 percent of Venetian patrician women were sent to monastic orders; in Milan 75 percent of patrician women were celibate in the first half of the seventeenth century. See "Family and Gender," 78–80.

78. Lack of a dowry may also have been one of the reasons that Fonte did not marry until she was in her late twenties. In Venice, the average age of marriage was sixteen in the second half of the sixteenth century. See Chojnacky, *Women and Men in Renaissance Venice*, 175 and 313. Fathers were known to fake downward the age of daughters to increase their chance of marriage after twenty-five. See Molho, "Deception and Marriage Strategy in Renaissance Florence," 204. Many women did go to court to get their due. See, for example, the case of Giulia Carriera reconstructed by Sergio Lavarda, "'Sempre parati al combatter.' Onore, risentimenti, ultime volontà in una famiglia padovana del 500," *Studi Veneziani* 30 (1995): 79–107.

79. Fonte, *Worth of Women*, 63. As Cox remarks, there is a will by Fonte's brother, drawn up three years after the author died, in which he complains that some of his property was still in his brother-in-law's hands, including many family documents and books ("molte scritture di casa nostra, e in particolare i libri"). In *Worth of Women*, 63 n. 30. Leonardo Pozzo's will is in ASV, Notarile. Testamenti: Crivelli, Girolamo fu Francesco, b. 222, n1176, April 23, 1595.

How many orphans today have no access
to the possessions that were their fathers'
for lacking, not someone who would court death,
but someone who would employ even his tongue in their favor?
As if speaking were a great concern,
if first their hand is not filled with gold,
few are the lawyers willing to undertake the task
of opening their mouths in their defense. (3.3)

The story of the original separation and of the father's differentiation between his offspring is told in almost the exact same terms twice in *Floridoro*, as if repetitions were necessary both to narrative closure and to cure some deeply felt anxiety on the part of the author. The chain of events that led one sister to pursue another in the name of equality is given center stage once at the start of the romance (2.30–37) and then again, almost verbatim, at the end (13.51–59). Both times this tale is accompanied by a combat in which Risamante fights (and defeats) a knight championing her sister, a combat in which it is paramount that she wound the enemy close to the groin ("between his belly and his flank," 2.21) or on the head ("into his head penetrates the cruel sword," 13.62) to suggest that the "right" hero wins because he is able to leave passions aside and think right, a technique that Aeneas had also used in his duel with Turnus at the conclusion of the *Aeneid*. Both times Risamante takes off her helmet at the end of the joust and reveals her sex under her armor, an event that thoroughly confounds the onlookers because at the same time that she is recognized as a woman, she is also misrecognized for being who she is definitely not: Biondaura.

The first misrecognition takes place as the public present at the duel between her and Macandro, king of the Parthii, realizes in utmost surprise that Risamante looks exactly like the woman in the painting that her adversary, whom she has just killed, left hanging on a tree (2.27).[80] Macandro came to the tournament to assert through a duel his belief that his idol, Biondaura,

---

80. In women's writing, unlike men's, portraits of beautiful women, authorized by women, do women no good. A striking example is that of the unnamed duchess in Giulia Bigolina's *Urania*, whose portrait, featuring parts described according to Petrarchan mythmaking codes, causes her eventual undoing. See *Urania*, 137–39. For how the "bellissima donna" has been portrayed in the Renaissance, see Yavneh, "Ambiguity of Beauty in Tasso and Petrarch"; and Elizabeth Cropper, "The Place of Beauty in the High Renaissance and Its Displacement in the History of Art," *Medieval and Renaissance Texts and Studies* 132 (1995): 159–205. For the inability of the ugly woman to function as an object of desire, as in the case of Ariosto's Gabrina, see Valeria Finucci, "The Female Masquerade: Ariosto and the Game of Desire," in *Desire in the Renaissance: Psychoanalysis and Literature*, ed. Valeria Finucci and Regina Schwartz (Princeton: Princeton University Press, 1994), 61–88, esp. 73–78.

was the most beautiful woman in the world, as her portrait clearly showed.[81] Now that he is dead the onlookers are puzzled: why would you indeed fight the woman you adore? Fonte uses here the image of the mirror to highlight the extreme resemblance between the sisters, one that in fact does not fade even when the real woman and the one painted are placed next to each other for comparison (2.29). The scene concludes with Risamante shedding the only sign of dissimilarity between her and her sister that Fonte mentioned when first describing them: clothes. At the insistence of the queen of Greece, Sorinda, and of her daughter, Celsidea, Risamante now takes off, even if just for the space of an evening, her breeches and dresses up in feminine attire for the official dinner.

Risamante's literal uncovering of her identity is repeated in the last octaves of *Floridoro*, after she defeats the second champion of her sister, King Cloridabello, who is now engaged in fighting not for Biondaura's beauty, as Macandro did earlier, but for Biondaura's kingdom. Were he to lose, Biondaura would be bound to let her sister have her entire land, including the capital city of Artemita. In seeing Risamante's face, a prostrate Cloridabello misrecognizes her for Biondaura and cannot understand why the very woman whose cause he is championing has chosen to fight him now (13.66). Fonte describes him as both dejected and befuddled.

As the story of Risamante develops, what is at stake is not so much who is right, but who is who. Throughout the narrative, what Risamante wants is not to be her sister but to have what her sister has—the kingdom of Armenia—because that will make her, just like Biondaura, her father's daughter. The only way Risamante can cure herself of the fear of being so unworthy of her real father's love as to have been literally forgotten by him, even on his deathbed, is to be so strong and successful that everyone can see that she too deserves to be loved. Thus when she has defeated Cloridabello and has the chance to show that her cause is just and moral, her fury against her

---

81. Macandro collects the shields of the warriors he bests (and he plans to do this now too) for the same reason as Rodomonte in the *Furioso*: self-aggrandizement. Alleging that Isabella, whom he killed because she wanted to keep her virginity, needs to be honored for that reason, Rodomonte challenges any passing knight in the *Furioso* to a duel. Just as Risamante does with Macandro, Bradamante denounces Rodomonte's twisted argument and tells him, indignantly, that she will joust only for Isabella and not for his invented program of angelology. For a thorough reading of what is at stake for men in women's glorification, see Valeria Finucci, "(Dis)Orderly Death, or How to Be In by Being Out: The Case of Isabella," in *The Lady Vanishes*, 169–97, esp. 191–95. The tie with the *Furioso* is further reinforced here by the image of a woman's painting on a tree branch, which recalls Orlando and Ferraù's duel in the *Furioso* (12.46). Orlando's helmet is temporarily put on a tree. In Boiardo too Rodamonte carries into battle the effigy of his beloved, which then falls to the ground, causing his rage. See *Innamorato*, bk. 2, 7–29, 14–20.

sister melts away. Seeing the king lying half dead on the bloodied battlefield, she breaks an all-encompassing epic rule—kill your adversary—and with a "pitiful hand" takes off his bloodied helmet and has him brought inside a tent to be cured (13.63). Having risked death in order to be "recognized," Risamante now nullifies her father's "No" by entering into an equal relationship with her sister based on blood ties. Through her woman warrior Fonte asserts that political inclusion is gender blind and women have the right to power sharing, as free individuals do, and thus are effective members of a contractual society. The rivalry/competition among sisters, like that among brothers, can be socially accommodated, therefore, once the father is out of the picture or rendered powerless.[82]

For once now, although still fully armed, Risamante is given an adjective that has so far marked only her sister, "soft" (*molle*). Fonte used softness to describe Biondaura's femaleness, but now she employs it to refer to Risamante's heart. Women warriors, she seems to suggest, have different issues at stake than men when they engage in combat. Respect for what they stand for is of primary importance, she argues, while useless violence and compensatory cruelty are better left to the other sex. Rivalry stops when truth is revealed, because women's heart is soft.[83] In short, women can choose to be generous when they have made their point, because their outward purpose is not to cancel their enemies but to make them come to their senses.[84] As Fonte puts it in *The Worth of Women,* "we women . . . among our other good qualities, are eminently mild, peaceable, and benign by nature," and it has been as a consequence of this natural disposition that this sex has often remained silent and composed in the face of discrimination.[85] The story of Risamante can thus end without the proper clear-cut closure that we are accustomed to

---

82. To observe how this rivalry works among brothers (and what the sisters have at stake in it) in a key Renaissance text, see Valeria Finucci, "In the Name of the Brother: Male Rivalry and Social Order in Baldassarre Castiglione's *Il libro del cortegiano," Exemplaria* 9 (1997): 91–116.

83. This stance also characterizes Bradamante in the *Furioso,* who is advised in canto 2 to kill Pinabello to save herself from a future betrayal, but does not.

84. On Risamante's new soft core, see also Francesca Behr, "Moderata Fonte's Lady Knight: A Different Perspective on Women, War, and Epic," *International Journal of the Classical Tradition* (forthcoming, 2006). According to Jennifer Low, women fight to get respect. They are also not overly vindictive or bloodthirsty: "Female characters engage in the duel (if they do so at all) with much less braggadocio than male characters, often agreeing to keep their combat unknown. Their purpose is not to punish their opponent but to change his view of what is due to women." *Manhood and the Duel: Masculinity in Early Modern Drama and Culture* (New York: Palgrave Macmillan, 2003), 140–41.

85. *Worth of Women,* 61. Enough of this restraint, Fonte adds in her call to arms, because men exercise their power too unreasonably and arrogantly, "treating us like slaves who cannot take a step without asking their permission or say a word without their jumping down our throats."

in epic romances but with a hint that now perhaps our woman warrior can embrace a newly discovered feminine "softness" and stop cross-dressing. Let us recall that Fonte explicitly made the difference in clothes between the sisters their only distinguishing sign of difference.

By entering adulthood through the establishment of her true bloodline and by taking possession of her filial assets—a kingdom—after a protracted battle of the wills with her estranged and yet so similar twin, Risamante stops being an "amazon," for as William Tyrrell writes, "amazons are daughters in limbo, neither men nor women nor nubile girls."[86] She will become a queen and, Fonte anticipates, will marry and mother a daughter. *Floridoro* did not reach the end that the events in the first few cantos anticipated, and we know nothing more of the iconic pair Floridoro and Celsidea; but once the semi-autobiographical part was under control, it could indeed be sent to press. All the other "heroic and magnanimous actions" that we were led to expect remained in Modesta Pozzo's overflowing drawers or perhaps just, and most comfortably, in her capacious mind.[87]

Valeria Finucci

86. "The Amazon myth," Tyrrell argues, "concerns the specter of daughters who refuse their destiny and fail the accepted transition through marriage to wife and motherhood." See William Tyrrell, *Amazons: A Study of Amazonian Mythmaking* (Baltimore: Johns Hopkins University Press, 1984), 65.

87. The words are in Fonte's letter to Francesco I: "su la base delle eroiche, et magnanime sue attionj." Carinci, "Una lettera autografa," 679.

VOLUME EDITOR'S
BIBLIOGRAPHY

PRIMARY SOURCES

Albizzi Tagliamochi, Barbara. *Ascanio errante*. Florence: Landini, 1640.

Alighieri, Dante. *La Divina Commedia*. Ed. Alberto Chiari. Milan: Bietti, 1977.

Apollonius of Rhodes. *The Voyage of Argo (Argonautica)*. Trans. E. V. Rieu. London: Penguin, 1959.

Aretino, Pietro. *Ragionamenti*. Ed. Romualdo Marrone. Rome: Newton, 1993.

Ariosto, Ludovico. *Orlando furioso*. Milan: Garzanti, 1974.

———. *Orlando Furioso*. Trans. Guido Waldman. Oxford: Oxford University Press, 1983.

Belloni, Antonio. "Il fallimento dell'ideale eroico." In *Il Seicento*. Milan: Vallardi, 1929.

Bembo, Pietro. *Prose della volgar lingua, Gli Asolani, Rime*. Ed. Carlo Dionisotti. Turin: UTET, 1966.

Bergalli Gozzi, Luisa. *Componimenti poetici delle più illustri rimatrici d'ogni secolo, raccolti da Luisa Bergalli. Parte prima, Che contiene le Rimatrici Antiche fino all'Anno 1575*. Venice: Antonio Mora, 1726.

Bigolina, Giulia, *Urania*. Ed. Valeria Finucci. Rome: Bulzoni, 2002.

———. *Urania, a Romance*. Ed. and trans. Valeria Finucci. Chicago: University of Chicago Press, 2005.

Boiardo, Matteo Maria. *Orlando Innamorato* (abridged). Trans. Charles Ross. Berkeley: University of California Press, 1989.

———. *Orlando innamorato*. Ed. Riccardo Bruscagli. 2 vols. Turin: Einaudi, 1995.

Boccaccio, Giovanni. *Decameron*. Ed. Vittore Branca. In *Tutte le opere*. Vol. 4. Milan: Mondadori, 1976.

———. *Famous Women (De mulieribus claris)*. Ed. and trans. Virginia Brown. Cambridge: Harvard University Press, 2001.

———. *Filocolo*. Ed. Antonio Enzo Quaglio. In *Tutte le opere*. Vol. 1. Milan: Mondadori, 1967.

Bouchard, Jean-Jacques. *Journal II. Voyage dans le royaume de Naples. Voyage dans la campagne de Rome*. Ed. Emanuele Kanceff. Turin: Giappichelli, 1976.

Castiglione, Sabba. *Ricordi o vero ammaestramenti*. Venice: Lorenzini, 1562.

Cortese, Isabella. *I secreti della signora Isabella Cortese ne' quali si contengono cose minerali, medicinali, artificiose, e alchemiche. Et molte de l'arte profumatoria, appartenenti a ogni gran signora*. Venice: Cornetti, 1584.

Cutolo, Alessandro. *I romanzi cavallereschi in prosa e in rima del Fondo Castiglioni presso la Biblioteca Braidense di Milano.* Milan: Hoepli, 1944.

D'Aragona, Tullia. *Il Meschino, altramente detto il Guerrino.* Venice: Sessa, 1560

Doglioni, Giovanni Nicolò. *L'anno dove si ha perfetto, et pieno raguaglio di quanto può ciascun desiderare, sì d'intorno alle cose del mondo celeste, et elementare, come d'intorno a quelle de' tempi et del calendario.* Venice: Rampazetto, 1587.

———. *Compendio historico universale di tutte le cose notabili gia successe nel mondo, dal principio della sua creatione fino all'anno di Christo 1594.* Venice: Zenaro, 1594.

——— [as Leonico Goldioni]. *Le cose maravigliose dell'inclita città di Venetia, riformate, accommodate e grandemente ampliate da Leonico Goldioni.* Venice: Imberti, 1603. Rpt., Naples: Liquori, 2003.

———. *Historia venetiana scritta brevemente da Gio. Nicolo Doglioni, delle cose successe dalla prima fondation di Venetia sino all'anno di Christo 1594.* Venice: Zenaro, 1597.

———. *L'Ungheria, spiegata da Gio. Nicolo Doglioni. Ove chiaramente si leggono tutte le cose successe in quel regno, da che prima fu così nominato, sino all'anno corrente.* Venice: Zenaro, 1595.

———. "La Vita della Signora Modesta Pozzo dei Zorzi, nominata Moderata Fonte." In *Il merito delle donne . . . in due giornate. Ove chiaramente si scuopre quanto siano elle degne e più perfette de gli uomini,* by Moderata Fonte. Venice: Imberti, 1600.

Dolce, Lodovico. *Dialogo della institution delle donne.* Venice: Giolito, 1945.

———. *Dialogo nel quale si ragiona delle qualità, diversità, e proprietà de i colori.* Venice: Sessa, 1565.

Ferri, Leopoldo. *Biblioteca femminile italiana.* Padua: Crescini, 1812.

Fonte, Moderata [Modesta Pozzo]. *Le Feste. Rappresentazione avanti al Serenissimo Prencipe di Venetia Nicolò Da Ponte, il giorno di Santo Stefano, 1581.* Venice: Guerra, 1581.

———. *Le Mérite des femmes.* Ed and trans. Frédérique Verrier. Paris: Editions Rue d'Ulm, 2002.

———. *Il merito delle donne . . . in due giornate. Ove chiaramente si scuopre quanto siano elle degne e più perfette de gli uomini.* Venice: Imberti, 1600.

———. *Il merito delle donne.* Ed. Adriana Chemello. Venice: Eidos, 1988.

———. *La Passione di Christo descritta in ottava rima da Moderata Fonte.* Venice: Guerra, 1582.

———. *La Resurrettione di Giesu Christo nostro Signore che segue alla Santissima Passione, descritta in ottava rima.* Venice: Imberti, 1592.

———. *Tredici canti del Floridoro.* Venice: Stamparia de' Rampazetti, 1581.

———. *Tredici canti del Floridoro.* Ed. Valeria Finucci. Modena: Mucchi, 1995.

———. *Das Verdienst der Frauen.* Ed and trans. Daniela Hacke. Munich: C. H. Beck, 2001.

———. *The Worth of Women Wherein Is Clearly Revealed Their Nobility and Their Superiority to Men.* Ed. and trans. Virginia Cox. Chicago: University of Chicago Press, 1997.

Guasco, Annibal. *Discourse to Lady Lavinia His Daughter* (1586). Ed. and trans. Peggy Osborn. Chicago: University of Chicago Press, 2003.

The Holy Bible. New International Version. Colorado Springs: International Bible Society, 1984.

Homer. *The Iliad.* Trans. Robert Fitzgerald. New York: Farrar, Straus and Giroux, 2004.

———. *The Odyssey.* Trans. Rodney Merrill. Ann Arbor: University of Michigan Press, 2002.

Lucan. *Pharsalia.* Trans. Jane Wilson Joyce. Ithaca: Cornell University Press, 1993.

Machiavelli, Niccolò. *Florentine Histories.* Trans. Laura Banfield and Harvey Mansfield Jr. Princeton: Princeton University Press, 1988.

Malatesta, Gioseppe. *Della nuova poesia.* Verona: Sebastiano delle Donne, 1589.

Marinella [Marinelli], Lucrezia. *La colomba sacra.* Venice: Ciotti, 1595.

———. *L'Enrico overo Bisantio Acquistato.* Venice: Imberti, 1635.

———. *The Nobility and Excellence of Women and the Defects and Vices of Men (La nobiltà et l'eccellenza delle donne, co' diffetti e mancamenti de gli huomini).* Ed. and trans. Anne Dunhill. Introd. Letizia Panizza. Chicago: University of Chicago Press, 1999.

———. *La vita di Maria vergine, imperatrice dell'universo.* Venice: Barezzo, 1610.

Melzi, Gaetano. *Bibliografia dei romanzi e dei poemi cavallereschi d'Italia.* In *Storia ed analisi dei romanzi di cavalleria,* ed. Giulio Ferrario. Vol. 4. Milan: Ferrario, 1829.

———, and Gian Paolo Tosi. *Bibliografia dei romanzi di cavalleria in versi e in prosa italiani.* Milan: Daelli, 1865.

Ovid [Publius Ovidius Naso]. *Metamorphoses.* Trans. Mary M. Innes. Harmondsworth: Penguin, 1955.

Passi, Giuseppe. *I donneschi difetti.* Venice: Somasco, 1599.

Petrarca, Francesco. *Petrarch's Lyric Poems.* Ed. and trans. Robert Durling. Cambridge: Harvard University Press, 1976.

Pisani, Sebastiano. *Ordini et decreti per le monache della città e diocese di Verona pubblicati et stampati di ordine dell'Illustrissimo et reverendissimo Sebastiano Pisani di Verona.* Verona: Battista Merlo, 1667.

Salvetti Acciaioli, Maddalena. *Davide perseguitato.* Florence: Caneo, 1611.

Sarrocchi, Margherita. *La scanderbeide.* Rome: Facis, 1606.

———. *Scanderbeide: The Heroic Deeds of George Scanderbeg, King of Epirus.* Ed. and trans. Rinaldina Russell. Chicago: University of Chicago Press, 2006.

Tarabotti, Arcangela. *Paternal Tyranny.* Ed. and trans. Letizia Panizza. Chicago: University of Chicago Press, 2004.

Terracina, Laura. *Discorso sopra il principio di tutti i canti dell'Orlando Furioso.* Venice: Giolito, 1550.

Ugurgieri Azzolini, Isidoro. *Le pompe sanesi, o' vero Relazione delli huomini, e donne illustri di Siena e suo Stato.* Pistoia: Fortunati, 1649.

Virgil [Publius Vergilius Maro]. *The Aeneid of Virgil.* Trans. Allen Mandelbaum. New York: Bantam, 1971.

———. *Opera.* Ed. R.A.B. Mynors. Oxford: Oxford University Press, 1969.

White, T. H. *The Book of Beasts, Being a Translation from a Latin Bestiary of the Twelfth Century.* New York: Dover, 1984.

Zorzi, Filippo, de'. *Dell'aria e sue qualità.* Venice: Rampazetto, 1596.

SECONDARY SOURCES

Abulafia, David. "Ancona, Byzantium and the Adriatic, 1155–1173." *Papers of the British School at Rome* 52 (1984): 195–216.

Allaire, Gloria. "Tullia d'Aragona's *Il meschino altramente detto il Guerino* as Key to a Reappraisal of Her Work." *Quaderni d'Italianistica* 16.1 (2005): 33–50.

Baldo, Vittorio. *Alunni, maestri e scuole in Venezia alla fine del XVI secolo.* Como: New Press, 1977.

Barbagli, Marzio. *Sotto lo stesso tetto: Mutamenti della famiglia in Italia dal XV al XX secolo.* Bologna: Il Mulino, 1984.

Beeching, Jack. *The Galleys at Lepanto.* New York: Scribner, 1983.

Beer, Marina. *Romanzi di cavalleria: Il Furioso e il romanzo italiano del primo Cinquecento.* Rome: Bulzoni, 1987.

Behr, Francesca D'Alessandro. "Moderata Fonte's Lady Knight: A Different Perspective on Women, War and Epic." *International Journal of the Classical Tradition* (forthcoming, 2006).

Bellavitis, Anna. "Patrimoni e matrimoni a Venezia nel Cinquecento." In *Le ricchezze delle donne. Diritti patrimoniali e poteri familiari in Italia (XIII–XIX secc.),* ed. Giulia Calvi and Isabelle Chabot, 149–60. Turin: Rosenberg and Sellier, 1998.

Bellomo, Mario. *La condizione giuridica della donna in Italia.* Turin: Einaudi, 1970.

Bellonci, Maria. *Segni sul muro.* Milan: Mondadori, 1988.

Bicheno, Hugh. *Crescent and Cross: The Battle of Lepanto 1571.* London: Cassell, 2003.

Braunstein, Philippe. "Le commerce du fer à Venise au XVe siècle." *Studi Veneziani* 8 (1966): 267–302.

Brown, Alison. "Pierfrancesco de' Medici, 1430–1476." In *The Medici in Florence: The Exercise and Language of Power.* Florence: Olschki, 1992; Perth: University of Western Australia Press, 1992.

Brucker, Gene. "The Medici in the Fourteenth Century." *Speculum* 32.1 (1957): 1–26.

Brundage, James. "The Crusader's Wife: A Canonistic Quandary." *Studia gratiana* 12 (1967): 625–41.

Brunelli, Vitaliano. *Storia della città di Zara dai tempi più remoti sino al 1409.* Trieste: LINT, 1974.

Bury, J. B. *The Invasion of Europe by the Barbarians.* New York: Norton, 1967.

Campbell, Stephen J. "Eros in the Flesh: Petrarchan Desire, the Embodied Eros, and Male Beauty in Italian Art, 1500–1540." *Journal of Medieval and Early Modern Studies* 35.3 (2005): 629–62.

Carinci, Eleonora. "Una lettera autografa inedita di Moderata Fonte (al granduca di Toscana Francesco I)." *Critica del testo* 5.3 (2002): 671–81.

Cavallo, Jo Ann. "Tasso's Armida and the Victory of Romance." In *Renaissance Transactions: Ariosto and Tasso,* ed. Valeria Finucci, 77–111. Durham: Duke University Press, 1999.

Cessi, Roberto. *Storia della Repubblica di Venezia.* Florence: Giunti Martello, 1981.

Chemello, Adriana. "La donna, il modello, l'immaginario: Moderata Fonte e Lucrezia Marinella." In *Nel cerchio della luna: Figure di donna in alcuni testi del XVI secolo,* ed. Marina Zancan, 95–160. Venice: Marsilio, 1983.

———. "Gioco e dissimulazione in Moderata Fonte." In *Il merito delle donne,* by Moderata Fonte, ed. Adriana Chemello, ix–lxiii. Venice: Eidos, 1988.

Chojnacki, Stanley. "Getting Back the Dowry: Venice 1350–1530." In *Time, Space, and Women's Lives in Early Modern Europe,* ed. Anne Jacobson Schutte, Thomas Kuehn, and Silvana Seidel Menchi. Kirksville, MO: Truman State University Press, 2001.

———. *Women and Men in Renaissance Venice: Twelve Essays on Patrician Society.* Baltimore: Johns Hopkins University Press, 2000.

Collina, Beatrice. "Moderata Fonte e *Il merito delle donne.*" *Annali d'Italianistica* 7 (1989): 142–64.

Comparetti, Domenico. *Vergil in the Middle Ages.* Trans. E. F. M. Benecke. Princeton: Princeton University Press, 1997.

Conti Odorisio, Ginevra. *Donna e società nel Seicento.* Rome: Bulzoni, 1979.

Cotterell, Arthur. *The Encyclopedia of Mythology: Classical, Celtic, Norse.* New York: Smithmark, 1996.

Cox, Virginia. "Fiction, 1560–1650." In *A History of Women's Writing in Italy,* ed. Letizia Panizza and Sharon Wood, 52–64. Cambridge: Cambridge University Press, 2000.

———. "Moderata Fonte and the *Worth of Women.*" In *The Worth of Women,* by Moderata Fonte, ed. and trans. Virginia Cox, 1–23. Chicago: University of Chicago Press, 1997.

———. "The Single Self: Feminist Thought and the Marriage Market in Early Modern Venice." *Renaissance Quarterly* 47 (1995): 513–81.

———. "Women as Readers and Writers of Chivalric Poetry in Early Modern Italy." In *Sguardi sull'Italia: Miscellanea dedicata a Francesco Villani,* ed. Gino Bedani et al., 134–45. Exeter: Society for Italian Studies, 1997.

Cranston, Jodi. "Desire and Gravitas in Bindo's Portraits." In *Raphael, Cellini, and a Renaissance Banker: The Patronage of Bindo Altoviti,* ed. Alan Chong, Donatella Pegazzano, and Dimitrios Zikos. Exhibition catalogue. Boston: Isabella Stewart Gardner Museum, 2003.

Cropper, Elizabeth. "On Beautiful Women, Parmigianino, *Petrarchismo,* and the Vernacular Style." *Art Bulletin* 58 (1976): 374–94.

———. "The Place of Beauty in the High Renaissance and Its Displacement in the History of Art." *Medieval and Renaissance Texts and Studies* 132 (1995): 159–205.

Crouzet-Pavan, Elisabeth. *Venice Triumphant: The Horizons of a Myth.* Trans. Lydia G. Cochrane. Baltimore: Johns Hopkins University Press, 2002.

Datta, Satya. "La presenza di una coscienza femminista nella Venezia dei primi secoli dell'età moderna." *Studi veneziani* 32 (1996): 105–37.

De Vivo, Filippo. "Historical Justifications of Venetian Power in the Adriatic." *Journal of the History of Ideas* 64.2 (2003): 159–76.

Donato, Eugenio. "'Per selve e boscherecci labirinti': Desire and Narrative Structure in Ariosto's *Orlando furioso.*" In *Literary Theory/Renaissance Texts,* ed. Patricia Parker and David Quint, 33–62. Baltimore: Johns Hopkins University Press, 1986.

Epstein, Steven. *Genoa and the Genoese, 958-1528.* Chapel Hill: University of North Carolina Press, 1996.

Erspamer, Francesco. *La biblioteca di Don Ferrante: Duello e onore nella cultura del Cinquecento.* Rome: Bulzoni, 1982.

Ferrante, Lucia. "Marriage and Women's Subjectivity in a Patrilineal System: The Case of Early Modern Bologna." In *Gender, Kinship, Power: A Comparative and Interdisciplinary History,* ed. Mary Jo Maynes at al., 115–29. New York: Routledge, 1996.

Ferraro, Joanne. *Marriage Wars in Late Renaissance Venice.* New York: Oxford University Press, 2001.

Ferroni, Giulio. "Il sistema comico della gemellarità." In *Il testo e la scena: Saggi sul teatro del Cinquecento,* 65–84. Rome: Bulzoni, 1980.

Finucci, Valeria. "The Female Masquerade: Ariosto and the Game of Desire." In *Desire in the Renaissance: Psychoanalysis and Literature,* ed. Valeria Finucci and Regina Schwartz, 61–88. Princeton: Princeton University Press, 1994.

———. "In the Name of the Brother: Male Rivalry and Social Order in Baldassarre Castiglione's *Il libro del cortegiano.*" *Exemplaria* 9 (1997): 91–116.

————. *The Lady Vanishes: Subjectivity and Representation in Castiglione and Ariosto.* Stanford: Stanford University Press, 1992.

————. *The Manly Masquerade: Masculinity, Paternity, and Castration in the Italian Renaissance.* Durham: Duke University Press, 2003.

————. "Moderata Fonte e il romanzo cavalleresco al femminile." In *Tredici canti del Floridoro,* ed. Finucci, ix–xxxix. Modena: Mucchi, 1995.

————. "La scrittura epico-cavalleresca al femminile: Moderata Fonte e *Tredici canti del Floridoro.*" *Annali d'Italianistica* 12 (1994): 203–31.

————."When the Mirror Lies: Sisterhood Reconsidered in Moderata Fonte's *Thirteen Cantos of Floridoro.*" In *Sibling Relations and Gender in the Early Modern World: Thicker Than Water,* ed. Naomi Miller and Naomi Yavneh, 116–28. Aldershot: Ashgate, 2006.

Fumagalli, Giuseppina. *La fortuna dell'Orlando Furioso in Italia nel sec. XVI.* Ferrara: Zuffi, 1912.

Grant, Michael. *A Guide to the Ancient World: A Dictionary of Classical Place Names.* New York: Barnes and Noble, 1986.

Graves, Robert. *The Greek Myths.* New York: Penguin, 1960.

Grendler, Paul. "Chivalric Romances in the Italian Renaissance." *Medieval and Renaissance History* 10 (1988): 59–102.

————. "Form and Function in Italian Renaissance Popular Books." *Renaissance Quarterly* 46 (1993): 451–85.

————. *Schooling in Renaissance Italy: Literacy and Learning, 1300–1600.* Baltimore: Johns Hopkins University Press, 1989.

————. "What Zuanne Read in School: Vernacular Texts in Sixteenth-Century Venetian Schools." *Sixteenth Century Journal* 13.1 (1982): 41–54.

Grubb, James. *Provincial Families of the Renaissance: Private and Public Life in the Veneto.* Baltimore: Johns Hopkins University Press, 1996.

————. "When Myths Lose Power: Four Decades of Venetian Historiography." *Journal of Modern History* 58 (1986): 43–94.

Günsberg, Maggie. "'Donna liberata'? The Portrayal of Women in the Italian Renaissance Epic." *Italianist* 7 (1987): 7–35.

Guthmüller, Bodo. "Non taceremo più a lungo. Sul dialogo in *Il merito delle donne* di Moderata Fonte." *Filologia e critica* 17 (1992): 258–79.

Hacke, Daniela. "'Non lo volevo per marito in modo alcuno': Forced Marriages, Generation Conflicts, and the Limits of Patriarchal Power in Early Modern Venice, c. 1580–1680." In *Time, Space, and Women's Lives in Early Modern Europe,* ed. Anne Jacobson Schutte, Thomas Kuehn, and Silvana Seidel Menchi, 203–21. Kirksville, MO: Truman State University Press, 2001.

Hempfer, Klaus. "Un criterio di validità per interpretazioni: L'epica cavalleresca italiana del Rinascimento." *Intersezioni* 4 (1984): 289–320.

Hibbert, Christopher. *The House of Medici: Its Rise and Fall.* New York: Morrow Quill, 1980.

Jaffe, Irma, with Gernando Colombardo. *Shining Eyes, Cruel Fortune: The Lives and Loves of Italian Renaissance Women Poets.* New York: Fordham University Press, 2002.

Javitch, Daniel. "*Cantus Interruptus* in the *Orlando Furioso.*" *MLN* 95 (1980): 66–80.

————. *Proclaiming a Classic: The Canonization of the Orlando Furioso.* Princeton: Princeton University Press, 1991.

Jordan, Constance. "Renaissance Women Defending Women: Arguments against Patriarchy." In *Italian Women Writers from the Renaissance to the Present: Revising the Canon*, ed. Maria Ornella Marotti, 55–67. University Park, PA: Pennsylvania State University Press, 1996.

Kisacky, Julia. *Magic in Boiardo and Ariosto*. New York: Peter Lang, 2000.

———. "The Perils of Power: Government in Moderata Fonte's *Floridoro*." Essay presented at the AAIS meeting, Chapel Hill, NC, April 2005.

Klapisch-Zuber, Christiane. *Women, Family, and Ritual in Renaissance Italy*. Chicago: University of Chicago Press, 1985.

Kohl, Benjamin. *Padua under the Carrara, 1318–1405*. Baltimore: Johns Hopkins University Press, 1998.

Kolsky, Stephen. "Moderata Fonte, Lucrezia Marinella, Giuseppe Passi: An Early Seventeenth-Century Feminist Controversy." *Modern Language Review* 96 (2001): 973–89.

———. "Per la carriera poetica di Moderata Fonte: Alcuni documenti poco conosciuti." *Esperienze letterarie* 24 (1999): 3–17.

———. "Wells of Knowledge: Moderata Fonte's *Il merito delle donne*." *Italianist* 13 (1993): 57–96.

Kuehn, Thomas. *Law, Family, and Women: Toward a Legal Anthropology of Renaissance Italy*. Chicago: University of Chicago Press, 1991.

Kunt, Metin, and Christine Woodhead, eds. *Süleyman the Magnificent and His Age: The Ottoman Empire in the Early Modern World*. London: Longman, 1995.

Labalme, Patricia. "Venetian Women on Women: The Early Modern Feminists." *Studi Veneziani* 5 (1981): 81–109.

Lane, Frederic. *Venice: A Maritime Republic*. Baltimore: Johns Hopkins University Press, 1973.

Lavarda, Sergio. "'Sempre parati al combatter.' Onore, risentimenti, ultime volontà in una famiglia padovana del 500." *Studi veneziani* 30 (1995): 79–107.

Low, Jennifer. *Manhood and the Duel: Masculinity in Early Modern Drama and Culture*. New York: Palgrave Macmillan, 2003.

Madden, Thomas. "Venice's Hostage Crisis: Diplomatic Efforts to Secure Peace with Byzantium between 1171 and 1184." In *Medieval and Renaissance Venice*, ed. Ellen Kittell and Thomas Madden, 96–108. Urbana: University of Illinois Press, 1999.

Mallett, Michael. "Venice and Its Condottieri, 1404–54." In *Renaissance Venice*, ed. J. R. Hale, 121–45. Totowa, NJ: Rowman and Littlefield, 1973.

Malpezzi-Price, Paola. *Moderata Fonte: Women and Life in Sixteenth-Century Venice*. London: Associated University Presses, 2003.

———. "A Woman's Discourse in the Italian Renaissance: Moderata Fonte's *Il merito delle donne*." *Annali d'Italianistica* 7 (1989): 165–81.

Mariotti Masi, Maria Luisa. *Una veneziana alla corte dei Medici*. Milan: Mursia, 1986.

Martelli, Daria. *Moderata Fonte e Il merito delle donne*. Venice: Centro Internazionale della Grafica, 1993.

Masetti Zannini, Gian Ludovico. *Motivi storici della educazione femminile. Scienza, lavoro, giuochi*. Naples: D'Auria, 1982.

Molho, Anthony. "Deception and Marriage Strategy in Renaissance Florence: The Case of Women's Age." *Renaissance Quarterly* 41 (1988): 193–217.

The New Century Italian Renaissance Encyclopedia. Ed. Catherine Avery. New York: Meredith, 1972.

New Larousse Encyclopedia of Mythology. London: Hamlyn, 1959.

Nicholson, Eric. "Romance as Role Model: Early Female Performances of *Orlando Furioso* and *Gerusalemme Liberata*." In *Renaissance Transactions: Ariosto and Tasso*, ed. Valeria Finucci, 249–69. Durham: Duke University Press, 1999.

Norwich, John Julius. *A History of Venice*. New York: Knopf, 1982.

Pace, Enrica. "Aspetti tipografico-editoriali di un 'best-seller' del secolo XVI: *L'Orlando furioso*.'" *Schifanoia* 3 (1987): 103–14.

Padoan, Giorgio. "*Ut pictura poesis*: Le 'pitture' di Ariosto, le 'poetiche' di Tiziano." In *Momenti del Rinascimento Veneto*, ed. Giorgio Padoan, 347–70. Padua: Antenore, 1978.

Panizza, Letizia. "Polemical Prose Writing, 1500–1650." In *A History of Women's Writing in Italy*, ed. Letizia Panizza and Sharon Wood, 65–78. Cambridge: Cambridge University Press, 2000.

Parigino, Giuseppe. *Il tesoro del principe: Funzione pubblica e privata del patrimonio della famiglia Medici nel Cinquecento*. Florence: Olschki, 1999.

Parker, Patricia, and David Quint, eds. *Literary Theory/Renaissance Texts*. Baltimore: Johns Hopkins University Press, 1986.

Pezzini, Serena. "Ideologia della conquista, ideologia dell'accoglienza: La *Scanderbeide* di Margherita Sarocchi (1623)." *MLN* 120 (2005): 190–222.

Phillips, Jonathan. *The Fourth Crusade and the Sack of Constantinople*. London: Pimlico, 2005.

Pitcher, Donald Edgar. *A Historical Geography of the Ottoman Empire from Earliest Times to the End of the Sixteenth Century*. Leiden: E.J. Brill, 1972.

Plebani, Tiziana. "Nascita e caratteristiche del pubblico di lettrici tra medioevo e età moderna." In *Donna, disciplina, creanza cristiana dal XV al XVII secolo*, ed. Gabriella Zarri, 23–44. Rome: Edizioni di Storia e Letteratura, 1996.

Pomata, Gianna. "Family and Gender." In *Early Modern Italy: 1550-1796*, ed. John Marino, 69–86. New York: Oxford University Press, 2002.

Queller, Donald. *The Fourth Crusade: The Conquest of Constantinople, 1201–1204*. Philadelphia: University of Pennsylvania Press, 1977.

———, and Thomas Madden. "Father of the Bride: Fathers, Daughters, and Dowries in Late Medieval and Early Renaissance Venice." *Renaissance Quarterly* 46 (1993): 685–711.

Quondam, Amedeo. *Il naso di Laura. Lingua e poesia lirica nella tradizione del classicismo*. Modena: Panini, 1991.

Ravegnani, Giorgio. "I dogi di Venezia e la corte di Bisanzio." In *L'eredità greca e l'ellenismo veneziano*, ed. Gino Benzoni, 23–51. Florence: Olschki, 2002.

Richardson, Brian. *Printing, Writers, and Readers in Renaissance Italy*. Cambridge: Cambridge University Press, 1999.

Ristaino, Christine. "Lucrezia Marinella's Oeuvre: Between Tradition and Innovation." Ph.D. diss., University of North Carolina–Chapel Hill, 2003.

Rogers, Mary. "The Decorum of Women's Beauty: Trissino, Firenzuola, Luigini, and the Representation of Women in Sixteenth Century Painting." *Renaissance Studies* 2 (1988): 47–88.

Rosenthal, Margaret. *The Honest Courtesan: Veronica Franco, Citizen and Writer in Sixteenth-Century Venice*. Chicago: University of Chicago Press, 1992.

———. "Venetian Women Writers and Their Discontents." In *Sexuality and Gender in Early Modern Europe: Institutions, Texts, Images*, ed. James Grantham Turner, 107–32. Cambridge: Cambridge University Press, 1993.

Saccone, Eduardo. "Prospettive sull'ultimo *Furioso.*" *MLN* 98 (1993): 55–69

Shemek, Deanna. "Getting a Word in Edgewise: Laura Terracina's *Discorsi* on the *Orlando Furioso.*" In *Ladies Errant: Wayward Women and Social Order in Early Modern Italy,* 126–57. Durham: Duke University Press, 1998.

Sperling, Jutta. *Convents and the Body Politic in Late Renaissance Venice.* Chicago: University of Chicago Press, 1999.

Stephens, J. N. *The Fall of the Florentine Republic, 1512–1530.* Oxford: Clarendon, 1983.

Treadwell, Nina. "'Simil combattimento fatto da Dame': The Musico-Theatrical Entertainments of Margherita Gonzaga's *Balletto delle donne* and the Female Warrior in Ferrarese Cultural History." In *Gender, Sexuality, and Early Music,* ed. Todd Borgerding, 27–40. New York: Routledge, 2002.

Trevor, Dean, and K. J. P. Lowe, eds. *Marriage in Italy: 1300–1650.* Cambridge: Cambridge University Press, 1998.

Tyrrell, William. *Amazons: A Study of Amazonian Mythmaking.* Baltimore: Johns Hopkins University Press, 1984.

Vickers, Nancy. "The Body Re-Membered: Petrarchan Lyrics and the Strategies of Description." In *Mimesis: From Mirror to Method, Augustine to Descartes,* ed. John Lyons and Stephen Nichols, 100–109. Hanover: University Press of New England, 1982.

———. "Diana Described: Scattered Woman and Scattered Rhyme." In *Writing and Sexual Difference,* ed. Elizabeth Adel. Chicago: University of Chicago Press, 1982.

Visceglia, Maria Antonietta. *Il bisogno d'eternità: I comportamenti aristocratici a Napoli in età moderna.* Naples: Guida, 1988.

Yarnall, Judith. *Transformations of Circe: The History of an Enchantress.* Urbana: University of Illinois Press, 1994.

Yavneh, Naomi. "The Ambiguity of Beauty in Tasso and Petrarch." In *Sexuality and Gender in Early Modern Europe: Institutions, Texts, Images,* ed. James Grantham Turner, 133–57. Cambridge: Cambridge University Press, 1993.

———. "Lying-in and Dying: Moderata Fonte's Death in Childbirth and the Maternal Body in Renaissance Venice." *Rinascimento* 43 (2003): 177–203.

Zanette, Emilio. "Bianca Capello e la sua poetessa." *Nuova Antologia* 88 (1953): 455–68.

Zarri, Gabriella. "Le istituzioni dell'educazione femminile." In *Recinti: Donne, clausura e matrimonio nella prima età moderna.* Bologna: Il Mulino, 2000.

———. "Monasteri femminili e città (secoli XV e XVIII)." In *Storia d'Italia, Annali IX: La chiesa e il potere politico dal Medioevo all'età contemporanea,* ed. Giorgio Chittolini and Giovanni Miccoli. Turin: Einaudi, 1986.

Zatti, Sergio. *L'uniforme cristiano e il multiforme pagano. Saggio sulla Gerusalemme liberata.* Milan: Il Saggiatore, 1983.

Zorzi, Alvise. *La Repubblica del Leone. Storia di Venezia.* Milan: Bompiani, 2001.

NOTE ON TRANSLATION

My translation of *Floridoro* is based on Valeria Finucci's 1995 edition and on the 1581 edition.

I attempt to follow the structure of the stanzas for the sake of those poetic elements I am able to reproduce, focusing primarily on the rhythm, rhyme words, and alliteration, but without trying to write English verse. My other primary concern is clarity of meaning. Along these lines, it was common in Renaissance chivalric poetry to employ personal pronouns without being overly scrupulous about identifying the character involved. For instance, it may take some thought to figure out who just struck the latest blow in a duel. In a few cases I have inserted the character's name for quicker comprehension.

Particularly challenging is the fact that in her narration, Fonte frequently switches back and forth between present and past tenses. A good example is canto 2, octave 89. The Pygmy king always refers to Princess Raggidora in the present tense; his beloved is always vividly before his mind's eye. But he recounts the Egyptian nobles' contemporaneous actions, in the same stanza, in the past tense. To smooth out the passages, I have adjusted some of the verbs (in this case, in verse 5, and elsewhere more extensively).

In the encomiastic passages dealing with the Medici and prominent Venetians I have retained variant spellings of people's names; it seems clear enough that Cosmo is Cosimo and Gradenico is Gradenigo.

Julia Kisacky

FLORIDORO: A CHIVALRIC ROMANCE

LETTERA AUTOGRAFA

Altiss[im]o et Ser[enissi]mo Principe etc[etera]

Havendo io già qualche anno speso parte de miej pensierj intorno à i dolci studij della Poesia, più tosto spinta da natural inclinatione, che allettata da alcuna speranza di acquistar lode, venni meco stessa considerando, che mi sarebbe di grand[issi]ma contentezza, et di altretanta gloria, se di queste piacevoli, et gratiose mie fatiche io facessi obbietto le regali Eccellentie di qualche honorato Signore, dando l'essere alle mie rime con la dispositione di tanta materia, et havendo molto discorso di cui trà molti dovessi far tal elettione, già mi haveria proposto nell'animo, che la gloria di v[ost]ra Altezza Ser[enissi]ma fusse quel lume, et quella stella, la qual sola in tanto pelago mi mostrasse la vera via di trovare il porto; Già era ella il fondamento di questa fabrica, era il segno, ove si drizzavano tutti i miei pensierj, et già haveva dato altero principio à i novi versi, quando d'improvviso si sparge per questa città, et intendo la nova feliciss[im]a delle splendide, et fortunate nozze trà v[ost]ra Altezza Ser[enissi]ma, et la Ser[enissi]ma Si[gno]ra BIANCA CAP-PELLO celebrate; La quale riempiendomj l'animo d'una solenne allegrezza (com'in parte mostrai subito alla Ser[enissim]a Al[tez]za di lei con una mia canzone)[1] mi fece con maggior animo confermar in questa opinione, et con maggior contentezza seguir l'impresa incominciata, includendovi anco il nome, auttorità, et meriti di lei, per esser una cosa istessa in amore con v[ostr]a A[ltezz]a Ser[enissim]a. Hor continuando io la compositione di questa opera, et non havendo potuto far di manco di non lasciarne qualche particella vedere ad'alcuni, che degli studij di essa Poesia sommam[en]te si dilettano, et ne sono peritiss[im]i. Da questi tali più volte, co 'l mezo di alcuni

---

1. The canzone Fonte speaks about is the one dedicated to "Don Francesco de Medici," which
she then published in *Floridoro,* and which is transcribed below.

FLORIDORO: A CHIVALRIC ROMANCE

DEDICATORY LETTER

Most High and Most Serene Prince, etc.

I had already for several years devoted some thought to the sweet stud-
ies of poetry when, more impelled by natural inclination than enticed by
any hope of winning praise, I came to consider that it would be a great
happiness to me, and just as much glory, if I made the royal and excellent
qualities of some honored lord the object of these my pleasing and gracious
labors, giving existence to my rhymes with the disposition of so great a sub-
ject matter. After pondering a great deal on whom I should elect among so
many, I resolved in my heart that the glory of your Most Serene Highness
was that light and that star which alone in so great a sea showed me the true
way to find the port.

Already you were the foundation of this edifice, you were the goal to
which all my thoughts were directed, and I had already commenced the
lofty new verses, when suddenly there spread through this city, and I heard
of it, the most happy news of the celebration of the splendid and fortunate
nuptials between your Most Serene Highness and the Most Serene lady
Bianca Capello. This news filled my soul with a solemn joy (as in part I
showed immediately to her Most Serene Highness with a poem of mine); it
confirmed me with greater spirit in my decision, and made me with greater
happiness persevere in the project I had begun, including therein her name,
authority, and merits, and considering her to be, through the power of love,
one same thing with your Most Serene Highness.

Now in continuing to compose this work, I could not help showing
some small parts of it to some men who in the studies of this selfsame poetry
take the highest delight, and are most expert at it. From such men as these
many times, through the agency of some friends of mine, I have been insis-
tently requested to send forth this initial part of the work. Finally to please

miei, instantemente richiesta à mandar fuori questo principio, finalm[en]te
per compiacerli (poi che le loro instanze, rispetto alla virtù, et meriti loro,
mi devono esser in vece di comandamenti) sono stata astretta di farlo, et così
hò permesso, che siano stampati questi—XIIJ—canti del Floridoro, che così
è intitolata l'opera; et ciò sotto imaginato nome di Moderata Fonte, poi che
'l mio vero, et proprio non hò giudicato esser bene di esponer alla publica
censura, essendo giovane da marito, et secondo l'uso della città obligata à
molti rispetti; Al che avendo risguardo, io hò così raccomandato alla stampa
questa finta divolgatione, per non dover celar poi, come faccio hora, la verità
alla candida, et benignissima mente di lei. Eccovi adunq[ue] Altiss[im]o et
Ser[enissi]mo Principe con la presente i novelli frutti del mio da se povero, et
sterile ingegno, ma divenuto in parte ricco, et abondante de i meriti, honori,
et glorie di v[ostra] Al[tezza] Ser[enissim]a, et della Ser[enissi]ma sua con-
sorte, quasi secco prato, che da spiranti zefiri sia riempiuto di vaghiss[im]i
et preciosiss[im]i fiori: La qual cosa, se conoscerò esser di qualche gusto al
Mondo, et specialm[en]te, alla v[ostra] Ser[enissim]a Alt[ezz]a (essendo già
totalm[en]te ordita l'opera, che arriverà à meglio di cinquanta canti) mi sforz-
erò con tute le forze mie di ridurla alla sua perfettione, sostentandola tutta
pure al solito sù la base delle heroiche, et magnanime sue attionj. Conche
facendo fine, et consacrando tutto l'ingegno, et saper mio, benche sia poco, à
i regalj meritj di v[ostr]ra Al[tezz]a Ser[enissi]ma le baccio l'Illustrissima, et
generosa mano, et humilissimamente me le dedico, et inchino.[2]

Di Venetia il dì 17.mo di Novembre. 1580
Di V[ostra] Ser[enissi]ma Altezza
Humiliss[im]a serva
Modesta Pozzo

PREFATORY SONNETS

AL SERENISSIMO
DON FRANCESCO DE MEDICI
GRAN DUCA DI THOSCANA.

Moderata Fonte

Folta, frondosa, e verdeggiante selva,
  Di sacri honor, non di Cipressi o Palme,

2. This transcription is based on the original letter by Fonte now in the Archivio di Stato
di Firenze, Mediceo del Principato, f. 741, 97r–v. To enhance reading, the letter *v* has been
modernized into the customary *u*.

them (since their repeated insistence, in respect of their virtue and merits, must stand me in the stead of commands) I have been constrained to do it, and so I have permitted the printing of these thirteen cantos of Floridoro, for thus the work is entitled. And I have done this under the imagined name of Moderata Fonte, since my own true name I have not judged it well to expose to public censure, being a young marriageable woman and, according to the custom of the city, obligated in many respects. Consequently, I have recommended to print this feigned disclosure, in order not to have to conceal later as I do now the truth from the city's candid and most benign mind.

Here then, Most High and Most Serene Prince, with this letter are the new fruits of my intellect, which by itself is poor and sterile, but it has become in part rich and abundant from the merits, honors, and glories of your Most Serene Highness, and of your Most Serene consort, like a dry meadow which by wafting zephyrs is filled with most charming flowers. And if it turns out somewhat pleasing to the world and especially to your Most Serene Highness, since the work is already totally plotted, and will reach better than fifty cantos, I will force myself with all my strength to reduce it to its perfection, supporting it all as usual on the bases of your heroic and magnanimous actions.

Making an end to this, and consecrating all my wits and knowledge, paltry though they be, to the regal merits of your Most Serene Highness, I kiss your most illustrious and generous hand, and most humbly I dedicate myself to you, and I bow to you.

> From Venice, the 17th day of November 1580
> Your Most Serene Highness's
> Most humble servant,
> Modesta Pozzo

PREFATORY SONNETS

TO THE MOST SERENE DON FRANCESCO DE' MEDICI, GRAND DUKE OF TUSCANY,[3]

[From] Moderata Fonte

A dense, leafy, and verdant forest
of sacred honors, not of cypresses or palms,

---

3. Francesco de' Medici (1541–87) succeeded his father in 1574 as Grand Duke Francesco I of Tuscany.

Produce il suol de le tue belle, ed alme
Virtù, là 've ogni stil vago s'inselva,

In lei non s'ode aspra feroce belva
Fremir, ma dolce suon di ben nate alme,
Che porta (ò gran Signor) tuoi pregi, e palme
Di Cittade in Città, di Selva in Selva.

Io, che d'entrar fra li sentier diversi,
E frà l'immense vie bramo, & ardisco,
Per quale hor deggio incaminar miei versi?

Scopriran li tuoi merti? o 'l valor prisco
De gli avi illustri? ò pur n'andran dispersi?
MA gloria è porsi ad honorato risco.

ALLA SERENISS. SIG.
BIANCA CAPPELLO DE MEDICI
GRAN DUCHESSA DI THOSCANA.

Moderata Fonte

Pioggia di gratìe in te perpetue piova,
Celeste Donna, onde tal luce abonda;
Viva ogn'hor la tua gloria alma, e gioconda
Co'l Ciel (non pur con la Fenice) à prova.

I preclari intelletti illustre, e nova
Tessino Istoria in lingua atta, e feconda,
Ch'al tuo merto, al tuo pregio corrisponda,
Al gran lume, al gran ben, ch'in tè si trova.

Te scelta il fior de gli almi Heroi già scelse,
Che d'amor vero, e di regal corona
Il tuo cor cinse, e le tue belle chiome.

Ed io scelgo tue lodi alme, ed eccelse;
nè maggiore hor desio l'alma mi sprona,
Che di por frà miei versi il tuo bel nome.

is produced by the soil of your lovely and bountiful
virtues; there every fine style[4] takes sylvan refuge.

Therein one hears no harsh, ferocious beast
roar, but rather the sweet sound of wellborn spirits
which carries along (O great lord) your worth and your victories
from city to city, from forest to forest.

To enter among the diverse paths
and among the immense roads I desire and dare—
onto which of them must I now send forth my verses?

Shall they reveal your merits? or the ancient valor
of your illustrious ancestors? or might they end up scattered?
And yet, there is glory in taking honorable risks.

TO THE MOST SERENE
LADY BIANCA CAPELLO DE' MEDICI,
GRAND DUCHESS OF TUSCANY,[5]

Moderata Fonte

Upon you may a shower of perpetual grace rain down,
O celestial lady from whom such light abounds.
Long live your immortal and radiant glory
which with heaven, not merely with the phoenix, contends.

May eminent intellects weave an illustrious and new
tale in language apt and fruitful,
corresponding to your worth, to your merit,
to the great light, to the great good which in you is found.

The flower of immortal heroes has chosen you;
with true love, and with a regal crown
he has encircled your heart, and your beautiful locks.

And I choose to sing your praises, immortal and unexcelled;
nor does a greater desire now spur on my soul
than to place among my verses your lovely name.

---

4. And by extension, every fine poet.

5. Bianca Capello (1548–87) was the second wife of Grand Duke Francesco. See also cantos
1.5 and 3.61–68.

DEL SIG. CESARE SIMONETTI. ALLA SIG. MODERATA FONTE.

Nobil Cigno del Pò sovrana gloria
    Cantò Ruggier con bellicosi carmi,
    Sì, ch'eterna via più che bronzi, e marmi
    Del sangue Estense il Mondo havrà memoria.

Nobil Sirena (e se per lei si gloria
    La Regina del Mar, ben giusto parmi)
    L'amor di Floridor cantando, e l'armi
    Tesse al gran Duce Thosco illustre Istoria.

Se già d'altre Sirene al dolce suono
    Chiuse l'avide orecchie il Duce Greco
    Saggio, accorto a schivar perigli, e morte;

Hor per questa udir sol benigna sorte
    Brama ogn'un mille orecchie in caro dono
    Tanta dolcezza, e maestade hà seco.

DEL SIG. BARTOLOMEO MALOMBRA.
ALLA SIG. MODERATA FONTE.

Piega, per honorar sì bella Fonte,
    Che de l'altre ogni gloria oscurar suole,
    Come al nostro Orizonte arriva il Sole,
    Di sacro allor la coronata fronte.

FROM CESARE SIMONETTI,[6] TO MODERATA FONTE

A noble swan, the Po's sovereign glory,[7]
sang of Ruggiero with warlike poems
so that far more eternal than bronzes or marbles
will be of the Estense bloodline the world's memory.

A noble siren (and it is most just, it seems to me,
if the queen of the sea[8] glories in her)
in singing of Floridoro's love and of arms,
wove for the Tuscan grand duke an illustrious story.

If formerly to other sirens' sweet sound
the Greek lord closed those avid ears
in his wisdom, alert to avoid perils and death;[9]

now solely to hear this one siren, everyone
desires a thousand ears as benign fate's dear gift,
so much sweetness and majesty she has in her.

FROM BARTOLOMEO MALOMBRA[10]
TO MODERATA FONTE

To honor so beautiful a Fount,[11]
which of other springs obscures all the glory,
when on our horizon the sun arrives,
that forehead crowned with sacred laurel bows.[12]

---

6. A contemporary poet, and judging from his contribution here, he must have belonged to Fonte's or Doglioni's circle. See also canto 10.32 and note.

7. Ludovico Ariosto (1474–1533) was a member of the nobility and a poet in the service of the Este lords of Ferrara, located on the Po River. His masterpiece, the chivalric poem *Orlando furioso*, narrates the adventures of Ruggiero, a fictional ancestor of the Este. Simonetti alludes to a famous passage (canto 35.14–23) where Ariosto describes great poets as swans who immortalize the names of those they praise.

8. Venice, Fonte's city.

9. In book 12 of the *Odyssey*, Homer tells how Odysseus (Ulysses) had his ship's crew plug their ears to avoid hearing the Sirens' singing, which would have lured them to their deaths.

10. Another poet friend of the author; see also canto 10.31.

11. Malombra plays on the literal meaning of Fonte's pseudonym: fountain or spring.

12. Apollo, the Greek god of the sun and poetry; wreaths made of his plant, the laurel, were used to honor poets.

Lascian Parnaso il favorito Monte
　　Le Muse, poi ch'in lei ciascuna vuole
　　Lavarsi il petto, e'l viso, onde si duole
　　Castalio, ed Hipocrene à noi sì conte.

E le Ninfe, e le Dee del Mare intorno
　　Le fan nobil ghirlanda, onde si stima
　　Di gran pregio l'humor, ch'in lei risorge.

Però, seguendo il portator del giorno,
　　Honorianla ancor noi frà l'altre hor prima,
　　Che stupore, e letitia al Mondo porge.

The Muses leave Parnassus, their favorite mount,[13]
behind, since in this fountain each of them wants
to wash her breast and her face—whence the grief
of the Castalian and Hippocrene founts, by us so highly esteemed.

And the nymphs and the goddesses of the sea round about
her make up a noble garland; therefore we deem
most precious the fluid which from her rises.

For this, following the example of the one who brings the day,[14]
let us now honor her first among the others,
for she provides amazement and delight to the world.

---

13. The Muses of Greek mythology inspired poetry. They lived on Mount Helicon, where they would wash in the Hippocrene spring. The Castalian spring is located on Mount Parnassus, a center of the cult of Apollo, with whom the Muses were closely associated. Both of these springs were said to confer poetic inspiration. See *New Larousse Encyclopedia of Mythology* (London: Hamlyn, 1959), 119.

14. Apollo, the sun god.

CANTO 1

ARGUMENT

Macandro arrives at Cecrops's walls
and fells all the knights of the court.
The Sican follows his destrier into a dark wood
far from the Palladian gates.[1]
A maiden narrates to him the adventure
of the garland and the fate of Parmino.
Macandro puts all Athens in great terror;
at last a knight comes to best him.

1

Choose from adorned and well-composed verses
the most beautiful flower, lovely Muse, and sing
the captured trophies and the fires extinguished
by time, of which Mars and Love still brag.
Tell of the cruel battles and the ardent flames
that issued from the arms and the holy torch,
when the fierce god had altars
and the Cyprian was adored as a goddess.[2]

---

1. Cecrops was the legendary founder of Athens. See *New Larousse Encyclopedia of Mythology*, 179. The Sicans were ancient inhabitants of Sicily. Pallas Athena was the patron deity of Athens.

2. Fonte may refer here to the tradition that Aphrodite (the Roman Venus), the goddess of love, and Ares (Mars), the god of war, had a love affair. See Robert Graves, *The Greek Myths* (New York: Penguin, 1960), 67. Aphrodite resided on Cyprus; it was an early and important center of her cult. See Graves, *Greek Myths*, 49. The Italian word for torch (*face*) might also refer to Aphrodite's face.

2

Sing the glorious deeds and the sweet affections
of illustrious knights and ladies.[3]
Make it so that of those hands, of these hearts
the merit and joy might live eternal lustrums;[4]
and match my style to those concepts
that emerge from my eager and industrious thoughts,
while in the most pure and divine light
of a noble couple I sharpen my dull wits.

3

Meanwhile she who is to be the light and escort
of the noble task I have undertaken
will favor along the way
that ardent desire which has kindled my mind.[5]
Otherwise this work would be
a too obscure and badly guided endeavor,
nor would I hope without her gracious light
to reach the so-much-desired end.

4

Most serene FRANCESCO,[6] splendor
of the fortunate realm of Tuscany,
you, without whose favor
I judge my every effort to be vain,
kindly deign, in the generosity of your heart,

3. Ariosto is echoed everywhere in *Floridoro*. He was the first author, after all, to make clear from the very beginning that romances of chivalry are also about love and women, and not just about heroic deeds and manly business. Like Fonte, he inscribed his poetic aim at the start of the *Furioso*: "I sing of knights and ladies, of love and arms, of courtly chivalry, of courageous deeds" (*OF* 1.1). But Fonte also echoes Virgil in the previous octave by calling on the Muse for help in her endeavor, as in *Aeneid* 1.13.

4. A lustrum is a period of five years.

5. The author probably refers to Bianca Capello.

6. For Francesco de' Medici, grand duke of Tuscany (1541–87), see the prefatory sonnet, and below, canto 3.59–62.

out of your noble and superhuman virtue,
to mull over from time to time my lowly intellect's
unpolished verses, which I sing herein.

5

And you, most illustrious BIANCA,[7] who, united
by an affection both chaste and connubial,
reign in joy and dispense high and lofty graces
into every heart subject to you,
you who are no less the support and hope
of the thoughts inflaming my breast,
do not disdain to accept this humble gift,
since I too, among so many, am your servant.

6

In the loveliest flowering of that lucky
and renowned epoch, in that early age
when in Athens propitious fate rained down
as many graces as a benign star can give,
there went a proud king, endowed with the well-favored realm
and with every noble, prized, and beautiful
virtue, no less prudent than he was courageous,
just, and humane. He was named Cleardo.

7

With a happy marriage, joyous and merry,
he had fulfilled his vows to his protector, Cupid:
the royal daughter of King Alismondo

7. Bianca Capello was born in 1548, the daughter of a noble Venetian family. In 1564 she
eloped with her lover to Florence. She became Francesco's mistress while he was heir to Tus-
cany. After the death of his wife Joanna of Austria in 1578, Francesco, now grand duke, married
Bianca secretly, and publicly the following year. At this news, the Venetian Senate declared her
a beloved Daughter of the Republic. Bianca and Francesco had a child together, Antonio (but
there are questions as to the maternity, let alone paternity, of that child), and they both died
in 1587; at the time it was rumored they had been poisoned by Francesco's brother and succes-
sor, Ferdinando, but some later historians have concluded they died of malaria. See John Julius
Norwich, *A History of Venice* (New York: Knopf, 1982), 496–98.

this king had taken from Sicilian to Greek shores.
With her he brought into the world a girl
who surpassed in esteem and acclaim all other beautiful women,
a girl endowed as well with excellent wits,
for an unworthy spirit cannot reign in a beautiful body.

8

This girl's gracious, noble appearance
(she was called Celsidea)
and her habits were so lovely and pious
that she seemed not a mortal woman but a goddess,[8]
such that her fame overshadowed that of all other women
throughout the world, nor did people speak of anything else.
And while every man talks and reasons of her,
every other woman loses the claim of being beautiful.

9

For his pleasure the king was accustomed by day
to seat this maiden by his side,
with around them the queen and more damsels
who were the finest ladies in the Greek state.[9]
Now it happens that when they were in the hall one day
with the Greek heroes, just as I've recounted,
there appeared among them a great and fierce giant,
to whom they all turned their eyes and thoughts.[10]

8. The name Celsidea—that is, *Ciel sì Dea*, "Such a goddess of Heaven"—may have been made up by Fonte to underline her heroine's celestial beauty. Similarly, Ariosto's most beautiful woman was Angelica—that is, "angelical," "heavenly."

9. Here, as later on, kings father mostly daughters—a feature of women writers' literature (see, for example, Valeria Miani's *Celinda*). Even when sons are in the picture in *Floridoro*, they are elsewhere at war or engaged in tourneys, while the daughter sits next to the father king. Most strikingly, the queen too is always present at her husband's side in state affairs. See also canto 2.58 where the Emperor Agricorno conducts state affairs with his wife next to him.

10. The opening narrative sequence in which King Cleardo witnesses the sudden entry of a "great and fierce giant" is closely modeled upon a similar scene at the start of Boiardo's *Innamorato* when King Charlemagne, he too surrounded by knights and court ladies, sees four "fearsome and enormous giants" appear in the royal hall. See *Innamorato* 1.1.21.

10

This fellow had departed from the Armenian kingdom
where he had long served in vain
a beautiful, marriageable young woman
who held that realm's scepter in her hand.
His heart wounded by her beautiful eyes,
he had all but gone insane for her,
and believing himself the one most in her good graces,
he held himself blessed over every other lover.

1 1

Not that the noble maiden loved him;
he was too coarse a lover for her.
Instead it was because she had a quarrel with her sister
and always feared some unforeseen problem;
thus with a joyful regard and with sweet words
she held him tight in love's tangle,
and for a time she kept him at court,
so that in a pinch he might help her.

1 2

Now while he, in Armenia's grand court,
was blissful and proud to serve such a great lady,
he heard how great a slur the acclaim
of this Greek damsel brought to her whom he loved so much,
and rage ignited his heart so strongly
that (if he could have) he would have killed the rumor.
Yet, since he could do nothing else, he planned at least
to give vent to this venom in the Achaean realm.

1 3

He armed himself and took leave of her
whose lovely face he bore impressed in his heart,
and, as I said, he went before
the king of the Achaeans in the great hall one day.
As soon as he arrived, that royal, illustrious young virgin
(whose beauty humiliated the sun,

let alone every other beautiful woman)
appeared before his dreadful, wicked eyes.

1 4

By her extreme beauty, on which the fierce, crude man
did not dare to rest his gaze,
he recognized her for that exceptional daughter
who was to be the heir of the Greek empire.
And he marveled greatly
that, as he gazed on his own goddess in his thoughts,
she did not seem to him as fair and beautiful as
this one, although he loved her very much.

1 5

Despite this, in order not to have come
in vain, and for the love that he bore her,
and to provide evidence of
his valor which he considered so great,
he determined not to remain silent and mute.
Turning to the king who waited attentively,
he spoke with a loud and haughty voice,
such that everyone heard his fierce speech.

shows the weakness of men PRIDE

1 6

"Because too widespread are the esteem and acclaim
which so honor your daughter,
and in order to fill up with glory the Parthian shore,
and to give light and splendor to Armenia,
I, Macandro, who in Parthia have my lair
and am high lord of so great an empire,
have come to prove with weapons in hand
that this acclaim is far from the truth.

1 7

"And I say, and I intend to prove in your lands
with whoever among your warriors is held in highest esteem,
that the beautiful Biondaura, who commands

the Armenians and also (what's worth much more) my valor,
in her fair visage and her noble and serene eyes
outdoes your daughter, and has no equal on earth.
I say that she has so beautiful and joyful a visage
that she surpasses this girl, and has no peer in the world.

18

"Let the trial with lance and sword
last for three days, and the one who ends up unhorsed
(this is the pact I want among us)[11]
shall give up his shield as the victor's prize.
And so that no other disturbance may occur,
you will assure me on your honor
that your warriors will observe the pact,
and no other quarrel will arise among us.

19

"I will go, if your judgment approves it,
outside of the city, next to the great olive tree.
There I will await whoever might come to the trial
against me, for I declare I will prove
not only that it is my queen alone
whose beautiful eyes and whose beautiful divine countenance
do not yield before any other's beauty,
but that there is no human face to match hers."

20

To everyone his proposal appeared
haughty and arrogant, and their expressions showed it.
But you, beautiful maiden, what was your countenance,
what your heart, at so strange a sight?

---

11. The joust launched to assert that one's opinion regarding a particular woman should be embraced by all men, with the loser meekly giving his shield to the winner, is part of the folklore of chivalric romances. Here the setup recalls a similar call for jousts in the *Furioso* where Rodomonte aggressively challenges all men crossing a bridge to joust with him for the sake of Isabella. If they lose, they must give up their arms. They all do, not knowing that Rodomonte himself has killed the very woman he now wants everyone to worship (*Orlando furioso* 29–39).

The king, who saw that that fierce giant
disturbed and saddened his beautiful daughter,
told her, "My daughter, let it be your care
to find someone who will defend our reputation.

21

"As for me, on my honor I promise
the knight that his pact will not be broken,
and since your noble and lovely aspect
spreads so clear and so lauded an acclaim,
will you not find a perfect knight
who will defend the esteem you command?
Let this warrior proceed, for someone will take good care
to defend you, I assure you."

22

Haughty Macandro noted that the request
did not frighten him even a little,
and he departed with a shake of his head,
as if despising everyone there.
When the wicked one had departed, in the court nothing remained
to discuss but the upcoming game,
which pleased them as much as the bold giant's
great pride displeased them.

23

A few days before, by pure chance,
to Athens had come Apollideo,
to whom was due the scepter of those walls
that the keen sound of the cithara founded,[12]
and the king of Sparta too, and old
Griante, so strong and so astute.
There was also Aliforte of Thessaly,
who craved to be the first to battle.

12. The legendary Prince Amphion's lyre music moved stones into position to form the wall of
Thebes. See Graves, *Greek Myths*, 257.

24

The bold king of Arcadia could not wait
to challenge fierce Macandro to battle,
and rejoiced to find himself there at the right time;
Polinide shared the same thought.
He came from the realm where,
when Typhoeus[13] sighs, Etna ignites and screeches;
nephew he was of the king through his consort,
and he had just arrived to visit the court.

25

I mean to say that his father was the brother
of the queen, Cleardo's wife,
for both of them were children of
King Alismondo, who was in his day so brave.
After he died, his son Brancardo
was made the new king.
He was the father of Polinide, as I've stated,
and crowned ruler over all of Sicily.

26

That whole day and evening the knights
who would go out against the foreign giant
spent tending their arms and destriers,
that they might not fall easily in battle.
Though every one hoped to be the winner
(if right gives victory in hand),
nevertheless no one failed to recall
every most proper and diligent counsel.

27

Dawn had barely appeared in the east
to perform her immemorial escort of the new day,
when great Macandro's formidable horn

13. Also called Typhon, he was the last of the Giants who rebelled against Zeus, who impris-
oned him under volcanic Mount Etna. See Graves, *Greek Myths*, 134.

resounded throughout the land.
Immediately in the square Apollideo made his appearance,
and answered the giant with insults and scorn.
Meanwhile the people, flighty by their nature,
ran in a great hurry to occupy the city walls.

2 8

The Theban prince took leave
first of the king, then of the royal daughter,
nor without her consent did he intend
to move even an inch his destrier's bridle.
Thence toward the great gates he turned his reins,
with a few of his household who followed him.
The king too, with his daughter and his wife,
came onto the wall to see.

2 9

The Athenian damsels make both prayers and vows
to the chaste and warlike goddess,
that their knight might not be unhorsed
and that he might uphold Celsidea's honor.
And he, praying that his thoughts
might not go empty of effect,
as he passes by, gazes at her who shines out amid
a hundred beautiful women, and who stirs up and kindles his heart.

3 0

Dazzled he remained, that knightly lover,
from the moment he gazed at her beautiful eyes,
and inside he melted like wax before
a blazing fire or snow exposed to the sun.
But Love did not make him so arrogant
that he dared to add words to glances;
silently he adored her divine countenance,
the sole relief for his burning heart.[14]

14. The vocabulary of this octave—with references to fire melting like snow, unanswered glances, godly countenance, and aching heart—was typical of all Petrarchist, courtly, and Neoplatonic poetry of the period.

31

At the opening of the gate, as proud Apollideo
emerged boldly outside,[15]
the giant's face shone and he rejoiced,
his heart all full of jubilation and love.
And certain of being the victor
and of putting Armenian merit before Greek,
he too advanced—but before he answered the challenger,
he turned his gaze to the Palladian frond.[16]

32

On a branch of the sacred olive tree Macandro had hung
a portrait of a magnificent and gracious lady,
with an aspect so noble and so divine
that rarely has anyone found its like.[17]
Before this image (which seemed not painted but alive,
so diligent a style had portrayed it),
the haughty and faithful devotee bowed,
and he broke heaven's peace with this shout:

33

"Although I am not worthy of such favor,
O queen of Armenia and of my heart,
since I, a lowly mortal knight,
try to exalt your divine beauty,

---

15. In this octave Fonte calls the Theban knight Ismeno. This could be a reference to the mythical Ismene, daughter of King Oedipus of Thebes. See *New Larousse Encyclopedia of Mythology*, 193. Ismeno was also a powerful magician ("mago Ismeno") in Tasso's *Gerusalemme liberata*.

16. The olive tree was associated with Pallas Athena. See Graves, *Greek Myths*, 60.

17. Showing the effigy of a beloved in battle has a literary antecedent in Boiardo's *Innamorato*, where the ferocious knight Rodamonte has the image of Doralice of Granada in his standard and "in looking at her during a fierce battle, he would become bold and more ferocious, for his valor would increase at that sight, as if he had her alive before his eyes" (2.7.29, my trans.). Fonte must have had this episode very much in mind, given the many similarities in the two stories. In Boiardo, for example, the giant Rodamonte meets a woman warrior, Bradamante, who, like Risamante in *Floridoro*, wounds the bold opponent on the side, although not mortally (2.7.6.) Hanging an object on a tree is also an image present in Ariosto. There Orlando hangs his helmet on the branch of a beech tree, because he does not want any advantage over the knight Ferraù, who famously lost his own helmet and was already trying to retrieve it in canto 1. See *Orlando furioso* 12.36–54.

even so accept the ready and loyal will
which adores your greatness and bows only to it,
and deign that for you I now defeat the Achaeans,
for next I want also to defeat the gods in heaven."

34

With this he slackened the reins and pricked the flank
of his destrier, which ran through the meadow;
no less did Agenor's warrior,
who straight toward him turned his course
and went to strike him so daring and bold
that all the bystanders marveled.[18]
In the encounter, by his horse's fault,
the fierce giant missed with his lance.

35

Not so the Theban, who hit right
in the center of fierce Macandro's shield,
but in vain he pricked it, for it was double-strength and ironclad,
although the blow was harsh and rough.
And because he put too much force in his arm,
he shattered his lance down to the naked iron,
nor did the giant bend or move,
as if he were a tower before the wind.

36

The horses, carried on by their impetus,
with little inconvenience passed on.
After they had gone a ways, the knights turned them round
and returned toward each other.
Macandro cursed the stars and the fates
when he recognized his manifest error,
and such a fury assailed him
that Alecto is more placable, and Megaera.[19]

18. Agenor was an early king of Phoenicia and the father of Cadmus, the founder of Thebes.
See Graves, *Greek Myths*, 195.
19. Two of the Furies.

3 7

Having drawn the sword with which he had slain many people,
the good Theban was coming forward,
when the giant hurled himself upon him.
Overcome by great choler,
he seized with his mighty arm and clutched
the helmet of Celsidea's champion,
and pulled it so strongly to his breast
that the knight was forced to fall.

3 8

By this everyone saw what extreme strength
the giant had, and no less dexterity,
and the king (not that this caused him to grieve or fear)
marveled greatly at his fierceness.
The Argive women so famous for their beauty,
and in whose hearts hope and fear struggled,
were much distressed that the Greek warrior
had fallen, and their glory with him.

3 9

But much greater was the shame and anger
of Apollideo from this event;
on account of it he wanted to pursue dire battle
with his sword to avenge the offense.
But the king, who foresaw this,
quickly sent a messenger who refused it to him,
and ordered him as well, according to the pact,
to leave the victor satisfied.

4 0

His shield, where Peneius's daughter
was seen adorning the earth with a new tree,
Apollideo therefore left to the giant,
and he returned ashamed into the city.
As the Cadmean youth entered,

out to the second battle came Aliforte,
who liked to dress in as many colors
as are found in that bow which announces peace.[20]

4 1

This boy was very brave,
but by nature vain and arrogant.
Therefore he boasted before King Cleardo
that he would bring back the giant's shield.
He came just as I said, nor slower
than he was his adversary to advance.
They ran the field and took their turn,
with lances lowered and reins slack.

4 2

The warrior of Thessaly caught Macandro
on the shield as well, but made so light an impact
that without opening either plate or mail
his lance flew to the sky broken in a thousand pieces.
Nor did the king of the Palladian throng see him
leave the battle any happier
than the good Theban, when in the helmet Macandro
struck him so that he threw him from the saddle.

4 3

The knight was no sooner on the ground
than he rose up and regained the saddle,
and to his adversary he handed his shield
with its begemmed insignia of a peacock;
then toward the city he turned his course,
and discontented he left the fight.
Meanwhile another knight already on the spot
undertook the task of jousting.

20. Daphne, daughter of the river god Peneius, was turned into a laurel tree to save her from
the attentions of Apollo. Cadmus was the legendary founder of Thebes. In Genesis 9, God
makes the rainbow the sign of his covenant not to send another flood.

4 4

This one of whom I speak was the lord of Sparta;
the Amphion-descended king's younger son
was so generous, so great a friend of virtue,
that Sparta had elected him as its lord.[21]
He came toward the victorious enemy
to amend his brother's error;
he too carried on his shield the laurel,
but on his helm he had a crown of gold.

4 5

The good Algier (so he was named) had
no better results than his brother Apollideo,
for at the encounter he hit the green earth
while his strong adversary stayed in the saddle.
After him Griante moved swiftly
(he was the most prudent knight at court),
and he challenged the disdainful and haughty Macandro,
for he was glad and proud to hold the fourth honor.

4 6

The same that happened to every other knight
with the haughty Macandro occurred as well with Griante,
for after the encounter he pressed the earth with his back,
and the king of the Parthians held himself in the saddle.
Arisen, the knight ceded his shield,
recaptured his horse, and went back.
Meanwhile the king of Arcadia, called Elion,
exposed his courageous breast against Macandro.

4 7

He had on his shield a painted panther,
and ash-gray weapons and surcoat.

21. For Amphion, see above, canto 1.23n.

His destrier's coat was tinted likewise,
but of a true and natural color.
Macandro, intent on acquiring the fifth
glory, as if he had put wings to his destrier,
came to strike him with such fury on the forehead
that he knocked him to the earth, and he would have knocked down a
mountain.

48

At this Polinide, who was the nephew
of the Greek king through his wife,
mounted his horse, and slackened and shook his reins,
and encountered Macandro who had already moved forward.
But still he could not bend him from the saddle;
rather he also fell, joining the others' band,
and he handed over to Macandro his green shield
whereon was painted an ear of wheat.[22]

49

He gave him his shield, and went after his destrier
to catch and remount it;
but the horse ran away so nimbly
that to gain it was a difficult task.
The knight did not cease to follow it,
that it might not hide and take cover.
The horse ran and gained such a lead
that in short order it went out of its lord's sight.

---

22. As the octaves above show, where six different jousts are delineated, Fonte seems to have had no problem in working through the dynamics of open field jousting, although the inability of women to know how this sort of manly engagement actually worked was regarded as one reason why they would not try out their skills in the epic genre. But, as was the case for men of the same generation such as Tasso, Fonte could easily appropriate the sine qua non of military culture by reading one of the many manuals published at the time on the subject. For a list, see Erspamer, *La biblioteca di Don Ferrante*. Like Ariosto (*Orlando furioso* 11.26–27), Fonte complains that modern artillery has put a stop to men's bravery and boldness in her time: "But artillery and guns have been the ruin of the brave knights of our time, for they prevent them from displaying their valor and courage to the full, and no army, however strong, is capable of resisting them" (*Worth of Women*, 229).

50

Yet Polinide went after its tracks
until he plunged into the middle of a dense wood;
and now on that path, now on this one,
he searched quite a bit, because he loved it well.[23]
At last a charming damsel stopped him.
She came toward him with her reins slack,
and holding the destrier that it might go no more,
she loosened her tongue and spoke these words:

51

"Tell me, O knight, would you by chance have
seen a warrior of daring and brave aspect
pass by here, with beautiful rich clothes
bearing the insignia of a white lily on green?"[24]
The good Trinacrian answered, "These eyes of mine
have never yet seen such a warrior.[25]
What name is his?" "I don't know," said the lady.
"I know him only by the clothes and by reputation.

---

23. A similar plot development—the hero's horse running away—determines the story line of canto 1 of the *Furioso* too, when the Christian hero Rinaldo abandons Charlemagne's camp to run after his charger Baiardo. The twists and turns created by this choice will make him unable to return to duty for a good while. Labyrinthine movements are of course key to the plot of desire informing all chivalric romances. For a brilliant analysis of such a fertile invention for the genre, see Eugenio Donato, " 'Per selve e boscherecci labirinti': Desire and Narrative Structure in Ariosto's *Orlando furioso*," in *Literary Theory/Renaissance Texts*, ed. Patricia Parker and David Quint (Baltimore: Johns Hopkins University Press, 1986), 33–62.

24. White was the key color of women warriors in all epics, and in fact it was because Clorinda in Tasso's *Gerusalemme liberata* did not wear her usual white armor that she was killed, after the Christian hero, Tancredi, failed to recognize her outside Jerusalem's walls. Fonte will repeat this presentation of Risamante with emphasis on the color white, but still without naming her, in canto 2.4. In the *Furioso* Bradamante's first appearance is conveyed likewise without naming her initially: "Out of the wood a knight appeared. Stalwart and proud was his mien. His raiment was white as snow, and a white plume crested his helmet" (1.60). On color symbolism, a topic that was in any case widely discussed by all social classes, see Lodovico Dolce, *Dialogo nel quale si ragiona delle qualità, diversità e proprietà de i colori* (Venice: Sessa, 1565). On white as a symbol of purity, see 29r. In *The Worth of Women* Fonte describes the reasons why colors signify different emotions and has her character Corinna argue for the importance of white armor: "I'd wear the white armor and white surcoat of the novice knight, and bear on my shield a golden yoke broken through the middle, signifying freedom" (231).

25. Trinacria was the ancient Greek name for Sicily.

52

"I need him to free me
from a great anguish that dwells in my breast,
since he wins all difficult struggles;
so much greater is his power than any other.
I would indeed tell you of my cruel torments
and of that suffering which surpasses every other,
if I were not in such a hurry to find
that noble knight who has no peer.

53

"I seek him in every land,
but fate, always contrary to my desire,
turns me and sends me to places far from him;
yet I have heard reports that he has been around here.[26]
Perhaps he is at the Castle of the Garland,
where every knight in search of adventure competes
in the trial newly appeared
in the land of Dacia in that castle."

54

"Ah," said Polinide to the damsel,
"tell me about this adventure, please.
Tell me how it's strange and how it's fair,
what the peril and what the glory might be,
because I plan to go to it,
and perhaps the victory will be mine."
When the lady heard this prayer,
immediately she dismounted from the destrier.

55

And she said, "If you wish to come with me,
mount onto the saddle, for I will ride pillion,

26. Again there is a similar episode in the *Furioso,* when Ippalca meets Ruggiero and Ricciardetto in canto 26 and asks for their help.

and just as I heard the report, I will recount to you
the high adventure where more than one has failed."
The knight, who desired to find himself
at that adventurous enterprise,
accepted the damsel's offer,
took the bridle, and leaped into the saddle.

56

On the horse's back the damsel placed herself;
then toward Dacia they took the path.
While riding, as she promised,
she began to narrate thus to the knight:
"The queen of Dacia's husband
was conquered by a cruel, fierce destiny.
As it pleased him, she remained his heir
in his splendid regal houses.

57

"And having that heart which in times past
chaste Dido had toward her consort
(as every widow should have),
which did not open the gates to vain desire,
the marital fidelity which she owed to her king
she planned to keep unto death.
Since she had lost her lord,
she planned to live without a husband and without love.

58

"Now unfortunately one day a knight
chanced upon that court,
and gazing at her lovely visage
(for she was still fresh and of graceful countenance),
he burned for her to such an extent that night and day
he loosed hot sighs from his burning breast.
The youth was the duke of Transylvania,
with a handsome visage and royal manner.

59

"He thinks of nothing else, he desires nothing else,
nothing else does the unhappy youth seek
but to obtain the desired lady
who alone can make him joyful and happy.
To risk his life, wealth, and reputation
in any way, licit or illicit,
is of no concern to him, as long as he might succeed;
for then he could die happy.

60

"At court there was a servant of lowly stock
whom the king had raised since childhood,
and the queen considered him the most trusted,
the dearest of many she held in her service.
The duke thinks he can render this fellow
ungrateful with money, and propose to him
every wicked deed. He finds him, and as best he can
he tests his mind with these notes:

61

"'You know, Parmino' (for this he'd heard was his name),
'that while I have been at this court
I have had service from you, and you courtesy
from me, and more than one rich gift.
It seems to me that we have contracted
so great a friendship that there is no
service so great that, if I thought
it might bring you pleasure, I would not perform it.

62

"'And I believe that similarly on your part,
if I revealed a certain need of mine,
you likewise would very readily
carry out what I wish and crave,

and you would accomplish my great desire
which, without your favor, I judge to be a dream.
Moreover, if in this affair of mine you are discreet,
you will be rich, and I content and joyful.'

63

"Parmino, who already knew from experience
that he was a rich and generous lord,
told him, 'By now you should know
of the love I bear you.
Tell me this new requirement of yours,
let me know what you have closed up in your heart,
for there's nothing in the world so great
that I would not do it at your least command.'

64

"The knight responded, 'Since I see
that you are so quick and desire to serve me,
know that for many days I have been raving
for the beauty of a lovely lady,
and every day I will go from bad to worse
if I don't obtain her whom my heart desires.
If you, Parmino, don't give me aid soon,
I have already come to the end of my life.'

65

"'Tell me who she is,' Parmino said,
'and have no doubt that I will conquer and tame her.'
'It's the queen who pierced my heart,'
answered Amandriano (such was his name).
'On her my desires are firm and fixed,
on her beautiful eyes and golden tresses.
I have told you; now that you hear it and know,
don't fail me in what you have promised.'

66

"Parmino was astonished and confused,
greatly regretting his promise,
but the knight, who was experienced in such practices,
at once placed a rich ruby on his finger.
Parmino said to himself, 'If I make excuses,
if I decline to accept this course,
when will the time ever come again to
get rich, if I don't do it now that I have the chance?'

67

"He took heart and said, 'Amandriano,
your request is weighty and I am quite distressed
that you want me to have a hand
in something so nefarious, which I am not at all used to doing;
yet so that my word will not be broken,
and for your kindness, I intend to do my best.
By all means tell me what you think I could do,
for I'm willing to do anything, provided that I please you.'

68

"The knight, who had planned beforehand
how he might deceive the queen,
informed Parmino fully
of the way he intended to dupe her.
Parmino left the enamored duke
and walked to the royal residence,
and found a good pretext
for the queen to send him to Belgirone.

69

"Belgirone was three leagues away,
a castle for recreation, pretty and decorated;
here (following Amandriano's instructions)
the wicked Parmino spent the night.
Then, when the sun rose from the ocean,

in a great hurry he made his return to the city.
He went to the queen and indicated he wanted
to make her aware of a circumstance he considered important.

70

"The queen listened willingly to him
(for everyone takes great delight in hearing of new things),
and with a single gesture she made
her damsels and menservants leave her presence.
Parmino recounted: 'My lady, I was just yesterday
at Belgirone as you bade me,
where, having executed your lofty command,
in the evening I went wandering through the courtyard.

71

"'While alone in the fresh air I wandered and strolled,
and gazed at the green meadow and the serene sky,
I saw the soil near me move
as if a mole was under the ground.
I stopped and looked, and in looking I realized
that the meadow was rising just like a gravid womb,
and shortly, produced from the ground
came a felicitous and monstrous fruit.

72

"'I saw it with these very eyes, and even I
can barely trust them, and yet it was true:
with a white coat and a small golden horn,
a fine and majestic bull-calf came forth toward me.
Under his foot flowered so beautiful a treasure
of bright gems that they dazzled me.
I say that every flower on which he trod
took the form of a pearl or ruby.

73

"'Confused by such a strange marvel,
I didn't know what I should do.

At first a desire seized and gripped me
to fill my hands with those rare stones;
but then a new thought counseled me
to try to acquire the fine bull-calf,
for I wouldn't envy the Eritrean coastlands
if I acquired the bull that makes gems bloom.[27]

74

"'I reach out my hand to grasp his horn,
but he startles and does not give in to my desire.
Still more I go circling around him,
and in vain I tire out my hands and feet.
At last I return to my first thought:
to make myself the heir of that treasure.
I bend and open my hand, but no less
does the bull clear off the ground under my palm.

75

"'Since to obtain that treasure I lack the ability and power,
I return to the bull, and he backs away and flees.
Now for one, now for the other I toil,
and pain and desire consume my soul.
The bull at last, seeing my torment,
turns to me, nor does he low like a bull;
rather, like a man who has intellect and the power of speech,
the goal of all this roving he lays open and reveals to me.[28]

27. Along with other countries on the west coast of the Red Sea, Eritrea has laid claim to being the fabulous land of Punt, which was highly regarded by the ancient Egyptians for its wealth of resources, including gold, ivory, and incense. The richest man in the *Furioso*, for example, is Senapo, emperor of nearby Ethiopia (Nubia), also known as Prester John. See *Orlando furioso*, 33.103–28.

28. This story of the bull-calf producing so many jewels as to tempt men and women's impertinent curiosity with its riches constitutes a reworking of Ariosto's tale of Judge Anselmo. The jealous Anselmo was unforgiving of his wife Argia's fickleness when she betrayed him with Adonio for the sake of possessing a dog producing jewels at whim. But then, in a degrading follow-up, Anselmo allows an Ethiopian, an ugly Moor, as Ariosto puts it ("brutto Moro"), to sodomize him for the sake of having for himself a palace of alabaster with gold friezes (*Orlando furioso* 43.72–143). This Ariostan tale was so well known that Cervantes, for one, gave the name of Anselmo to an overly curious husband in *Don Quixote*.

76

""""This strange and most felicitous adventure,
Parmino," he tells me, "is not made for you,
nor is anyone allowed to touch my treasure,
and others attempt in vain to catch me.
Your queen alone can go off happy
with the goods, than which nature has made none greater.
The rich pickings to her alone are due,
for a cruel trouble that she must have before long.

77

""""Know that shortly a strong and powerful king
will make war on her and cause her great sadness,
because lacking gold she will lack people,
and she will be in grave necessity and scarcity.
Therefore a wise magician who is her kin,
having foreseen her cruel circumstance,
placed in my foot this wealth,
so that she might acquire it at need.

78

""""Now that the time has come, I have revealed myself
to you, the most faithful of all her people.
Therefore tomorrow find her and lay open to her
the goods which I enclose and harbor.
Tell her to come alone, and let her coming
be hidden, nor let anyone hear word of it;
let her arrive by night and, except for you, let
no one else accompany her.

79

""""She will catch me, and she will be victorious
only through the virtue of the precious stones."
So saying, within the concealed den
together he withdrew his stones and himself.
Then the grassy earth joined together again,

and I remained thoughtful with lowered eyes.
I could not sleep all night,
so much did I desire to make my way to you.'

8 0

"The simple queen, who through long experience
had great faith in Parmino,
heard and believed everything that he told her
when she should least have lent him credence.
She believed it that much more
because it was true she had an uncle
highly learned in Medea's art,[29]
who could have created the adventure.

8 1

"At once she begins to mull over which king it might be
who will wage war on her, and how and when;
and more than one iniquitous and treacherous discourse
comes back, disturbing her anxious mind.
As if the band of enemies were already
near her, she plans to start preparing.
She is a woman; the circumstance pressing her is grave
and the time brief; thus, she has reason to fear.

8 2

"It is true that she takes much hope and comfort
from what her faithful Parmino has told her,
that a lucky bull-calf he'd sighted
can pluck her from every harsh and cruel fate.
Therefore it seems to her the day will never
end so she might set out on her path;
she cannot wait for evening to arrive
in order to go to Belgirone with the darkness.

29. The mythological Medea was skilled in magic.

83

"The night is rather long and the way short,
so that she hopes to make her return quickly,
nor will Dawn make her usual escort to the sun
before the queen will have returned to her own bed.
As the night brings the stars into the sky
and everyone is in their proper place,
Parmino makes ready two swift horses,
and waits for the people to sleep.

84

"But Sleep has barely overcome every soul and scattered
his drops of forgetful oblivion,
and Morpheus is representing in varied scenes
more than one good or bad incident to mortals,[30]
when the great desire to acquire this good fortune
leads the queen out from her home.
The untrustworthy Parmino, in whom she trusts,
goes with her and is her companion and guide.

85

"They spurred their good destriers so much
that in less than an hour they reached the castle.
Inside, Amandriano kept watch from a corner,
for at a certain signal he was to open the door.
He listened intently; in time Parmino made the signal,
nor did the duke wait to ask who it was,
but quietly he opened, and in the dark
the queen made her way inside.

86

"In the darkness Parmino draws the incautious woman
into a vacant dwelling.

30. Morpheus was the god of dreams.

Instantly Amandriano, who burns and sighs,
comes to force her beautiful person.
But the matter does not go as he desires;
for often it happens, as in the proverb,
that in punishment for his sin
the deceiver ends up at the feet of the deceived.

87

"Amandriano believes he has in his arms
the beautiful woman whom he loves and desires;
but instead he embraces a person
who doesn't seem to him to be the queen,
who clutches and encumbers him so much
that pincers could not clutch more tightly.
It does him no good to struggle and writhe,
for in the end he is captured and carried away.

88

"The same is done to Parmino.
The queen remains alone in the dark;
she hears more than one 'Alas!' nearby,
which alarms and distresses her.
She no longer hears Parmino; she calls Parmino,
and hears not a word in answer.
She sees no bull, she sees nothing at all,
and she begins to fear for her life.

89

"Not knowing what to do, afflicted and silent,
without sleeping a bit, with much anguish
she waits until Dawn, arriving in the heavens,
uncovers her shining golden cloth.
As every wakened bird greets the day,
and the time of year makes the beautiful morning greener,
the lady finds before her
a lofty edifice, stupendous and new.

90

"It is shaped in the form of a pyramid,
and it shines, transparent, like a crystal.
On the high summit is placed a garland
of flowers much redder than coral.
The astounded lady approaches it
and sees inside Parmino and the Transylvanian duke
in penance for their offense,
for the wall is clear and translucent to her gaze.

91

"The queen recognizes each of them,
but she cannot yet fully discern the truth of the matter.
Then in the stone in golden letters
she sees united the characters and the notes
which reveal to her the fiction of the bull,
and make known to her all those duplicities.
Next she reads that Parmino and the foreign duke
from the prison will never emerge,

92

"unless there comes a knight so clever
and so valorous that he can break that enchantment,
and strip the fateful pyramid
of the garland placed on its summit.[31]
'When (there was written) someone should take wing
and fly to acquire these priceless spoils,
if he is a king who gets so rich a token,
he will never be driven out from his kingdom.

93

"'But if he is a private knight
who takes the garland into his power,

31. Enchanted garlands were often woven into the narrative of early modern works. For another example of their importance, see Bigolina, *Urania* (2005), 138–47.

he will in time gain an empire,
nor will he ever be driven away from his state.
If the lofty circle should come into the hands
of a lady or a maiden, she may be sure
that her chastity will be guarded
against any treacherous or ungrateful mind.

9 4

"'And so that everyone may know
who made such an important artifact,
know that he who guarded you from treachery,
noble queen, is old Celidante.'
The queen, understanding the cruel intent
of the greedy servant and the audacious lover,
revealed herself to the castle's people,
and made plain to them the iniquitous and treacherous incident.

9 5

"The news spread, so that more than one person tried
thereafter to acquire so great a crown.
A great golden hammer is hung there,
to beat the marble, which resounds.
Then a door opens, and out comes an armed
king who resembles in his face and person
the king of Dacia, the deceased beloved
husband of the queen of whom I have told you.

9 6

"This man fights with such great power
that he overcomes every brave and strong warrior,
and drives him perforce into that dwelling
whence he issued, and then locks the doors;
and if he is not called to a new dance
by a new sound, he does not come out into the courtyard."
Thus while riding the woman spoke
to the knight, who listened attentively to her.

97

But I do not intend to tell you so much of these two
that I forget to return to the Greek realm,
where the giant had taken the victor's palm and the credit
from the hands of every most worthy warrior.[32]
I told how Algier, who in Sparta had the royal dignity,
left him his shield as a token, and also the Theban,
Elion, Aliforte, and that prudent
Griante, and finally Polinide.

98

In addition to these Macandro stretched on the plain
many others, and gained new victories.
The shields which he took as prizes from them,
he consecrated one and all to that beautiful image.
When the king discerned no one else
at that point preparing to ride in his defense,
toward his palace he returned,
for the sun was already near midday.

99

Macandro, the delighted victor, remained behind
to gaze at his goddess, a happy lover
whose fervent love persuaded him
to perform here so many acts of valor.
All the people returned to their houses
discussing the giant's strength.
All the maidens sorrowed
at having lost their much-cherished reputation.

100

But Celsidea more than any was disheartened
that her glory was so soon extinguished,

---

32. Fonte deftly uses here the much-imitated Ariostan and Boiardan technique of interweaving
narrative strands in order to keep the reader's attention high. For a sense of how well this zigzag
narrative works, see Javitch, *"Cantus Interruptus."*

although her modesty did not permit
her to show herself afflicted and unhappy.
That day and the next no man dared and attempted
to go forth through the gate against the giant.
On the third there appeared a knight
of whom I hope to tell in the next canto.

CANTO 2

ARGUMENT

The foreign warrior kills the wicked giant
and gives news of himself to King Cleardo.
The king proclaims a tourney. Good Silano
suffers the sea's harsh and vigorous assault.
From Egypt to Thrace the dwarf makes his way.
To him Prince Risardo promises
to liberate the lovely damsel in distress,
and he gives them news of her predicament.

1

No one must think so highly of himself
that he disdains everyone else,
even if he is as rich and honored
as a man of royal and illustrious blood can be.
Even if he wore the royal mantle
and shone with eminent valor
and possessed all of Phoebus's knowledge,[1]
he should not, to praise himself, disparage others.

2

Every person must be humble
and display benevolence and love,
for humility binds every noble heart

---

1. As god of the sun, Apollo was also called *Phoebus* (brilliant); the sun saw and knew everything
that happened on earth. See *New Larousse Encyclopedia of Mythology,* 113, 142.

with a sweet and most gentle chain.
Pride on the other hand is boorish and base.
It urges its followers on to their own detriment,
and it made Niobe and Pentheus and others perish
at the peak of their pride and brashness.[2]

3

When most strongly these people believe they are on the wheel's upswing
and they enjoy Fortune's uncertain goods,
which she purposely revolves and wheels,
then she makes them experience a thousand certain pains
and casts them down, and makes known to them
what penalty awaited their unworthy acts—
just as with King Macandro you will be able to hear,
you who are about to read these pages.

4

I left off on the third day, when the sun
was lowering his aged head, warm and yellow,
and the king waited with the others, grieving
because he saw no one else coming to the dance.
A knight in search of adventure,
richly adorned, both he and his horse,
entered by chance into the city,
where he heard what had happened, as I have narrated.

5

The knight seemed vigorous and brave
in appearance, and daring over all others.
His insignia on a green shield was a white

2. The wife of Amphion, Niobe was so proud of her seven sons and seven daughters that she disparaged Leto for having only two children. These two, Apollo and Artemis, took vengeance by killing all of Niobe's children, and Zeus turned her into a statue. See Graves, *Greek Myths*, 258–59. Fonte may have known the story from chapter 15 of Giovanni Boccaccio's *Famous Women* (*De mulieribus claris*). King Pentheus of Thebes attempted to imprison Dionysus, who drove Pentheus's mother and other Theban women mad. When Pentheus followed the women up a mountain, they tore him to pieces. See Graves, *Greek Myths*, 105.

lily, his clothing was green and white.
He had barely entered when a hundred people rushed to his side
and offered him hospitality and pleasant welcome.
Some to the high king carried news of him;
others recounted the situation to him and moved him to compassion.

6

Therefore he came immediately to the king,
and like a courteous man with a bold heart,
he offered before the decreed deadline
to demonstrate his valor against the giant.
One can believe that the king, who did not hope
for help from elsewhere, accepted with all his heart.
All the people then ran to the battlements,
and made haughty Macandro marvel.

7

The knight, because the hour was late
on the day fixed in advance as the last, as I've recounted,
with the king's permission returned outside
well mounted, equipped with noble weapons.
A great and notable thing was seen then,
for as soon as he emerged, onto the meadow fell
the portrait which hung high in the branches,
the one great Macandro esteemed so much.[3]

8

As much as the giant regretted and sorrowed
to see his goddess press the earth,
that much delight was born in the Greeks' hearts,
for they held it to foretell a successful outcome for that battle.
The knight, who liked the omen,
challenged Macandro and began his charge.

3. In Boiardo too the effigy of the beloved falls to the ground, an event that upsets Rodamante
so much that he goes on to slaughter all the Lombards in fury, for "he had nothing in the world
more dear or pleasing to him, since the woman with those features was his love and his entire
hope" (2.14.20, my trans.).

Macandro, full of rage, also stretched forward,
and so they charged one against the other.

9

The unknown knight, who was a master
of the game, came to strike cruel Macandro
under his shield in such a way
that the hauberk did not withstand the great blow.
The lance in many splinters flew to the sphere of fire,
but the wound in his flank held the iron,
whence in great abundance the blood sprayed out
and tinted the pure steel with a red adornment.

1 0

As from a high mountain an internal spring
issues furiously, and descends violently
in a twisted path down the rocky cliff face,
and leads to the river and widens it in the plain,
just so from the living and animate mountain
that Macandro resembles, the blood
spreads and stretches out eagerly and furiously,
and makes a lake appear on the sand.

1 1

By the impious one the warrior was struck in the helmet,
but it didn't pass through, for the helm was of excellent tempering.
The lance shattered and the knight was very
close to finding himself on the grass;
yet he held himself back, quickly gathered up the reins
(which had fallen), and hurriedly pricked his destrier.
The great shock of the encounter had pushed it down
on its rump, but it rose up at once.

1 2

At the very effective blow which the knight
had given the haughty giant,
everyone in the Greek state rejoiced,

and the king beamed at it with Celsidea.
Haughty Macandro meanwhile had returned.
He suffered much from the wound;
still, his belief that he was the victor
tempered somewhat his grave pain.

1 3

But when he saw the knight against him
with his sword in hand and still in the saddle,
such a mighty rage encumbered and wounded his heart
that the tempestuous sea does not shake so much.
At once he too took in hand his sword
and went against the warrior who feared nothing,
and he burdened him with such heavy loads
that it made all the Greeks' hair curl.

1 4

So strongly he hit him in the center of the forehead
that he left him senseless, and he would have given up
his dazed soul to the realm of Acheron,
if the fine helmet had not defended him.[4]
With his tremendous and ready strength gone astray,
his destrier ran flat-out through the meadow.
Irate Macandro lost no time then,
and set off to follow through the green grass.

1 5

But just as a lofty and firmly rooted tree,
against which a mighty wind employs its every force
(which however does not uproot it or snap it at the base,
but bows down and bends somewhat the high branches),
once that furor has ceased, with just as much
strength straightens up and spreads its foliage to the sky;
just so the warrior, after the blow Macandro
struck made him bend down, soon rose again.

4. The Acheron is a river in the Greco-Roman underworld.

16

With that extreme fury which one can
imagine pain and anger placed in his heart,
he turns his horse after he rouses.
He swings his sword at his enemy,
and on the right shoulder where he strikes him
he gives back with great force his answer.
He opens what he touches, and onto his thigh fall
both armor and flesh, and he cleaves every protection.

17

Macandro again directs a blow at the knight's
helmet with all his power.
He raises his shield, and on the graceful insignia
of the lily the impetuous sword strikes.
The knight who rules in Parthia is quite sure
he'll make him fall dead in two pieces to the ground;
he cuts the shield and he cuts the crest as well,
but the helmet withstands the cruel and horrendous blow.

18

Stunned by the mighty blow, the Greek champion
stretches out on his destrier's back.
The harsh buffet so blinds him
that if it's night or day he cannot discern.
Ferocious Macandro, who certainly does not intend
to employ any courtesy with him,
seizes his left arm, and trusts with certainty
that he'll pull him down to the earth, and believes he'll triumph over him.

19

But while he pulls, the knight
comes back to himself bolder than ever,
and risen again he stays in the saddle.
So Macandro takes another tack
and tries (but he doesn't manage it) to grapple
with him, and invites him to it,

but the expert warrior with sword in hand
keeps him distant by the sword's length.

20

Disdainful Macandro knows
that none of his plans is effective,
since the warrior holds tight with both thighs
and does not let him approach chest to chest.
To give him (if possible) the extreme anguish
and send his spirit to the Stygian abode,[5]
he takes up again his sword, and directs the harsh blow
at a place the shield does not defend.

21

At the left shoulder a great downstroke
which he would have delivered all the way to the saddle
he aims, but the warrior immediately
dodges with a jump the cruel blow.
Then he drives his harsh and biting sword
over the thigh of the impious and unruly soul;
he passes its deadly point between his belly and his flank
two spans deep, and deprives him of life.[6]

22

Bloody from four wounds falls
the Parthian king, yet before he dies,

---

5. According to Greek mythology, after death people's shades cross the River Styx to enter the underworld.

6. The terms of this combat—Macandro repeatedly trying to wound the enemy on the head and Risamante aiming at the lower part of her opponent's body—are typical of epics where the "good" hero, that is, the moral one, is destined to win because he uses his head, while the "wrong" hero will need to be reminded that he has been governed by lower carnal passions. Fonte reinforces her choice by describing Risamante as holding "tight with both thighs" (2.20)—an image that also reflects her heroine's chastity. Likewise, in the *Aeneid* Turnus is killed by Aeneas's spear which, "hissing, . . . penetrates his thigh"(12.1235). See also the Volume Editor's Introduction. For more on rules of combat governing jousts in the early modern period, see Klaus Hempfer, "Un criterio di validità per interpretazioni: L'epica cavalleresca italiana del Rinascimento," *Intersezioni* 4 (1984): 289–320.

since love still rules him,
he says that he does not grieve for his fate,
but that, in order to exalt that beauty
which he loves, he wishes he'd been stronger yet;
and he regrets only, and it gives him infinite pain,
that he no longer has life to serve her.

2 3

Already from the city walls the whole incident
Cleardo together with all Athens had discerned,
since the battle had been waged
nearby, and everyone could see it well.
Therefore, as the Fate cut that king's
thread and gazed at him lifeless on the sands,[7]
everyone descended from the wall and ran,
and adorned and crowned the victor with praise.

2 4

He had returned his sword to the sheath,
and was coming away at a slow and sluggish pace.
Once arrived at the grand gates where the grateful king
waited, he left the saddle right away.
The delighted king embraced him and wanted him by his
side, exalted him and praised his courage,
but much more he praised his courtesy,
which had relieved him of that burdensome nuisance.

2 5

The warrior, who was noble and courteous,
in thanking the king loosened his tongue
and rendered all the honor to his daughter,
for he was determined to cede all the praise to her.
The king entreated him at this point please
to show his face, so he removed his helmet

7. The three Fates were believed to spin the thread of each person's life. Clotho would spin the thread, Lachesis measured it, and Atropos cut it when it was time for the person to die.

and revealed that the warrior so strong in the saddle
was a most noble maiden.[8]

26

She removed her helmet and uncovered the blonde
tresses, clearer and more luminous than gold.[9]
And two stars appeared, so joyful
that for envy the sun hid itself in the sea.[10]
Her fresh, rubicund cheeks moved
the lilies and crimson roses to envy,
and her hand, which she had bared as well,
seemed whiter than snow.

27

As she revealed her beautiful visage to all,
for all were gazing fixedly at her,
she appeared to everyone that same lady for whom Macandro
had directed his course to Cleardo's kingdom,
that lady to whom the wretch had offered the shields
before death cast its dart at him.
They marveled no less at this fact
than at the valor they saw manifest.

28

Just as one who is present when
a woman holds a mirror before herself,
and now gazing at the natural face,
now at its likeness in that glass,
examining every part, cannot discern
anything that might differ between them,

---

8. Fonte uses masculine pronouns until Risamante's face is revealed.

9. The removal of the helmet, which in turn leads to the revelation that the warrior is a woman because of her golden hair falling down onto her shoulders, is a topos of chivalric romances. It marked the audience's discovery of the woman warrior's sex in Boiardo (3.5.41–42), Ariosto (43.41), and Tasso (3.21). Women writers used it too, as in the case of Margherita Sarrocchi's Rosmonda, with whom Vaconte immediately falls in love. See *Scanderbeide* 13.86.

10. In Latin and Italian poetry, especially in the Petrarchan tradition, the beloved lady's eyes are often called stars or lights.

just so this woman seemed to resemble in all her parts
the beloved of the king of the Parthians.

29

The king ordered that the portrait
be brought there (it was still lying on the ground),
and the painted and the true appeared identical
when they were close, no more, no less.
The king beseeched her to tell why she had removed
from life one who rendered her honor clear
and bright, for there was no other woman who shone so,
and the courteous maiden explained the whole matter.

30

So that you may know the truth, this damsel
by whose hand Macandro lay dead on the ground,
who goes by the name of Risamante,
with beautiful Biondaura was born at the same birth.
Daughters of the king of Armenia both the one and the other,
they are equal in everything between them as the heavens pleased,
except that one is soft and delicate,
and the other goes armed as a warrior.

31

At her birth, because the stars
inclined her to lofty and gracious works,
the great wizard Celidante, when she was still
a little child, stole her from her father.
Consequently the king, grieving at such news,
once his wife was no longer a mother,
left in dying to the daughter who remained
the inheritance of his royal households.

32

Not for this did Celidante cease
with diligence and paternal love
to raise the child Risamante,

whose skill and valor he had foreseen.
Consequently, afterward she surpassed all others
in arms, and thereby gained eternal honor.
She stayed with him a long time concealed
in a castle founded in the middle of the sea.

3 3

But after the sun had wandered seventeen years
through the circle whence it brings the heat and the ice,
the good wizard informed the royal offspring
of her honorable paternal stock.
Therefore she sent with humble words
to her sister the message that since heaven
had made them born of one father and so much alike,
in dominion as well they should be equal.

3 4

She meant to imply that, as was only right,
she should agree to divide between them their father's kingdom.
But her sister pretended artfully,
although from many she had heard the truth;
and so she responded that on her
part she would never so lightly have
thought, let alone believed, that she
might be her sister by blood.

3 5

Once she'd had a sister, but fate had placed her in the hands
of a thief who killed her with his own hand.
Even if she were the one whom heaven produced
together with her, and that were plain to her,
let her not claim that hers by right was
half of that realm she had in hand,
since the dying king bequeathed this royal burden
to her alone, and did not even name the other.

36

For this harsh answer Risamante
was angry at her with a just anger,[11]
and, valorous and with an excellent heart,
armed she seeks out every city, every realm,
and she helps people here and there so that her
many courtesies might accomplish her design.
She does good deeds for this and that lord,
so that in her need they might come to her aid.

37

The lofty warrior recounted the situation
to King Cleardo, and added that the giant[12]
had come for her sister's sake;
her beauty had kindled and pricked his heart.
The king heard the whole true story,
and since to his benefit the lady had slain
the impious giant, he offered her his gratitude,
and proffered his help to her in everything.

38

Risamante thanked the good king,
and because by now night was overcoming the day,
the king with the others took to the saddle
and returned to his palace.
But the queen and courteous Celsidea
came immediately to Risamante,
and in a room they removed her armor
and adorned her in feminine clothes.

---

11. Biondaura's answer to Risamante, which causes "just anger," as Fonte puts is, is remarkably
in contrast with the reaction that Marfisa and Ruggiero have in the *Furioso* when they are told by
the wizard Atlante that they are twin brother and sister. "With great joy Ruggiero recognized
Marfisa as his sister, and she him," Ariosto writes. "They embraced each other . . . And as they
recollected details of their early years—things done and said and experienced—they discov-
ered with greater certainty that all that the spirit had told them was true" (36.67).

12. Fonte here misspells the name Cleardo, obviously an invented name, into "Cleandro."

39

I decline to tell of the party and the cheer
with the honor that was paid to the maiden,
who as a woman possessed as much beauty
as she did valor as a warrior in the saddle.
Already Celsidea so loved and appreciated her
that she wanted to spend that night with her,
and so they went together to their repose
until the fresh dawn appeared in the sky.

40

As the next morning woke and roused them,
the beautiful ladies rose from bed;
the one girded on her womanly garment,
the other her accustomed steel save for the helmet.
But Celsidea came out grieving and sad,
for the warrior had already said she would depart;[13]
and she pleaded with the king to entreat her
to remain with her for three days yet.

13. As every contemporary reader would have noticed, this scene closely recalls one of the most piquant and well known in the *Furioso*, reworked from the last canto of the *Innamorato*, when the Spanish princess Fiordispina invites Bradamante—whom she takes to be a knight when she first sees her, because she is wearing armor and has short hair—to stay in her castle. Fiordispina then has Bradamante take off her manly attire and wear female clothes, so that she can undeceive herself of the love she has conceived from the very beginning for the newly arrived woman. After dinner, the two share a bed, as was customary. Throughout the night a sleepless Fiordispina, still wishing that her bed mate were a man, keeps checking Bradamante's body just in case "something" could be found to confirm the sex of the person she wishes she had next to her. Tired by the ruckus, Bradamante tells Fiordispina the morning after that she is leaving right away. Her twin brother, Ricciardetto, hears that day of his sister's adventure and comes back to Fiordispina's castle, dressed in the clothes that Bradamante was wearing. He is able to show the princess the following night that he possesses precisely what she was looking for: "She saw and touched the object she had so craved, but she could not believe her eyes or her fingers or herself, and kept wondering whether she was awake or asleep" (*Orlando furioso* 25.67). No sexual implications and no ad hominem winks are, however, present in Fonte's rereading of this story, no matter how much Fonte uses the same vocabulary to highlight the thematic similarities. For a reading of this episode in Ariosto, see Finucci, *The Lady Vanishes*, 201–25.

41

And so at their entreaties she remained
three more days, and then she took her leave
to general sorrow, so much was she welcome;
indeed, she moved everyone to love her.
Armed, she passed from Europe into Asia
and went so far that she found herself in a beautiful garden.
But I intend to leave her here, because it is fitting
for me to remain now with Cleardo.

42

For cheer at the victory
won against barbaric boldness,
he proclaimed in public the most solemn
tourney that had yet been seen.
The news of it he ordered
trumpeted everywhere,
and he provided a lucky opportunity to the world
to see Alismondo's granddaughter.

43

The king of Syria made his passage there,
and the king of Persia, and a strong brother of his.
The king of Africa made the voyage as well,
and a thousand others left their own courts.
Only to see the noble Achaean lineage
did each one move toward the Palladian gates.
Each planned to come to the Achaean shore
only to see that worthy girl.

44

Italy too heard the fortunate proclamation
in which Athens extolled her merits to the skies,
such that Silano as well, with faithful Clarido,
left the lofty hill of Latium.
Silano, only prince of the Saturnian

shore—he too entrusted himself to the gentle waves,[14]
and for two days he had propitious for his intent
the air clear, the sea quiet, and the wind from the stern.

45

For two days and two nights Fortune smiled
on the ship such that the helmsman could not ask for more,
but the following day killed his hope,
for the sky, the wind, and the sea broke faith.
A wind rose then which into the air brought
dark clouds; the sun is no longer seen.
The sky around them is bright with frequent lightning;
the wind, the air, and the sea threaten disgrace.

46

The swollen wave grows little by little,
and clashes with the north wind and rebels against the heavens.
The water bounds up to the sphere of fire,
for it seems to want to enclose the stars in its bosom.
Jove makes the lightning bolt move about,
and strikes towers and uproots trees.
The sky, and the wind, and the sea make such war
that it sinks the wind, the sea, the air, and the earth.

47

The wretched helmsman is pale and wan;
although he's dazed by great terror,
still, industrious and alert, he does not cease from doing
what's fitting to the craft of navigation.
He commands this one and that, but the wind carries
away his shouts and he is disappointed,
for none of the sailors hears him,
yet each one attends to his duty.

14. Saturn's grandson, Faunus, was one of the first kings of Latium, the region in which Rome
was founded. See *New Larousse Encyclopedia of Mythology,* 207.

48

The sad helmsman shouts for them to release
the rope which holds the largest sail,
for he still hopes that the weather might turn,
but he cannot make his speech heard.[15]
The arrogant sea meanwhile swirls round and turns
the ship, which groans and is torn apart.
Not only has the water carried off some lifeless parts,
it's also penetrated everything to the core.

49

The sailors consider themselves lost
when they spot the enemy wave entering the ship,
and with most bitter cries and weeping
they ask for mercy from the highest eternal realm.
Only courageous Silano and his faithful companion
do not lose heart among so very many,
nor do they give the least sign of cowardice,
for they have steady hearts and a strong and bold demeanor.

50

Some of the sailors run in a great hurry
to plug the fissures where the sea enters.
Others with buckets into the sea throw back
the salty and bitter waves that entered earlier.
Behold meanwhile a sudden thunderbolt,
cast by the celestial hand onto the mast.
It shatters the pole and burns the rudder, and with it
sends the wretched helmsman into the world of darkness.

15. The failure to hear the helmsman's orders just before a momentous shipwreck is a classical
topos. See, for example, Ovid's *Metamorphoses* 11.465 and Boiardo's *Innamorato* ("everyone was
screaming and nobody could be heard," 3.4.5). A similar scene is also in Marinella's *Enrico*: "the
pale helmsman screams and orders, but the heavy rains make it impossible to see" (5.10). My
translation.

5 1

This was indeed the harsh and disastrous shaft
that killed only one yet pierced the hearts of all,
for it was now quite clear and manifest
that there was no escape from that deadly furor.
Therefore with Silano Clarido was quick
to take the decision which proved the best.
They ran to the nearby boat
to escape the pitiless ocean's pride.

5 2

Many wanted to follow their example,
but they forbade it with naked sword.
They released themselves from the ship and from those men,
who ended up prey to the harsh and voracious sea.
They didn't know if they were near the Indus or the Moor,
for clouds acted as shield and shelter from the daylight.
It's true that the lightning often opened the veil,
yet it showed them nothing but the sea and the sky.

5 3

How with the good Clarido young Silano
later found himself in a better state,
and how later to the shore he was saved
from the fury of the harsh and mad sea,
in another place will be recounted;[16]
for now, for a little while, I direct my style afar,
and I leave these two in so dubious a predicament,
to go to the splendid court of Thrace.

5 4

There is a city placed on the extreme shore
which the Bosphorus separates from Bithynia.
On this side Helle's sea appears between Sestus and Abydos;

16. Silano and Clarido's shipwreck and their landing without any other crew member on a
"fortunate" island are closely modeled upon an adventure of Homer's Ulysses, who in escaping
the cannibals reaches the domain of the sun god's daughter, Circe. More on this later.

on the far side the Euxine strikes and stings the coasts.[17]
Byzantium it is called, whose proud acclaim
reaches from the low center to the supernal heavens,
and the west has not, nor the east,
a more ferocious and warlike people.

55

For a long time Agricorno had been
emperor there of Mars's great people.
The fame of his valor spread round about,
giving subject matter to the most learned writings.
He had a son adorned with every virtue,
with every excellent endowment and every noble art,
who in all lofty, noble, and gracious works
was rare in the world, and greater than his father.

56

Besides this boy, who was named
Risardo, he had also a daughter;
while her brother was courteous and brave,
she was among the most beautiful.
She was called Ersina, and Love's dart
for her sake had not yet caused fresh wounds;
she had not yet been in another's heart
the cause of joy or the opposite effect.

57

This is because she is so wise, and modest,
and of such decorous and noble habits
that she does not display her great beauty,

17. The Bosphorus is the strait which connects the Black Sea to the Sea of Marmara and separates Europe and Asia. Byzantium (today Istanbul) is on the European side of the strait, while the ancient country of Bithynia was on the Asian side. Helle and her brother fled from Greece eastward on a magic flying golden ram. The strait where Helle fell into the sea was thereafter called the Hellespont. (See Graves, *Greek Myths*, 226–27.) This is the modern Dardanelles, connecting the Aegean Sea to the Sea of Marmara. Sestus and Abydos were cities on opposite shores of the Hellespont. For more on classical names, see Michael Grant, *A Guide to the Ancient World: A Dictionary of Classical Place Names* (New York: Barnes and Noble, 1986), 2–3. The Euxine, or Black Sea, has salt water.

and she keeps hidden her two lovely eyes
because, being no less virtuous than beautiful,
she does not want anyone to be torn and consumed.
She does not want anyone to feel affliction because of her,
for if her face is tender, her heart is stony.

58

Now while the emperor is happy
with this lofty virgin and his son,
and with him one day in the hall is the empress
with her grave countenance and serene expression,
and also the victorious ranks of Thracian heroes
with all his royal council,
there appears among those lords a little dwarf,
with clothing rich, lovely, and exotic.

59

With such rare beauty is the dwarf adorned
that no painter portrays Cupid better.
The gaze of all around is drawn by
that beautiful color which graces and tints his face.[18]
Sad and humble, the dwarf bows
to Agricorno and to the others, and constrains them all to pity.
He forces himself to speak, but in his throat
grief closes off his words.

60

At last desire inflames his breast so much
that he breaks the bitter chain of grief,
and he opens the way for his sorrowful affection,
despite his suffering, his pain.

---

18. Dwarfs are common features of chivalric romances, but in women's narratives they seem to be cast as the most faithful and honest human beings, perhaps because their diminutive size makes them less threatening. A case in point is Bigolina's *Urania*, where even in the name, "Giudizio," the dwarf reflects his inner power. For Ariosto, however, the dwarf is a figure of sexuality gone awry, as the queen of Lombardy, for example, is made to show her perversion through her choice of a dwarf over her handsome husband, King Astolfo (*Orlando furioso* 28.35).

He lays out his doleful thoughts,
which he intersperses with sighs and tears,
and he makes every soul light up with pity
while he spills out lovely tears.

61

"Hoping to find in you just piety,[19]
supreme high emperor of the Thracians,
I have sought," he said, "these lands,
leaving the impious and deceptive Egyptian fields,
in order to save an angelic beauty
from the tyrannous, harsh, and rapacious hands
which, having killed King Galbo of Egypt,
laid on his niece the blame for the crime.

62

"By now it is twenty days since he was killed,
and there is no sure proof by whom.
They accuse of the misdeed the young woman
wherein all faith, all goodness reside.
And because Miricelso, her wise brother,
elsewhere his valor demonstrates and proves,
the impious and perjured faction has become so bold
as to imprison the sweet, noble lady.

63

"To usurp that kingdom from the innocent damsel,
they have placed her in a harsh and cruel prison,
for there was no closer and nearer kin
to the deceased lord than she.
For love of her all Alexandria is sorrowful.
By what is said, in vain one hopes for
her liberty, because they have sentenced her
to stay locked up thus until the end of the year.

19. The Italian *pietade* (or its variant *pietà*, which appears elsewhere in the poem) could also be
translated as "compassion" or "pity."

64

"During this time the unhappy girl
must find a champion to defend her
from a knight who slanders her, and says
that against everyone who might take up her defense,
he intends to prove that she, iniquitous and treacherous,
was the cause of that king's horrendous death.
He will maintain for the whole year
that she carried out such a cruel plan.

65

"Alas, if a knight does not come in the meantime
to prove that Raggidora is innocent
(this is the name of the woman I love so much),
guiltless she will reach her final hour." [20]
His voice failed at this, and the handsome dwarf's
weeping increased, for he was troubled, and he moaned, and wept.
When he had proceeded to that pitiful point,
perforce he put a period to his phrases.

66

The lofty emperor who was seated on high,
and had around him a crown of princes,
seeing grief so wounded the dwarf
that he could not give the breath he desired to his speech,
although he did not ask him for succor and help,
well knew that to no other end did he hold forth.
So he turned his eyes to his people near and far,
and thought which ones he should send with the dwarf.

20. In romances of chivalry, it is not important whether a woman is innocent or guilty. Her future, as well as her reputation, depends on the man who will take up her cause with a joust: if he wins, she is good; if he loses, she is bad. Likewise, when Ginevra in cantos 4 and 5 of the *Furioso* is accused of being unfaithful, it is because the man who takes up her defense wins that joust that she can be declared innocent.

67

All the young and strong Thracian warriors
were eager for such a righteous venture,
and they yearned to see beautiful Raggidora
defended from others' wrongs;
but because everyone had realized
that Risardo had his heart most set on it,
not one revealed his thoughts,
nor dared to speak before him.

68

Risardo stood, and with his father's
leave, he said to the dwarf, "Now be at peace,
for I promise and swear to you in the presence
of my lord, and of all the Thracian people,
to liberate this woman from such a sentence,
if it is (as you say) unjust, impious, and false,
and to see to it that she acquires that kingdom as well."
And he went to prepare instantly.

69

Consoled by such a promise, the dwarf
dried the sad moisture from his beautiful eyes.
While his son adorned himself
with polished steel, minister to his valor,
and to the admiral of the fleet the order was given
to have the best ship prepared,
the king bade that to the empress the dwarf express
more particulars of the strange case.

70

Let him tell the reason why he alone comes
to procure for her such desperately needed help,
for out of so many that the Egyptian cities contain,
no one (except for him alone) has come.

He could perhaps be a spy for Athens
(the astute emperor mused to himself),
and come with this swindle and this deception
to learn how things are going here.

71

At that time a great dispute between the Thracian realm
and the Greek had arisen as to their borders,
and of this uproar, of this resentment,
perhaps the cause was ungrateful Thrace.
Now this king, who had in mind the impious design
to destroy (if he could) the Greek army,
thought that King Cleardo on his part
desired to do him the same harm.

72

Drawn aside next to the queen,
by the king's will the dwarf was seated.
With his angelic and divine voice,
with a progressively more joyful and gracious visage,
he began: "Errant and wandering Fame
had given notice to the Orient,
so that on every tongue, in every pen
was the extremely beautiful virgin of the Nile.

73

"The exalted report proceeded from shore to shore,
there where I am king in the Pygmies' realm.[21]
She so kindled my heart with this acclaim
that I forgot myself and everyone else for her,
such that leaving my friendly and faithful kingdom,
alone to Alexandria I journeyed.

21. Fonte may never have seen a Pygmy because not only does she make him a dwarf rather than dramatically short, but she also erases all his racial characteristics and describes him as white, with features that make him handsome according to current understanding of classical male beauty.

There arrogant Love gave me to her as a gift,
and dedicated me as her perpetual servant.

74

"Once there I found that very far
was her reputation from the truth, for everything I had heard
was a modest and scant report,
compared with what I then saw and understood.
I shall not recount her superhuman beauty,
for it is too great a weight for my shoulders.
It suffices that wherever the sun spreads its rays
a greater beauty it never saw on earth.

75

"I loved her and could not find
peace with this love near or far,
if not when heaven sometimes allowed me
to see my goddess's beautiful visage.
In order to mitigate the flame that burned me,
I did not care to send letters or messengers.
Rather I changed my royal garments for ones rough and lowly,
and I saw to it that she welcomed me as a servant.

76

"Since I judged myself not apt to practice
illustrious feats and to demonstrate valor,
and through prowess with weapons
to gain for myself her lofty love,
in another fashion I planned to help myself,
and of such wealth to become the possessor.
I pretended to be of humble station; I saw to it that she
accepted me among her own and called on me to be her servant.

77

"No man was more alert than I
in serving her, among so many that she had;

in my eyes and speech I was modest;
always with great readiness I served her.
She looked with so much favor on my every gesture,
my service, my diligence,
that she commanded me alone, and used to say
that no one understood her better than I.

78

"Into my hands she entrusted
her most valuable things, gold and silver,
every richest and most prized garment,
gems, garlands, every ornament.
I had the care of her apartments,
regal and ornate as was fitting for her.
And my love grew so, little by little,
that my heart was scant fuel for so great a fire.

79

"Despite all this, never did I become so bold
as to reveal myself to her, for always some
damsel used to serve her with me,
so irksome to my eager thoughts.
At last one day, propitious to my desire,
Fortune came my way—
one day when she was spreading out her beautiful hair in the sun,[22]
without the company that was usually there.

80

"As I found myself alone in her presence
and I thought of revealing myself,

22. Venetian women of Fonte's period would bleach their hair by going to a sunny rooftop, spreading out their hair, and applying henna. See Irma Jaffe, *Shining Eyes, Cruel Fortune: The Lives and Loves of Italian Renaissance Women Poets* (New York: Fordham University Press, 2002), 409. For a contemporary book on how to do it, see Isabella Cortese, *I secreti della signora Isabella Cortese ne' quali si contengono cose minerali, medicinali, arteficiose, e alchemiche. Et molte de l'arte profumatoria, appartenenti a ogni gran signora* (Venice: Cornetti, 1584).

the respect I had, the reverence,
the fear that I might disturb her sincere heart,
and that in anger she might send me away and out of her service,
calling me foolish and presumptuous,
had hemmed in my heart with so much apprehension
that I nearly went out of my mind.

8 1

"Her beautiful tresses she unbinds and lays out
on a balcony where the sun passes.
In such a way she shakes, arranges, and spreads them out
that every hair enjoys the solar ray,
and with the pure, toothed ivory she takes pains
to make numerous voyages for their entire length.
I suddenly heave a sigh so hot
that it makes her lift her beautiful eyes to my face.

8 2

"However, she does not say a word to me; and in vain I judge
she seeks what concerns her so little.
Thus, sadly I add the second to the first,
and I release the third one hotter yet.
She, seeing I do not express my pain,
in order to learn of it opens her mouth,
and asks me sweetly the reason
why I sigh so hotly.

8 3

"I do not answer this question of hers,
but I lower my eyes and heave more abundant sighs,
so she repeats it to me and asks again,
and yet I keep silent and do not respond.
At last as my mistress she commands me
to make plain to her the pain which I hide inside.
She marvels at me, and is vexed
that I do not want to reveal my thoughts.

84

"As I see her so burning and avid
to hear what I want to disclose to her,
I make her swear that what I must tell her
will cause her neither wrath nor sorrow
and, though too boldly I err and rave,
I will not lose that favor to which I am accustomed;
rather that she will have on me some pity,
in consideration of my youth.

85

"She who would have thought of anything else
swears and promises to me generously,
and I with a sad and ashamed face
humbly narrate my royal status.
Then I disclose the flame of love
which for her beauty burns my mind,
with the submission that is my duty,
and in the best way that Love dictates to me.

86

"It seemed that at first she was disturbed,
and shame painted her face;
not however that that great news which clutched her heart
urged her to my detriment.
She was silent first a little while as if thinking,
and to respond then she opened her lips—
but at that moment we heard the royal household
fill the sky with cries and laments.

87

"To learn the cause of that weeping,
with her hair neglected on her shoulders,
the maiden moves, and I, spurred by love,
by her side run in a great hurry.

She wants to know the cause of so great an uproar,
to take care of the matter as is her duty.
To the king's hall first she goes,
where the greatest shouting and tumult she hears.

88

"From this room to that one her anxious foot
takes her where she hears the sad accents,
so that she arrives at the woeful door
and enters among a good hundred ladies and maidens.
When she glances inside she is stunned,
for she sees her uncle the king lifeless,
lying among the sad and tearful people,
bloody from more than twenty wounds.

89

"She becomes so disconsolate then
that she throws herself with her hair in disarray
over the cold cadaver, and out
from her beautiful eyes issue two hot fountains.
While she languished and cried and wept,
dukes, marquesses, and counts filled the room,
for having heard the sorrowful announcement,
they tried to find out who had killed him.

90

"Among these knights was one Lideo,
who from Euboea to those parts had come.
He was skilled, and often combated
the most famous, and always gained the victory.
This one, having arrived among the others at the scene of the crime,
having seen the king dead, made a bad judgment.
The cause I cannot say which moved him to it;
it is enough that he judged it was so.

91

"He said, and he made everyone believe, that no one
would have conceived, let alone accomplished, a plan
for the king to lose his life,
unless they hoped to inherit the state.
As there was no one in that realm
who might have sinned for such a cause
(for rumor held Miricelso was dead),
the guilt he attributed to that lady.

92

"He speaks freely and haughtily,
and his authority makes him trusted.
He shows that the profound grief he harbors in his heart
makes him say what he would rather not say.
He says that she merits a just and bitter
death; and so much he incites and spurs every heart
that many who have malign thoughts
say that he speaks ill, but tells the truth.

93

"All have hearts greedy to rule,
and they believe him, or they make a show of believing.
The most noble barons are in accord
with Lideo, who shows anxiety and apprehension.
Following his judgment and his memory,
without anyone forbidding it, they give the order
that in prison my lady be placed,
as if she were guilty of the deed.

94

"With her as well were taken pages and maids
who, overcome by threats and promises,
confessed to the iniquitous and treacherous minds
that so great an error took place because of her.
No one spoke to the contrary;

therefore out of fear the true yielded to the false,
and the innocent was taken and overcome
by cruel and duplicitous malice.

9 5

"I saw the beautiful hand, white and pure,
restrained (alas!) by a rough, ignoble bond.
I saw her into a dark and abominable prison placed,
that lady the world is not worthy to hold.
With the innocent creature buried away,
they divided up between them her fair realm.
Only the people, the commoners alone,
lament for the unhappy damsel.

9 6

"Now since unjust and stingy Nature
did not give me strength consistent with my spirit,
to be able to liberate so rare a lady,
who forced me to follow the footsteps of Love,
I have sought out this bright and illustrious land
where there is justice, where virtue does not sleep;
and I pray that it please you to give me aid
against the wicked Egyptians with your arms."

9 7

Thus the enamored dwarf recounted
the wretched damsel's predicament,
and meanwhile to punish mad Egypt
good Risardo was set in order.
But since he has finished narrating
the strange circumstances, as he had been entrusted,
I too intend to close here this canto;
later I will tell what befell them.

CANTO 3

ARGUMENT

Risamante kills the fierce serpent,
loses her destrier, and descends into the grotto.
Before her come the Phrygian lady and her son;
this lady gives her an account of herself.
The fay appears and gives her the diamond,
then in a mirror shows her
her renowned descendants; and, upon exiting,
she finds her horse and good lodging as well.

1

O great virtue of the knights of the past,
who with so much pity employed their arms! [1]
Without obligation, courteous and agreeable,
always for innocents they wielded the sword.
Among so many perils where they were
called, their own lives they risked
to save those of strangers,
neither their countrymen nor their kin.

2

I believe in our age few there would be
who would put themselves at risk for others.

1. This first verse recalls Ariosto's famous and ironic line, "O gran bontà de' cavallieri antiqui!" (O great goodness of the knights of old!) in *Orlando furioso* 1.22. This is the narrator's response when Ferraù offers Rinaldo a ride in their hot pursuit of the object of both their desires: the beautiful Angelica, who wants neither of them.

Far from leaving the bosom of the fatherland
to go in defense of I don't know whom,
they'd prefer their father to pass away,
or even others worthier than he,
rather than, without reward, help with a word,
let alone expose their life, of which we have only one.

3

How many orphans today have no access
to the possessions that were their fathers'
for lacking, not someone who would court death,
but someone who would employ even his tongue in their favor?
As if speaking were a great concern,
if first their hand is not filled with gold,
few are the lawyers willing to undertake the task
of opening their mouths in their defense.[2]

4

But among those few I have reason to praise heaven
for some who are not of that sort,
who seek with faith and friendly zeal
to relieve me where I am so oppressed.
I will never cease to thank heaven for their
immense courtesy, their good offices,
recognizing their gracious works
as much as I can with deeds and with words.[3]

2. Here Fonte uses the masculine plural for "orphans," but she may well have been thinking especially of women's situations, as described in *The Worth of Women*: some fathers neglect to provide for their daughters, but there are some "who are lucky enough to be left a dowry by their father, or to receive a share in his estate along with their brothers if he dies intestate, but who then find themselves imprisoned in the home like slaves by their brothers, who deprive them of their rights and seize their portion for themselves, in defiance of all justice" (62–63).

3. Fonte's own father died when she was an infant. Here she acknowledges the importance of her uncle Giovanni Niccolò Doglioni for her upbringing and the recovery of her inheritance. In his "Life of Moderata Fonte" Doglioni mentions that when the poet and her brother were orphaned, "their relatives, close and distant, fell over one another to take the orphans into their care—along with their inheritance" (*Worth of Women*, 33).

5

So many others, in whom impious avarice rules,
should also imitate these of whom I speak.
Each of them with this worthy example
should also be pity's friend.
Let every fair mind imitate Giovan Giacopo, the
honor of the Gradenico lineage.
Let him imitate illustrious Giovan Vincenti, and the rare
and good Tomaso Cernovicchio likewise.[4]

6

There must be many others yet
of such goodness, or the world would be in a bad way,
but how could I distinguish them out
of so great and endless a crowd?
These who defend me hour by hour,
these who have taken on the weighty task of helping me,
by their effects I know them and by the goodwill
they have toward me, without desire of gain.

7

A noble warrior was Prince Risardo
for demonstrating such goodness then,
when he was not slow to undertake the task
of liberating beautiful Raggidora.
And although later the brave young man
to a new path turned his prow,
as I will recount to you, *I* do not blame him,
for nevertheless with this goal he left the court.

---

4. In *The Worth of Women*, Fonte gives a longer list of good lawyers (196–97), in which she includes Vincenti again. The Gradenigo are a noble Venetian family which gave Venice three doges and countless bishops and ambassadors. The Cernovicchio family was from the Balkans, ennobled in Venice in the fifteenth century.

8

All the greatest lords of the Thracian realm,
with his magnanimous son the king sent off.
He wore over his armor a worthy mantle,
which by her own hand Ersina had woven him.
He tied on his shield with its design
of a lovely wandering damsel
who, gazing at the sky, was intended to show
the hope he had of winning forever.

9

But because the subjects are varied, and the verses
varied, and they contend with each other over which will continue,
I am like a child who of diverse
flowers intends to form a beautiful garland,
and in order to take advantage of the beauty of each one
takes not always the lily or the violet,
but now one, now the other, and in varying the color
makes use in the end of his every plucked flower.

1 0

Therefore leaving good Risardo for a little while,
to Risamante I want to return.
She, just as I said elsewhere,
arrived by chance one day in a beautiful garden,
lovely and adorned with acanthus, jasmine, narcissus, and crocus,
and with every other beautiful flower,
and encircled by a distinct green wall
of boxwood and juniper saplings.

1 1

In the middle was a wide and beautiful shady grove
of beautiful and blooming vermilion rosebushes.
The rest was all clear and spacious,
with only a meadow and budding flowers.

The odor of the flowers and the song of the birds
drew the lady to repose there.
She dismounted from the saddle and removed the horse's bit,
took off her helm and sat in the cool shade.

1 2

In the gentle shade of the humble wood
she planned a sweet and quiet sleep,
but she was barely arranged on the grass
when she heard a great din in the rosebushes.
She got up at once and replaced her helm in a rush,
and moved her foot with a mute and quiet pace;
but then she paused at the sudden appearance
of what she saw come toward her.[5]

1 3

She saw a serpent come out amid flowers and leaves—
I don't know if it was a jaculus or an amphisbaena,
which in Africa outdoes all the others
in its size and amount of venom.[6]
Haughty in its gold and green skin,
its venomous tail it shook around.
It leaped out hissing from the tufts,
and destroyed with its breath the grass and the flowers.

1 4

From amid the wood of flesh-pink roses,
which it burned up completely and crushed with its furor,

5. The scene closely mirrors canto 1 of the *Furioso*, when Angelica finds a similar pleasant grove, with equally enticing tender grass, birds singing nearby, and a thicket of red roses. There too Angelica steps into the bower, lies down, and falls asleep, soon to be awakened by a loud sound—the knight Sacripante approaching (*Orlando furioso* 1.37–38). The setup became such a cliché that we find it everywhere in the period, most famously in Spenser's *The Faerie Queene*.

6. Both of these snakes are legendary. The jaculus would dart through the air and pierce whatever it encountered; the amphisbaena had a second head in its tail (see Lucan, *Pharsalia* 9.720–23). To the ancient Greeks and Romans a "dragon" was a huge snake; but since Fonte's monster leaps and runs, it would seem to possess legs.

it emerged suddenly, and in the lady struck
I don't know what anguish and terror.
But nonetheless she replaced her shield at her neck,
took her lance in hand, took heart again,
and with the lance prepared to contend
against the beast who was coming to make a meal of her.

1 5

The greedy beast with mouth open
rushed upon her, and yet it could not catch her.
Rather, incautiously it swallowed the iron of the lance
which the lady wielded against it, and pierced and struck itself.
The lady centered the point more and more
so that in vain the dragon rolled and circled around.
The dragon pierced itself, and in its dire distress
as much as it could it shook itself and drew back.

1 6

A similar battle in that bygone era
Cadmus waged with a horrendous and dire dragon
(for, having seen the beloved bones of his companions,
he knew they had reached the final torment),
since no less immense were the members
of this one than of the one the Tyrian killed,
nor does Risamante have less skill and valor
than the generous son of Agenor.[7]

1 7

She followed the dragon valorously,
and the more it drew back the more she advanced.
Futilely by drawing back the serpent
tried to flee the death it had before it,
because in backing away incautiously

7. Cadmus was the son of King Agenor of Phoenicia, where the city of Tyre was located.
When preparing to found Thebes, Cadmus sent his men to fetch water. The serpent of Ares
killed them, and then Cadmus slew the serpent. See Graves, *Greek Myths*, 194–96.

it fell into the hole from which it had issued earlier;
the lady had not discovered it before,
since the wood had held it closed over and covered.[8]

1 8

The maiden nearly fell
(she was coming after it) into that dark tomb,
but the moment the treacherous beast went over the edge,
she let go of the lance, and it was to her great good fortune.
Released from that disturbance, she planned
to depart in search of other adventures,
but she found that her destrier had fled
elsewhere for fear of the snake, and she knew not where.

1 9

All at once she suddenly heard a voice
that said, "O most noble lady warrior,
I advise you not to depart from this beautiful garden
without first descending into that cruel tomb,
for from there in reward for killing the serpent
you will come out rich and proud with the prize.
Enter by all means there where the horrendous serpent
fell, if you want to see something stupendous."

2 0

At that cry Risamante turned,
and though she saw no one she did not delay.
In order to know what was in that place
she approached the hole and bowed her head and looked.
Having seen some large rocks
jut out, the courageous young woman

---

8. Although the entire episode was often treated in romances of chivalry and although Ariosto,
as we shall see later, is the main model here, Fonte may have also had Boiardo in mind in the
episode of the knight Mandricardo who faced a monstrous serpent in a garden, killed it, and
then fell into a dark cave in which, as here, he found a well-appointed abode and a fairy. See
Innamorato 3.2.21–37.

with her hands grasped the rim and lowered her feet,
and made those rocks her support and stairs.[9]

21

The virgin thought to herself while descending
that she'd have to step on the head or the belly
or some other part of that horrendous dragon
to regain her lost lance.
But she saw, having reached level ground,
that all she had thought was a dream and nonsense,
because she found there, instead of the dragon,
a noble matron and a handsome boy.

22

The young boy had not yet reached
thirteen, and he was as fresh and beautiful
as a lily which at dawn's birth
opens its leaves and gives off a new scent.
In him so much delicacy dwelled
that his face and hair seemed made by a brush;
it looked just as if his limbs were painted,
and he was so white he seemed made of snow.

23

Very blond was his hair, and curly,
and the rich veil that adorned his beautiful body
was of a delicate white silk
that looked extremely wanton.
In his eyes his demeanor was so sweet and agreeable
that he drew out the heart from the breast of whoever gazed at him.
Of him in short one could say no more,
but that he was all love and charm.[10]

9. This episode is modeled on one in Ariosto's *Orlando furioso* cantos 2–3 (later imitated by Spenser in the *Faerie Queene*), in which the lady knight Bradamante gets into Merlin's cave.

10. What makes this description startling is that it is applied to a boy; these constructions are mostly used for nymphs.

24

The maiden was astonished when she understood
so beautiful a child had been enclosed in that tomb.
He approached her reverently,
as if accustomed to mix in great courts.
The noble matron turned her eyes
to the maiden who had just climbed down there,
and courteously greeted her,
saying, "Be welcome.

25

"At last that dear and longed-for day has arrived
when I am drawn out of every peril,
and this my sweet and ill-regarded son
will avoid death's bitter blow.
Now we can go outside into the bright daylight,
for the end of our long exile has arrived.
And you, Risamante, have been the cause
of freeing us from prison."[11]

26

"For this I praise you and thank you so much
that as long as life's spirit is in me,
I will never forget how great
an obligation I have to you for so welcome a deed.
And so that you may understand the whole situation
that makes me give you infinite thanks,
let us sit together, for I want to make it clear to you,
if you would like to hear the whole story."

---

11. Dark, tomblike prisons from which women need to be released abound in *Floridoro*. Not
only in this instance does the noble matron need to be freed from her "cruel tomb," but Rag-
gidora is condemned "to stay locked up thus until the end of the year" (2.63); and later on
Circetta is enclosed in a "closed and secret cavern" (7.46); and Lucimena, Nicobaldo's lost wife,
is "cruelly locked in prison" in an ominous castle (6.65).

27

The lofty warrior was astounded
that this woman knew her name,
and she desired to hear the matter made plain:
why she came here, and when and how.
Therefore she removed the helm from her head
and showed forth her crinkled golden tresses;
and she sat next to that lady,
proving herself both courteous and beautiful.

28

That boy gazed at her intently,
for in all his days he had seen no other beautiful face;
but at his tender age he did not feel love,
and with simplicity he regarded her and laughed.
The mother began, "Of the powerful king
of the Phrygian plain who was named Aclide
I was the wife, and I lived for a time within bounds,
content with such a husband and such a kingdom.

29

"But that powerful god, I speak of Love,
who tames monsters and in heaven even overcomes the gods,
envious of my happiness, came to disturb it,
and interrupted all my pleasures.
While my king went to help
the Lydian realm against the wicked Syrians,
a courteous king at my court arrived,
and kindled and pricked my heart with love.

30

"This man had come all the way from the west,
where he ruled the whole Iberian country.
Being valorous and powerful,
he had left his happy dominion,

and he went seeking through all the east
every adventure, every harsh peril,
eager to show his prowess,
and make himself immortal and glorious.

3 1

"The gods know what I did to root out
the new passion from my frail heart,
but I was not able to shield myself
from the invincible weapons of Love.
I confess that I should sooner have taken my
own life than ever commit so great an error;
but then when I look at this beautiful fruit
that was born of it, I am even more sluggish to repent.

3 2

"I say that by that king, who showed himself
no less ardent for me than I for him,
I became pregnant while
my lord was involved in that war.
Then when from Lydia he returned,
gravid he found me with a child not his;
I could not cover my fault well enough,
for he discovered the matter.[12]

---

12. As this queen plainly shows and as later another "queen," Circe, exemplifies, there are consequences to sex in women's narrative that seem to be altogether absent in male writing. Both women become pregnant, one with a son and the other with a daughter, as a result of their more or less passionate adventures. But no matter how many women betray their husbands in Boccaccio's novellas, how many are "seduced" in Boiardo, Ariosto, Dolce, and Tasso's epics, how many are pro-active in Aretino and Machiavelli's comedies, and how many are scolded in conduct books, there is hardly a child appearing on the horizon nine months later in these authors' narratives to trouble their male characters' conscience, if not their purse. If there is an offspring, he will soon disappear. In the episode I mentioned above of the queen of Lombardy making love to a dwarf in *Orlando furioso* 28, for example, there is a child born of that union in the first, 1516, version of the *Furioso*, but he is eliminated in the final, authoritative, 1532 edition in order not to burden men's fantasies with social responsibilities. This is not the case, as far as I know, of women's narrative in Italian in the early modern period. Here either the sex is relegated to a time beyond the writing itself after a proper marriage has taken place to make it legal, or these

33

"From me he had been divided for a year
when he returned from Lydia to me.
Having discovered my amorous deceit,
he wanted with his sword to cause me the final humiliation.
I escaped his fury, and with anxiety
I came and brought forth here this child to the light;
here, moved to pity by my peril,
a fay helped and counseled me.

34

"And because of my husband's
unceasing persecution from all sides
(for he still wanted to punish me for the sin
I had committed in betraying him),
she warned me that with the sweet newborn
I should stay in this closed-up and solitary place,
because my life could not be secure
until the king's was completed.

35

"So that no one of those
who went spying for my person might
find me in this grotto and hand me
over to his irate monarch,
she placed here that serpent
to guard me against everyone;
and she told me, 'From here do not depart
until the dying dragon vanishes,

---

women become pregnant. Celinda, for example, in Valeria Miani's tragedy *Celinda*, dies preg-
nant—one reason why sex is hardly in the cards in women writers' texts. In *The Worth of Women*
Fonte makes one character notice, quite sarcastically, that the reason why adulterous women
are punished by law while men are not (here she refers to the Augustan Roman legislation) is
that men make the laws: "'Well, the reason is obvious,' replied Corinna. 'Men may be wicked
but they aren't stupid, and since it was they who were making the laws and enforcing them, they
were hardly going to rule that they should be punished and women go free'" (96).

36

"'because at that time, in that same moment
that the slain dragon disappears,
your lord will perish,
and released you will be from this prison.
And know that that dragon is not to be
overcome by the valor of any baron,
but by the hand of a noble virgin,[13]
who has no peer from Bactria to Thule.'[14]

37

"She told me your name is Risamante,
and whose daughter you are she informed me."
The lady wanted to continue further,
when before them suddenly arrived
the noble fay she had mentioned earlier,
who greeted them with a joyful visage.
Standing up, they and that courteous boy
at once to that fay returned greetings.

38

The beautiful fay who loved her dearly
embraced Risamante like a daughter,
and a thousand times she kissed that beautiful face
and that mouth as vermilion as purple dye.[15]
And then, taking from her own finger
a ring, she handed it to her and said, "Take it.

13. In early modern iconography, Saint George would kill the dragon in order to save the virgin, who was occasionally represented dressed in white like a bride. Fonte regenders the story by having a woman, Risamante, take up the case of another woman punished for having been unfaithful. The myth of Saint George and the virgin is central to Tasso's *Gerusalemme liberata*.

14. Bactria was a country in southwestern Asia. Thule was the northernmost part of the habitable ancient world.

15. The fay here is modeled on Ariosto's sorceress Melissa. In the *Furioso* (also in canto 3), inside Merlin's cave Melissa shows Bradamante her glorious posterity.

This ring which gives out such splendor,
I present to you as a reward for your great valor.[16]

39

"Know that it has a great hidden virtue
that avails against every enchantment and every fear,
and renders the soul courageous and daring
against every strange, horrible adventure.
But so small a thing is not enough for me,
because I intend to do you a greater favor;
I hold your merits so dear
that I want to render you a greater service.

40

"I want to show you, if you like,
many of your illustrious and worthy progeny
in a mirror where everyone can
see his bloodline before it comes to be.
But truly no one can have this mirror,
and in vain do some plan to acquire it,
because it is reserved for a knight
who is not yet born, of the Greek empire."

41

So saying she opened a small door
where none had ever yet entered.
The maiden inside there set her foot,
and entered with her an enchanted abode.
By the virtue of that ring she dispersed
many wicked shadows that came upon her from the sides.
The matron and her comely son tried as well
to enter, but they were constrained to withdraw.

16. Angelica too is given a magic ring to break spells and save others (as well as herself) by becoming invisible. The ring is already present in Boiardo's *Innamorato*, where she uses it, for example, to free Orlando from the enchantress Dragontina.

42

Dark was the place where the fay passed,
as if night had its shelter there;
but when she raised the curtain
which impeded the mirror from shining,
immediately by it she was illuminated,
and it appeared that with that ray the sun shone there.
The fay uncovered it and revealed it to the light,
and it mirrored her with its light.

43

That beautiful crystal on the wall was hung,
enclosed in a small frame of bright gold.
When Risamante set her gaze there,
within she saw infinite people sway.
From what she comprehended at the sight,
all were excellent in mind and spirit.
Some had helmets on their heads, others a crown of gold,
but she recognized none of them.

44

There were many ladies, beautiful and adorned,
of whom one came before the warrior.
"This one," said the fay, "in beauty,
intelligence, and valor, outdoes you, I believe;
not only you, but she will surpass as many women
as will be born in her age.
With the king of Cyprus by you she will be conceived,
an only child, called Salarisa.

45

"He will marry her to that handsome and lofty king
who will be the son of Celsidea
and of another famous knight
whose soaring glory will spread throughout the world.
Not yet does he wear armor or possess a kingdom,

but I do not find, from one pole to the other,
nobler blood anywhere the sun shines,
since his lineage descends from the heavens.

46

"From Ulysses comes the young man's line,
he who was grandson to the king of the highest chorus.[17]
Floricelso your son-in-law will be called;
see him there, holding the golden scepter.
See Cleardo, not the one who now is subject
to the heat and ice, but a successor of theirs,
then Celsidoro, and then Florideo
with two sons, Ippolito and Liseo.

47

"All these must reign in Athens,
and others as well of these ancient offspring.
Because they are so many, it is better
that I not tell you all their names one by one.
Behold, Silvestro comes after these;
he will be nourished in the ancient forests
of Nauplia, the prized naval city,
which from that time on will be named Naples.[18]

48

"While his father by the Thracians is besieged,
secretly he will put the boy outside.
Once grown, he will then be the remedy
for his kingdom through his great valor.
He will cast off from Athens the long trouble,
and will be its legitimate lord;

17. In book 13 of the *Metamorphoses*, Ulysses claims his father, Laertes, was the son of Arcesius, who was a son of Jupiter, the king of the gods.

18. The city now called Navplion is a port city in the Peloponnese (southern Greece). Naples (Napoli) is an important port city in Campania in Italy. Fonte's motivation for linking the two cities is unclear. Perhaps the name Silvestro made her think of Iacopo Sannazaro's *Arcadia* and Naples.

he will sit in the regained seat,
after driving away the impious tyrant.

49

"Therefore, having healed his native realm
from most bitter and mortal wounds,
he will acquire that illustrious and worthy name
which will descend in his regal seed.
Medic of the fatherland, who in intelligence
and in valor surpasses the immortal gods,
by all Greece he will be called and hailed
as more perfect than Phoebus and Aesculapius.[19]

50

"For a very long age his successors,
still with the name of Medici, will then be
of Naples and of Athens possessors,
and they will be the flower of all the heroes.
From the line used to producing emperors
I see then a branch bear its fruits
into noble Etruria, and set firmly there
its excellent roots and its illustrious and divine seeds.[20]

51

"Among them see one named Giovanni who in appearance
does not deviate from his line's ancient splendor,
whose skill will defend Florence
from the Milanese, its cruel enemy.
With an undefeated mind and singular prudence
behold Vieri, virtue's friend.

---

19. In the original, *medico* (doctor); Fonte is creating an origin tale for the Medici family, in her time the rulers of Tuscany. In addition to his other attributes, Phoebus Apollo was a god of medicine, and so too was his son Aesculapius.

20. Tuscany was called Etruria when it was ruled by the Etruscans, before the Romans conquered it. The Medici grand dukes seized on this name for political purposes, since ancient Etruria had included territories owned in the Renaissance by the pope.

See another Silvestro, of such glory
that writers will immortalize his history.[21]

52

"Cosmo follows thereafter, with such valor
that all Tuscany will not have a better—
very rich, courteous, and generous,
with a bright and supreme reputation in his times.
After him of equal virtue is Pietro,
possessed of wisdom and goodness far more than human.
That other is Giuliano (ah, hard fate!)
who will die by treachery.[22]

53

"Lorenzo, most noble and esteemed
as much as any other of this elect band,
is this one who comes to him from the right-hand side;
and in fact, I affirm and tell you, O excellent warrior,
that among so many I have shown you so far,
there is no nobler and loftier soul.

---

21. In 1351 Giovanni de' Medici made heroic efforts to defend against an invading Milanese
army. See Gene Brucker, "The Medici in the Fourteenth Century," *Speculum* 32.1 (1957): 14. The
banker Vieri (or Veri) di Cambio de' Medici (died 1395) amassed a large fortune. See Brucker,
"The Medici," 6–11 and 22. His "virtue" may refer to his generous donations to religious insti-
tutions. A more provocative possibility, considering that the *Floridoro* was written during the
Medici principate, is that Fonte may be recalling an episode reported by Machiavelli in the
Florentine Histories, bk. 3, chap. 25, when during a political upheaval Veri was offered the rule of
Florence but refused it, causing Machiavelli to characterize him as more good than ambitious.
Salvestro de' Medici was prominent in Florentine politics; he participated in the revolt of the
Ciompi (cloth workers) in 1378. See Brucker, "The Medici," 15–21.
22. Cosimo the Elder de' Medici (1389–1464) was the de facto ruler of Florence from 1434
until his death. Immensely wealthy from the family's banking business, he was an important
patron of the arts. See Christopher Hibbert, *The House of Medici: Its Rise and Fall* (New York:
Morrow Quill, 1980), chaps. 4–5; and Giuseppe Parigino, *Il tesoro del principe: Funzione pubblica
e privata del patrimonio della famiglia Medici nel Cinquecento* (Florence: Olschki, 1999). Cosimo's son
Piero the Gouty (1418–69) ruled Florence from 1464 to 1469. He continued the family tradi-
tion of patronage of artists and scholars. See Hibbert, *House of Medici*, chap.8. Enemies of the
family assassinated Piero's son Giuliano (1453–78) in church during Mass. See Hibbert, *House
of Medici*, 138.

Giulio is that one then who will have such worthy burdens
of honor that he will change his clothing and his name.[23]

5 4

"This one from Giuliano; but from his brother
Lorenzo, what a fine lineage!
Another Pietro and another Giuliano
and another Giovanni it provides to the world.
This latter, prudent, splendid, and humane,
wears another mantle and takes another name,
and pontiff he will be called by the world,
which will then be a rank second to no other.[24]

5 5

"This is a nephew of his, the duke of Urbino,
called Lorenzo. That lady next to him,
with an aspect truly august and divine,
who you see wear the crown and mantle,
is his daughter Caterina, who will have
a destiny so happy and fortunate
that she will be a king's wife and a king's daughter-in-law,
mother of three kings and of a daughter as well.[25]

---

23. Lorenzo the Magnificent (1449–92) was another important patron of the arts and a great statesman as well. See Hibbert, *House of Medici*, chaps. 9–13. The illegitimate son of Giuliano, Giulio de' Medici (1478–1534), was elected Pope Clement VII (1523–34). See Hibbert, *House of Medici*, 239.

24. Lorenzo the Magnificent had three sons. Piero the Younger (1471–1503) ruled Florence from 1492 to 1494, when he fled the city before the French invasion. See Hibbert, *House of Medici*, chap. 14. Giuliano (1478–1516) became duke of Nemours. See Hibbert, *House of Medici*, 222. Giovanni (1475–1521) was elected Pope Leo X (1513–23). See Hibbert, *House of Medici*, 217.

25. Lorenzo di Piero de' Medici (1492–1519) took over the Duchy of Urbino with Pope Leo's support. See Hibbert, *House of Medici*, 220–24. Orphaned young, Caterina (1519–89) married Henry of Valois (later King Henry II of France), second son of Francis I. See Hibbert, *House of Medici*, 252. She had nine children, including the three kings Francis II (r. 1559–60), Charles IX (r. 1560–74), and Henry III (r. 1574–89). Her daughter Marguerite of Valois married Henry of Navarre, who became king of France in 1589. See *The New Century Italian Renaissance Encyclopedia*, ed. Catherine B. Avery (New York: Meredith, 1972), 221–22.

56

"To France she will go to wed;
but her brother, that one who comes close by her,
called Alessandro, will be betrayed
once he's the duke, and cruelly oppressed.
He will leave Guido. Ippolito, clothed
in virtue, is that one; and that is Asdrubal with him.
But leave this branch and regard that one:
that is Lorenzo, great Cosmo's brother.[26]

57

"See Pietro Francesco; and see together with him
Giovanni his son, who will take
a wife come from the Sforza's seed,
from whom the other Giovanni will come to the light.
Behold the one who through lofty and supreme feats
will adorn the world with so bright a light;
I speak of the second Cosmo, who in valor
will surpass his every other predecessor.[27]

26. Pope Clement VII gave Alessandro (1511–37) the rule of Florence in 1530; he obtained the ducal title in 1532. He outraged the Florentines with scandalous and tyrannical behavior and was assassinated by his partner in crime, Lorenzaccio de' Medici. See Hibbert, *House of Medici*, 251–56. See also J. N. Stephens, *The Fall of the Florentine Republic, 1512–1530* (Oxford: Clarendon, 1983). Lacking any pertinent Guido, this could be a reference to Alessandro's illegitimate son, Giulio, who died in 1600. See Hibbert, *House of Medici*, 257 and 266. An alternative translation would be that Alessandro will leave Guido cruelly oppressed. Ippolito (1511–35), illegitimate son of Giuliano, duke of Nemours, was created a cardinal by Pope Clement. See Hibbert, *House of Medici*, 252. No identity can be found for Asdrubal. Lorenzo di Giovanni di Bicci de' Medici (1395–1440) was the younger brother of Cosimo the Elder. See Hibbert, *House of Medici*, 32.

27. Pierfrancesco de' Medici (1430–76) was raised by his uncle Cosimo the Elder. During his lifetime, political and financial disagreements led his sons to break with the elder branch of the Medici family. See Alison Brown, "Pierfrancesco de' Medici, 1430–1476," in *The Medici in Florence: The Exercise of Language and Power* (Florence: Olschki, 1992; Perth: University of Western Australia Press, 1992). Giovanni il Popolano (1467–1514) married Caterina Sforza, ruler of Imola and Forlà. Giovanni delle Bande Nere (1498–1526) was a famous military leader. See *New Century Italian Renaissance Encyclopedia*, 623. The son of Giovanni delle Bande Nere, Cosimo (1519–74), was called by the Florentines to become duke after the assassination of Alessandro. In 1570 he became Cosimo I, the first grand duke of Tuscany. See Hibbert, *House of Medici*, 257–58 and 266.

58

"Duke he will be of Florence as a young man
of eighteen, that generous son,
for his merits and his lineage elected
by the will of that whole council.
Thereafter called grand duke of Tuscany,
which he will guard from every peril;
nor certainly a worthier man will
the sun ever see, which spreads everywhere its rays.

59

"But what shall I say of his fair progeny,
of sons, and of daughters illustrious and rare in the world?
This one is called Giovanni, and that one Garzia,
here Ferdinando and there Pietro appears.
Behold Maria, Lucrezia, and Isabella,
but eminent and singular above all,
see FRANCESCO, lover of virtue,
worthy enough for Apollo to write and sing of him.[28]

60

"He is the second grand duke of Tuscany,
with a heart so magnanimous and distinguished,
and with intelligence so acute and so profound
that human reckoning cannot equal him.
He will demonstrate clearly his descent from that eloquent
Ulysses, and in this will be even more splendid and rare.
O Francesco, forever fortunate
for talents so admirable and divine.

---

28. Giovanni (1543–62) became a cardinal; Garzia lived 1547–62; and Pietro 1554–1604. Ferdinando (1549–1609) became Grand Duke Ferdinando I in 1587, after Francesco's death. Maria (1540–57) and Lucrezia (1545–61) died in their teens. Isabella (1542–76) was murdered by her husband. See Hibbert, *House of Medici*, 269–79. For Francesco, see above, Fonte's dedicatory sonnet and note, and canto 1.4n.

61

"Yet far happier and more fortunate,
since, by the grace of a benign fate,
the noblest lady who ever was
is destined to you by heaven for your wife,
after you will have lost that first one
due to bitter, inevitable death
(I mean Joanna of Austria, by whom will be
conceived young Filippo Cosmo)."[29]

62

So said the fay, and added then,
directing to Risamante her words,
"Mirror your eyes in that lady,
who will be a second dawn to so beautiful a sun.
Time in his annals has not yet
noted a worthier descendant than she.
This lady will be born in that land by the sea,
of a generous and benevolent lineage.

63

"In the glorious and fortunate bosom
of the Adriatic a city is to be founded;
heaven will not see on the earth another
of more grandeur or greater beauty.
With a chain of love, without other restraints,
its people will live united in liberty.
The name VENICE will be bright and joyful,
and will last to the end of the world.

---

29. The sister of the Holy Roman Emperor, Joanna married Francesco in 1565 and died in
1578. See *New Century Italian Renaissance Encyclopedia*, 622. Her son, Filippo, born in 1577, died
in early childhood. See Hibbert, *House of Medici*, 275, and above, canto 1.5n.

64

"The nobles of that dominion could
rightfully be called princes,
because they will have many realms to rule,
and for their ancestors' nobility,
and because all born to that council
can become princes.
One after the other will be almost certain
of being the first in the city, if he is worthy.

65

"From one of these illustrious and worthy houses,
which is the elect family of the CAPPELLI,[30]
this lady of the regal emblems will come
in time to the light, and will be called BIANCA.
She through her virtue dims the glory
of every other member of her perfect lineage;
or rather, with her valor she increases
her excellent ancestors' lofty splendor.

66

"Besides this noble, courteous, and beautiful
lady, abode of wisdom and of eloquence,
so dear to her husband and he to her,
both of them so dear to Venice and to Florence,
this most illustrious house CAPPELLA
will produce spirits of rare excellence,
and before this lady it will adorn the world
with a thousand bright, eminent demigods.

30. Here the family name, Cappello, is given in the masculine plural form, Cappelli, referring to its members in general. In octave 66 the feminine singular form accords with the Italian word for "house." English language sources often use "Cappello," the masculine singular form. Renaissance women would often be registered with their family name in the feminine, so Bianca was known at the time as Cappella. The modern Italian spelling is Capello for single members of either sex and for the family at large.

67

"Among them one named Nicolò with a lively ray
will spread through those seas his splendor.
Afterward from so divine a noble lineage
I see great Vicenzo issue, and Vittore,
then Bartolomeo, courteous and wise,
worthy father of the great Bianca.[31]
But you cannot see them manifest,
because these are not of your line.

68

"Bartolomeo will dress Bianca in the beautiful bodily veil
which will bear such privileges from heaven,
nor will his fertile stalk
blossom only with this lady's merits.
For a son as well he will praise heaven,
an illustrious young man with eminent habits;
Vittor too will make him fully blessed
for so many excellent qualities that will abide in him."[32]

69

Beautiful Risamante stayed to hear,
while the fay discoursed thus.
The dear seeds she saw before her,
and now at one, now at the others she gazed with love.
The noble fay, after so many praises
that she gave to these and to others of her line,

31. Nicolò was active in Venetian politics in 1296. Vincenzo di Nicolò was ambassador to England and two popes. An experienced admiral, he was captain general of the Venetian navy in 1540 as part of the Christian coalition against the Turks. Vittore di Giorgio (1402–66) was a naval commander and heroic defender of the Peloponnese against the Turks. After Bianca's elopement, Bartolommeo requested Venice's Council of Ten to put a price on the head of her lover and to bring her back to be locked up in a convent. When she became grand duchess, he was reconciled with her.

32. After Bianca became grand duchess, her brother Vittore was made Knight of the Golden Stole, like his father Bartolommeo.

with the veil re-covered the holy glass,
and with the girl went back.

70

They returned where with the beautiful boy the noblewoman
waited. Turning to her, the fay
said, "Now you can go and stay among people,
for your persecutor's life is over.
And know that in a very brief time
this boy, wherein one sees encompassed
so rare an angelic beauty,
will be one of the foremost heroes of this age."

71

So saying she disappeared, and the warrior
took her leave of the matron then.
Regaining her undamaged lance
which she found there, she did not stay long,
but returned to the place where she had descended.
Though with great difficulty, nonetheless she returned outside,
and found that the rosebushes were remade
more than ever joyful and merry with beautiful flowers.

72

Among dense thorns therefore and shady branches
the lady set off until she emerged;
once she was in the spacious meadows,
she followed her interrupted path.
To find other perilous places,
other strange adventures, was her desire.
On foot she left the green and blooming garden,
and regretted the destrier that had fled her.

73

But she did not take many steps before the destrier,
which had hidden earlier for fear inside a hedge,

came toward her in the middle of the path,
as if at her arrival it had placed itself there.
Delighted, the lady caught it easily,
and once she regained the saddle,
she spurred it so that that evening she arrived
at a hamlet called Francariva.

74

At that hamlet a gentleman had
a farm with a rich mansion,
and if a lady or a maiden arrived,
or a knight, he gave them lodging.
He was rich and always spent abundantly
in practicing courtesies devotedly and by intent.
On account of this, in all that countryside
he was called the courteous knight.

75

In fact, he was at the door
of the courtyard, which was broad and spacious,
when the lady passed, and by him she was perceived
as a warrior of valorous appearance.
The gentleman urged her to dismount,
for it was time for lodging and repose.
By his prayer and by need overcome,
the maiden stopped and dismounted from the saddle.

76

At once a servant took and lodged her destrier,
unharnessed it, and set before it plentiful fodder.
Others from various places either descended or stood,
and prepared dinner in an instant.
The knight led beautiful Risamante
to a loggia to disarm.
But here I put an end to the present discourse,
and I intend to rest both my hand and my mind.

CANTO 4

ARGUMENT

The good helmsman puts into Risardo's heart
the Greek king's tourney and daughter,
so that he has him conduct him to the Greek domain
to gaze at her stupendous and unique beauty.
There he fells one and the other of Odoria's
knights, and she kindles and steals his heart.
Lideo, burning with wrath against his beloved,
accuses her of murder and usurps the kingdom.

1

Women in every age were by nature
endowed with great judgment and spirit,
nor are they born less apt than men to demonstrate
(with study and care) their wisdom and valor.
And why, if their bodily form is the same,
if their substances are not varied,
if they have the same food and speech, must they
have then different courage and wisdom?[1]

---

1. This is the most famous octave of *Floridoro*—a full-fledged hymn to women's worth. Male authors too praised women along the same lines from time to time as part of a Renaissance tradition of praise of women. Here is Ariosto's passionate endorsement: "Women have proved their excellence in every art in which they have striven; in their chosen fields their renown is clearly apparent to anyone who studies the history books. If the world has long remained unaware of their achievements, this sad state of affairs is only transitory—perhaps Envy concealed the honors due to them, or perhaps the ignorance of historians" (*Orlando furioso* 20.2).

2

Always one has seen and sees (provided that a
woman wanted to devote thought to it)
more than one woman succeed in the military,
and take away the esteem and acclaim from many men.
Just so in letters and in every
endeavor that men undertake and pursue;
women have achieved and achieve such good results
that they have no cause at all to envy men.[2]

3

And although of so worthy and so famous
a status there are not a great number of women,
it is because on heroic and valorous acts
they have not set their hearts for various reasons.
Gold which stays hidden in the mines
is no less gold, though buried;
and when it is drawn out and worked,
it is as rich and beautiful as other gold.

4

If when a daughter is born the father
set her with his son to equivalent tasks,

2. Fonte will return to women's skills in the military in *The Worth of Women:* "if women do not bear arms, that isn't because of any deficiency on their part; rather, the fault lies with the way they were brought up. Because it's quite clear that those who have been trained in military discipline have turned out to excel in valor and skill, aided by that peculiar feminine talent of quick thinking, which has often led them to outshine men in the field" (100). Lucrezia Marinella will borrow from Fonte in approaching the topic: "But in our times there are few women who apply themselves to study or the military arts, since men, fearing to lose their authority and become women's servants, often forbid them even to learn to read or write. Our good friend Aristotle states that women must obey men everywhere and in everything and not search for anything that takes them outside their houses. A foolish opinion and cruel, pedantic sentence from a fearful, tyrannical man." See *Nobility and Excellence of Women,* 79. Marinella was not alone in citing the first four octaves of this canto (55, 78–81); Arcangela Tarabotti quotes octave 4 in *Paternal Tyranny,* ed. and trans. Letizia Panizza (Chicago: University of Chicago Press, 2004), 104; and Luisa Bergalli Gozzi quotes octaves 1–4 in the introduction to her *Componimenti poetici delle più illustri rimatrici d'ogni secolo, raccolti da Luisa Bergalli. Parte prima, Che contiene le Rimatrici Antiche fino all'Anno 1575* (Venice: Antonio Mora, 1726).

she would not be in lofty and fair deeds
inferior or unequal to her brother,
whether he placed her among the armed squads
with himself, or set her to learn some liberal art.
But because she is raised in other pursuits,
for her education she is held in low regard.[3]

5

If the magician had not proposed the military
to Risamante, nor disposed her heart toward it,
she would not in the end have carried out with her own hands
so many glorious feats of valor.
I said that this outstanding young woman
was by the courteous and generous lord
led into a loggia to disarm herself,
where dinner was to be made ready.

6

But while I discourse and sing of her,
the Thracian knight comes to mind.
He, as I narrated in the other canto,
had girded on his bright, polished steel
in order to go to Egypt to rescue from tears
and from prison the innocent young woman.
Having said farewell to his kin, he left his
native shore, and entrusted himself to the troublesome and unreliable sea.

7

All happy and joyful, he had already released
to the north wind's breath the twisted linen,[4]

3. According to her uncle Doglioni, Fonte educated herself by studying her brother's school-
work because she had no other opportunities. See Fonte, *Worth of Women*, 34–35. For infor-
mation on women's education and for women writers' arguments about its necessity, see the
Volume Editor's Introduction. Arcangela Tarabotti quoted this octave when claiming forcefully
that "if we women do not have the means of acquiring learning, we do not lack ability." See
Paternal Tyranny, 102, 106.

4. The ship's sails.

nor could he wait in his secret heart for the time
when he might see the Egyptian port.
He had in the ship a wise and skillful helmsman,
with a lively and sensible mind,
who liked to hear tales
of what was occurring in lands near and far.

8

Seeing the wind to his course
was propitious, and the sky clear and delightful,
and that to go to the Alexandrian port
both the air with its breeze and the sea were favorable,
the helmsman came with a reverent gesture and a bow,
like a man both reasonable and experienced in the world,
among those lords. Once arrived in their presence,
he too obtained permission to speak.

9

He said, "It must already be plain to you, lord,
the so dear and so welcome news
which draws to Athens to honored feats
from every region, from every country,
all the warriors in whom prowess is found.
There King Cleardo launches a tournament,
and the lofty acclaim of so praiseworthy an event
has already turned the whole world upside down.

1 0

"Everyone runs to the Attic slopes,
and all the more because he has an only daughter
who is a phoenix of beauty in the world,
and steals the prize from all other beautiful women.
That man could indeed be considered happy
who will enjoy so noble a girl,
for along with the beauty that adorns her,
she is endowed with every admirable virtue.

11

"And furthermore, to her alone is due
the inheritance of so famous a kingdom,
because this lovely girl
is (as I said) her father's only child.
This is the reason, I believe, that entices
every worthy warrior to go to Greece,
for they hope the king will make her the wife
of the bravest and strongest one among them."

12

While this fellow speaks, handsome Risardo
turns over new thoughts in his mind.
He listens to him intently, and his face and his gaze
are fixed on him, and he barely breathes.
The helmsman continues, "Every strong and brave man
who desires to show his prowess,
or to gaze at her beautiful visage,
now goes to the competition on the Achaean shores.

13

"Great is the fame which circulates
of the high esteem of this excellent maiden;
but the other day when I arrived in those parts,
I found the truth overwhelms every expectation.
Her grace and beauty are so great
that one can say her fame is nothing beside it.
I saw her, lord, and yet I barely believe
what I saw with my own eyes.

14

"Crinkled gold is her hair. Her forehead
resembles ivory more clear and limpid than the sky.
You would say that ebony are her lashes,
from which Love pours out fire and sweetness.
Her cheek seems white and vermilion,

snow sprinkled with carmine or cinnabar.
Her mouth seems to outdo minium;[5]
from there are born gentle, life-giving words.

15

"Her slim neck is select alabaster,
round as a column; and crystalline
is her ample, firm, and delicate breast;
her hand of pearls and her nails of coral.
In short, everything in her is beautiful and perfect.
Nature committed no error in her,
but the splendor of her eyes and their charm
surpass all the rest in beauty.

16

"Who could tell of her gestures' grace and loveliness,
corresponding to the beauty of her face?
Who could tell of the gentleness
of her sweet words and sweet smile?
Her gracious habits give notice
that in her modesty and courtesy reign,
such that I do not believe her peer could be found
anywhere the sun heats and the sea encircles."[6]

5. Red lead.

6. The description of Celsidea follows what has been termed the "short" canon of a Petrarchist representation of the fragmented female body, one that starts from the woman's hair, moves down to every part of her face, then to the neck, and stops at her breasts. Ariosto reserved such a depiction, for example, to Angelica, while he preferred the "long" canon, in which also the legs are properly examined, for Alcina. This characterization of female beauty was such a cliché in the early modern period that women writers used it too, as in this description, made by a fictional painter, of an unnamed duchess in Giulia Bigolina's *Urania*: "Please, look closely here, my lord, how the gold and curly hair seems like a net to entrap a thousand hardened hearts. See the spacious and highly polished forehead, the eyes, which resemble two stars, although one cannot fully discern their natural liveliness, the lashes curly and black as ebony, the well-proportioned nose, the rosy cheeks, the small mouth, the lips that surpass the corals in beauty . . . and also the very proportionate chin, which is neither slight nor redundant in any part. It seems that each says, 'Love has his kingdom here and not elsewhere.' But what shall we say of the throat and chest that surpass the snow in whiteness? And of that little protruding apple, which no one, admiring it fully, can see without feeling his heart melt out of desire?" (137). On the similarity between literature and art in representing women, see Giorgio Padoan, "*Ut pictura poesis*: Le 'pitture' di Ariosto, le 'poetiche' di Tiziano," in *Momenti del Rinascimento*

1 7

Indeed the helmsman could not find a better
subject than this, or more delightful news,
to wage a greater assault on the Thracian's heart,
and arouse in him a new desire.
When Risardo has heard his account,
no longer does he care to go to beautiful Alexandria,
and he commands the helmsman right then
to turn the prow toward the Achaean homeland.

1 8

The helmsman obeys. No one dares
open his mouth against his command,
all the more because every soul there yearns
to acquire fame and demonstrate courage.
They all share the desire to be present
at that noble and famous tourney.
Anyone with a strong and courageous heart yearns
to go to Athens before Egypt.

1 9

Having already left Selybria and Perinthus on the right-hand side,
the good helmsman passes the strait
where Leander and Hero loved in vain,
and which became for one and the other sepulcher and bed.
Crete is in sight, though far off,
and on the left side the Phrygian roof;

---

veneto, ed. Giorgio Padoan (Padua: Antenore, 1978), 347–70; on the piecemeal representation
of women, see Nancy Vickers, "Diana Described: Scattered Woman and Scattered Rhyme," in
Writing and Sexual Difference, ed. Elizabeth Adel (Chicago: University of Chicago Press, 1982).
As Fonte plainly puts it in *The Worth of Women,* "Whatever people say, there is no better subject
for poetry than the praise of feminine beauty. It's a subject . . . that offers poets much fine
inspiration. What would the divine Petrarch have done if the physical and spiritual beauties of
the woman he loved, which he describes so sublimely, had not provided him with such ample
material for him to forge his way to immortality?" (216). For the overuse of Petrarch in the
period, see Quondam, *Il naso di Laura.*

and he comes close to the island
of Tenedos, and he plows the Aegean Sea.[7]

20

He enters then the sea which took its name
from the daring son of Daedalus,
who ascended to the sky with waxed feathers
and then fell, and ended his life and his flight.
To the Capharean promontory then he came,
where he does not cleave the green sea's
unstable soil in a straight line toward the south,
but toward the west he extends his voyage.[8]

21

Andros he leaves behind on the left, and Negroponte
on the right side, and the southern wind blows so well
that in a short time it pushes the vessel to Mount Sounion,
and at last he espies the beautiful Cecropian land.[9]
Once arrived, the Thracian has the gangplank thrown to earth
and disembarks, and turns his eyes here and there.
Following Risardo's example,
every brave warrior disembarks to the shore.

7. Selybria and Perinthus were cities on the northern coast of the Sea of Marmara. See Grant, *Guide to the Ancient World*, 486–87. The strait is the Dardanelles, or Hellespont. Leander, from Abydos, loved Hero, a priestess in Sestos on the opposite shore. He swam the strait nightly to see her, but one night her lantern blew out, and he became lost and drowned. Upon hearing the news, she threw herself from her tower. See Arthur Cotterell, *The Encyclopedia of Mythology: Classical, Celtic, Norse* (New York, Smithmark, 1996), 52. Phrygia, a territory in Asia Minor, included the western part of the central plateau. See Grant, *Guide to the Ancient World*, 504.

8. The Icarian Sea is in the southern Aegean between the Peloponnese and Asia Minor. To escape from Crete, Daedalus made wings for himself and his son, but Icarus ignored his warning and flew too near the sun, which melted the wax that held the feathers. See Graves, *Greek Myths*, 312–13. The Capharean promontory is a peninsula on the island of Euboea. In verse 8, Fonte refers to Favonio (from the Latin Favonius), or the west wind, to stand for the westward direction: "Ma ver Favonio il suo viaggio stende.".

9. Negroponte is another name for Euboea. Fonte calls this particular wind Volturno, a southeast wind, also named euro, one of the eight Roman winds. Cape Sounion is the southernmost point of Attica.

22

He does not plan to go openly,
but prudently hides himself from all,
because of the hate and enmity which had arisen
between the Achaean kingdom and his paternal shores.
The Thracian heir first wants to learn better
whether the royal proclamation answers to his will;
he wants to know whether in those august and happy days
Cleardo safeguards even his enemies.

23

He does not yet want to enter the city,
but goes about through the grassy countryside
contemplating those lands with his men;
and he discovers now one thing, now another.
Then he sees before the famous city,
passing through the most heavily traveled streets,
three knights with black weapons and destriers,
lacking insignia on their shields and crests.

24

At first sight, each one seems brave.
With no decoration of gems or gold,
they seem to others' eyes and judgment
to show dignity, grace, and decorum.
When he sees them, young Risardo
plans to test their prowess;
in a thoroughly courteous manner,
he challenges them to joust, and sets his lance on his thigh.

25

The one of the three knights who comes in the lead,
who does not know how much the boy is worth in arms,
accepts the invitation, and without a doubt expects
to be the victor in the battle.
The others stop to see which of them is

worthy of greater regard and of higher esteem.
Indeed, the Thracians move away somewhat,
and the other two warriors do the same.

26

Risardo, intent on the upcoming assault,
holds back somewhat his destrier's bit.
He drives it at first in fits and starts,
dexterous and nimble, with skill and reason.
Then, once turned round on the grassy course,
he presses it to a speedier pace;
he so slackens the reins and grips with his spurs
that to meet his enemy he drives it.

27

The unknown knight, no less daring,
ready, and master of the joust than he,
turns skillfully his destrier's rein
from the left side, and pricks it with his right foot.
With such quickness it presses the earth
that its nimble and dexterous foot leaves no prints.
Both aimed their hard lances toward their opponent's helmet,
and in midcourse the knights crashed together.

28

Risardo, to whose daring, to whose vigor
only one other man in his age can compare,
brought into the proud blow so much valor,
with no inconvenience to himself,
that, the victor of the encounter,
he continued his charge with abandon.
The other, who left his saddle at the fierce blow,
with little honor ended up on the ground.

29

At so fierce and so vigorous an encounter
everyone marvels, and praises and approves it.
Eager for good Risardo's valor,
they long to see some new feat.
He, having turned Ruggipardo,
comes boldly to the second trial,
and the other, who sees him come from afar,
prepares his heart, skill, and strength.

30

He takes the field, and crudely threatening
to avenge if he can the other's defeat,
at the fierce encounter he passes the Thracian shield,
and breaks his lance between the hauberk and the cloth.
But Risardo finds his unarmored breast
and puts him in such distress, in such apprehension,
that if he had not stretched out on his destrier's
back, the fierce blow would have killed him.

31

He was near falling, yet held on;
but while rising up and as he drew his sword,
I don't know how the horse came to stumble,
so that by necessity he fell.
Since Risardo gained the second victory
(for there was no reason to joust again with that knight),
as if fortune would always smile on his honor,
arrogantly he challenged the third knight.

32

But that one, making no corresponding gesture or motion
to joust with the Thracian,
moved his destrier toward him at a slow pace,
and with a very humane and pleasant voice
said, "O knight, make me happy;
let me know in whom heaven hides such merit.

Tell me what father and fatherland destiny gave you,
your kin and the country where you were born."

33

That sweet and humane utterance which he makes
with quiet and very gentle speech
seems strange to Risardo as he listens;
it seems not a boy's but a maiden's voice.
Responding to the humble and quiet entreaty,
with all courtesy he too speaks and declares,
"Although I like always to conceal myself from others,
nevertheless with you I am content to reveal myself.

34

"I am Risardo; I was born of King Agricorno,
emperor of ancient Byzantium.
But you who show by your elegant speech
that you are a lady most worthy of honor,
tell me who gave you to the world and the daylight,
and whether I judge truly or am in error.
Your clothing makes you seem a virile man,
but your voice is that of an august and noble lady."

35

Indeed, he does not act contrary to Risardo's desire;
rather, uncovering the beloved face,
she says this to the amorous prince:
"See that yours was a true judgment.
I am a lady of high and famous rank.
Beyond the Ganges is my happy state;
my kingdom and my native abode
are the most felicitous Sabaean fields." [10]

---

10. As in canto 2.25, Fonte continues to use the masculine pronoun until the lady's face is revealed. The prosperous ancient kingdom of Saba, the biblical Sheba, was located in present-day Yemen. The scene of Risardo's encounter with a fully armed knight who seems to be a woman and is indeed one, Odoria, is modeled upon a scene in the *Furioso* in which Astolfo and Sansonetto meet a knight who likewise "looked like a man, to judge by attire and movements: she was a woman, however, and a remarkably fierce warrior. / She was the virgin Marfisa . . . Day

36

As the polished steel, shiny and heavy,
leaves uncovered the maiden's visage,
and the very sweet and gentle sight
suddenly catches his barbarous heart,
he is so stunned, he trembles so and fears,
and becomes so amazed and conquered by her
that he no longer deserves the name of victor;
and Love carries off all the praise.

37

As soon as he sets eyes on her
and sees her golden hair drifting in the wind,
Love, who draws his bow in those beautiful eyes,
to cast down that barbarous daring,
with an arrow wounds his heart so deeply
that he deprives him of every honor, of every ornament.
Already with such desire he burns and binds him
that he doesn't know what to say or what to do.

38

In a gracious manner at last he speaks, and dares
to ask what cause now makes her depart
from her famous, blessed homeland,
and seek realms distant and foreign to her;
and whether her journey's end lies
in the less fertile and less healthy Achaean fields,
or if instead she is traveling to yet another place,
to make it illustrious and lofty with her light.

39

The virgin, who is named Odoria,
has realized from his gestures and his words

---

and night she was always armed" (*Orlando furioso* 18.98–99). Marfisa will then join the knights
on their way to Damascus, just as here Risardo joins Odoria, who is not a woman warrior but
dresses as such to travel safely, on the way to Delphi.

how much the Thracian mind is inflamed
by her divine and unique beauties.
Though she is not agreeable to the first question,
the second she does not mean to deny.
She is silent about why she left the Orient,
but she obliges his curiosity as to the rest.

40

She says that to go by the most traveled
and shortest road to Delphi is her desire,
for in the Orient she had heard the fame
of the fateful pronouncements of the blond god,
who predicts through the holy and pious oracle
the things to come in others' lives.[11]
And because she has two doubtful thoughts in her heart,
she wants to know which of them is more perfect.

41

When the lady reaches this point,
Risardo decides to go to the temple as well,
to find out from the eternal and divine voice
whether the maiden's heart is compassionate or pitiless.
He wants to know whether she prizes him or shuns him,
whether he will have delight or destruction from the new love.
He turns aside his heart from his other undertaking,
and offers to accompany her.

42

The damsel consents to the noble youth,
for she esteems him highly for his prowess.
Meanwhile she considers privately
how she might see his handsome face.
Already, shortly after she uncovered her brow

11. Delphi was the site of a very famous oracle of Apollo. People came from far and wide to consult the oracle on matters of grave importance. Vapors from a chasm would drive Apollo's priestess, the Pythia, into a frenzy, and her words were set in verse by interpreters in answer to the questions.

the Thracian band had gathered there,
profoundly amazed that a noble
young woman was going about in men's clothing.

43

The damsel went thus armed,
not because she had strength or courage,
but in order not to give those who traveled with her
grounds to demonstrate their valor often.
Since she was a maiden and so beautiful,
they might often come to blows for her;
they might find more than one warrior on the route
who for love of her would resort to arms.

44

Therefore, in order not to have so many disputes
that might delay their journey,
the lady decided to cover
from others' gaze her august and divine face.[12]
Risardo apologized courteously
to the two warriors who stood with heads bowed,
and he showed great sorrow and regret
at having caused them this inconvenience.

45

These warriors were highly esteemed
by her, for she had seen great things from them;
that they were unhorsed by Risardo
astonished her, and shamed them.[13]
Now once they had regained their saddles,
beautiful Odoria replaced her helmet,

---

12. Whether women traveled dressed as men for reasons of physical security in the early modern period is debatable, although there is circumstantial evidence that they did. The short story tradition often refers to it. See for example Boccaccio, *Decameron* 2.3 and 2.9; and Bigolina, *Urania*, 87.

13. The shame of which Fonte speaks recalls the shame ("vergogna") of the three kings coming from Iceland with Ullania in the *Furioso*, whom Bradamante briefly engages in a joust and bests in order to enter the Castle of Tristan. See *Orlando furioso* 33.72–76.

although Risardo, displeased by this decision,
beseeched her to keep her face uncovered.

46

But when the dwarf hears that Risardo
desires to follow the Sabaean tracks,
that he is abandoning the enterprise of Cleardo
and means to accompany this woman to Delphi,
weeping, he is not slow to implore him,
by the faith which men have in the gods,
not to put off any longer the promise
he had made to help his oppressed lady.[14]

47

Risardo comforts him and promises
soon he'll do what he must for him.
If he does not set foot in Egypt first,
and if following him seems hard to him,
let him return to Alexandria and await him
(he says) for he will come as soon as possible,
and let him not doubt that then he will
deliver her from every trouble and liberate her.

48

Since prayers, weeping, and laments do not avail
to make Risardo change his course,
the dwarf departs, angered and discontent,
and he tells everyone of this wrong.[15]
He goes to find a man more faithful to his wishes,[16]
who would defend the innocent young woman;

14. The dwarf's request for help, also accompanied by tears and laments, recalls an episode in the *Innamorato*, where a dwarf begs Ruggiero and Gradasso "per pietate e per mercede" to accompany him to a tower (3.7.37–41 and 3.7.54–55).

15. In Fonte's hands, Risardo is the poster child for male inconstancy, in sharp contrast with the dwarf's single-minded steadiness in love and purpose toward Raggidora. In *The Worth of Women* Fonte satirizes fickleness in men with an incisive sentence: "Their love is no more than a flash in the pan; their loyalty, a laugh in the tavern; their devotion, a day out hunting the hare; their fine appearance, a peacock's tail"(74).

16. Or "more faithful in his nature" ("uom più fido al suo talento").

and at last he meets a foreign knight,
after much winding through mountains and plains.

4 9

Risardo's knightly companions,
whom the Thracian emperor sent with him,
at the will of the brave prince
returned back to their lord.
But I leave these people, and now of that sharp dart
with which Raggidora pierced Lideo's heart
I intend to tell you, and how in Egypt he killed
the king, blaming her for the crime.

5 0

From the dwarf you heard in what manner
she was treated in her realm,
but he did not know to tell you the whole reason
why she was accused of the offense.
Now I want you to hear the true story,
and I say that she was imprisoned for love,
for a love so cruel and wicked
that it made the knight Lideo err so greatly.

5 1

Once the damsel's great beauty
had bound and clutched the warrior of Euboea,
who had reached beautiful Alexandria by chance,
he remained a prisoner of her lovely countenance.
Since he found her feminine mind
rebellious and contrary to his amorous affection,
he tempted her with the many ways lovers use:
feasts, verses, tourneys, entreaties, and weeping.

5 2

The cruel young woman never
had pity for him who had given her his heart.

Never toward him did she direct courteous eyes;
never did she do him the least favor.
Therefore the wretch kept in continuous woe
his soul wrapped up in so vain an error,
since, more deaf than an asp and harder
than a stone, she relished his affliction.

5 3

When in the end service of any sort
did not move that haughty and pitiless heart,
and Lideo found himself despairing,
he wanted with his own hand to kill himself.
Then thinking again of so ungrateful a soul,
he wanted not to die but to avenge his fate.
He planned to kill the king secretly
and blame her, who was innocent.

5 4

The wicked thought did not lack people to favor it,
for besides the fact that fortune smiles on evil,
the splendor of gold has so much power over servants
that in the king's own room he found and killed him.
He went unpunished for so great a fault,
for no one realized it, no one saw him.
And then to safeguard his weak point,
he killed those who knew of the deed.

5 5

With guilt added to guilt, harm to harm,
by the most hidden and most secret ways,
as soon as it was known to all and everyone knew
that the king had crossed Lethe's waves,[17]
the better to cover up his cruel deceit

17. Passage through the River Lethe into the underworld removed a soul's memory of life on earth.

and to satisfy and enjoy his desires,
he accused Raggidora, and offered and hoped
to uphold the cruel calumny as true.[18]

56

Although the knight of Euboea had not
too handsome and gracious a countenance,
yet his manner was so benign,
his conversation so loving and straightforward,
that, added to the great valor shining in him,
everyone felt for him love and respect.
Raggidora alone did not love him,
and did not esteem his deeds and his fame.

57

Lideo, with the means and the favor he obtained
from the greatest personages of that realm,
little by little came to such preeminence,
with skill, shrewdness, and intelligence,
that after Galbo he became its lord.
And his plan succeeded to such an extent
that with no dispute from the people
he was publicly hailed as king.

58

But although he is heir to so great a kingdom,
and wears the regal mantle and crown,
love does not allow him to rest.
Even more than before it stirs him up and spurs him
for Raggidora, who possesses his heart
and denies him her beautiful person.

---

18. To accuse a woman of coldness for being unresponsive to a man's love was a recurrent topos
of both prose and verse fiction. We have examples in Boccaccio as well as in Castiglione. For a
similar take in Ariosto, see the episode of the Princess Ginevra defamed by the knight Polinesso
(*Orlando furioso* 4.59 and passim).

She is so opposed to his desires
that she wants to die sooner than be his wife.

59

He, who loves her and has offended her so much
only because of her ingratitude,
comes to admire that blessed visage
not once each day, but five and six times.
To placate her he prays and weeps
that they might celebrate their proper nuptials.
Scornful, she disdains him and does not bend,
and at last out of pride she refuses to look at him.

60

The enamored king endures everything;
her every cruelty he takes peacefully,
for he hopes to make her compassionate
more by acting humble with her than bold.
And although she, proud and scornful,
shows that she bears him a pertinacious hatred,
and is sparing of her looks and words,
he honors her, and loves her, and wants to love her.

61

No longer does he keep her in a dark and shadowy place,
but in a free, illustrious, and lofty abode.
He shares with her all those goods
which his splendid domain can give.
He shares every grace in his generous heart
which can make her happy.
Precisely as if she were the queen,
he gives her an abundance of every treasure, of all his goods.

62

He makes a vow to visit in Paphos and in Cnidus
the goddess of delights and pleasures,

so that gentle Cupid
might bend the beautiful lady to his wishes.[19]
She who is the abode and nest of every grace
does not, however, change her haughty habits,
but every day expects the dwarf to return,
bringing in other hands her vengeance.

63

From moment to moment she expects the Pygmy king
to return with some champion
who will take from the unjust and wicked tyrant
not only her, but the kingdom, and the air and the light.
Indeed, she guessed that fierce Lideo
had committed the ultimate ignominy against the king.
Many times to herself she had reasoned
how that event must have occurred.

64

Thus, far more than before, and with good reason,
she held the treacherous king in hate and anger.
In vain he wept and sighed,
nor could he draw out the passion from his heart.
Overcome by the sorrow that pained and tormented him,
he sent a messenger hurrying to Stellidone,
that he might come to keep his word against the haughty
young woman, that she might finally perish.

65

A rumor had come to Alexandria
that many knights of highest daring,
in order to defend the lady,
had set off and were due to arrive.
The king, who had arranged the unjust plot
and felt so much torment on her account,

---

19. Paphos in Cyprus and Cnidus in Caria were chief centers of the cult of Aphrodite. See *New Larousse Encyclopedia of Mythology,* 130.

for his own honor's sake no less than for the pain,
wanted his brother to take on that task.

66

Of three most worthy brothers
who ruled the island of Euboea,
this Lideo of whom I tell was the eldest;
the last, Stellidone of whom I spoke.
The other, Tisandro, was much better.
Of him Lideo had no news;
so on Stellidone he based his plan.
But I have arrived at the end of this canto.

CANTO 5

ARGUMENT

To Ithaca the storm transports
Silano. There the magic damsel
transforms a knight into a tree,
and saves him from the bestial throng.
The Greeks reach the king. The jousters make a fine
spectacle. Risamante informs
her noble host of the way she obtained
the ring, and how she killed the treacherous dragon.

1

Ah, what can that wicked tyrant Love not do,
if in striking and wounding a heart he drives away good sense?
From some he wrests away life, from others honor,
from others their possessions and true friendships.
Some because of him go mad,
and are forced to act against duty.
For each one who seems wise from his sparks,
he drives a thousand to madness.

2

For one whom Love makes well-mannered
and reverent, courteous and noble,
infinite are those who retain a malicious,
treacherous, disgraceful, and base mind.
If the lady to their ardent desire
does not show herself humble right away,

if she does not give in to impious and annoying entreaties,
behold them quick to hate, to vengeance.

3

Let ladies avoid even more than sin,
more than death, the undertaking of love,
for most men have ungrateful hearts,
from what I read and often hear tell.[1]
Still, from the impious, unjust, and villainous,
one cannot guard oneself well in any way,
for evil comes to whoever loves; and worse yet
befell Raggidora for not loving.

4

She, by not consenting to the great desire
of the knight insane from too much love,
caused him, overcome by the torment,
to show himself rough and boorish toward her;
although afterward, as I will tell you,
he tried to placate her, but always in vain.
Now let her wait there, for from the sea's
furor I want to extract the Latin prince.

5

Boreas, impetuous and firm in his severity,
did not cease until the third evening,
constantly shaking the little skiff
through the fierce and injurious ocean.[2]
On the third day, when they had no more shelter from it,
the haughty fury seemed to wane somewhat,
and the air opened up a bit on the horizon,
and revealed the setting sun's face.

1. Renaissance women writers often commented on the risk for women of falling in love in a system in which marriages were arranged and dowries determined a partner's choice. See Bigolina, *Urania*, 107, 121; and Fonte, *Worth of Women*, 74–75.
2. Boreas is the north wind. See Graves, *Greek Myths*, 27.

6

Little by little the wind again welcomed birds' wings,
and returned soothed to his great overlord.
The sea as well abated its rage and furor,
and returned to its former state.
Then a sweet contrary breeze wafted forth,
which dispersed the clouds and made room for the light.
Cynthia showed forth her beautiful tresses,
and the sky adorned itself with scintillating stars.[3]

7

Dawn appeared then in the east,
and decided that day to array herself in pearls.
Shining golden Aurora followed,
winding a fresh garland in her hair.
From sleep she released the knights
who had passed that night far more sweetly,
for they had disembarked (not knowing in what lands)
on a charming and beautiful island.

8

As delighted as one can imagine,
both of them greeted the desired shore;
and they took to the land in those unknown parts,
and they turned their backs on the troublesome and unreliable sea.
With pious, holy, and devoted words,
since they had been drawn to a safer nest,
they thanked the eternal, divine spirits,
with eyes and hands upraised to heaven.

9

They were on foot with all their armaments,
for each warrior had saved them.

3. Aeolus was the ruler of the winds. See Graves, *Greek Myths*, 160. Cynthia was the moon
goddess.

Thus through merry and verdant meadows,
through that beautiful plain they set off walking.
They saw the beautiful fields starred with flowers,
where more than one roe deer glided nimbly,
and then not far away the golden wheat stalks,
trembling, imitating the sea's waves.

1 0

In the grove of laurel and juniper
they saw between two sweet and untouched streams
a dear and secret shelter for fallow deer and hares,
which hid them from beasts and plowmen.
Sweet Love, you who with thorny shafts
make hearts sore and alleviate the wounds,
when in Cythera did you have, or in Paphos or Cnidus,
so joyous and gracious a nest? [4]

1 1

Everywhere as the warriors advanced
they discerned new beauty, new loveliness.
They heard harmonies; they listened to songs
of lovely birds with competing melodies.
The two warriors, happy among so many pleasures,
swore that this alone delights and does good;
nor in their judgment was there a joy more complete
than the delights and the beauty of springtime.

1 2

The streams' source was unknown to them,
for they couldn't tell from where the water issued,
which, coming out from afar on two sides,
descended more limpid and cooler than amber.
The land, split in three by the two rivulets,

---

4. Cupid's sharp golden arrows cause love, but his blunt, lead-tipped arrows put love to flight.
Aphrodite rose from sea foam and first stepped ashore on the island of Cythera, before going
to Cyprus. See Graves, *Greek Myths*, 49. For Paphos and Cnidus, see canto 4.62n.

made nature increase her treasures.
On the sides were a thousand fertile plants;
in the middle was the wood which I mentioned earlier.

1 3

The streams flowed bright and crystal clear
into a pleasant and flourishing meadow,
which had around it a graceful and beautiful wall
of myrtle shrubs and of azure and purple-black violets.
Here joined by nature into one,
they formed in passing a little river
that had colorful banks shaded
by every most rich and fruitful frond.

1 4

They discerned here and there a thousand trees all
loaded with lovely and merry golden knobs,
for the trunks supported the fronds and fruits
which decorate Bacchus's shining blond hair.
With such good order nature produced there
the branches and in them the dangling grapes,
some golden and some tinted with the color purple,
that they seemed depicted and feigned by art.[5]

1 5

Silano's body was weak and miserable
from the harsh and inclement weather,
and he suffered hardship from the long fast.
His spirits rose at so charming a vista,
and to drive away hunger at his ease
he stopped next to the dangling objects.
Clarido stripped the branches of fruit,
and satisfied him and that avid desire.

5. Bacchus was the Roman god of wine. The *locus amoenus* (pleasant place) is a common motif
in literature of the period, from Boccaccio's *Filocolo* to Bembo's *Gli Asolani*. Fonte had already
composed a similar poem on the topic, which her character Corinna recites at the conclusion
of *The Worth of Women*.

16

It was their good fortune they did not touch
any fruit of the trees within,
nor pluck flowers, nor taste of that clear
river, for they would have broken their fast badly.
They were even luckier they did not pass into that grove
of which I spoke, for everyone perished there.
Silano was lying down well within the meadow,
but Clarido outside it was plucking fruit.

17

Whether chance or their prudence fills up
their stomachs, there they both restore
their afflicted spirits, and then in the scented shade
of an amorous myrtle they sit.[6]
That sweet time clears away all sadness.
Soft breezes blow a gentle breath.
But they stay there only a little before at a great noise nearby
they stray from so cheerful and refreshing a sojourn.

18

They get up, and through the grassy vale,
equipped with shield and sword,
toward that noise they take the path
which leads them to the more traveled road.
They discover then the broad shoulders of a mountain
which ascends to the divine, bountiful region,
and its foot is circled by a well-built wall
which blocks the passage securely from wanderers.

19

One cannot swear that the wall
is of Parian marble or alabaster,
because its splendor is such that it dazzles every eye,

6. The myrtle was the plant of Aphrodite.

however steady and distant it may be.
No diamond that gives similar light
equals so wondrous a stone.
It is not of carbuncle nor crystal,
not silver nor the finest metal.

2 0

It is of such clear and distinguished material
that it exceeds and surpasses every human thought.[7]
Thus, gazing at so rare a work,
Prince Silano is stunned.
Clarido with his hands protects his eyes
from the great brightness of the rare workmanship,
and finally they both judge
that this is a magical artifact.

2 1

You might ask me the reason
why they had not seen it before,
and I will say the magic incantation
hid it from them, although it was right in front of them.
But once they emerged from the meadow where Pluto[8]
had his forces, and walked forward,
on the secure path they were undeceived,
and they discovered far-off the mountain and the wall.

2 2

They went farther, and the great noise they heard
struck and pierced their ears far more.
Once they were a stone's throw away
from that magnificent ring,

---

7. This passage recalls Ariosto's famous description of the walls encircling the city ruled by the evil and seductive enchantress Alcina. See *Orlando furioso* 6.58–59.

8. Also called Hades, Pluto was the ruler of the underworld. See *New Larousse Encyclopedia of Mythology,* 165.

they saw a door open, not of sapphire
but of a richer and more precious stone;
and out of the great circle came a damsel
who was leading a knight as a prisoner.[9]

23

Part of her curly blond hair
she kept spread over her beautiful neck;
part was gathered in a braid at the border
of her lovely ears; and it was wispy on her forehead.
Her beautiful, angelic, and divine eyes
would have burnt every asp's and tiger's heart.
Her gaze was vivacious, shrewd, and enchanting,
and her visage in every part august and lovely.

24

Noble Love in her courteous glances
conveyed his sweetly proud arrow,
and already her prisoner felt the sweet
and severe assault of the amorous darts.
In the end the two brave men stay to see
where the lady leads the knight.
She keeps him bound with a chain of gold
and approaches, cheerful and proud.

25

When she comes near them, with a humble gesture
they make their reverence to the divine beauty,
and she with a kind and noble expression
returns their greeting, and walks on.
Clarido already feels the tinder and steel
of Love, who sharpens his arrows in her beautiful eyes;

9. The precise word Fonte uses here for "circle," *girone,* was employed by Dante to refer to a circle of Hell. See also canto 6.76.

he feels his breast take flame little by little,
and he already sighs for his new fire.

26

On the path by which they arrived at the mountain,
the beautiful lady leads the knight.
Over a stream was placed a little bridge,
by which into the woods she conducts the wretch,
who barely touches the plain when he changes form,
loses the life-giving air, loses the light.
Silano and Clarido watch it and see it,
yet can barely believe it themselves.

27

Like senseless statues they stand immobile
to gaze from afar at that hard circumstance.
The fright and agitation in their hearts
are such that they nearly go out of their minds.
The knight, leaving his carnal garment,
becomes a tree trunk at a simple conjuration;
his arms become branches, and the new stalk
spreads its graceful green foliage to the sky.[10]

28

When she has increased the untrustworthy forest
in number and in beauty with the new plant,
the beautiful lady returns toward the fortress,
and passes before the prince and Clarido.
Clarido no longer esteems that beauty
which nested in his heart so quickly;
and, wounded and healed in a single moment,
dismayed, he and Silano gaze at her.[11]

---

10. This passage echoes a well-known episode in canto 6 of *Orlando furioso*. When the evil fay Alcina tires of her lovers, she transforms them into plants. One of these castoffs in tree form, Astolfo, warns Ruggiero against Alcina, but he disregards the warning and is seduced.

11. Fonte's allusion to Petrarch's famous verse, "piaga per allentar d'arco non sana" (a wound is not healed by the loosening of the bow), points up the contrast between Petrarch's decades-

29

She, contemplating the knights' expressions
which show fear and astonishment,
says, "Let neither of you, stupefied,
take any fright from what you have seen,
because I will show you a greater miracle
than what I have done through my power.
Whoever wants to pass with me beyond that wall
to see its effect, I assure his safety.

30

"Come, adventurous knights,
and fear no strange peril."
Ah, wretched maiden, you try to cut short
your peace and wound your healthy heart!
How much better it would be if with contrary
accents and with haughty and discourteous speech
you drove away the bold knights
whom you invite with such dear little words.

31

She goes on, "I will tell you that adventure
which the world cannot yet know.
Together with it I will narrate my misfortune
which keeps me closed up in these unknown valleys,
for I too am subjected to a hard fate,
and I sprinkle my cheeks with tears,
hoping in vain for the arrival of a knight.
Who knows if one of you is not that very one? [12]

long love and Clarido's brief infatuation. See *Petrarch's Lyric Poems,* canzone 90. When Fonte
quotes this same Petrarchan verse in *The Worth of Women,* she applies it to women who continue
to love men even after discovering the men have only pretended to care for them and who
commit illicit acts out of "naiveté and their wish to satisfy the desires of the men they love"
(121)—this is Circetta's fate.

12. In the diminutive Circetta, Fonte combines elements of Ariosto's half sisters Alcina and
Logistilla and his sorceress Melissa. For more on this radical rewriting of the myth of the seduc-
tress Circe, see Finucci, "Moderata Fonte e il romanzo cavalleresco al femminile," xxxix–xxxv;

32

"He through his rare and profound valor
is to free me from this place,
and this fertile island will be his,
once he overcomes the monsters' rage."
So well does she project her kind and joyful
voice from those sweet lips
that the knights, somewhat reassured,
trust her sweet and truthful speech.

33

Nor is either of them so discourteous
as not to accept her benign invitation,
and the damsel makes her way
to the wall by which the great mountain is encircled.
Silano then turns his eyes to the summit,
and sees there a temple of burnished gold.
To Clarido he shows it on the high peak,
for neither saw it before.

34

When they reach the magnificent gate,
the damsel is not slow to pass through,
and she urges and coaxes the knights
to follow her and not take fright.
Encouraged, Silano follows his escort,
and Clarido with him shows boldness,
since the young woman affirms and swears
that she guarantees them against any treachery.

Kolsky, "Moderata Fonte's *Tredici canti del Floridoro*," 170–75; and Cox, "Women as Readers,"
142–43. Lucrezia Marinella's Erina in *Enrico* and Margherita Sarrocchi's Calidora in *Scander-
beide* are imagined along the same lines as Circetta. Described as "a young woman honest and
marvelously wise, most graceful, sensible, and charming" (7.52), Circetta is throughout more
virginal than witchlike, and rather than seducing, she is seduced, although only platonically.
As Fonte shows through the actions of Risamante, women can get what they want only if they
themselves pursue their goals. Circetta's and Raggidora's problem is that they have to wait for a
man to take up their cause and free them. The wait will be long.

35

But they have barely set foot inside
the great, lofty threshold between the wall and the mountain,
when a million pitiless beasts
leap toward them ready to harm them.
Silano, who does not mean to fear them,
draws his sword and with a bold front
charges among them, and with horrendous strokes
from their bothersome fury defends himself.

36

Bears, tigers, lions, wolves, and serpents,
rough enemies of the sight of men,
with sharp claws and voracious teeth
make a hard assault against the two faithful friends.
But the pious damsel, who can command
the elements with her rare artifices,
with the power of a single word
soothes that whole beastly herd.[13]

37

Down different paths, here and there,
all the horrendous host scatter.
By so stupendous an act she leaves
the knights downcast and ashamed.
The most sweet virgin, laughing,
with a discreet and gracious word
then takes both men by the hand,
and apologizes for the strange and awful event,

38

saying, "I gave you safe conduct
from the power of the magic spell,

13. Likewise, in *Orlando furioso* Alcina's realm is surrounded by wild beasts, which impede men's
entry. But the most immediate reference is to Homer's Circe (*Odyssey* 10), who is able to tame
wild animals through words.

not from the other accidents to which man
is subject, and against which he can employ his wisdom and weapons."
Silano to her with a gracious pleasantry:
"Neither wisdom nor valor will be able to help me
at all against you if with sweet accents alone
you overcome bears, lions, tigers, and serpents.

39

"Nor do I believe that anything enchants a heart more
than a lovely visage and sweet speech.
I see them clearly in your beautiful countenance,
for my intellect fears no other force."
The lady lowers her honest and chaste eyes
at that speech which is by no means unwelcome to her,
and adorns her face with the beautiful color
that the rose reveals in the morning sun.

40

A pleasant street, quite wide and capacious,
turns between the mountain and the luminous circle.
At the foot of the mountain lies an ample door,
through which one goes into the deep cavern.
Here the lady, who is secretly pleased
by the amorous young man's discourse,
strikes the door; it gives way to her,
and she and the warriors set foot within.

41

What the knights did then within
that mountain, and what followed after,
and of her who later suffered so many shames
from love for an ungrateful and wicked boy,
I must tell you elsewhere.
For now, I turn my speech to King Cleardo
and his warriors, who with a magnificent show
wanted to go out to the honored joust.

42

Already, so that the plan of the jousting,
which had been made public for many days, would not go awry,
and to effectuate the order given,
Cleardo, who held the reins of Greece in his hand,
had gathered every warrior of his
happy state, from near and far.
They, having heard of the general concourse,
had run in a great hurry to obey the royal edict.

43

Indeed, all the kings, dukes, marquesses, and counts
who were lofty King Cleardo's vassals
had been quick to come to court
to honor his magnificent reign.
They passed rivers and forests and valleys and mountains,
since their paths were diverse,
except for those who had not left the court
after haughty Macandro died.

44

Alarco left Megara as the news
spread, and King Amarinto left Macedonia.
The dukes of Corcyra and of Zakinthos
hurried to the promulgated competition.
Among the others, wise and noble Silvarte
had passed the isthmus of Corinth;
to him for his faithful goodness
the king had given Mycenae to govern.

45

He had come, and had brought with him
his extremely good-looking son Floridoro;
since he was born into the nourishing and blessed daylight,
the sun had seen the bull sixteen times.[14]

14. The zodiacal sign of Taurus runs April 20–May 20.

The expression of his comely face was so agreeable,
so lovely the splendor of his beautiful, golden hair,
and his appearance was so divine,
that every heart, even a harsh one, was inclined to love him.

46

With his shrewd father came the noble son,
in delightful and lovely clothing.
Love laughed in his tranquil brow;
rather he appeared Love's very image.
His splendid white and vermilion complexion
made every eye eager to contemplate him.
Every part of him, except his speech,
appeared that of an illustrious and beautiful girl.[15]

47

The young nobleman had never yet
practiced the feats of Mars,
but by nature he was quite brave,
endowed with great dexterity and courage,
and he had always taken delight
in arms and horses and seeing jousts.
Thus, with his father leaving Mycenae,
he wanted to go with him to Athens.

48

They presented themselves before King Cleardo,
who welcomed them with a benign expression.
Turning his gaze to the sweet visage,
he liked him so and took him into so much favor
that, until Love with his biting dart
induced the beautiful boy to wrong him,

---

15. Floridoro's first description echoes that of the boy in the grotto (3.22–23), and it is re-
markable for the accent on his feminine traits rather than on the manly qualities we would
expect for the title character. For more on Floridoro's characterization, see the Volume Editor's
Introduction.

to the dishonor of the royal Greek blood,
he always loved him like a son and kept him with him.

49

To obey his royal decree
Stellidone came as well from Negroponte;
this was before the Egyptian messenger
landed in Euboea to find him.
Thus the knight reached Athens
with his heart sad and brow troubled
for his two brothers, who were brave and strong;
but he does not know if they are living or dead.

50

The one is Lideo, who accused in Egypt
the beautiful lady for whom he burns with desire.
The other is the warrior who in the place described
Silano saw transform into a plant.
For them the good brother is distressed,
and feels in his heart bitter torment;
yet now he consoles himself a bit with the hope
of seeing them together at that tourney.

51

Not only had every lord of the Greek realm
repaired to the Palladian land,
but each most worthy barbarian warrior
came as well from all over the world.
This ship and that one cluttered up the Achaean port;
already this destrier and that one walked the earth.
Everyone had already repaired to the city,
for to all the king gave safe conduct.

52

The day of the tourney everyone
ate earlier than on other days.

And then the prince of Thebes, Apollideo,
did not wait long to come outside.
That plant decorated and colored his shield
which hid Peneius's daughter from the sun.[16]
The same branch crowned his crest as well,
for it is the prize and crown of the most illustrious heroes.

53

Next to him the Spartan king, named Algier,
magnanimous and courteous, took his place;
because the one was the other's brother,
they had their exploits in common, as well as their kin.
The first came at a gentle and even pace
on a white Turkish horse, and took the first place.
The other rode a country-bred Spanish horse,
and his colors denoted love and hope.

54

On a slim and fast Barbary horse appeared
the lord of Thessaly among hundreds.
His armaments and his ostentatious and beautiful clothing
adorned him, as was his custom, with a hundred colors.
He was young, and in so large a group
he too intended to show daring that day.
He too, who was called Aliforte, wanted
to enter among the others, and he took the third place.

55

After him Elion, who was lord
of Arcadia, the shepherds' paradise,
entered the lists where he hoped to take
part in the efforts and in the honors.
Painted on his shield he had a panther
with its charming, many-colored coat,

16. For more on the laurel, see above, canto 1.40n.

and with so beautiful and so lovely a sight
it deceives and saddens the simpler beasts.[17]

5 6

Sirio, stronger and more mature in age,
who held in his hand the reins of Lacedaemon,
came carried by a dark bay horse
which had a faint stocking on one hind foot.
His arms and shield were azure;
therein was depicted a book in a hand
since, besides his regal blood and name,
he was a lofty and eminent philosopher and poet.

5 7

Satirion did not fail to appear,
he who commanded the island of Corcyra.
His horse's coat was black and white;
only one star on its forehead could be seen.
His shield portrayed a tired Nereid
who was pulling a large conch onto a rock.
The oyster hid a great treasure of pearls,
and showed the richness of those waves.

5 8

Seventh in the martial group appeared
Clizio, king of the Epirotes near the sea,
mounted on a large and worthy destrier
with rich adornments, golden and fine.
His helm was girded with a rubicund insignia
of precious and splendid rubies.
His emblem was the king of melted ice,
who was striking the sea with his triple-toothed dart.[18]

17. In *The Worth of Women*, 76, Fonte makes the panther represent faithless, deceiving lovers who abandon their lady once she yields to their desires.

18. The god of the sea, Neptune (Roman) or Poseidon (Greek), carries a trident.

5 9

The other was that Stellidone, who not with a joyful
face had crossed the untrustworthy sea,
adorned with black and dark gray silk;
he moved and walked in accordance with his grief.
The king of Cyprus and the king of Crete were missing,
for they were supposed to make a perfect ten.
Indeed the king and all the Attic kindred
marveled at their lagging.

6 0

These ten young men, illustrious and lofty with great esteem,
were selected by the king
as the most valorous and most perfect.
They were to stand against the foreigners,
one by one proving with the results
that they were bold and courageous knights,
with one or more lances in the great square.
But they could not employ rapiers or clubs.

6 1

Upon being knocked down, each of them could
return to the saddle for a new joust;
but against him by whose hand he had been
felled, he could not make a new attempt.
The barbarians had certainly heard the news
of all the rules the king had set.
The order was known to everyone point by point,
and already more than one had appeared on the spot.

6 2

It was a great delight to see
now here, now there, some warrior emerge,
in rich garments according to his own custom,
with varied destriers, shields, and crests.
But in order not to sing always of one subject,

I now turn my thoughts to Risamante,
whom I left with the courteous knight;
she had dismounted and was removing her harness.

6 3

When at the removal of her helmet the knight
knew Risamante was a maiden,
he became so confused in his thoughts
that for quite a long while he looked at her and did not speak.
Meanwhile a clever squire of his
brought a beautiful mantle to the beautiful warrior,
for the gentleman was accustomed to use such courtesy
with those whom he held most worthy.

6 4

Having washed their hands, they sat down
at table. The menservants, ready and willing,
at their command set about serving,
bringing in now new dishes, now cool wine.
While of various boiled and roasted foods
the lady and the knight were partaking,
by chance the knight saw the ring,
illustrious and beautiful, which the lady had on her finger.

6 5

I mean the diamond of infinite value
which the lady had acquired just before.
The knight gazed at it quite a long while,
judging it a jewel of great worth;
and although he was accustomed to seeing gems,
yet he valued and esteemed this one over every other.
Therefore he courteously asked the lady
from whom she had had it, and where.

66

"While I gaze," he said, "at the illustrious ring
which adorns your hand, noble warrior,
I doubt whether one could see
a richer jewel near or far.
This seems to me the most beautiful of diamonds.
I don't know whether it's Arabian or Indian,
but if I judge from its clear color,
then it comes from India, which sends us the best.

67

"All my days I have always delighted
in seeing jewels, and I know a little about them;
but among all the beautiful Nabataean stones,
this which I see here and now is the most beautiful.[19]
Oh, tell me how you enriched yourself with it,
for I desire to know the person and the place.
I want you in courtesy to reveal to me
(if it is not a bother) the way you obtained it."

68

Risamante was not opposed to his
entreaty, though it was quite reluctantly
that she narrated to others her successful feats
and made known her lofty triumphs.
So she made plain to the knight
how she had put an end to the dragon's fierce bites,
and after entering the grotto
she had acquired the gem as a reward.

69

When the knight heard that Risamante
had released the fierce beast from life,

19. Nabataea was a kingdom in northwestern Arabia. See Grant, *Guide to the Ancient World*, 416.

he raised his hands thankfully to the holy and eternal places,
since that plague was dead and buried.
"Now the traveler will be sure,"
he said, "that his life will not be taken,
and the villager and the wanderer
can enjoy the beauty of that garden.

70

"I am happy for that, yes, but far more joyful
because I hope that you might be the lady
who is to liberate me from that trouble
in which I have lived most of my days,
and from whom I hope to have before I die
that treasure which I desired so much and then lost.
And so, I pray heaven that I
have guessed the truth of this matter."

71

Said the lady, "When I find a way
to expose myself to some dangerous undertaking,
I don't draw back; rather I enjoy it more
when it's held for an impossible thing.
Every good knight must have a soul
ready and eager to untie every
intricate knot, whenever it might help
people, as in this matter of the serpent."

72

He added, "Urged by the noble zeal
which usually urges a generous heart,
I too would have set about that feat
for the safety of others and for my honor,
but I doubted whether I might be overcome
because of some magical horror.
I fear enchantments far more than death,
for in that case being bold and strong does not avail."

7 3

So saying the knight let forth
a great sigh, and his face became sad,
nor could he conceal the bitter torment
which showed clearly in his eyes.
The lady burned with pity and desire
to know the cause of this.
She prayed him to tell what new concern seized him,
what great cruelty drove him to weep.

7 4

The knight answered, "Great distress
I felt in recalling the enchantment,
distress for one who has endured it for many years in a castle,
and this caused me pain and tears."
But I hope to recount to you in the next canto
the hard and unjust fate which this fellow had.
There you will hear how man often,
through ignorance, bewails his good fortune.

CANTO 6

ARGUMENT

Nicobaldo recounts to the woman warrior
how he came to be Lucimena's lover
and gained her for his wife, and of the cruel
lady who caused him to undergo great torment,
the deceit she practiced on him and the manner
she used to draw him into her net,
how he then released himself from that tangle,
and the prediction the friendly wizard gave him.

1

No one can guess the end of his venture,
whether it will be unhappy or joyful,
nor what heaven destines for his life,
no matter how learned and intelligent he may be.
Just as, when still in the morning hours,
if dawn opens the way for the bright sun,
or if in rising the sun emerges among clouds,
who knows whether the day will end up clear or dark?

2

Because of this no one must go sure
of his fortune when he lives in a happy condition,
nor should he ever despair when fate is dark,
contrary, and opposed to his desire.
For often a man believes that some
thing is harmful to him, and hates and avoids it,

189

but it turns out to his benefit; or he believes a thing
will bring him good, and yet it ends up badly for him.

3

Just so it happened to the knight
who gave hospitality to the courageous maiden.
He risked wasting away
over something which was later very agreeable to him,
as I will recount to you point by point,
if you come to hear the story I have planned.
I said that a bitter torment gripped his soul
and the lady asked him the cause.

4

"A cruel cause," answered the knight,
"which makes my days disturbed and sad,
having returned now to my mind,
forced me to weep as you saw,
because I remembered the cruel enchantment
(I don't know if you have ever heard of it),
which has lasted many years in a castle
called the Castle of Fear.

5

"There, if a lady or a knight arrives,
so great a fright comes upon that person's heart
that he cannot avoid being captured
or killed there, with fierce, bitter torment.
The beautiful eyes for which I lived content,
perhaps they too were deprived of the light there.
My beloved, my life, and my comfort
(who was captured there, alas) perhaps is dead.

6

"But so that the harsh grief which torments
and scourges me may be more open and clear to you,
know that some years ago Love gripped me

for the beauty of a noble maiden.
Nor can I complain, since beautiful Lucimena's
heart was always directed to me.
Lucimena is her name; I am Nicobaldo,
who burned for her with amorous heat.

7

"In a rich and prosperous city
in Lydia I was born of honored parents.
I wish I had not been, or that heaven had taken me
in my most beautiful and charming years,
before my greedy and furtive eyes
had come to see the angelic countenance.
She was born in the same city,
of equal condition, of the same age as I.[1]

8

"The time had come when a solemn
holiday was celebrated in honor of Minerva,[2]
when all the virgins always assembled,
for the city observes this custom.
Here with others Lucimena came;
here she saw me and became my servant,
and I came into her service,
for I pleased her eyes, and she pleased mine.

9

"We started to reveal to each other our new affection
with sighs, faithful ministers of love.
We stole each other's heart with our glances,
and, silent, we alternately gave out shouts.
All the others enjoyed various delights:
seeing jousts, hearing sounds and cheerful shrieks,

---

1. The idea that the damsel should be the same age as the man was certainly not common in the fiction of the time, which was instead crowded by suspicious mature men and vulnerable damsels in distress.
2. The Roman goddess of wisdom.

admiring pomp, horses, and armed heroes;
we that day saw nothing but each other.

10

"Once the divine and honored holiday
is ended with the clear and shining day,
grieving and sad she leaves me,
and bitter and distressed I part from her.
But her noble countenance remains in my heart,
nor can I ever get it out of my mind.
Rather, the new thought which Love impresses on me
drives away and pushes aside every old thought.

11

"Since every hour my great desire
gets hotter, and my affection grows and abounds,
and since constantly the strength grows in my breast
of that flame which burns it and encircles it,
since I cannot forget her,
I strive at least for her to share my feelings;
for the man who catches and falls into a grave illness
immediately has recourse to the doctor.

12

"Since from her alone can come the medicine
which will heal my afflicted and infirm heart,
I find a way to entice my queen,
and I reveal to her my firm and tenacious ailment.
The beautiful lady bends to my prayer,
for she too finds no defense against love;
but because decorum restrained her,
perhaps she loved more and showed it less.

13

"Beyond the looks, the greetings, and the happy gestures,
which with a chaste mind she gave me,
such grace and such great favor I obtained

(since she was never rebellious against me)
that I came to honest conversations with her.
Therein I find her as courteous as
she is beautiful, and favorable to my desires,
provided I am disposed to make her my wife.

1 4

"Nothing else do I seek and plan
(for this is the goal of every good lover);[3]
when I hear her plan in conformance with mine,
you can well imagine whether I was delighted.
We had no other delay, no other restraint
from making plain our secret feelings,
except that at that time, to our distress,
Lucimena's father was not in Lydia.

1 5

"For this reason it does not seem right to me to say anything
to mine, because I hope in a few days
every delay will be made null and void,
when the one whom I desire as father-in-law returns.
Then I will have my father ask for the girl
without waiting any longer,
for if I reveal my heart to him at the wrong time,
perhaps he will change his mind before that time.

1 6

"Meanwhile I often find easy and adroit ways
to feast my eyes on her beloved countenance,
nor is her sweet and gentle gaze removed from me,
whether in the temples or at her window.
Often she welcomes me to speak
with her, for she comes to a room on the ground floor

---

3. Notwithstanding Nicobaldo's sweeping statement, in this period it is exclusively in women's literature that men "naturally" desire to marry the women they love before they aim at satisfying any sexual desire. Orlando and Rinaldo in the *Furioso*, for example, "love" Angelica, but they are already married.

with a low iron balcony
that overlooks an unfrequented place.

17

"There, on account of the long delay which oppresses us,
we give out frequent and fervid sighs,
and we complain bitterly together.
I weep for her torments, she weeps for mine.
Then each gives the other comfort and hope
that we will soon reach the goal of our desires,
saying that evil is followed by good,
and the sun always comes after the rain.

18

"Now, with matters standing thus, my father was obliged
to leave home as our king commanded;
he wanted to send him to Syria
to the king, who happily welcomed him as ambassador.
Think whether I regretted it,
whether Lucimena grieved with me,
because if her father returns first,
we must still delay as before.

19

"But neither of them came, for with weeping and pains
we saw the sixth new moon come out.
Whether awaiting someone who never comes
is a great torment, we had proof of it then.
Our desire grew, our hope dwindled.
At last I rejoice to hear
that my father is coming back; and (where I had thought
to feel joy) at his coming, I feel immense anguish.

20

"With the royal business completed, my father returns,
and upon his return increases my suffering,
telling me that shortly he hopes and believes

he will give me a beautiful and honorable wife.
With this word he wounds my heart;
he takes my life, blood, and soul,
such that I can barely move my tongue and breath to tell him
that at the moment I do not want a wife by my side.

21

"He is by nature irascible,
and only a small flame warms his heart.
When he hears me contradict him,
he is all filled with wrath and furor.
I hide from his paternal ire,
and full of sorrow I run to my goddess;
I tell her the plan of my father,
too obstinate, harsh, and capricious a man.

22

"'Wretched us,' she answers, 'for we are
oppressed by precisely the same misery.
This morning my father too arrived,
which made my heart extremely happy,
hoping that at last the hour and the moment
had come when my soul's pain would lessen,
and we might put an end to so much desire,
which has made me constantly sigh and weep.'

23

"So saying she burst out in such pain
that her tears prevented her continuing,
and she so confused and interrupted herself
that she strove hard but was unable to speak.
Although I cannot hear it, her torment
breaks the restraint of my steadfastness,
and I too weep for the unspoken pain
which so afflicts Lucimena's heart.

24

"At last, sobbing strongly, she says,
'Now our sorrow is truly ended.
You will be the husband of another consort,
leaving me, who adore and venerate only you;
and I will take a husband of another sort,
who is not you, who alone had the right to me.
Alas, I want to die before
anyone has me but you, my sweetheart.

25

"'Know, my darling, that I heard my father
tell my mother in secret
how from a distance he arranged a marriage
for me; I know not with whom, for he doesn't say.
It suffices that soon he intends to give me a husband
with whom, in his opinion, I will be happy.
In the meantime he wants her to see to
tidying up the house and putting it in order.

26

"'My father,' she added, 'is no less fierce,
no less harsh than yours, nor less cruel.
Therefore I must either die, or stay under
his rule and set my course to another love.
Oh, our ill-founded and vain plan!
How will you turn out, O faithful love of ours?
Ah, my Nicobaldo, what way, what method
can we ever employ to untangle such a knot?'

27

"As if a mountain fell on me,
I am oppressed by the heavy weight
of the sad news. I cannot give
her a ready answer, and I am paralyzed.

I was not before so overcome and beaten down
as I am now, seized by the new trouble
which burdens me and clutches me so strongly
that I seem to be on the point of death.

28

"I use every art to console her, every deed.
I leave there languid and sorrowful,
and to think on it I betake myself
to the now hateful paternal walls.
I find the whole house turned upside down,
since my father is determined to make me a husband,
and against my plans and my desires
he wants me to obey him and take a wife.

29

"Now I boldly refuse, now I make entreaties,
so that he might change and turn away from his decision,
and not bind me to the hateful yoke,
and dissolve the completed arrangements.
But it does not avail that I beseech and refuse him,
for he wants me to take a wife despite myself.[4]
If I don't do it he threatens to drive me
out of the house and, what's more, to disinherit me.

30

"He says he does not want to make an enemy
of such a family through my foolishness,
nor for people throughout the city to say of him
that he dissolves and breaks his promises.

---

4. Women's inability to marry without their father's approval has often been remarked upon, but men's need to follow a father's fiat in the same matter has received only scant attention. Yet it was specifically to control both men's and women's choice of a marriage partner that the Counter-Reformation imposed the rule that marriage banns had to be posted for an extended period of time at a church's door before a wedding could take place. For more on marriage laws, see the Volume Editor's Introduction.

Besides, there is no woman in all Lydia
more noble, more modest, or possessed of greater beauty
than she whom he can give me,
with a rich and honorable dowry.[5]

31

"When I understand my father's
obstinate mood which keeps getting firmer,
all night, desperate, I think
of risking myself in every rough, cruel venture,
and of being deprived of all my possessions,
of suffering every hard and sharp pain,
rather than ever abandoning the beautiful lady
who was always so courteous to me.

32

"To flee Lydia and take her with me
would have been a good plan,
to go to the Italian or Greek realms
or some other distant region,
and live for some time as an exile with her
until heaven sent a better season;
but I cannot do this in an instant,
and the impious nuptials were too far advanced.

33

"Indeed I don't fear for myself, but what matters
is that she perforce will be rebellious against me;
for if a man is forced to submit to his father,
what can a weak damsel do?
I fear also that the pain she bears
will kill the unhappy girl, and me with her.
If she dies, I cannot live,
for I breathe with her breath, she with mine.

5. Valeria Miani will express the same concepts in setting up the love story of her Celinda in Lydia, a region of Turkey. See *Celinda*.

34

"This cruel thought becomes so fixed
in me that I seem already to see her lifeless.
Already such great torment afflicts my heart,
and my soul is bound with so much pity,
that before the virgin shade, sundered from her
mortal body, might pass the dark Stygian wave,
I am indeed content (ah, fierce and unjust fate)
that another take her in hand, provided she does not perish.

35

"As she and I have tried every way
to destroy her father's cruel plan,
and since she cannot impede wicked destiny
from going forward and running to its goal,
rather than that she kill herself with poison
or the sword, or be overcome by unworthy grief,
I am content that the new husband have her
in his power, and that she be another's instead of mine.

36

"With this opinion, when the day comes
I jump out of bed. As love inflames me,
I go out from my home and return to the window
where the distressed maiden awaits me.
I see her hair more adorned than usual,
and she is all shining with gems and gold.
This was a dagger in my breast,
for then I suspected what was actually the case.

37

"From this sudden change I reason
that she is to take a husband that day,
and such great agony I feel in my heart
that I decide to live no longer.
It is true that I would die less unhappy,

if I didn't believe her death to be imminent.
Therefore I entreat her, my lady and goddess,
that if she cannot be mine, let her be another's, and live.

38

"Let her not be so distressed that she takes
her own life and dries up the flower of her youthful years,
for I promise her as well to ease my grief
with every effort, and to mitigate my anxieties.
Not that my heart will ever be released from that net
in which love's snares captured me,
for although our bodies may be separated, together
our hearts will live until our final hours.

39

"Weeping, she wants to answer me,
but in that moment she is called (I believe) by her father.
So she leaves, and I go wandering
like a doe pursued by greyhounds.
More than one relative with a friendly and pleasant
expression approaches me with greetings,
rejoices with me and takes delight
in that one thing which grieves and vexes me.

40

"All are around me, and my old father,
weeping from bliss and sorrow,
and my dear mother with many ladies
who have come to do honor to my nuptials.
I go amid the hateful crowds
and, overcome by the rage in my heart,
made audacious by ire, I protest to them
that they might lead me wherever they please,

41

"yet I will never consent to what
they plan to do against my will.

With this speech my weeping overflows,
so that I can barely see where I'm going.
Meanwhile they go, and I with them, to the place
where I must unwillingly take a wife,
where the bride, so much hated
by me, must be ready and waiting.

42

"I swear at her and curse her forever,
although she is not guilty of my torment.
As if I had some long-established hate against her,
I wish her every ill fortune.
My father was so great a friend of the king
that he was content for my union
to be celebrated in the royal palace,
and so all of us went there.

43

"We climbed the magnificent royal stairs
and arrived in the hall, where there was a great
court of men and women, all adorned and sumptuous
as befitted their status.
These were the bride's relatives,
who desired to make me her consort.
Richly adorned, she too was seated
among these friendly and honorable people.

44

"But when, exhausted and overcome by sorrow,
I raise my eyes, still sighing,
and I look the maiden in the face
(she in seeing me becomes disconcerted and pale),
I am nearly beside myself
from a joy which suddenly seizes me—
because I see her, and I recognize her, and I barely believe it,
for this is my dear Lucimena:

45

"she whom I bear constantly fixed in my heart,
and who values me more than her own life;
she whom I had so much sorrow
in leaving that even thinking of it breaks my heart.
I cannot tell you which was greater in us
then, whether wonder or happiness.
Each of us looks at the other and says not a word,
brought from one extreme to the other.

46

"We realize we have made the passage
from an extreme torment to an extreme joy,
when we were most deprived of every hope,
when our hearts were most wretched and afflicted.
Of necessity I brighten up my sad expression,
and show clearly my pleasure in my face.
At this all of my people are cheered, for they perceive
the great change which comes over me.

47

"I learned then that when our fathers were
traveling back toward our homeland together,
since each one's stock
was quite similar in wealth and lineage,
they had contracted between them the marriage
which made us happy beyond all hope.
But what good is it, if my happiness was
late and slow in coming, and quick to disappear?

48

"I cannot express to you precisely
with what unhoped-for bliss and what joy
I was then joined in matrimony

with her, whom I will love forever until I die.[6]
But to come to the tearful moment
which gave me torment and trouble again,
and so that you may know that among us no good fortune
ever lasts, listen to a cruel disaster.

49

"After our most sweet nuptials
were legitimately celebrated,
and we were by the gods' grace
married with a most solemn ceremony,
and I bring to my home her
with whom I had so greatly desired marriage,
all my cares and all my thoughts
are to give her each day entertainment and pleasures.

50

"One day (wretched me!) I lead her outside
into this villa full of delights:
clear waters, green plants, pleasant flowers,
delightful hills, cool shade, serene air.
I find dogs, horses, and hunters
to give new delight to Lucimena.
Desiring to do something to please her,
I go out with her one morning to hunt.

6. The figure of the faithful, loyal, and honest Nicobaldo seems to be drawn upon that of Zerbino in the *Furioso*, whose constant faith Ariosto fulsomely celebrates: "A pledge, whether sworn only to one or to a thousand, ought never to be broken. And in a wood or cave, far from towns and habitations, just as in the courts amid a throng of witnesses, amid documents and codicils, a promise should be enough on its own, without an oath or more specific token" (21.2). But faithfulness is also at the core of Brandimarte and Fiordiligi's story in the *Furioso* and of Brandimarte and Fiordelisa's story in Boiardo's *Innamorato*. Fonte too praises the devotion of the true lover in *The Worth of Women*: "The man who loves from the depth of his heart desires nothing, hopes for nothing, and demands nothing except to be loved in return; he keeps within the bounds of decency; stands in awe of the woman he loves; loves her in her presence; praises her in her absence; interests himself not only in her but in everything that concerns her, as though it were his own business" (80–81). Still, in tune with her usual characterization of men, Fonte constructs Nicobaldo as essentially powerless, first victimized by his father and then by a witch. He even needs a woman, Risamante, to free his wife.

51

"Some people spread on the plain fine nets
to entangle the robust animals.
Others lie in wait at the most secret passages
and hold in hand a lance, or a skewer, or a dart.
Some hold the leash of the bold and excited dogs.
No one is lazy or slow to act.
Meanwhile a nimble roebuck springs forth,
and I spur my destrier after him.[7]

52

"Lucimena, companion most sweet,
urges her horse to full speed as well.
Because she never departs from me,
we both chase the slim and agile beast.
The beast emerges from the wood into an open,
ample countryside, and we follow it.
It took us so far
that we no longer heard the hunters or dogs.

53

"In the end we lost sight of the animal,
so we were about to turn back,
when a lady with a merry expression
came toward us on a destrier.
As soon as she laid eyes on me,
she was struck in the heart by Love's arrow.
So charming my face seemed to her
that in a moment it kindled and burned her heart.

---

7. The scene in which Nicobaldo goes after an elusive roebuck and loses himself in the Castle of Fear recalls a similar scene in the *Innamorato* in which Brandimarte, who is looking for his wife Fiordelisa, is attracted by the stag of the Treasure Fairy and spurs after him, but, as in Fonte, "its spell was so strong, no man could catch it, even if he flew, and Brandimarte chased in vain for all that day, across the plain" (2.12.60). Unlike Nicobaldo, Brandimarte will be able later to find Fiordelisa in the hands of a wild man.

54

"Having noticed my lady, who was lovelier
than she, she immediately thought that I
had set my heart on this lady,
and that all my thoughts were of her.
But feeling the new wound
which was consuming her with fervid desire for me,
she thinks to herself, in order to have me with her,
she will see to the demise of the girl I have with me.

55

"This woman was an impious enchantress's
maid, sent around by her
to draw to her unhappy walls
all the warriors of Lydia and the region.
She is no less a betrayer of every
damsel, nor does she cause them less outrage and humiliation.
So with various lies, some sad, some cheerful,
she constantly draws some incautious person into the net

56

"and leads him to that sorrowful castle,
the Castle of Fear as it's called,
where dwells the deceitful sorceress
who lays snares for everyone in the Lydian state.
Now this iniquitous woman, her servant,
has thought up a new invention;
facing my beautiful lady,
so false and wicked she speaks and says,

57

"'Are you not going, beautiful lady, where so many
damsels compete with each other in beauty,
with this your fair husband or lover here,
to that new and adventurous undertaking?
There is in a castle not far away

an adventure where everyone vies;
and because there one employs neither lance nor sword,
the endeavor is charming and pleases all.

58

"'The case is this: on the shore of a lake
is a mermaid bound to a tree
with a golden cord. As a wizard has said,
she can never be freed and unbound
if by good fortune a knight does not reach this shore
with the most beautiful image
of a lady born in the world today,
and he the most faithful man alive in the world.

59

"'He through the excellence of his fidelity
must release the knot with her help,
through her beauty which surpasses all others,
and so she will have the boast of being the most beautiful.
Every warrior who sees himself as faithful
runs to the trial, and every noble damsel.
Some loosen more, some less the tight cord,
depending on how beautiful the visage, how faithful the heart.[8]

60

"'He who releases her will be blessed in the world,
for besides being considered the most faithful,
he will acquire that rich and joyful cord
which has great virtue against every cruel heart.
The man who bears so rich a weight
will never find his lady unfaithful,
for the fateful chain will have the power
to make her always turn her heart to him.

8. Mermaids are typically used in fiction to pursue, mirror, or fulfill erotic aims. To use a mermaid as a test of faithfulness is a new narrative twist.

61

"'To this point no one has ever yet been so worthy
as to release the biform creature.
Yet when I gaze at you,
with your warrior here who is so close a match,
I seem to see the bond released by you both,
since you surpass in form the most beautiful
women who have reached this shore,
and thus this man has cause to be faithful to you.'

62

"Alas, having faith in her words,
we beseeched her to accompany us,
because my lady is a sun of beauty,
and in fidelity I yield to no one.[9]
She, who perceives her plan goes just as
she wants, makes our trip delightful.
We rode several days until we reached
the bridge where knights are so greatly shamed.

63

"Beyond the bridge is the castle of which I spoke,
where the iniquitous sorceress dwells.
Without any suspicion I cross the bridge
behind the lady, and Lucimena too.
Suddenly such fright fills up my breast
that I don't rightly know what to do then.
I tremble with great fear, and wish to flee
elsewhere and hide, and I don't know where.

9. Trials in which men defended their women's superior beauty were typical in chivalric lit-
erature, but tests of a man's fidelity to his lady reflect a fresh new way of looking at gendered
relationships and at what most matters to women.

64

"I throw myself from my destrier, for even that
frightens me. I forget my lady and everything,
and I flee like a timid lamb
that fears the greedy wolf's fangs.
The water that flows under the little bridge
encircled the castle, as I recall;
someone had raised the bridge,
so there was no escape for me.

65

"Now to conclude, I was taken and bound
by wicked people who approached me,
and cruelly locked in prison;
and the same happened to Lucimena.
For many days then I was so scourged
that I don't know which of the gods kept me alive.
At last one night the deceiving woman
comes where I abide unhappy and alone.

66

"I speak of the one who used on me the deception
of the mermaid and who was so inflamed
for me, who caused me the harm
at which my soul will always be offended.
The wicked woman feels my horrible anguish
in her breast, weighing down her heart;
she steals the key to my gloomy prison,
and comes alone in the dark to find me.

67

"Having no way to make the excuse
that she did not bitterly offend me,
confessing her error, she accuses Love,
who placed the wicked thought in her mind.
She says she has enclosed in her heart such a wound

for my love that he must indeed be powerful.
To beseech she came; and if I will be
her friend, she intends to release me from that predicament.

6 8

"She promises and swears to liberate me
from the prison, provided that I favor and love her,
and to extract me from the Castle of Fear,
a name that's certainly appropriate.
I care only for Lucimena,
nor shall I ever adore and desire another.
Since I heard this proposal
from the one who had so betrayed us,

6 9

"you can imagine what rage came to me then,
when she laid out her lascivious thought to me.
If I had not been bound in chains,
by Jove, she would not have departed in one piece!
But I must perforce restrain myself,
and swallow my ineffectual fury.
I make no response to the impious and dishonest woman,
but I tremble like the sea in a storm.[10]

10. The story of the "iniqua donna" (dishonest woman) is modeled upon that of the "iniqua femina" or "femina iniqua" of Ariosto (*Orlando furioso* 21.15, 21.19)—the perfidious Gabrina, who set her eyes on her brother-in-law, Philander, and put him in prison when he refused to have sex with her. Like Fonte's witch, "almost daily she [Gabrina] visited him in prison, for she had the keys and let herself in at her pleasure./She kept assailing my brother, even more boldly than before. . . . 'If you do my pleasure I shall see to restoring your freedom and your reputation'" (21.29.31). But in Nicobaldo's case, the refusal to have sex comes from his decision not to be unfaithful to his wife, while in Philander's case he denies himself because his act would be incestuous: "'Never!' cried Philander. 'Never hope that my fidelity will prove false to itself. Though I endure such merciless treatment, quite at odds with my deserving, and everyone thinks the worse of me, it is enough for me that to the all-seeing One, who can revive me with eternal grace, my innocence is plainly evident.'" (21.32). Unlike Ariosto, Fonte refuses once more here, as in the Circetta episode, to create a totally evil woman—or even a completely ugly one, the two attributes that defined failed womanhood in the literature of the time. Instead, she makes her deceiver eventually repent of her "fallo" (the Italian word works both in the sense of "mistake" and in that of "phallus," an irony that was surely intentional).

70

"She entreats me, and in beseeching finds
all the terms of humility that she can.
Since her prayers and weeping prove useless,
she adds these to her first notes:
'Cruel man, since loving you does not help me,
nor bathing my eyes and cheeks with tears,
since it doesn't please you to give me an answer,
I mean to depart; stay in peace.

71

"'It grieves me, for you will wish, once it's too late,
that you took my trustworthy advice.
I want to tell you what you don't know,
and Jove knows how much sorrow I take at it,
for tomorrow you will certainly be
taken from prison and led to the ultimate peril,
for this custom always abides here.
Today it was another's turn, tomorrow yours.

72

"'Whenever another warrior does not arrive here,
they will lay hands on the damsels next,
and your consort might easily
be one of those in a very short time.[11]
How much better it would be (if you care so much for her
that you don't want to betray her for another woman)
if you save yourself, for perhaps before she dies
you will yet find a way to save her.

11. The custom in which one person per day is sacrificed in an abandoned, lugubrious place
recalls Ariosto's description in the *Furioso* of the Island of Ebuda, on whose shores one chained
beautiful woman per day is destined to be eaten by a marine monster. Angelica is the first to be
threatened by the fury of the sea orc until Ruggiero rescues her in canto 10; then the paladin
Orlando liberates the new would-be victim, Olimpia, before killing the marine monster in
canto 11. See also Boiardo's Crudel Rocca. Ovid's Ariadne (*Heroides* 10) is, of course, the clas-
sical source for the story.

73

"'Great was my error. I know and I see
that I should not have thought, let alone done this.
But I don't know how I might undo what's been
done, although I am sincerely repentant.
Ah, why do you seek to go from bad to worse?
You have lost part and you want to lose the rest.
Ah, do not let that punishment that I
deserve come to you, my lord.

74

"'Don't persist in doing such harm to yourself
for the great hate that, with good reason, you bear me.
I don't want to be comforted by anything else,
if not that I have put you outside of the castle.
And so that you may know as well that it matters to me,
how much the error I committed weighs on me,
I promise you to place my own life at risk
to give (if I can) aid to your lady as well.'

75

"Confessing an error with humble acts,
with infinite tears and with entreaties,
has great power over noble minds,
just as I learned then from experience.
I hear the true and subtle reasons
she finds, and already more than half
the vengeful resolve fades in me,
so it seems to me that she speaks the truth.

76

"After I had reflected privately somewhat,
more to give some aid to my goddess
than for my sake, I agreed to be helped
by her, who had become so repentant.

So I was unchained—my arms and back
and legs and feet were all in irons—
and taken by her out of the prison,
and even out of the fatal castle's encircling walls.[12]

77

"But when I found only myself at liberty,
without her whom I prized more than myself,
think for yourself what apprehension and compassion
I felt for her, and what was the state of my heart.
I went sighing through the streets,
and I didn't know (like a blind man) where I was going.
And it was true that I was blind,
for my sun's ray was not with me.

78

"I came to wish to return to the castle
where my heart had been stolen and taken from me,
and to undergo for her every cruel danger,
for it's not good with one captive and the other released.
But a wizard made my thoughts restless.
Turned to pity by my great miseries,
all compassionate he came to find me
so that I might take some repose.

79

"'Calm down,' he told me, 'Nicobaldo,
for you cannot be happy for a few years.
It's enough that she whom you love dearly
will not be taken to the final torment.
Consider my words firm and steadfast,
for you must await the arrival
of a regal girl, illustrious and beautiful,
who will go armed like a warrior in the saddle.

---

12. Again Fonte uses the word *girone*. See above, canto 5.22n. The devilish connotation is more obviously appropriate here.

80

"'So that you may have true knowledge
of your fated consoler,
know that one evening she is to lodge
in your shelters (happy host!),
and she will tell you she was victor
over a fierce serpent in a garden.
But before she will make your soul joyful,
she must become a queen and a wife.'

81

"He told me of the ring and that it has power
against every fierce and frightful enchantment,
so I know I am not in error,
and you are the one I have awaited so long.
Thus at your coming I take heart,
royal maiden, and I am consoled somewhat,
seeing everything the wizard told me then
has in fact come true now.

82

"So I implore you, please
remember me, a poor lover,
once you have effected your plans
of which the wise Celidante told me."
Here the warrior put an end to his words,
leaving Risamante very glad,
because the wizard in his narration
was hers, the one she loved like a father,

83

the one who raised her from childhood
after he took her from her father the king,
the one from whom she learned the discipline
of wearing arms and showing valor.
Now since she truly must be a queen,

she plans to put into effect the thought in her heart;
she plans to unite many peoples together,
and then to move against her sister.

84

She does not delay to offer
her forces thereafter to the courteous knight.
Meanwhile the servants, since the hour was late,
had brought many lighted candles.
At their coming, the courteous lord took
the brave young woman by the hand,
and conducted her to an exquisite abode,
where she slept until the day appeared.

85

But I promise to tell you in another place
what happened with this maiden.
I intend to say no more of her now than what I have said,
nor how she found herself in various places
where, with that perfect valor she had,
she performed great feats and strove in such a manner
that the knight of the white lily
was deemed brave and courageous over all others.

86

Nor shall I say that when she had united together
her peoples whom she gathered from many realms,
she waged against Biondaura a terrible war,
so that in Armenia she took every city from her;
because I am returning to Athens where the desire
for glory gathered daring peoples into one place.
But in order not to be tedious to those who listen to me,
it will be good for me to discourse of it at another time.

CANTO 7

ARGUMENT

*As the prize for the tourney, the king proposes
a royal crown. Silvarte's son
wishes to compete, and the king opposes his
desire. Filardo makes him leave with a deception;
he returns armed. Love, who makes him the prisoner
of Celsidea, again makes him withdraw.
Circe's daughter welcomes
Silano, who kindles her heart with his handsome visage.*

1

Two spurs strongly grip our heart.
One is the common desire to acquire fame;
the other the natural stimulus of love
which a man bears for her whom he adores and desires.
Very powerful by itself is the zeal for honor,
and likewise amorous desire alone;
but when joined, what heart is so constant
that it could resist both the one and the other emotion?

2

These were the powerful reasons
that made so many strong kings and valiant knights
from extremely distant regions
come then to the Attic city.
For no other cause did so many people arrive there

215

than to see the angelic beauty
of Celsidea, of whom they had heard the news,
and to go forth to compete in that tourney.

3

All the people of Greece are already in place
to judge and examine the knights,
and they are discontent because not immediately
do they see lances shatter, destriers unburdened.
Now while they are disposed to await
that signal loved by the fiercest minds,
behold, the lofty prize which is reserved for the victor
is carried by with superb and magnificent pomp.

4

Bright and shining, of rich gems
a crown was formed, and of gold.
Vulcan at his blazing forge
never made a worthier or nobler work.
The wife of that god who coursed through
the Orient and carried away the triumphal laurel
never wore such on her beautiful locks
before it shone in the sky among the other stars.[1]

5

Every illustrious soul admires the promised gift
as much for its workmanship as for its richness,
but more because it is to be a gift from that palm
which everyone praises and esteems so much.
As a reward to the knight who will gain the victory,
she who surpasses all others in beauty,
the noble Celsidea, with her own hand
is to give that superb and rare prize.

1. The god Dionysus traveled through Egypt, India, and Thrace, overcoming repeated armed resistance. Later he married Ariadne and placed her bridal chaplet among the stars as the constellation Corona.

6

Meanwhile youthful Floridoro
near Cleardo leans on a balcony,
gazing at the worthy and regal assembly
of so many illustrious heroes in the field.
With them are other kings, other princes,
who encumber all the levels of the loggia.
The ladies, far scarcer in view,
have not yet appeared at the windows.

7

Although the king with the most senior
princes stays to admire so worthy a show,
Sorinda the queen, and with her Celsidea,
out in the hall do not yet show themselves.
Because of the great concourse of lords
who had come to honor the tourney,
they did not want to come forth, but stayed
withdrawn several days far from the crowds.

8

Now, as I said, the gracious son
of Silvarte, who holds Mycenae in guard,
is admiring that noble converse
near prudent Athena's king.
His eyes blaze and his face is vermilion.
The blood boils in his every vein,
so inflamed is he by a noble urge
to join the fair and elect number.

9

He cannot have repose, peace, or quiet,
his youthful furor consumes him so.
With tacit and unspoken words
he condemns the king's excessive fear,
since for too much love he does not let him

release from his heart so honorable a thirst.
The king does not grant him leave to arm himself and joust,
for he does not believe valor is found at so tender an age.

10

He loves him like a son, and consequently fears
that he might suffer an outrage.
The more he entreats him the less he consents,
for he wants to enjoy his beautiful radiance longer.
He calls him an incautious and imprudent boy
who seeks to engage in so perilous an attempt,
who tries to expose himself to certain peril,
when he is unfit and inexperienced with weapons.

11

Like a generous and noble destrier
that wants to run in a pleasant green field,
if by a wise and experienced rider
he is restrained against his will,
he stamps now and again the path with his foot,
and snorts impatiently and gnaws the bit,
nor can he stay still in that place nor in this,
but he circles around and breathes flame and fire;

12

just so the daring youth who desires and yearns
to go out among so many knights
is all enraged with resentment and pain,
since the king who loves him so much holds him back.
He feels that if he goes out on the field and has courage,
he too will acquire splendor and fame.
Now while he waits in such affliction,
a messenger arrives and presents him with a paper.

13

A dear companion of his, who had risen
from his side before lunch,

who loved him with a sincere and holy love,
and was called Filardo of Crete,
with whom he held in common laughter and weeping,
good and ill, the sad state and the glad,
in order to do him a particular favor, performed
a fine act, which I now want to impart to you.

1 4

He had noticed the young man sorrowing
because the king did not want him to go to the joust;
so, knowing well how valiant
he was, and at an age to employ the lance and sword,
he had considered prudently
which was the best way in that affair
to fulfill the youth's plans,
without the king's finding out and getting angry.

1 5

Once he had conceived the way
(for he was full of shrewdness and prudence),
at the right time he loosened his tongue
and asked the king's permission to depart.
All intent on his planned deception
he left the lofty presence of so many heroes,
and provided himself in secret
with arms and horses, diligently and speedily.

1 6

With no other delay before the deed
(once he was provided with arms and destrier),
he girded on the shining metal,
and called in a great hurry one of his squires.
Pretending to be sad, he threw himself
swiftly ahorse, and pensively
handed him a false letter,
and ordered him to take it to Floridoro.

17

He feigned a sorrowful and pious face,
so full of pity, so lacking in pride,
that the sanest judgment could err,
and believe his deception and his grief.
The servant set out timidly after Floridoro
and presented him with the consigned paper,
precisely when his heart was blazing
with ire and vexation, as is told above.

18

In King Cleardo's presence the boy takes
and opens and reads the writing he's received,
which the name signed below informs him
is by the hand of Filardo's father.
The tenor is that an all-too-vigorous illness
had so oppressed and afflicted the spirit
of his wife, Filardo's mother,
that it had brought her to the point of death.

19

He says that if she matters to him at all,
if his desire is to see her alive,
let him come away swiftly to her before that illness
sends her soul to the cruel Stygian realm.
Before she makes her last farewell,
he entreats him to come and perform every pious act;
nor let there be anything elsewhere which might impede
her son from seeing his mother's bones.

20

He adds that she has nothing else on her tongue
than her Filardo in that extreme suffering,
and often she comes to recall as well
Floridoro whom she considers as a son.
In these two she places all her hope

for a single last loving comfort.
Thus he too as a father exhorts him
not to wait to hear that she is dead.

21

Floridoro reads and is so upset,
he is so moved with compassion,
that he cannot hold back from his eyes the tears
which, streaming down his beautiful face, fall to his breast.
He comes then to remember how much
he went through in Dictaean regions,
when he as a tender infant made the passage to Crete,
where he received so much affection.[2]

22

Recalling the writer and her who, infirm,
is at any moment about to close her eyes,
he knows in his heart he has a firm and stable
obligation to her, such that he could never repay her.
And now he sees it confirmed
by the compassion she demonstrates in her extreme woe,
the maternal love and zeal which she bears
him while yet she enjoys the mortal veil.[3]

23

For this, weeping he bows to the king
and with a most sweet and gentle voice
he beseeches that he might plow the Idaean waters
to see the lady to whom he has such an obligation.[4]
The noble and divine speech moves the king
to grant him grace to take ship.
Again he bows to the king and to Silvarte,
and thence to reach Filardo departs.

2. Mount Dicte is located on Crete.
3. This is not the only time Fonte refers to the earthly body as the veil of the soul.
4. Ida is another mountain on Crete.

24

As when Phoebus hides his golden rays,
the world remains blind and shadowed,
just so that court is left dark and sad
at so much beauty's being removed from there.
Now while Floridoro intends to depart,
for the desire to joust no longer bothers him,
he sees a knight of fierce aspect
come toward him on a white destrier.

25

The knight adorned with white armaments
aims his lance and comes to encounter him.
The youth rides unarmored,
nor does he have other weapons than his sword,
and in the street no living man is seen,
for all the people gather in the square;
yet he does not want to flee from the knight
who so discourteously comes to assail him.

26

He stops his horse and with great heart awaits him;
he wraps up his cloak and takes his sword in hand.
The other, who comes quicker than an arrow,
when near him pulls back the reins,
and raises his lance and uncovers hurriedly
to Floridoro his sought-after face—
for the boy, raising his gaze to him,
recognizes his most sweet Filardo.

27

With the pleasure one has in suddenly
obtaining an unanticipated delight,
he embraces tightly his dear companion,
as true friendship requires.[5]

5. The "true friendship" that distinguishes the relationship of Floridoro and Filardo echoes
classical examples, such as Homer's Achilles and Patroklos; Virgil's Euryalus and Nisus; and

Having satisfied in great part their affection,
Filardo recounts how he took this
course and used this deception
to draw him away from there, and do him a favor.

28

He adds then that he is holding
aside for him a strong suit of armor,
and a fair destrier far whiter than snow
that he found by chance in a stable;
nor, in his opinion, should he wear
any insignia on his left side or his helm.
Floridoro is delighted at this announcement,
and I could not tell how much he thanks and praises him.

29

And embracing him again, he tells him,
"My dear Filardo, you alone in the world
can make me glad and happy,
and on your account I may say I am the happiest of all."
While he praises and blesses him,
together they enter a secret dwelling,
which, far from the town squares and the tumult,
seems apt to their hidden need.

30

There Filardo had already prepared
arms for Floridoro which would humiliate
pure snow, and, both having dismounted,
he and a page help him put them on.
Then with a mantle of delicate silk

---

most closely Ariosto's Cloridano and Medoro and Ruggiero and Leone. It is perhaps to under-
line this similarity that Fonte's Floridoro—the knight who will fall in love with the most beauti-
ful woman in the world, Celsidea—has a name etymologically close to Ariosto's Medoro, the
knight who will end up with the most beautiful woman of the *Furioso*, Angelica. Both indeed, as
their names imply, strike gold. Although male friendship has been profusely celebrated, Fonte
argues in *The Worth of Women* that women's friendship too should be examined because "women
make friends with other women more easily than is the case with men, and their friendships
are more lasting" (123).

(it too was white), he makes him even more adorned.[6]
Thereafter he leads him to that destrier so beautiful
that it fills him with amazement and eagerness.

31

This was the destrier of a great lord,
who had come among the barbarous company;
he had such strength, such heart,
that he never feared any dire peril.
Now a wise man took this racer from him,
for he loved the noble and handsome Floridoro.
The way I will not tell which he used to take it;
it suffices that it came into the hand of his Filardo.

32

It was the wizard named Celidante,
who took care of all the princes;
I mean those who had fine
spirits and benign, noble natures.
He is the one who raised Risamante,
and makes sure to aid and favor her.
Next after her he esteems and loves Floridoro,
and wishes to help and advance him.

33

Floridoro is infinitely pleased
with so lovely and noble a destrier,
which from its features and its golden equipment
he judges to be some great warrior's.
Based on its beauty, gems, and gold,
he judges it must be quick and nimble in the race
and in dressage. Therefore, content he takes
the bridle in hand and leaps into the saddle.

---

6. For a more in-depth look at the unusual association of Floridoro with the color white, see the volume editor's introduction.

34

The wretched boy prepares his sorrows
while he joyfully seeks to arm himself.
He rejoices and makes merry
at what will bring him hard and cruel pain.
Luckier for him if he had gone far from this
country a thousand miles or more seeking adventure,
so that the fierce arrow would not strike him,
the arrow a pitiless archer prepares for him.

35

The good Dictaean, who descended earlier
from the saddle with the page to help him,
sets about himself the heavy weight of armor
so well made for his back, for his waist.
When he sees Floridoro mounted on the destrier
with such quick agility,
he too mounts his horse, and takes
two lances chosen beforehand from among dozens and dozens.

36

One for Floridoro, for himself he keeps
the other, and they both command the servant
that if by chance anyone comes seeking
them, he should answer thus to whoever asks:
he saw them leave Athens in a hurry,
but he does not know where they plan to go.
With this speech the knights, incognito,
direct toward the great square their destriers.

37

Meanwhile the king with a legal edict
had given the orders that he must,
and had interdicted every word, every act
that might cause brawls and scandals.
Having given leave to that undefeated band,

to whom a mere moment seems a long delay,
he returns to the palace, and places himself to view
the bellicose contest from the royal balcony.

38

The noble queen comes then, and with her
her daughter, and she shows her noble and joyful visage.
At the appearance of her beautiful face,
a new sun seems to shine in the world.
Astonished, every soul, whether faithful or rebellious to the king,
contemplates Alismondo's granddaughter.
She has already overturned the whole field,
although she employs neither lance nor destrier.

39

Just as when a comet appears in the sky,
all people turn their eyes to that new flash;
or when one sees all the crowd raise their heads
if Cynthia opposes her brother's light;[7]
in the same way when the virgin appears,
each person turns to that illustrious and beautiful radiance.
With good Filardo meanwhile, Silvarte's son
arrives and hears the common whispering.

40

While every man stands astonished and intent
on contemplating the sweet young girl,
Floridoro comes along, glad and content
with that delightful company.
He is adorned with white silk and silver,
with a pure mantle and unsullied cuirass,
and the feathers of his helmet's crest
are that color which is most opposite to black.

7. Cynthia, the moon goddess, is associated with Artemis, the sister of Apollo, the sun god.

41

Ah, Floridoro, ah, don't lift your gaze,
for to your misfortune you will see that sweet smile!
The boy arrives and heedlessly
raises his eyes to that celestial visage,
and immediately Love with an invincible dart
pierces his attentive heart.
Cruel wound, from which one suffers and languishes,
feeling the pain and not seeing the blood.

42

Of the thousands and thousands of arrows which the cruel archer
cast from those beautiful eyes in a single moment,
this was the cruelest, this the fiercest,
which pricked and struck noble Floridoro.
Caught thus while lost in thought, the boy
was all dumbfounded, all startled.
Love delights in the fine stroke; and in those blond
tresses he hides himself, his bow, and his crime.

43

The boy remains so changed and full
of great fright and lofty wonder,
that his hand no longer knows how to hold the rein,
and he leaves the bridle to his destrier's judgment.
It, feeling free where least
it should, decides to twist its course;
it no longer cares to go forward,
but returns back to where it left just before.

44

The young man nearly fell out of the
saddle, so stunned did he remain.
Filardo did not notice him, and gave it no
thought, for other places had attracted his eye.

He gazed a good while at the infinite number
of so many illustrious, lofty people.
He saw as well that stately damsel,
but with a mind more healthy and more sound.

45

He believed Floridoro was doing likewise,
and he turned to tell him something;
and when he did not find him at his side
he was astonished and thoughtful.
Then, seeing him neither in that corner nor this one,
he did not rest in his thoughts or on his destrier;
nor for all his gazing and turning about
was he gladdened by the sight of him.

46

How the Cretan knight found him later
full of fierce and powerful grief,
I hope to make plain to you in another place,
for now Silano disturbs me and forbids it.
He had entered the closed and secret cavern,
together with that other knight
and with the lady whose powerful words
freed them from tigers and serpents.

47

The Latin king's son believed
she would take him to a dark and blind place,
and he went timidly with her
like a man who for honor's sake follows peril.
But when he arrived in the subterranean cave
with good Clarido, they both raised their eyebrows,
filled with wonder; for inside
there was greater light and splendor than outside.

4 8

On first reaching those hidden rooms,
they gazed at three beautiful ladies gathered in a band
with majesty, grace, and decorum,
seated around a rich and beautiful artwork.
They kept their eyes and hands intent and turned
to distributing gems, silk, and gold;
and they kept their minds fixed and faces bowed,
embroidering that excellent and divine cloth.

4 9

But at the opening of that little door
and the entrance of the stately damsel,
they all raised immediately their lovely faces,
and paid their respects to the newcomers.
The wellborn lady, in appearance rather grave and severe,
commanded the noble band
for the time being to leave off their needlework,
and prepare lunch for the company.

5 0

At the first word the ladies quickly
left the beautiful, unfinished garment.
One took on the burden of cooking the foods;
one dressed the table with white linen.
The other to another exercise set her heart;
her mind was ready and her hands quick.
Already Ceres and elect and holy Bacchus
filled every corner of the long tablecloth.[8]

5 1

While they took care to prepare thoroughly
the diverse boiled and roasted viands,
and with pepper and honey they had in abundance

8. Ceres is the goddess of the harvest, and Bacchus is the god of wine.

they made ready cakes and compotes,[9]
she who held the reins of the beautiful country,
like a courteous and most kind hostess,
with sweet speech made the delay
seem less bothersome to her guests.

52

She was the daughter of that Circe
who was so learned and so perfect a sorceress,
a young woman honest and marvelously wise,
most graceful, sensible, and charming;
such that whoever turned his eyes to her
felt his heart rent with a sharp wound.
If good Silano had lacked love,
he would certainly have given his heart to her beautiful visage.

53

But because he kept impressed in his mind
the great beauty of the Athenian lady,
as fame's report sculpted it deeply
into him in his own kingdom,
no other lady could have the power
to create in his heart a new desire.
The beautiful countenance which gave him the rough blow
was his shelter and shield against any other arrow.

54

Since each of them felt secure,
the two warriors both removed their helmets;
and the lady, turning her eyes to them,
praised to herself aspects so noble.
But the handsomer Silano kindled her heart
and seemed to please and delight her more—

9. Pepper and honey were key elements of any Renaissance meal, and Venice was a main port for the importation of pepper and of all the various spices that—like today's sauces—then accompanied local dishes.

not, however, that she gave her beautiful eyes
too much license to gaze at his august form.

55

Handsome Silano entreated and implored her
please to narrate what she had promised:
the noteworthy fortunes of the island and herself,
and all the matter of the pitiless animals.
She astutely took care
to be gazed at often by the handsome youth,
and answered full gladly his entreaties
with what in the other canto I will tell you.

CANTO 8

ARGUMENT

*Circetta narrates to the knight Silano
her father Ulysses' long, strange wandering,[1]
and the horrendous and strange enchantment which Circe cast
after the cruelties and mad acts she committed.
Floridoro laments and weeps in vain
for his new, too-elevated amours.
He wants to conceal himself from Filardo; and the more he beseeches
him to tell him what's the matter, the more he hides and refuses.*

1

Circe in olden times by the virtue of herbs and words,
with lofty lore not revealed to anyone today,
could obscure the illustrious face of the sun,
turn the poles and often stop Cynthia,
make roses and violets bloom
when the field is most oppressed by snow,
dry up meadows and turn the air black
in the loveliest, greenest springtime.

2

That she could perform, against the statutes
of nature, works so worthy and admirable

---

1. The Italian "errori" could refer to Ulysses' voyages or his mistakes, or both.

makes me marvel, since not seen
today are miracles so great.
But that she changed men into
brute animals with her words, at her commands,
seems so light a matter that I am truly amazed
she deigned to give it a thought.

3

It seems to me she did not do much in changing
human bodies into bears, wolves, and bulls,
when in our age men in erring
are transformers of themselves.
I see them go around changing themselves
with such facility, without employing verses or potions,
that I esteem that art little,
since our century so frequently takes part in it.

4

Each man is so good a magician with his own form
that she could not match their skill at that time,
when she employed to change our image
so many herbs, so much study, and so much time.
Each man is so eager to stray from himself
that he does not thereafter find the time to return.
Not of all, but of most men I discourse,
who like to seem what they are not.

5

I would tell you how now this man, now that one,
often takes on the semblance of a greedy wolf;
others of the muddy and filthy animal;
others of the stolid bear, fell and treacherous.
But I recall that I am awaited
by the lady of the mountain, to whom the young
Latin seems so handsome that her only desire
is to please him. Therefore she begins to speak:

6

"That knight who lived many years ago,
whose virtue had no peers in the world,
who in Greek and Phrygian fights
showed divine knowledge, profound valor—
that so prudent and valorous Ulysses
who was more daring and eloquent than any other,
was lord of this island which was
called Ithaca, and now Circetta's isle.

7

"Before the Greek torch in that age
had kindled and burned proud Ilium,[2]
there appeared among the worthiest Greek heroes
Ulysses, quick and lively in speaking.
Against that strong man with scarce any pity toward himself,
that so famous and wrathful Ajax,
he obtained with lofty and ornate words
the strongest Achaean's honored arms.[3]

8

"And after to the regal and lofty Spartan camp
he had brought the placated wretch Philoctetes
(who in Vulcan's irate cliff
kept Alcides' bow and arrows,
without which the king of the Greeks awaited in vain
on the Phrygian wall his final revenge),[4]

2. Troy.

3. Ajax went mad and fell on his sword after the dead Achilles' armor was awarded to Ulysses.

4. Philoctetes inherited the bow and arrows belonging to Hercules (also known as Alcides). On the way to the Trojan War, Philoctetes was bitten on the foot by a snake, and the Greeks, unwilling to endure his screams, abandoned him on Lemnos, an island sacred to Hephaistos (the Roman Vulcan). A later prophecy that the bow and arrows would be necessary to take Troy caused Ulysses to be sent back to persuade Philoctetes to come to Troy, where he was healed and reconciled with the Greeks.

he set out to attempt again the waves' anger
toward this his homeland, toward this realm,

9

"so much did he yearn
to see again his fair progeny
and his chaste wife faithful to her husband,
who thought only of him and spoke only of him.
But the great ruler of the swollen and angry sea,
irate, moved a most bitter storm against him,
the champion of the Achaean crown
and destroyer of Idaean greatness.[5]

1 0

"He hastens to manifest his hate
to avenge his proud wall.[6]
While he, irate, aspires to vengeance
and plans to send Ulysses to the dark, infernal realm,
the wind transports him to a little island,
where on a hard and infamous cliff
he finds the Cyclops sleeping on the mountaintop,
and steals the eye from his terrible forehead.[7]

1 1

"Then he spreads his sails and abandons the island
to flee the infamous and impious Polyphemus.
He goes to the king of the winds, and speaks so well
with his unprecedented sweet style
that Aeolus takes them all and gives them to him,
so that he might escape the threatened destruction;

5. This Mount Ida is near Troy.

6. Poseidon built the walls of Troy.

7. The Cyclops Polyphemus trapped Ulysses and his sailors in his cave and killed and ate
several of them. Ulysses got him drunk and put out his eye while he slept.

but all in vain, for more than one unfaithful servant
deprives him of the gift, and of his beloved shore.[8]

1 2

"The greedy ones released the cruel and fickle wind,
and the sea renewed in the sea the cruel tempest.
The fleet was dispersed, and the proud duke
wandered with the ship that remained to him.
At last the fierce and injurious weather
drew him to Circe's illustrious forest.
Circe the beautiful and virtuous fay
welcomed Ulysses and his companions.

1 3

"And be silent, you who say unjustly
that she transformed his companions into beasts,[9]
for she never, if not forced,
caused displeasure to whoever turned to offend her.
The prudent knight came to the fay,
and received from her joy and pleasure.
By one and the other I was conceived,
and at birth I was named after her: Circetta.[10]

1 4

"The powerful warrior Ulysses was my
father, my mother that goddess
who was the daughter of the luminous god
who drives away the shadows and animates the extinguished day.[11]

---

8. Aeolus gave Ulysses all the adverse winds tied up in a bag to facilitate his return home. When Ulysses fell asleep, his men, thinking the bag contained wine, opened it, and the winds blew them farther from Ithaca.

9. In the *Odyssey*, when Ulysses landed on Circe's island, she turned his scouting party into pigs.

10. As in the case of Risamante's daughter, Salarisa, daughters get their mother's stamp in their proper name in *Floridoro*, and not their father's.

11. Circe was the daughter of the Titan Helios, the personified sun.

After she had given me to the light, Ulysses showed
himself reluctant to her desire,
and with the cunning at which he was an expert and learned,
one day he stole away without saying a word.

1 5

"He gave oar to the waters, and with a more propitious fate
he and his friends arrived here,
where, with his image transformed by time,
he was barely recognized as their dear lord.
Circe realized her beloved duke
had departed, and poured out a river of bitter tears.
She would have followed him, but her own power,
which Ulysses had learned, denied it to her,

1 6

"because while he looked on my mother with favor
and liked the fair Saturnian hill,[12]
and became father of a little daughter,
he wanted all Circe's art laid out.
She, unable to withstand his graceful manners,
with various magical verses and various ampullae
made every science plain to her lover;
and to please another she harmed herself.

1 7

"Now since Circe lacked the power
to impede my father from departing,
for the same art in which she was excellent
favored the fugitive Ulysses,
she closed her grief in her afflicted mind,

12. In the *Argonautica* Apollonius of Rhodes situates Circe's island, Aeaea, on the west coast
of Italy, which was linked to Saturn. See canto 2.44. Another tradition locates Aeaea not far
from the mouth of the Po River. See Graves, *Greek Myths*, 157. Also, Saturn is the Latin name
of Cronos, the brother of Circe's father, Helios. An intriguing possibility is contained in the
legend that Ulysses and Circe begat Latinus, the ancestor of the Latins, and two other sons.
See Graves, *Greek Myths*, 721. Is Fonte drawing attention to a tradition she ostensibly ignored?

and waited until the knight died
to take her vengeance on this island,
which his presence had forbidden.

18

"When the people, filled with grief and compassion,
had made the dutiful, customary, and holy pyre,
and enclosed in the traditional sacred urn
the mortal cinders of my father,
Circe to give an outlet to her desire,
since no one disturbed or forbade her,
came here, and her lofty and fateful charms
made her invisible to mortals.

19

"She covered every city with dark fog.
She made lions, tigers, and serpents appear,
and they were the ones that guard those walls
which you were content to pass with me.
The sound of her magical accents redoubled in them
that ferocity which they have by nature,
so that venom, claws, fangs, and horns
desolated all the cities around.

20

"After she was sated with exercising
that great cruelty born of love
(for while she roamed around the island,
she perceived nothing left unharmed by her furor),
she sought with her opportune spell the favor and grace
to immortalize her lord's name.
She wanted Ulysses' merits to live in the world,
and for his fame to be splendid and alive.

21

"With her strong enchantment she forced the wind
to penetrate into the center of the earth.

There she closed the ways in every corner
so that in vain it roamed and wandered to go out,
but natural desire drove it so much
that with great fury it waged war on the land.
Overcome and forced, the land rose and swelled
like a balloon when someone gives it breath.

2 2

"The earth ceded to the wind and formed the mountain—
the mountain which encloses us around and above.
Circe then with adroit and ready words
employed her wisdom in an even rarer artifice.
On the lofty yoke, on the elevated brow,
she made then a far more wondrous work.
A temple she made; and wherever the sun shines and circles,
nothing more beautiful than this does it see.

2 3

"The arches, the bases, the capitals, and the roof
she divided with equal proportion,
without a teacher, without an architect,
with the virtue of her magic incantation.
Once she saw her work perfected
with the aid of Orcus and Pluto,[13]
into the greatest city she descended alone,
and stole the holy relics of Ulysses.

2 4

"Besides the ungrateful lover's ashes,
which she found and took from the sacred mausoleum,
the glorious and triumphant spoils
of Peleus's son she found there as well.[14]
Those arms whose temper Vulcan made,
hung up and scattered, she detached and gathered;

13. Orcus is the Roman god of death. Pluto is the Roman name for Hades, ruler of the underworld.

14. Achilles was the son of Peleus.

and she transported them to this faithful abode,
as to a worthier and more glorious nest.

25

"I was present at all these feats,
for my mother had no other comfort
than to contemplate in me naturally
that comeliness which in Ulysses was extinguished and dead.
She did not, however, want to educate my mind
as to how one can outrage and wrong others;
she taught me the good which can come from that art,
and hid the ill in her puissant pages.[15]

26

"As pleased the hard and iniquitous stars,
my mother then determined
that as a pitiless rebel from human commerce
I should stay in this cliff, which was later named after me.
She also placed with me the three damsels
who provide me with service and company;
and she made the enchantment, unknown to all the world,
which was to endure until a future century.

27

"She established that Time could not
make a trophy of my youth,
and that it should keep me at that same age
as when she placed me in this cruel enchantment.
One can see well how much her wisdom
availed, for she did not perform the work in vain,
since from then till now so many years have
passed, and yet I am fresh and youthful.

15. Or "in her magical book" ("nelle possenti carte"). Fonte implies that Circe, like medieval magicians, used a book of spells. See for example Julia Kisacky, *Magic in Boiardo and Ariosto* (New York: Peter Lang, 2000), chaps. 1 and 3.

28

"With me as well, of those who while my father
lived showed themselves contrary to him,
Circe (who attributed to them a longer age
than the stingy heavens ordered)
placed the heirs here to guard Ulysses'
arms, until a warrior of virtue equal
to his might come to draw me from this prison,
and become lord of the island and of the arms.

29

"As the beloved duke came to her
not through his will but by chance,
so she did not want fame to induce anyone
to attempt the extraordinary adventure,
but rather for fortune to lead him here by chance
to prove if fate is friendly or hard to him;
nor did she want anyone to be able to enter the temple
who is not equal to Ulysses in cleverness and in valor.

30

"When someone audacious but of little merit
forces his entrance into the infernal walls,
he is punished so that he lives the rest
of his life, however long, under another skin.
Just now you saw the deed manifest.
You saw me force nature;
that warrior was seen by you just now
to lose his flesh and acquire wood.

31

"Now if it seems to you that you are such knights,
if you have the heart to enter through that door,
then when you have passed the pitiless and mortal
battles, and the great terror the door evokes in you,
from the most rich and fateful paving stones

you will see something emerge which matters much more:
Colossus and Tantalus, each one immense,
who will want vengeance for Polyphemus.[16]

3 2

"But let's assume that the ferocious impious giant
is wondrously killed by you;
who will defend you from great Theante,
who will suddenly assault you?
From his head to his heels he is inviolable,
nor by any iron blade can he be conquered.
As with his father, his fleshly garment is enchanted,
and he desires to avenge Ajax's harm."[17]

3 3

The young woman's discourse
makes the Latin souls very thoughtful.
The desire for honor entices them both
to attempt those lofty and divine deeds.
But fear of the chastisement that awaits
whoever does not reach the desired end,
namely, to be constrained to change into a tree,
makes them doubtful, nor do they know what to do.

3 4

But the astute Silano, who from peril
tries to draw himself with cleverness and wits,
turns often toward her his courteous brow,
and shows her this and that sign of love,
for without gaining her grace and counsel
he does not hope to reach the destined point.[18]

---

16. The Colossus of Rhodes was a giant statue of Helios. Tantalus incurred the wrath of the gods by serving up his son to them at a banquet; he was punished in the afterlife by being near delicious food and water that he could never reach. He was not a giant. There is no clear connection between these two, or between them and Polyphemus.

17. Ajax was invulnerable except in his armpit. His son was Eurysaces, not Theante.

18. Silano is modeled upon Homer's Ulysses, and as these verses make plain, he shows the same scheming penchant, astute thinking, and manipulative personality.

Without her favor he does not consider himself sufficient
to deal with so important an undertaking.

35

Now, while he is in suspense, a damsel
enters that place and with a kind invitation
calls the kind lady and the knights,
for the feast is already set in order.
They moved, therefore, and passed into a rich and
beautiful hall which she pointed out to them.
It was so rich and marvelously beautiful
that again the Ausonian eyes were amazed.[19]

36

It had three great windows in the east
with columns of elect alabaster,
three toward the south, and the sun through as many
toward the evening illuminated the roof.
The last face, a wall of diamond,
was divided by three doors of pure ivory.
The sills and hinges were of silver,
and the floor of brilliant rubies.

37

The roof was of gold, and the architrave, and also
the cornices, and over and around the doors
was a great festoon of oriental pearls
which spread outside; adorned with other gems,
it feigned then a vine, which had grapes
so natural they outdid the true ones.[20]
Between the architrave and the cornice was a frieze
with an excellent foliage of emeralds.

19. The Ausonian people lived in central and southern Italy.

20. A possible reference to Zeuxis, the Greek painter who "produced a picture of grapes so successfully represented that birds flew up to the stage buildings [where pictures were hung]." Pliny, *Natural History*, trans. H. Rackham (Cambridge: Harvard University Press, 1995), 9:309 (35.65–66). Fonte is imitating Ariosto's description of Alcina's island in the *Furioso* here.

38

But let's allow that the great hall gave
a wondrous splendor of gems and gold,
or rather that it was all one gem,
distinct in a rare and immortal artwork.
I set every other loveliness as nothing
with respect to that which surpassed every treasure;
I speak of the illustrious, adamantine walls,
with which art deceived nature.

39

In that hard gem, strong and solid,
or perhaps infinite gems were joined into one
as in wax that is heated at the fire,
a thousand beautiful figures were sculpted.
As to whether they were cold stone, whether living and warm
flesh, anyone's judgment would be set in dispute,
for artifice had so little part there
that art seemed to be hidden in art.

40

Silano on first arriving mistakes its significance;
it seems to him that one speaks and another breathes,
for the relief, the color, the line, and the shadow
show that their lips laugh and their eyes gaze.
That illusion so encumbers him,
and the false belief to such a foolish pass draws him
that, judging them to be true and living people,
he goes to pay them his respects.

41

But he better perceives his error when
they do not respond to his courteous act.
The girl watches him and laughs,
and has him approach his finger to the hard intaglio.
His hand proves his eyes untrustworthy,
so that the false idea is dispelled.

For the shame that seizes his heart,
he turns vermilion all over.

42

Returning to himself stupefied,
smiling he admires the celestial artwork.
Then he says, "I am quite satisfied
with what you promised us earlier on the way,
when by you that knight was drawn
out of his natural human garment—
namely, that in following you I would see things
much more miraculous than in the past.

43

"I implore you earnestly to narrate to me a little
of what these sculptures are meant to signify—
if the beautiful and noble figures were made
to adorn this beautiful place,
or if instead they are alive someplace
in our age or in future ages,
or if they are the natural forms
of people of past times."

44

Says the lady, "You see quite clearly
that these stories depicted before us
have not been nor are yet, but stingy Time
will bring them at the hour prescribed in heaven.
Those indomitable people will possess merit
so illustrious and rare, so much honor,
that by the fay from whom they were not hidden
they deserved to be sculpted in diamond.

45

"But because it takes a long time
to tell of the glories not yet manifested in the world,
and the lofty history of the future time

which her magical art showed to Circe
(hence she portrayed them here before their time,
and gave me news of them one by one),
I mean to beseech you that we dine first,
since it is time and we have the foods before us."

46

She gave them hope she would tell of them afterward,
so the two Latin warriors agreed,
leaving off gazing at the room for the time being,
in order to taste those bountiful and divine foods.
Meanwhile with kind and fair good manners,
and with modest and reverent bows,
two ladies entered and set out to serve them
with their sleeves reaching only to their elbows.

47

One carried in her hands a rich gilt vase
full of rose water for whoever must wash,
and over her left shoulder a delicate
cloth which surpassed snow for whiteness.
The other carried a golden bowl, wide and hollowed
in the bottom, which received the poured liquid.
They began to wash the hands
of the lady and the foreign knights.

48

Once she had sprinkled one after the other their hands
with that liquid which gave off a sweet odor,
and wiped and dried them with that white linen
which the lady had on her shoulder for that very purpose,
Circetta raised her beautiful visage to the knights.
Sweet in speech and grave in aspect,
she conceded to them the most honored places,
and wished as well that they be seated first.

49

Then she too sat down, and to the welcome viands
they set their hands with immense and highest joy.
The two damsels, accustomed to the task,
flew around the superb table.
One served with the knife; one into the gilt
goblets placed and dispensed the nectar-like wine.
That one filled the plates with new food;
this one cleared and carried away the used plates from the linen.

50

While that honorable company
was savoring that merry lunch,
the third damsel entered, who in the world
had no peer in grace and loveliness.
With the cithara and with eloquent words
she played a most sweet harmony,
such that the two warriors knew
that there they enjoyed all the pleasures of paradise.

51

But I reserve for myself at another time to tell
of this pair and the charming girl,
because Filardo wishes to find
his Floridoro, whom love wounds and injures.
Although Filardo looks all around,
he cannot satisfy nor content his eyes;
looking up and down, all over
he goes seeking him, and never finds him.

52

Full of great amazement, full of suspicion,
since in vain he turns round his horse and his gaze,
with little hope he directs his vigorous destrier
back toward the accustomed shelter.
There the sad youth arrived

long before the arrival of his Filardo;
and he is confused and beside himself
from the extreme grief enclosed in his heart.

53

Like a man who, while sleep oppresses his senses,
deals and converses with various false thoughts,
and with evil semblances into his heart impresses
something which his heart hates and his taste abhors,
so that then the image which sleep impresses
with every cruel emotion that goes with it
is fixed, and becomes so powerful in him
that even waking for many days he still feels it,

54

just so Floridoro is no longer equal to drawing out
that divine image from his heart,
where, as if in a hard and solid diamond,
Love sculpted it with his own hand.
Solid and constant, at every moment that memory
reinforces the living ardor in his breast.
The pain increases at every moment; the affection increases
in his simple and still tender breast.

55

Afflicted and tired from the heat and the anxiety,
he disarms his beautiful, pale face,
and stretches out his beautiful limbs onto a bed,
which he finds just in time in that hidden dwelling.
The flame which melts his left side
distills the blood gathered around his heart.
Transformed into pure water, it ascends
and out through his eyes in great abundance descends.

56

Just as a graceful, untamed young bull
used to going free among green fields,

if he feels placed onto his yet rebellious neck
the hard yoke, flares up in anger,
and in vain groans and roams all about
to get free of it, unable, however, to escape—
just so Floridoro, caught by the new cord,
in vain moans and tries to get out of his predicament.

5 7

Unspeaking a while, in tears and sighs
he gives vent to his grave, unwonted torment.
Then, overcome by his new, bitter agonies,
he joins words to weeping.
"Alas, what unaccustomed, lofty desires
disturb my peace and happiness?
What new sorrow, what new anxiety is this,
which leaves me so afflicted and troubled?

5 8

"If this sweet pain is born in me and comes
from the sweet good I perceived just now,
how did the sudden bliss not set free
my soul, unused to feeling so much good?
If perhaps Love, to give me greater pains,
did not strive to cause my death,
it was certainly that cruel and wicked tyrant
who knew how to temper together absinthe and honey.

5 9

"Wretched me! I know well that that insolent,
rough boy has caught me unaware with his snare.
Like a fleeting and timid deer,
wounded I flee in vain the bitter blow.
But how will I ever dare to call myself his servant
for so rare a subject?
Descended among us from the starry cloister,
she is a miracle and the honor of our age.

60

"Ah, by God, let there be no one who hears and listens to
such rash boldness, so insane a desire.
Let my pains stay here closed and buried,
nor let any human mind comprehend them.
For when I have tried in vain many times
to banish so foolish an idea,
in the end this sword alone will be the remedy
which will draw from my heart so hard a siege."[21]

61

While, all troubled and tearful,
the beautiful, enamored Floridoro
thus gives vent to his fiery thoughts,
and tries to relieve the great agony,
his dear friend, uncertain and jealous
of him who was his joy, his treasure,
arriving hurriedly at his torments,
interrupts his tears and laments.

62

His steps strike the boy's ears,
so he stands up, and with fine cleverness
runs to his destrier with hasty feet,
and makes a show of arranging the bit and saddle.
But in vain he strives and expects to conceal
that fierce new passion of his,
for Filardo on arriving finds his
face much transfigured.

21. Floridoro's love-tormented tossings and turnings recall a similar troublesome night in the corresponding canto of the *Furioso* in which Orlando is kept awake, anguished by his love for Angelica, who has run away. Dreaming later that she is asking for his help, he begins that long "amorous quest" (9.7) that leads to his undoing many cantos later. See also Virgil, *Aeneid* 4.522–32, where a sleepless Dido behaves likewise.

63

To Floridoro it seems so great an error
to have lifted his thoughts so high,
that while he conceals it as much as he can,
his visage turns now crimson, now pale.
He condemns and blames the horse
for his departure at the amorous assault,
but sensible Filardo is quite certain
that he has received some harm and wants to keep it hidden.

64

The good Dictaean is astounded when he understands
that Floridoro wants to conceal himself this way,
for he is accustomed to manifest to him every pain
that offends his heart, every thought.
So much compassion kindles his soul
that he moans and grieves more than Floridoro does,
and he cannot keep from telling him,
"Ah, Floridoro, by God, don't hide.

65

"Don't hide from me what I well realize:
that a new passion is born in your heart.
The cause of it, however, I cannot discern,
nor do I know why you want to keep it concealed."
At this Floridoro streams a whirlpool
of weeping over his delicate cheeks.
Filardo comforts him, and dries his beautiful
eyes with a linen cloth, and implores him to speak.[22]

22. This verse, "gli occhi belli/Col lin gli asciuga," is a reworking of a famous and much-imi-
tated line in Petrarch, where a kindhearted Laura is imagined doing the same ("asciugandosi
gli occhi col bel velo," drying her eyes with her lovely veil). See *Petrarch's Lyric Poems,* canzone
126.39.

66

With great effort and art the youth
at last extracts such an answer as this:
"Ah, my friend, flee from association with me, and go
to a place far from my imminent danger!
This unworthy son of good Silvarte
intends to leave behind his mortal prison.
In order never to be seen again by anyone,
he desires at so youthful an age to give himself to Pluto.

67

"Flee before strong grief or the bold sword
sunders this fleeting and fragile veil.
And don't be distressed, by God, if I hide and conceal
the cause which disturbs my peace,
because the lofty thought which burns and undoes me
is of such excellence that I shall not reveal it.
Let it suffice you to know that too bold
and too daring a soul quits this life.

68

"Don't sigh for my sorrows,
for it is reasonable that I alone grieve and perish.
Nor do I sorrow to die, when my mind
in dying must be released and sound.
But this alone burdens my heart: that death will be
able to part so much true friendship,
and our internal love will be divided,
when I believed it must be eternal."

69

With this his pain grows and grips his heart
so that it doubles his anguish and weeping.
So much torment encompasses his friend
that in his heart he weeps and grieves just as much.

But pity for them now constrains me
to stray from here, and put an end to the canto.
How afterward their torment diminished,
I will tell in the next canto to whoever listens to me.

CANTO 9

ARGUMENT

So much Filardo implores the noble son
of Silvarte that he reveals to him his secret.
He comforts him and gives him hope and advice,
such that he returns gladly to the tourney.
The Thracian releases Gracisa, and into sempiternal exile
he sends an unreasonable warrior.
They go together to the oracle, and they admire
the god's sumptuous and divine temple.

1

What minds happier and more joyous
live on earth than two who are united?
What greater contents, what benefits,
does generous heaven bestow upon a living man?
The dear union of true friends alone,
time cannot overcome nor fortune knock down.
These can take away possessions and liberty,
but the heart's treasure they cannot touch.

2

Oh, blessed are those to whom the stars gave
as their lot so much happiness in the world.
Even if their two fates vary,
love makes the hearts of both sad or merry.
There is nothing which brings torment to one,

which does not cause sorrow deep in the heart
of his friend; and if one finds pleasure,
the other enjoys and experiences the same well-being.

3

That one's heart is oppressed
by grave trouble, as sometimes happens,
and his dear friend for love of him
exposes his life, not to mention his wealth;
in so doing he steals away half of his friend's pain
through his help, his compassion.
Oh, how sweet to unburden your suffering soul
with one who feels grief at your sorrow!

4

That other one's breast is full of such bliss
that he would die if he did not tell it to someone,
and, finding a close companion of his,
he reveals it to him and shares it with him.
With this he doubles his delight,
for the good that one felt, two enjoy.
He makes a new gain of lofty pleasure,
experiencing the joy in his companion's heart.

5

But what am I saying? Friendship extends
its power so that even in death it keeps it,
since a man is not contained completely in himself;
his friend holds half of him,
and in exchange gives him half of himself.
Thus if one of them comes to death,
half the dead man in the living one lives still,
and half the living man in him must die.

6

A love so powerful and so vigorous,
souls toward each other so compassionate—
truly in those days Filardo and Floridoro
must have possessed them, and with these two I wish to proceed.
The young nobleman who had raised his gaze
too high, and with it his youthful desire,
felt so much shame that he desired to conceal
his torment not merely from others, but even from himself.

7

Despite all this, in the end he did not keep it hidden
(as you will hear) from his dear companion.
As I recounted to you, he came to console him
with great pity for his bitter sorrow,
and he took on half of his grief
(although he did not show it openly).
I said that he was grieved
at the wild answer Floridoro gave him.

8

Grieving deeply at the hard answer
(that he will die of the great pain),
Filardo beseeches and implores him
to reveal now this illness of his.
"So," he tells him, "our love will not endure
at least until the final torment?
You say that your death must end it,
and it seems while still living you intend to cut it short.

9

"Why don't you disclose to me what strange circumstance
has just now affected your thoughts?
Why does your judgment, formerly wise and sane,
witless now and infirm, fall into such foolishness

that you desire to leave this delightful human life,
and expose yourself to a base death?
You must kill whoever desires to kill you,
not take soul and fame from yourself.

10

"If perhaps the fear weighs down your heart
that my deceit has been revealed to the king,
that he might have realized or been told
that against his will you armed yourself,
by all means strip from yourself every suspicion
and lay on me all the sin.
I committed the error; your guilt is null,
and you can swear you knew nothing about it.

11

"Even if you have not the heart to take up
the martial invitation among so many knights,
if their infinite number affrights you
so that you despair of victory,
the way to leave here is easy:
let the results of our feigned intentions come true.
But I don't believe this afflicts your heart,
for you would not have clamored so much for it earlier.

12

"Ah, if the trouble in which you are freshly entered
is so powerful for another cause,
this trouble which so encumbers your mind and wits
that it blocks you from the honors you ought to gain,
why don't you open up and unburden your sorrowful heart
to me? For you well know that I would not tell it,
and if I am able and know how to give you aid,
I'm ready to exchange my life for yours.

1 3

"Why don't you reveal your new desire
to our sincere, long-standing trust?[1]
I would already have explained my thought to you,
if the sorrow which wounds your heart pressed me.
One does not confirm in such a way (I believe)
that true law of friendship which is in effect.
One friend must open his breast to the other,
and show him his heart without suspicion.

1 4

"Surely you know, my Floridoro, that I esteem and love
all that you equally love and esteem.
I praise, adore, and desire only
what I know you desire, adore, and praise.
On the other hand I hate mortally and defame
whatever you mortally defame, hate, and despise.
I laugh with your good fortune, and with your ill I grieve;
and in every vicissitude I want to be with you."

1 5

So he says, and with such good arguments
he struggles with the young lover's heart.
He by now is no longer able to refuse,
and must express his thought to him.
The modest boy, as if his amorous
affection were a serious crime,
staining with red his moist cheeks,
begins with these heartfelt sorrowful notes:

---

1. The rhetoric of trust (*fede*) is capital in romances of chivalry. See Eduardo Saccone, "Prospettive sull'ultimo *Furioso*," *MLN* 98 (1993): 55–69. The ties of mutual reliance, courtesy, moral obligation, allegiance, and honor that characterize Filardo and Floridoro's friendship come from the fertile model offered by Ariosto in his depiction of the much-touted friendship between Ruggiero and Leone.

16

"Would to God I had never come to Athens
with my father on his journey,
or if indeed I had to leave Mycenae,
would I had first been blinded for my own good!
Then I would not have seen the one for whom I suffer such pains,
the lofty splendor of regal Greek blood,
nor at finding myself in so wretched a condition,
would I seek death by my own hand.

17

"The singular beauty, divine on earth,
of Cleardo's magnificent daughter
has waged such powerful war on my heart,
that I could not express how I have burned and burn
since the moment when, to bury my destiny underground,
that beauty made me direct my gaze to her great light."
He continued no further, for grief occupied him so much
that his words failed and his weeping increased.

18

Filardo is astonished and unhappy
no less than Floridoro at this grim announcement,
since he knows that neither wits nor daring
can help the great desire which gnaws at his heart.
Nor must he base a plan on his knowledge,
for here neither fiction nor deception avails.
The less he hopes to give him aid,
so much more he fears for his life.

19

He thinks and considers now this matter, now that,
and not immediately does he respond to Floridoro.
While he is in suspense and does not speak,
Floridoro pours out with greater abundance a stream of tears,

for he sees clearly that this news
disturbs and confounds his faithful friend.
But the sensible Dictaean with ready advice
quickly makes him change that weeping into laughter.

20

Although he would rather weep,
he forces his heart to spare his friend more pain,
and at the new desire which sprouts in him
he laughs with a kind and serene brow.
Then he says, "So Love rules your desire?
A new love restrains your liberty?
How you used to make fun of me
when I recounted my amorous fire.

21

"Don't fret, for this wound is unaccustomed and new
to you, but to me it is familiar and long-standing.
A thousand times I have experienced it,
and I know how much harm it does when one gets entangled in it.
My heart, however, does not find in so many troubles
fate so inimical to its desire
that, overcome by the pain and torment,
in desperation it seeks to die.

22

"I well know, Floridoro, how much the pondering
of two impossible things weighs on you,
for you have little hope of either one,
and so you wish to end your life's course.
The first is to drive away the lofty and supreme
desires and to rein in the new love.
The other is (if indeed you remain in such torment)
to attain the desired goal.

23

"Although love does not want to hear reason,
be willing to listen to my reasons in peace.
Drive away for a moment your passion from your heart,
and begin to think where to turn.
You will see that you have a foolish and vain idea,
that you have welcomed misleading thoughts into your heart.
Loving without hope is a vain thing,
and you well know how far she is from you.

24

"Try your heart a bit, since not yet
firmly set is the pitiless root.
When one takes care at the start,
one can avoid every unhappy state.
Then if imperious Love remains,
nor can you expel him from your mind,
try every way to arrive at the goal
before you make plans to die.

25

"You are the handsomest, the most graceful lover
that one might find from the Indus to the land of the Moors.
A more valorous and more excellent spirit
than Floridoro's one cannot imagine.
Besides your inner graces, celestial and holy,
you are rich in gems and treasure.
Although you do not possess an empire or a kingdom,
at least you are as worthy of them as anyone else.

26

"Your flourishing youth, your beauty,
grace, virtue, daring, and skill,
courtesy, valor, nobility,
and your every other meritorious and praiseworthy part

will perhaps have power over her whom your heart esteems,
so that you will obtain part of her grace.
Do not speak of dying, Floridoro, without
essaying your fortune.

27

"It is better for you to serve her discreetly,
for a lofty love brings too much peril.
But reveal your valor so clearly
that every other glory remains overshadowed and null,
and make your acclaim reach the ears
of the illustrious and wise royal girl.
Make plain to her your valor
but not your name, however worthy of honor.

28

"Perhaps your outstanding and unique fame,
on reaching those grand and illustrious ears,
will awaken in her some lively spark
of desire to meet and see you.
Believe me, Floridoro, a man arrives
only by such paths at the goal of his will;
only through the ways of virtue does one obtain
the highest happiness, the highest good.

29

"Therefore, not to fail on your own part
to do what you owe to yourself,
dry the wretched tears from your eyes
and begin to hope for a happy outcome.
Let us return to the field to show how much
the lofty thought impressed in your heart can do.
Let so much prowess come forth from you today
that you may hope to be a happy lover."

30

This reasoning and other arguments even worthier,
Filardo lays out to the sorrowing youth;
they console his melancholy heart
and quiet his disturbed mind.
With his pain fading little by little,
his sighing is rarer and less ardent,
so that, reinvigorated, he raises his face,
dries his eyes, and embraces his dear friend.

31

What kind of answer he gives him, and of what sort,
for the infinite obligation he has to him
one can well judge, when he knows his life
through him has been saved from death.[2]
With the gates to sighs and tears closed,
his cheek returns to beautiful and rosy.
He takes heart; his earlier longing returns,
when gaining glory inflamed his breast.

32

As a languishing flower, which has held its corolla
bowed under a long rainfall,
at the sun's appearance dries its errant
leaves and stands gazing at the sky,
just so returned the bountiful and divine beauties
of Floridoro, or in a similar fashion,
after the rain ceased from his eyes and at the same time
he enjoyed the rays of newfound hope.

2. Again Fonte mirrors Ariosto in that the "infinite obligation" of Floridoro, who feels he has
been saved from death by Filardo, is metonymically close to Ruggiero's feelings toward Leone:
"I am infinitely beholden to you, and I promise to sacrifice the life you restore me at whatever
moment you claim it" (*Orlando furioso* 45.48).

33

That sweet hope has such force
in the youthful heart burning with love
that it increases and strengthens the vigor in his breast,
and the sweet visage is restored to its former honors.
Indeed he wants to delay no longer; with pride he strives
to regain the time spent uselessly.
Love makes him more proud, handsome, and vigorous
than Filardo has yet seen him.

34

They remounted their horses, happy and glad,
but Filardo more in his face than in his heart
(for he was one of the most prudent and discreet
of youths, and he feared the end of this love).
They returned silently and secretly
to the great multitude, to the noise,
where they found that of the foreign group
three knights had fallen to the plain.

35

Prince Aliforte was the warrior
who had overcome the barbarian knights.
One possessed the great empire of Persia;
the other ruled the people of Syria;
the third to fall was the African Riviero.
The first had a sun on his shield,
the second a falcon, and as insignia
Riviero bore a lighted torch.

36

The powerful youth and his Filardo
having reached meanwhile the proud lists,
varied thoughts take each one's attention.
They begin to gaze differently,
for Floridoro feels faint

at the joyous sight of Celsidea.
While the good Dictaean gazes at the jousting,
he turns his eyes to her on the loggia's upper level.

3 7

But his companion, a faithful minister to his honor,
steals him away and diverts him from this sweet object,
so that he comes to occupy the place
which should have accommodated the king of Crete.
The last place, dedicated to the king of Venus's
shore, serves for his companion,
because the king did not choose in their stead
others to make up the number ten.[3]

3 8

If his nephew were at court
(I speak of Polinide the great Sican),
and good Griante still strong in old age,
he would make them go down to the plain in their stead.
But fate forbids the one from returning;
the other he needed to send afar
with many people some days before,
to help and favor Risamante.

3 9

The great king praises, the proud squads praise
the fair and daring pair of Greek heroes.
Celsidea with her queen mother
gives them praise no less rare and infinite.
Every eye watches and every hand points out
the fair armor, white and graceful,
and the foreigners no less than the Greeks wish
to know who the knights are.

---

3. Venus's shore refers to Cyprus. Cleardo chose ten champions for the Greek side in the tour-
ney, but the kings of Crete and Cyprus have not come to Athens (see canto 5.52–60).

40

Of the fair tourney and who gained the acclaim
I will tell elsewhere later, for now Risardo diverts me
from it. He was going to the illustrious and sacred temple
in company with his beautiful Odoria,
and with those two who went always by her side.
Their hearts were filled with envy and jealousy,
since they were overcome by excellent Risardo,
whereupon the lady took him in such high esteem.

41

They arrived one morning at a crossroads
which split their path in two.
Suddenly a cry, a distressed voice,
reached their ears from the right side.
Risardo urged his swift destrier
toward that place whence the noise came,
and the damsel and the two warriors no less
spurred forward their destriers' flanks.

42

They had not gone far, when they discerned at a distance
a damsel tied to a large pine.[4]
Weeping, she lamented in vain,
all red in the face and disheveled.
Risardo, who was kind and humane,
ran toward the grieving damsel.
Once dismounted, he stretched his hand to the trunk—
but at that moment a knight surprised him.

---

4. The episode of the damsel tied to a tree recalls Boiardo's scene in the *Innamorato* where a woman is tied to a tall cypress tree, undressed, and beaten by a giant while her sister screams for help. See *Innamorato* 2.2.7–29. See also Orlando's liberation of Orrigille, hung up by her hair (1.28.52–53).

43

A knight, who was hiding there
among green plants near the tree,
revealed himself, haughty and disdainful.
"Do not," he shouted to him, "release this woman from the pine.
Knight, do not be pitiful toward her.
Leave her be and return to your path,
because in loosing her bond you could
get yourself into a graver predicament with me."

44

And still speaking and threatening,
because Risardo did not stop at his cry,
he drew from the scabbard his sharp sword,
and aimed a great blow at his head.
Risardo, who saw it descend like lightning,
left the sad and afflicted lady.
He took a leap so that he might not reach him,
raised his shield, and gripped his own sword.

45

Saying nothing else, they began the rough
battle and gave mighty blows,
now here, now there; and to the naked
flesh many times they found their way.
Odoria now trembled, now sweated for fear
that her Risardo would be harmed.
Meanwhile one of those other two released and untangled
the damsel and set her on his horse's back.

46

The lady still trembled like a leaf
for fear of the boorish warrior,
lest he take her back again
from the knights' hands to torment her.

But mighty Risardo, who wanted strongly
to castigate that rough and insane man,
had already brought him to such a state
that he was beginning to be overcome.

47

He had taken away his shield and opened his helm
in four parts, and broken plate and mail.
He was all covered with his own blood,
so much did the warrior wound and afflict him,
such that the wretch in repayment for his arrogance
lost his life together with the battle.
Unfortunate was he who unknowingly attacked
one of the good warriors in the world.

48

When Risardo perceived the knight
was brought to his life's bitter end,
he resheathed his sword and remounted his destrier,
and so they returned to their voyage.
Odoria, once they gave themselves to riding,
entreated the lady to make clear and manifest
what cause for resentment the dead warrior had against her,
the reason why he had kept her tied to that pine.

49

Said the lady, "I came, sent
by the queen of the Armenian people,
who is besieged by her sister
and now holds only one city for herself.
There the unfortunate lady has escaped with a few others,
although she has little hope of finding refuge
from her sister, who with so many people
assails her constantly, and who is called Risamante.

50

"My queen, oppressed from every side,
secretly made me go forth,
so that I might find some benign and kindly
king or knight who would come in her favor
and restore her to her former state,
and Risamante's valor would not avail her.
Thus to serve her I took to the road,
and I saw and passed through many countries.

51

"But I have not yet been able to find a knight
nor a king willing to go to her.
Those who at first gave her aid,
having had enough of losing, now decline to come.
Others refuse to help her
because they love Risamante's daring;
they love her valor, boldness, and skill,
and they with their arms are on her side.

52

"So, since for many days I wandered in vain,
this morning I was making my return to her,
when to my misfortune I encountered
the knight who today was taken from the light.
I entreated him to come with me,
so as to travel secure from every ignominy.
The knight, feigning courtesy,
accepted my entreaty, and we rode away.

53

"When we arrived where the way splits
into two paths (which we just left behind),
he directed his horse to the right-hand side,
and did not follow the course I had taken.

Alas! When I saw him go aside
in a way different from the one I knew
(being fully instructed about the route to Armenia),
I was bewildered and very disturbed.

5 4

"At once and with good reason the fear seized
my heart that he planned to wage war on my honor.
Yet, pretending to think there was another cause,
I told him he was mistaken and erred as to the road;
and if he did not want to be my champion,
if he did not want to come with me to my land,
he should at least let me go at liberty
alone (as I had been), and follow my path.

5 5

"But when I saw that entreaties did not avail,
that he was holding my reins and going forward,
for the anger and sorrow which assailed me
I raised grieving to heaven my shrieks and tears.[5]
I swore at him and cursed him so much,
with so many insults and execrations,
that, overcome by the great wrath that seized him,
furiously from my destrier he threw and knocked me down.

5 6

"Then he too dismounted and took me by the hair,
and struck and tore my whole visage;
but while he beat me and disheveled my hair,
he could not silence my tongue.

5. The episode of Gracisa (we will know her name a few octaves later), who defends her virginity by shrieking and rebelling, recalls a similar scene of misplaced trust in the *Furioso*, when Isabella, entrusted by her beloved Zerbino to the care of Almonio, finds herself close to rape. To Ariosto's "[I] Shrieked to the high heavens" (13.28) and Boiardo's "loudly laments and tears her locks" (*Innamorato* 2.2.7) corresponds Fonte's "I raised grieving to heaven my shrieks and tears."

At last he decided
to bind both my arms to that tree trunk.
Taking a chain from I don't know where,
he bound and chained me thoroughly to that pine.

5 7

"I believe he intended to scourge me
awhile yet, and then leave me in that state,
when he heard more than one destrier spurred
by you who came in time to free me.
So he at once got off the path
to espy if anyone was coming to take me
from his hands (I think). The rest
since your arrival to you is manifest."

5 8

So said the lady, and then she requested
the knights with a beseeching entreaty
that they be willing to go with her in defense
of her queen, so that she might not perish.
Owing to the lofty valor she perceived in one,
she hoped so much from all together
that if they went to her of whom she spoke,
the defeated lady would end up the victor.

5 9

The knights answered Gracisa
(for so the damsel was named)
that they would go just as she devised
to help the besieged city,
but that they intended to go first in any case
to Delphi, for this was the course they had taken.
When they have been to the sacred temple,
then they will go with her to the Armenian kingdom.

60

The lady gave them highest thanks,
and determined to go as well to the temple
to hear from the blond and shining god
what must be for her noble queen.
So in agreement they spurred equally
their destriers, and each one proceeded so
that shortly they were in Delphi and they reached the holy
temple, which they desired so much.

61

The eminent, incomparable mass
was composed of celestial architecture,
a truly worthy abode for the great god of the sun
in its richness, intaglio, and structure.
The roof and the proud walls shone
all of gold and unique and elect stones.
The pavement, the columns, and the frieze
were all gems of incredible worth.

62

The lofty and holy windows appeared
between illustrious and valuable columns,
which seemed to be all of one piece,
of the finest diamond from the foot to the summit.
The bases where all the second
series and the first rest
were incised by subtle work,
with figures and foliage expressed in gold.

63

The rich capitals projected out,
over which many nude and beautiful boys
were seen seated in relief;
they seemed to perch there alive.
With their hands they supported on every

side a festoon of enamels and jewels,
arranged and spread with good judgment,
which encircled the arch formed by the balcony.

64

Over the first order was the second,
of columns equal in artifice;
and over that one the third no less pleasing,
no less rich in oriental gems.
It is true that a white and rubicund frieze
of pearls, rubies, and such jewels
was distinct between one order and the other,
all girded with laurel fronds on the borders.

65

The splendid wall all around
flamed with lively carbuncles,
which illuminated all the air and the earth
at night no less than in the bright day.
Above, the structure proved
to be covered with silver all around.
The doors were interwoven with ivory and gold,
with figures of noble and celestial intaglio.

66

The blond god who opposed the fierce Python
appeared there sculpted with highest industry,
as he removed from the world the cruel and harmful bites
of the venomous, horrible dragon.[6]
The cautious archer and the serpent seemed alive;
Apollo was represented in so fine a gesture against
Python, and he worked his bow so well,
that nothing more belongs to truth.

---

6. The goddess Hera sent the dragon Python to kill Apollo's pregnant mother, Leto, but Poseidon hid her. At four days old, Apollo fought and killed Python with an arrow.

67

Risardo and his companions paused
astounded awhile to contemplate from outside
that illustrious edifice and those portraits.
They praised the architect and the sculptor,
those masterpieces and those works of art so well made
with so many gems of various colors.
Once they had admired the whole from outside,
having dismounted from their destriers they entered the temple.

68

Within, the sacred, famous, ample edifice
was no less shining and beautiful than outside,
no less filled with richness and artifice,
with illustrious stones and works of the chisel,
and with figures that had different tasks
expressed on the wall on this side and that.
Everywhere a window did not appear,
sumptuous and rare statues shone.

69

The months all figured in gold
were seen around the transparent wall.
They were sculpted six here, six over there,
of varied colors and varied workmanship.
On the right side a strong and secure man
appeared portrayed; he was the first of them,
adorned with helm, shield, and every trophy,
like a warrior prepared at arms.

70

Because at the end of the winter the experienced
and expert soldier goes out to battle,
the man covered with strong mail
and finest plate represented March.
Next to this one a peasant with his head uncovered
encumbered the wall.

With a ruffled beard and neglected hair,
he appeared to be a shepherd from his clothing and aspect.

71

At his feet, for his legs were bare
to the knee, a she-goat lay;
she was languishing with grave pain,
and seemed to give birth to two little kids.
The shepherd was playing bagpipes,
and in this figure one recognized
April, when the glad and joyful shepherd
leads to pasture his fecund herd.

72

Next followed a youth of immature
age, fresh and rosy in visage.
His clothing was all lovely and superb
with flowers and gold, reaching all the way to his feet.
It seemed he was in a grassy meadow
enriched by Zephyr with a thousand flowers.
A fresh garland of pretty flowers
wafted sweet odors from his lovely hair.

73

His hands were full of scented herbs, roses,
lilies, violets, and acanthus.
A light breeze came around, lifting up
his golden, white, and vermilion clothes.
To those who understood well it seemed
the graceful boy resembled May.
So many herbs, so many flowers, so many ornaments
show May's lovely and delightful days.

74

A field of very beautiful greenery
was next in order to this fellow.
In the middle of it one discovered the figure

of a laborious and rough peasant.
The sculpture portrayed around his head
a garland not of roses but of linen.
He had a dart at his side; he held the crooked scythe
with both hands, and aimed at and cropped the grass.

75

It meant June when in the sunny
countryside the peasant cuts the mature hay.
Another behind him cut the blond
ears of grain, and curved and bowed his back,
and with these important toils of his,
with such signs, he showed he was July.
A hat on his head was his shield from the sun,
and everywhere except his flanks he was naked.

76

The last image which appeared on the right-hand side
was another man likewise naked as he was born.
His flank alone was concealed
by a small cloth, as pleased the maestro.
Before a bath of fresh clear waves,
he seemed to wash in those limpid waters.
With his right hand he held a cup to his lips,
with his left he held up the little cloth.

77

This thirsty fellow, who seemed to swallow
the cool draft and bathe his feet and arms,
appeared to be August, when with such assistance
men temper and banish the heat of the dog days.
The other half of the year, where the sun follows
its course, was on the facing wall.
But it would be too much if I let
six more months pass before I rested.

CANTO 10

ARGUMENT

In the sacred and hallowed place Risardo sees the flower
of the yet-unborn renowned minds.
Apollo gives an answer to the worthy prayers.
Floridoro is victor of the tourney.
Filardo pretends to come from the farthest
realms with Floridoro. Celsidea burns
with love for Silvarte's son,
and gives him the gem. The two youths withdraw.

1

Ah, why in our age is there not
a pious, holy, and truthful oracle,
who could make our minds recognize
what harms us and what helps us?
I well know that at such a proof we would see
more than one war converted to peace.
A man could escape a thousand harms,
a thousand ruins, if he could guess the end.

2

Oh, how many marriages have proceeded
and still proceed for not knowing
whether they would in fact be successful.
If the end could be foreseen,
how many people who are betrayed by their own kin
in their honor, lives, and possessions

277

could instead, in guarding themselves from them,
save their honor, their persons, and their gold.

3

More than one man remains in sin and does not correct himself,
in the hope of living a long time;
perhaps he would make a dutiful correction,
if he saw his end imminent.
But, not having anywhere to get advice,
people live blindly in error.
Even if a man finds someone who foresees his harm,
since that one is a man like him, he does not believe him.

4

Although in that time the world gave faith
to falsehood, and rendered honor to a vain idol,
yet one believes that he often told the truth,
to keep every soul in that error.
To him people then erected that temple;
you have heard of its magnificent exterior.
I left you when I had described the one
wall inside, and was turning to the other.

5

First the celestial craftsman laid out
a rough and loutish man with bare legs,
at whose foot arose a fountain
of clear wine which went streaming down the plain.
On his shoulders his hair was spread out and even,
and he held a vine in his left hand;
with the other he gathered the grape stalks in great
abundance and pressed them with his mouth.

6

As the grape harvester is accustomed to trample
the grape with his feet to make the must come out,
this man with his mouth, with his hands alone,

was apt and disposed to different tasks.
Thus with such an effect he wanted to imply
that month which succeeds hot August;
and it is surely reasonable that he resembled
the fruitful month of September.

7

The second image was a young man
who did not yet show the first beard on his face.
He had a veiled head and wore a white doublet,
clean and very tidy.
It is true that it was tight to his sides,
and the rest wide open and loosened in the wind.
The sculptor had left only his legs and feet
intentionally bare and undressed.

8

This fellow with many cages of little birds
seemed to have planted a thousand branches
in the middle of a meadow, and that whole field
was encircled by tangled cloths.
The wandering birds aloft
could not see the trick he used,
and those in the cages appeared hidden and glad
to invite the others to come down into the nets.

9

One saw the hidden bird catcher
along the meadow, intent on his prey.
In catching more than one bird,
he seemed to laugh at their simplicity.
This man who laid snares for the sparrow and the linnet
was meant to signify October,
when birds go together in swarms
toward the country where the year is warmer.

10

Then a rustic plowman was seen
as well, doing his utmost in the noble theater,
and prodding the suffering oxen
which pulled behind them the plow.
His clothes were all torn;
the color of his visage was swarthy and dark.
On his hair, which he had short and loose
in the wind, he wore a woolen hat.

11

With his right hand the plowman held
the plow, which those two exhausted animals
were pulling, and in the ground he sculpted
with his left hand his labors.
The blood which issued from the punctures
of one and the other weary ox
so gracefully was sculpted,
that it seemed issued from living animals.

12

The figure of which I tell indicated
the month of the Pleiades.[1] At its borders
was one who wore a better garment,
whiter in his face and with longer hair.
His smooth beard showed no
hair which rose or bowed more than the others.
In his left hand he had a basket of grain,
which he went scattering over the tilled plain.

13

That was December, whose season
requires one to sow the grain in the field.
Nearby a very robust boy

1. The seven stars of the Pleiades set in November.

was seen, fierce in aspect and in spirit.
His portrait revealed that he was going hunting,
for he urged the greyhounds after the prey,
and laid the snare for the timid hares;
he caught some with dogs and some with nets.

14

The robust and capable youth showed
his well-groomed beard and his trimmed hair,
but he girded his legs, arms, and torso
with a very tight and tidy garment.
The dogs, which had an avid taste for hares,
went by his side playing with him.
He flattered them and stroked their heads;
they gave him a warm welcome with their tails.

15

This daring boy bore a close resemblance
to January, when the hunter usually
goes outside with nets and dogs,
as is his habit, through the snowy paths.
The last one to encumber this room
was seen to be an old man, laden with horror,
who near a great fire sat wrapped
in thick furs and all huddled up.

16

The white-haired, trembling old man
represented the harsh and icy days of February,
for he stayed with his limbs curled and wrapped up,
with his hands stretched out before that great fire.
One saw the varied designs
vary all the figures;
as the sculptor was well-advised,
the hair was one color, the visage another.

17

With such fine art each was expressed
that they seemed alive and moving and breathing;
the gold circled by pearls and sapphires
was well placed among the gems.
The figures did not have identical positions,
but with diverse arranged motions
they performed the task suitable to their times,
with a gesture that was proper to each one.

18

Nor above them did they lack their own signs:
Aries, Taurus, Gemini, and the rest.
It seemed then that each planet dwelled and ruled
over the houses appropriate to it.
All those portraits and those designs
which belonged to the shining deity,
the reliefs, the imprints, the heights and the hollows
were encircled and divided by green laurels.

19

The floor was all paved
with pictures made of alabaster and corals.
In the center rose the grand and sacred altar,
of marble far more lustrous than crystal.
Over it Phoebus was figured standing,
all of one piece of the most beautiful metal;
of massive gold, in the middle of the sacred altar
shone his divine and excellent simulacrum.

20

His bright and splendid golden hair was
crowned with verdant laurel.
In his right hand the cithara and plectrum appeared,
in the other his bow and golden arrows.
Closed in a chapel was the sacred altar
with incised columns of porphyry.

Between one column and the next stood
the Hours, ready to serve the author of the year.

21

The priests with golden stoles
go through the temple mutely and quietly.
The winged temple flies now here, now there,
for in the long run it discovers all secrets.[2]
But what shall I say of the superb school
of glorious and noble poets
who were sculpted around the divine altar,
although in that time they were not yet born?

22

In the anterior facade among them
a man worthy of every honor and reverence
was in the middle, whose light and decorum
seemed to have preeminence among the others.
From his regal presence, he merited
more than of laurel, a crown of gold;
it seemed that among those he had nearby
there was no other man so venerable.

23

He was seated, with a grave and serene face,
wearing a toga of glorious purple.
Everyone strove to approach him,
but few were those who reached his side;
yet it seemed he called every soul
to come forward, and showed himself agreeable to them.
His name was in pure and merry gold:
DOMENICO VENIER, light of the world.[3]

2. Fonte identifies the temple with the sun, with which Phoebus Apollo is associated.

3. A Venetian poet, politician, and patron of the arts, Domenico Venier (1517–82) was a cultural leader who hosted important gatherings of writers and artists. He promoted women writers such as Gaspara Stampa and Veronica Franco. See Rosenthal, *Honest Courtesan*, 89–98 and passim.

24

The one closest to him on his right was
youthful, of generous aspect.
One discerned clearly in his visage and manner
that he was a charming and noble intellect.
One read the lofty and illustrious soul's
elect name in letters of silver;
from this one could understand clearly
that he was the rare and famous MAFFEO VENIER.[4]

25

Another by his side was sculpted,
his follower and companion of his honor.
He blocked his mouth with a finger,
almost as if for him being silent were praise and gain.
The silver distributed in notes above
his head said: the noble CELIO MAGNO.[5]
The famous and worthy man, from his presence,
seemed of clear and excellent mind.

26

Next to him was a man of lofty and profound
doctrine in appearance, and of excellent habits.
It seemed he instilled virtue through his gaze,
and with his splendor he lit up the earth.
He had a long mantle, and his face abounded in years;
on an open book he fixed his eyes.
Above, BERNARDINO PARTENIO appeared,
in one and the other language a singular man.[6]

4. Maffeo (1550–86) was one of the most original Venetian poets of the century. His best poetry is in the local dialect. See Rosenthal, *Honest Courtesan*, 49–50 and passim.

5. Magno (1536–1602) was a Venetian poet and politician.

6. Pseudonym of Bernardino Franceschini (d. 1589); he wrote Latin verse and prose as well as a treatise in Italian about poetic imitation.

27

The one admiring on the left
the most bright father's lively ray
had a black beard and a humane visage.
He seemed a man of wise and sensible judgment.
The note said ORSATO GIUSTINIANO,
happy spirit, honor of his lineage.[7]
Just like the first ones he wore a long garment,
which brought gravity with reverence.

28

A man of mature age succeeded him.
At Orsato's back he seemed to hurry his pace,
and from what one could discern from his appearance,
he had no less noble and celestial a mind.
He was not wearing the long garment,
but short was the mantle adorning and clothing him.
In his caption, which the writing exposed,
ERASMO, one read, di VALVASONE.[8]

29

A person finished this facade
who demonstrated, by his grave and worthy aspect,
that he must have tasted the water in Helicon,
and in verse must surpass others' achievements.
VINCENZO GILIANI the caption rang,
filled with elevated knowledge and wits.
In this portrait such virtue was expressed
that my verse does not convey its merits.[9]

7. Giustiniano (1538–c.1603) was a well-known Venetian poet. Fonte is now describing the figures to the left of Domenico Venier, the central figure and "most bright father."

8. Valvasone (1523–93) was a poet and translator from the Friuli region.

9. Mount Helicon was the home of the Muses. People who drank from the sacred springs there received poetic inspiration. There is no information on this writer available.

30

At the head of the altar on the left side,
a younger noble man followed.
In his aspect he seemed no less
learned, honored, and full of courtesy.
Let it be clear he is ALBERTO LAVEZUOLA,
who never tires of following the blond
Apollo; for him that great city
will rejoice, in which the fair Adige flows.[10]

31

Then one saw a man who similarly
seemed born for study. In his heart he was very
benign, and of elevated mind,
if one can discern the character from the face.
The charming and cultured spirit possessed
those years which make a man most prudent.
He was blond, and his mantle encumbered him down to his feet,
and for him was written BARTOLOMEO MALOMBRA.[11]

32

An affable and discreet person
came to fill the picture on that side.
His mind was wise and beautiful, from what
his worthy and gentle face showed.
He seemed to stop the sweet waters with his song,
and to be no less worthy a poet than the others.
He had a short garment, and his note
showed and denoted him as CESARE SIMONETTI.[12]

10. Alberto Lavezuola wrote a commentary on Ariosto's *Orlando furioso*, *Osservationi sopra il Furioso . . . nelle quali si mostrano tutti i luoghi imitati dall'autore nel suo poema* (Venice, 1584). See Javitch, *Proclaiming a Classic*, 60–70. The Adige River flows through several cities in northeastern Italy.

11. Malombra published poetry with religious overtones in Venice in the 1570s. See also his prefatory sonnet to *Floridoro* (above).

12. Simonetti's *Rime* were published in Padua in 1579. See also his prefatory sonnet to *Floridoro* (above).

3 3

On the opposite wall, still at the head
of the sacrosanct altar, but on the right-hand side,
another image was shown standing,
portrayed with lofty and lordly presence.
He wore splendid and graceful clothing,
and the letters superscribed
declared him GIULIAN GOSELIMO,
of most felicitous and divine mind.[13]

3 4

Another of youthful age was seen
near him, who seemed to come in a hurry,
almost as if he regretted and was not pleased
that another person set foot ahead of him.
The place where he was sculpted persuades
that he was of a rare and perfect virtue.
The note he had made plain
he was the learned CESARE PAVESE.[14]

3 5

Nearby the chisel had portrayed
a man of younger and fresher age,
who in going among the noble band
seemed to increase his strength and courage.
He had a long mantle and on his head a hat.
Although among these he came last,
he was, however, first among a thousand other scholars.
Above was GIANMARIO VERDIZZOTTI.[15]

13. Giuliano Gosellini (or Goselini) (1525–87) was well known in intellectual circles in the period. He published poetry, letters, and historical-political works.

14. A poet and translator who published in late sixteenth-century Venice.

15. Verdizzotti (1537/40–1604/7) was a Venetian painter and poet.

3 6

On the last facade, which was sculpted
in back where there was little light,
a solitary young woman stayed.[16]
She did not dare come out with the others into the light,
quite ashamed that she, too bold,
aspired to the way which leads to heaven,
having as low and dull a mind
as her design was clear and sublime.

3 7

She wore a long white skirt,
as for the virginal state is appropriate,
and she seemed at an early and youthful age
to have lofty thoughts kindled in her heart.
This damsel had no caption
to make her plain to the other senses,
for the sculptor who fashioned her portrait
did not wish that her name be known.

3 8

The high chapel's ceiling was adorned
as well with elect figures of azure and gold.
The seven arts were impressed round about;
liberal they are called and named.[17]
In the middle a noble man made his sojourn;
it seemed that each of these seven
competed to gird his rare and illustrious head
with an immortal crown of laurel.

16. Moderata Fonte's representation of herself here as a shy, self-effacing poet who does not even dare to come into the light, or to name herself in the next octave, is a poetic conceit that aptly hides the boldness of her poetic enterprise.

17. The seven liberal arts are grammar, rhetoric, dialectic (logic), arithmetic, geometry, astronomy, and music.

3 9

Although he was girded and filled with age,
as one could discern from his appearance,
the wonderful portrait seemed
to show his breast overflowing with true glory.
His brow had an air both pleasant and serene,
which rendered him happier and more amiable.
Of GIOSEPPE ZARLINO the silver revealed
the name, and a long mantle clothed and covered him.[18]

4 0

After the religious and pious young Risardo,
with all his companions, for a while
had nourished his covetous gaze
on the fateful temple of the blond god,
devoutly he knelt, and was not slow
to explain to that deity his desire.
Likewise each one of them knelt
with their hands joined, their faces disarmed.

4 1

The principal minister, who consecrated
the victims to Apollo and adored him,
climbed the steps of the sacred altar
and, as was his custom, prayed to and worshiped him.
The priest implored him for a prediction
in order to have a response, whether sweet or bitter.
The burning lamps hung round about,
giving light to the one who lights up the day.

4 2

The minister, draped in a golden gown,
barely finished praying to the blazing deity,

18. Zarlino (1517–90) was a composer and important music theorist from Chioggia; he
worked in Venice from 1541.

when the torches doubled their holy light,
and every column in the great temple trembled.
Then they heard, beyond any human understanding,
"He will have the lady, and the man the man, and the lady,[19]
and the couple will unite with the couple
who against their own blood bring together so many arms."

43

The obscure answer left quite confused
those suppliant and devout souls.
With sorrowing hearts and lips closed,
they were unable to comprehend the obscure notes.
Then, full of furor the highest prophetic priest
opened his mouth
and cried loudly, "O ladies, O knights,
hear the great god's true announcements.

44

"The one of you who in the clothing of a strong man
hides her true feminine sex
will be the consort of this knight,
who has a damsel impressed on his shield.
For the other two another fate is reserved,
as the auspicious oracle has expressed to us.
In Armenia, where they make war and quarrels,
are the sisters whose husbands they are to be."[20]

45

Filled with inestimable happiness
at the answer, the young Thracian

19. As the text explains below, the true meaning of this incomprehensible verse is: the man who has a lady (in his shield) will have the lady who dresses as a man.

20. This notation makes us understand that Risamante and Biondaura will make peace at the end and marry, a development that in *Floridoro*, which is unfinished, Fonte does not flesh out. See also above, octave 42, "and the couple . . ."

thanked that god propitious to his desire,
since heaven too wanted what pleased him.
He rose to his feet and was not slow
to embrace his goddess, who blushed and was silent.
From that day on, Risardo wanted
her to relinquish the lying clothing.

46

The other two knights were quite pained
and sad at it in their secret hearts,
but they did not dare to complain about the celestial
pronouncements, so they stayed mute and quiet.
Toward Armenia they were quick to ride,
where they still had hope of being happy;
with Gracisa they took the route
specified by the divine interpreter.

47

Risardo, who was benign and courteous,
moved by pity for these knights,
decided to go with them,
and traveled the same roads.
It is true that not so quickly did he find himself
in that country, for love persuaded him
to spend some days alone in repose,
since one could say he was a newlywed.

48

But because I fear my tale will bore you,
if I continue with them and the two sisters,
it will be good if I defer their story till later,
and now of the king of Greece I give you news.
I said that ten of his knights,
with arms and surcoats rich and beautiful,
had gone forth to gain the laurel,
counting with them Filardo and Floridoro.

49

I left off when by Prince Aliforte
three knights had been knocked to the plain:
Brandilatte, who held court in Syria;
Acreonte of Persia; and the African.
Now I say that, while the nobility of the Greeks
and the foolish people were exalting the strong warrior,
a knight came out from the other side,
who seemed from his aspect a new Mars.

50

Miricelso of Egypt, who had the same father
as the innocent Raggidora,
having come as well against the Greek squads,
was the man who came forward against Aliforte then.
At once by his lovely gold and vermilion arms
he was recognized by everyone when he came forth.
Each one knew the prince of the Nile
by his insignia of the crocodile.

51

They took to the field, and the encounter was such
that it bent over the knight of Egypt,
and he showed more than one sign of falling;
he lost the stirrups and yet remained upright.
But they did not share the same fate;
the Greek was so afflicted by the great blow
that, having lost his strength together with his reins,
he was forced to fall to the ground.

52

After him Miricelso knocked down and threw
the king of Arcadia[21] clean out of his saddle.

21. Elion.

Then he made King Clizio press the grass,
and next to the duke was Satirione.
Satirione wanted to avenge
Aliforte, Clizio, and Elion,
when great Thebes's famous prince[22]
came forth haughty and disdainful to the joust.

53

The knights, brave beyond measure,
came toward each other and lowered their lances.
The Egyptian wanted his iron to pierce his belly;
he broke his lance on his belt.
But the Theban struck him on the head,
and proved his shoulder was harder.
The Egyptian could not protect himself enough,
and Apollideo won the bout and the right to boast.

54

After Miricelso fell, Apollideo
over the ferocious Marcane gained victory;
he was the lofty king of Persia's brother,
and his shield was white and blackish.
Then a warrior came forth; nature did not make
anyone prouder than he, and more rebellious against the gods.
He had azure arms, and on his shield he showed
a mountain on an azure field for his insignia.

55

Twenty-four years the ferocious youth
had already completed, and his strength was extreme,
such that in every peril and atrocious situation,
it seemed that even death feared him.
Love, who is so arrogant, did not harm him;
from that cruel heart he hid and trembled.

22. Apollideo.

This man was the good destrier's lord,
of which Floridoro was now the possessor.

56

His name was proud Sfidamarte,
to whom was due the rule of Trebizond;
the lofty acclaim of his bright deeds encircled
the whole earth in every part.
Daring and skill did not avail the good Theban
against this man who abounded in such strength;
although Apollideo put up a good defense,
he threw him to the ground far from his destrier.

57

At the encounter with Stellidone, Sfidamarte broke his lance,
but neither one fell from his destrier.
Since the first encounter was not enough for them,
with new lances they made another trial.
The Greek fell, and the other still clashed
with Satirione, Sirio, and Algiero;
each of them with little resistance
he overcame and felled through his great valor.

58

Now the Greek heroes' hope was founded
only on Filardo and Floridoro,
who remained to try their prowess
against the warrior who feared no opponent.
To crown himself with palm and laurel,
Sfidamarte pitted all his strength
against Filardo, who moved up in a hurry;
and he threw him a body's length from the saddle.

59

It is true that after Filardo struck,
his destrier was not steady on its feet,

and seemed sluggish to rise and slow,
so great a blow the good Dictaean gave.
But if Floridoro did not prove himself stronger
than he, the barbarian would win;
the Greeks would lose the triumphal honor,
if Floridoro was not better than he.

60

To Floridoro remained the last trial
against this man who knocked everyone else to the earth,
and the barbarians surely believed they would
bring news of victory to their country.
Already Floridoro, whose heart benefited
from that flame with which love burned him so,
had taken his lance onto his thigh
and turned his reins against Sfidamarte.

61

He really seemed in his actions, his gestures, his proud
movement, in his grave, heroic, and courageous appearance,
to be the flower of the group, and in daring
and strength to surpass all the others.
As if he had played this game a hundred
thousand times, haughtily he came forward;
his destrier raced out in such a flash
that it seemed he alone held that whole field.

62

Great was his advantage, for besides the valor
he had by nature, love increased his vigor;
and what's more, he rode so good a racer
that another like it could hardly be found.
Sfidamarte, who did not yet feel love
and who sat a weak destrier's back,
came haughtily to meet him, and on the center
of the boy's shield he broke his lance.

63

The barbarian was struck in the helmet
by Floridoro, whom he had not moved,
and the destriers crashed chest to chest.
In such a fashion each horse was struck
that Sfidamarte's was constrained
to collapse with its lord on its back;
he at such an encounter felt more wrath
than if he had lost his own kingdom.

64

At the serious blow Floridoro's
horse also set its rump to the earth,
but paused only briefly before rising again,
as soon as it felt at its flanks the accustomed pricking.
Everyone was astounded at Sfidamarte's failure;
wonder and fear gripped everyone.
Now to the joust the king of Arabia came,
who had a phoenix emblem, and he too had to fall.

65

With him overcome (who with white and gold
was adorned, and was named Lucidaldo),
the kings of Media and of Tartary
one after the other assailed Floridoro.
Norando, the former, had for insignia a bull;
the other a lynx, and he was named Anachia.
Floridoro lowered his lance,
and knocked one and the other from the saddle.

66

After these the youth threw onto the meadow
the kings of Hyrcania and of Sufiana.[23]

23. Hyrcania was an ancient province of Persia, on the southeast coast of the Caspian Sea.

The former, who was named Androcaspe,
designed and laid out as his emblem a cruel tiger.
Frangileo, the other, bore
a wild man in the middle of a spring.
Already all the people hoped and felt
the white warrior would be victor of the tourney.

67

But the barbaric host did not intend
for Floridoro to end up the victor.
At once every one of them took another lance
and remounted his racer.
Floridoro did not lose heart; rather he was kindled
to greater daring and more vigor.
He hit his horse and caught Miricelso,
who came first, and removed him from his destrier.

68

He unhorsed Riviero. He knocked down the king of Persia,
who proudly met and opposed him.
He hit Marcane, he struck Brandilatte,
and made the one and the other end up on foot.
In short, the knight whiter
than milk defeated everyone.
For joy then every trumpet sounds,
and the people's shouts resound to heaven.

69

The king rejoices, Celsidea is glad,
all the people laugh. They all enjoy
their side's having the victory,
and on the other hand the barbarians resent it.
Because the lofty name of the victor
is not known, they cannot give him praise;
yet they honor his merit with those names
which one can give to an uncertain knight.

70

At once the high king by a public announcement
issues an invitation to the illustrious victor,
because he wants, with everyone present, to give for his honor
the rich treasure which awaits him.
Rather, he wants the exceptional girl
to give it as a favor to the greatest knight;
and he commands everyone from the great court
to accompany the strong and famous warrior.

71

The most illustrious lords accompany
the lofty, unidentified knight.
To King Cleardo he presents himself;
he comes before him trembling and mute.
That magnanimous king places him next to himself,
and wants him to be seen by everyone.
He honors him, commends him, and gives him praise;
and in the same way everyone reveres and praises him.

72

O king, if you recognized the knight
whom you exalt so much and honor above all others,
I don't know if he would be so dear to your heart
as now when you are ignorant of his fair name.
Or rather, he would be; but if you knew the truth
of his new love (a love unwelcome to you,
since you are too haughty, too proud),
you would be his pitiless and bitter enemy.

73

Dukes, princes, kings, counts, and marquesses
had converged in infinite number
in the great hall, where at the royal invitation
the barbarians with the Greeks show courtesy.
There Marcane and the bold king of Persia

are with Riviero, upstairs with all the rest—
except Sfidamarte, who for wrath
right then departs the Greek realm.

7 4

Having received a sweet and dutiful welcome
from this and that lofty, eminent person,
Floridoro trembles in the royal presence
and, confused, does not speak and does not converse.
He cannot wait to make his departure
and acquire the triumphal crown;
still he stays reserved and mute,
for fear of being recognized.

7 5

The king is astounded. Everyone marvels
that the knight does not give forth his voice,
and the regal daughter grieves to herself,
for already more within than without she esteems and honors him.
The king entreats him to uncover his brow,
and say the name that will be famous forever.
He wants him to do such a favor to his highness,
that he and all the others might see his face.

7 6

The other lords urge Filardo
to remove now his helm from his head,
and to make plain to King Cleardo
their lofty and glorious lineage.
The good Dictaean is not slow to answer
those who constrain and bother him.
He knows very well how to pretend and deceive
with his voice and gestures, so he begins to say,

77

"Most serene king, we are brothers
of Tanafrè, the great prince of the Scythians.
Not for being malign, impious, and rebellious
have we departed from our bountiful land;
rather the acclaim of your fair and illustrious feats
has drawn us in good time to your famous shores
where, if today we have shown valor,
we want to offer it all for your favor.

78

"Our lord was pleased at our departure
to give us this statute and this law:
while we are in your kingdom,
we must never strip off our arms.
Therefore since I have declared our blood and our homeland,
do not complain if we do not intend to show ourselves;
for justice and reason cannot permit
us to disobey so great a king.

79

"Do not marvel, lord, if my brother,
who is called Biancadoro, does not speak to you,
because a fierce, unjust, and evil accident
has taken from him words and the power of speech.[24]
To satisfy further your desire,
call me, Calindrano, to your service;
I will be ready at your commands,
no less than these honored heroes."

24. The name Biancador, as Floridoro is now called by Filardo to hide his true identity, again calls attention to a color, white, that is often reserved for women in narrative, and that is indeed, as mentioned earlier, Risamante's color. Later on Fonte will also use white to distinguish King Cloridabello, whose shield sports a distinctive white dove (see canto 13.51).

80

These plausible excuses the king, who is prudent,
pretends to accept with a sensible and joyful face,[25]
and with his example all the people
remain tranquil and quiet in their thoughts.
Only the royal girl feels herself burn
with a contrary wish in private,
nor can she unburden her heart of the great desire
she feels to see that mute knight.

81

For a hundred charming youths thereabout
who contemplate her beauty
she does not care; she only keeps her eyes intent
on the knight whom she so admires and esteems.
"If his other parts are not different,"
she said to herself, "if his visage has such grace
as his aspect demonstrates, there is not in the world
a knight more handsome and more pleasant.

82

"Happy the one who saw his lofty valor,
which earlier cast down all the others,
but happier yet the one who might
gaze at his divine face's splendor."
So she goes turning through her heart
one thought and another that follows.
She does not know what love is, nor does she know how to name
the new affection; and she burns and does not know why.

---

25. For the second time, Fonte characterizes the ideal king as one who is typically wary of appearances and guarded in judgment. Confronted by a knight who refuses to reveal his identity and yet has just shown his valor by winning a joust, Cleardo "pretends" to believe the knight's reason for choosing to remain hidden, as astute princes do. Earlier the Emperor Agricorno likewise wondered whether the Pygmy who had arrived alone at his court was rather a spy sent from Greece, and thus remained on guard (canto 2.70).

83

Inexperienced, the virgin to the hard troubles
of love gives way, and secretly languishes and suffers.
She does not understand at so tender an age
that it is Love who burns her and chains her.
But she sees well that her sweet harms
would find a remedy, and her sweet pain,
if she could gaze at the beloved object,
but this is prevented by her virginal respect.

84

Floridoro realizes that he is gazed at
with much affection by his goddess,
and says to himself, "O lucky Floridoro,
if Celsidea considered you as such,
and not as what the knight of the Dictaean
island pretended and imagined!
Lucky you if she knew the truth,
and her heart was no longer fierce toward you!"

85

At this moment the king with gracious brow,
not to fail in any of his duties,
recalls sweetly to his beloved daughter
that by her the knight must be satisfied.
She blushes more vermilion than a rose,
lowers her eyes, and with a reverent gesture,
as the prize of the highest victory,
she gives the warrior the merited glory.

86

She gives, but that giving of hers is of such power
that she takes from him far more than she gives.
She gives him the crown, she takes his heart—
strange exchange and, with no toil, high payment.
Ah, for among those gems Love is hidden,

like a snake among flowers—and the wretched youth does not see it—
to remind him later, with the charming gift,
of his sweet, greedy co-giver.

87

From that beautiful hand of carmine and snow,
the gift is too welcome to the knight,
and while he readily receives the great favor,
the whole time through gestures he offers her his life as a gift.
With the ceremony completed properly,
the knight who can give forth sounds
asks leave of the king. To deny it
he certainly does not dare, so he speaks in this way:

88

"Famous knights who have come
to my shore, with the valor you have
shown to the world (for which eternal will be the acclaim),
you preserved the honor of our realm.
I sorrow that I am unable to repay in part,
at my own hearth, your great merit.
I regret and sorrow only at your departure,
for I would like to perform actions, not say words.

89

"If the generous heart finds a place
for any debt of nobility,
I pray you stay here where we prize
virtue and valor more than anywhere else.
With general joy and contentment
you will be the first heroes of this place,
nor will you have here less grace and favor
than you have with your own emperor."

90

For the courteous offers the good Dictaean
gives infinite thanks to King Cleardo.
His fully courteous response confirms
they are disposed to leave the Achaean field.
With Algier Apollideo grieves;
everyone grieves who hears of their departure.
But Celsidea sighs so much from her heart
that her mother turns her eyes toward her.

91

To prevent all the inevitable scandals
which from too much delay could arise,
Filardo then departs instantly,
and sends off Floridoro almost by force.
Oh, how hard it is for an ardent lover
to leave the woman he loves and desires so much!
I believe that Floridoro at that parting
was near the final torment.

92

They descend the stairs and leave all
those great lords sad at their departure.
Pretending they want to plow the wavy
billows, to the port they turn their coursers.
Returned again afterward into the city,
they strip off their arms and the white colors.
No one notices their return,
for it is already evening and no one is going about anymore.

93

The illustrious Greek and the Cretan youth
assemble in their comfortable abode,
and they hide away their arms and those spoils
which could make them known to people.
Orfil takes care to prepare

dinner for Floridoro and his master;
Orfil is Filardo's servant,
faithful, secretive, sensible, and diligent.

94

But Floridoro, too sated and listless
from the assiduous thought that bothers him,
can taste no food that is pleasant to him,
and stays with his face languid and sad.
He pretends he is all tired and troubled,
his whole life torn and crushed;
he does not want the servant to know his thought,
for more than one good reason.

95

With the unwelcome and solitary dinner
concluded between them in a brief period of time,
the inflamed Floridoro, who at every moment
feels in his heart the pain increase,
with Proserpina's ray goes outside[26]
where his too unrestrained desire leads him,
and returns to the palace—but I perceive
the page is already full, so I must rest.

26. Proserpina, the queen of the underworld, was identified with the waxing moon.

CANTO 11

ARGUMENT

Floridoro goes secretly to spy on
the royal dinner, and fate directs his feet
into his beloved's room. He writes down
his pain, descends by the balcony, and goes away.
Celsidea finds the paper and sorrows and suffers.
One Persian kills the other. Floridoro has a fierce
dispute with Marcane. For the Persian's death
the barbarian kings assign Cleardo the blame.

1

What vigor and power dwell and rule
in the virtue which resides in a noble breast,
one has seen and sees from a thousand proofs,
from a thousand clear signs, on a thousand occasions.
Its strength extinguishes hate
and resentment, and in their place kindles love and faith.
Virtue not only calms and extinguishes wrath,
but pulls man back from many iniquities.

2

Let every man strive to acquire some virtue,
for at some place and time, in some way or other,
it cannot be that it will not help him,
and give him some benefit, something useful.
Its strength often releases a man from servitude,
and wards off from him both prison and cruel death.

From ancient and from modern times
I could advance a thousand apt examples.

3

Virtue well disposed in a subject
makes its possessor renowned and noble,
and the man who loves it and adorns his heart
with it (whoever he may be) cannot be called base.
By poverty a man cannot be constrained
when he follows virtue's praiseworthy style,
whether in arms or learning, for he will be rewarded
by more than one courteous and agreeable spirit.

4

It is not to be wondered at
(for it gives men such grace and favor
that it extracts goods from others' hands, and takes
great rewards either for doctrine or for valor)
if the virtue of that mighty youth in person,
who had won the tourney and the crown,
can extract the heart from the breast
of the Greek king's proud daughter.

5

I left you with the valorous youth,
not very proud of his so great victory;
after a brief period of repose,
he had left Filardo and the groom.
Driven by the amorous goad
which makes a man court every peril,
toward the royal palace he turned his steps,
nor (beyond his sword) did he take any armaments.

6

He entered among the infinite throng of servants
who in the happy dwelling were bustling up and down.

Without any thought for his life
he dared to climb the royal stairs.
Fortune, which often helps the bold,
was to him so propitious and liberal
that no one gave him a thought; no one said,
"Who are you?" nor even sought from where he came.

7

Everyone solicitously studied and attended
to complete the task imposed on him,
nor did they care to look into others' chores,
to carry out their own all the quicker.
In the royal kitchen the fire shone
on diverse animals boiled and roasted;
they made pleasant viands in abundance,
of as many sorts as one can imagine.

8

In the splendid golden hall, bright
from the lighted candles in every corner,
the feast proceeded solemnly
among the ladies and the warriors whom I honor and sing.
The cautious Floridoro secretly
placed himself in the darkness. He could see all
the people, but by no one could he be seen,
let alone described and recognized.

9

On first arriving he sees the king of Persia
invite the regal girl to dance.
She courteously rises from her seat,
her hand united with the barbarian hand.
He watches her move now one, now the other foot
with such flowing grace and elegance
that simultaneously love assails him,
and cruel, mortal jealousy stings him.

10

The dance was guided couple by couple
in a long line at a grave and slow pace:
a happy opportunity, convenient and welcome,
for lovers to reveal their torment.
One regarded his goddess piteously;
one mutely asked her for mercy.
That whole regal abode was feasting and games;
every bliss, every good pleasure reigned in that place.

11

It was in the season of renewal
of Bacchus's most sweet liquor,
when the mature peach tree favors the taste buds
with its most durable and best fruit,
and the sun far from the new grape harvest
increases the hours of the nights and shortens those of the days—
the time when it is customary to dine
at night in the splendor of the waxy candlelight.

12

After they had consumed a good part of the evening
in so much cheer and so many pleasures,
the tables were set, where there was
a great abundance of as many foods as could be desired.
Citharas and lyres, harmonizing
so as to humble every fierce soul
with their song sweeter than a siren's,
accompanied the sumptuous dinner.

13

There was no lack of illustrious, lofty poets
who with felicitous and pure minds,
according lovely and joyous verses with the music,
praised every famous and worthy warrior;

nor did they celebrate (since they were discreet)
the eternal heroes any less than those of the Greek realm,
nor were they less pleased to raise above the stars
the virtue of the adorned and beautiful ladies.

14

The king of Athens had granted as the immense
and highest favor to the knights from the different lands
that they might sit together at one table
with the Greek virgins.
Here (since fate dispenses favors
at its pleasure) such a place the king of Persia held,
that the very beautiful daughter of Cleardo
was seated before his lascivious gaze.

15

By love of her that king was so kindled
that from moment to moment he released ardent sighs,
and, become impatient, his offended breast
revealed with his gaze his new torments.
He gazes at her, he yearns for her, and stays in suspense
so that she might understand his desires.
He turns now all ice, now all fire;
nor can he taste much nor even a little food.

16

Floridoro, hidden, watches it all.
Love consumes him and envy devours him.
Love afflicts him, inflames him, and torments him
for the beauty the whole world adores.
The jealousy that distresses him and breaks his heart
kindles his breast toward vengeance and wrath,
nor can he bear to see King Acreonte
placed across from his dear lady.

17

He numbers the sighs, he counts the looks
which too frequently that king directs toward her.
As if in his heart he feels stinging darts,
with jealousy and impatience he is consumed.
Sometimes (although it is not so) he thinks that she looks at him,
that Celsidea loves Acreonte and favors him;
when the beautiful lady merely raises her eyes
Floridoro reacts with anxiety and distress.

1 8

Overcome by rage in the end,
so that his wretched heart serves while languishing,
he wants to leave with all haste.
But his oppressed memory does not serve,
for in the dark he enters an access where he hears
a great murmuring of pages and serving maids;
to flee it he descends to his left,
and wanders far away from the stairs.

1 9

The youth, confused and belatedly repentant,
goes from that room to this one,
and truly regrets that he ever came to the feast
without anyone's invitation.
If he is discovered he will lose his head.
As a thief and malefactor he will be punished,
for the law says that from life a man will be released,
if in another's rooms at night he is caught.

2 0

As the greedy lover permits his too audacious
foot to encumber the third room,
a light strikes his eyes which reflects
from the fourth to the third, and frightens him not a little.

He fears there might be people there, so he takes
not another step toward where the fire shines,
but sets his trustworthy ear to the door
to listen in case he hears anyone speak.

21

When his attentive ear brings the sense
that in his judgment no one is there,
and makes his soul aware without a doubt
that within no one speaks or converses,
his emboldened hand opens the door
(though very quietly), and he casts a look around.
He sees a royal and ornate bedroom,
by a splendid gem illuminated.

22

The well-proportioned room,
of excellent architecture, is equal on each side.
Dressed with purple are its superb walls,
which the gold cornice encircles and embraces.
In the middle a very beautiful figure
lies on the frieze opposite the great door;
so admirable is its perspective
that it seems to all a natural and living form.

23

The image of a rare and illustrious lady,
or rather of a lovely and well-adorned goddess,
has a blonde head shining with many gems,
where a carbuncle burns like a torch.[1]
At once Floridoro's judgment declares
that so worthy a virgin is Celsidea,
so he begins to take hope
that this is Celsidea's room.

1. Boiardo presents a similar marvelous shining gem in Morgana's underwater palace (*Innamorato* 2.8.18–19).

24

At this partly he thanks the celestial gods,
partly he fears profound shame and ignominy;
for it's not good that he stay in that room,
and he does not know how to go back again.
Varied thoughts, some consoling, some sad,
in his youthful heart make a painful sojourn.
He is not sure of her; he fears everyone;
and in death alone he places his last hope.

25

While he is in suspense his eye is caught
by an inkstand with paper and pen.
He approves of writing, then he rejects it,
for this thought sets off profound fear.
He resolves in the end not to remain mute;
love makes new hope flare up in his heart.
He takes the hard plume, then stains it
in the black ink, and in the following manner he paints the page:

26

"I defeated the world and by one woman alone I was
bound and captured; and I enjoy being defeated
by her no less than being the victor over others,
nor for any better feat do I boast and praise myself.
Blessed and most happy the man
who will be worthy of her marital knot—
not only if he is a man, however illustrious and worthy,
but even if he is a deity and god of the sempiternal realm."[2]

27

In this way the timid boy thinks
to make plain his hidden flame,

2. Again in Fonte what proper men want from the very beginning is to marry the woman they
desire, which is in the end what women want.

and he prays Love to awaken in her a dram
of the fire which in his heart burns and blazes.
Having concluded without delay the epigram,
he begins to think about what matters more:
he begins to imagine which way to choose,
how to flee, how to save himself.

28

After considering various options it comes to him
that it would be best to climb down from the balcony,
which he considers a safer and better path
than going back to get entangled in so many doors.
Therefore, not having feathers to fly,
he thinks to appropriate a rope.
Fortune, who proposes to aid him,
at that moment places a rope into his hand.

29

He takes the rope, and having tied it good and tight
to the plank of the balcony,
he hurries as much as he can to descend,
for already he seems to hear people coming.
He attaches both fists to it, and in a hurry
down by the cord he lowers his body;
nor does his deft hand release it
before the tip of his toe touches the ground.

30

When he is on the ground, he finds he has descended
into a garden adorned with fruits and flowers.
The moon shines as bright as day,
so that he still fears being seen and captured.
Therefore, he quietly sets himself to linger,
stretched out in dense greenery amid the flowers,
waiting for Cynthia to leave the dark
sky, so that he might depart safely.[3]

3. On Cynthia, see above, canto 5.6n and 8.1.

31

The first thing that comes to his mind
(because no greater thought presses him)
is she for whom his heart is so ardent:
the beautiful princess Celsidea.
He would like to stay forever in her presence.
Then remembering the king whose
breast burns so with his same ardor,
he gets all enraged with wrath and vexation.

32

Meanwhile Celsidea in her mind holds fixed
Biancadoro's aspect and beautiful appearance,
so that feasting and so many pleasures
are of little use to heal her pierced and conquered heart.
After in dances, games, and laughter
more than half the night is spent, and in music and songs,
toward her bedroom she directs her feet,
where just before her lover has been.

33

There, afflicted and discontent, the beautiful
and enamored girl shuts herself in.
Inside for her service she brings
only Carinta, a faithful maid of hers.
While she unties her garments,
she converses of various things with her,
perhaps to decrease her sad heart's
ardor, which is growing ever greater.

34

While mulling over the past games,
she unfastens her pearls and crowns,
undecorates her fair neck and her fair hair,
and puts away all her ornaments.
By chance she comes to see that paper
where Floridoro exposes his fire,

the obscure enigma the young man wrote,
in which his hidden flame is described.

35

She takes it in hand, reads it, and gets all
confused, and her heart and her body tremble.
She feels that that paper manifests
a great love, without naming anyone.
She reads and rereads; at last she finds that this
comes from the man who won the crown,
the one who that day won the proud tourney,
and then received from her the prize in the evening,

36

that noble knight whose merit
she received with such force in her heart
that in no case will she change the plan
she has to serve him and bear him love.
Once she has read well the open meanings and the mute ones,
and interpreted well the whole tenor,
a pleasure full of fear and wonder
encircles and seizes her doubtful mind.

37

Wonder and fear fill up her heart,
for she does not know how he brought it here.
The brief time does not lead her to suspect
that to some servant's hand he might have entrusted it,
because together with her that day and evening
the whole band stayed among delights.
Ladies and maids and pages all day,
near or far, were always about her.

38

But however it happened, she is overcome.
With so much ardor her soul is kindled
that when Carinta looks at her face,

she wonders and trembles and stays in suspense.
Although Celsidea is all undressed,
it displeases and weighs on her to go to bed;
yet perforce she leaps to her repose,
not to make her servant more suspicious.

39

Carinta, in locking up the balconies (as every evening
she was accustomed to do), finds the rope tied
where Floridoro earlier climbed down,
and without saying a word she releases it.
Thus the diligent maidservant
wards off much shame,
for, if others saw the tie, Celsidea
would be wrongly considered immoral.

40

The wretched girl dismisses the servant,
who sleeps in one of her antechambers.
Once she is alone and no one sees or hears,
she opens the way to sighs and weeping.
She who was so happy and so cheerful
before, now is sad and full of agony.
She who did not know what sorrow
was, now is all sorrow, and the blame is Love's.

41

Just as a pretty bird which loose in the air
with free wings once flew,
which when it least expected finds itself entangled
in the ready snares and the strait cage,
in vain turns round and grieves at being caught,
in vain leaps up and down and rages;
with sweet song in vain one hears it lament,
while the cautious bird catcher laughs and rejoices;

42

just so was the enamored virgin,
who formerly had her desires free and joyful,
and had lived many years proud and beautiful—
until she burned with amorous thirst.
Now she grieves to no effect, she hammers herself,
for she cannot release herself from the net.
To no effect she laments, to no effect she shrieks;
and Love, who holds her in prison, laughs at her.

43

Above all things it torments her
that the knight went away so quickly;
for if it's true that for her he feels such pain,
why did he not accept the king's invitation?
How can it be that a man consents to leave
his beloved, when he can stay united with her?
He should have contrived to stay by her side
and not depart, even when entreated.

44

"If only I knew at least," she says, "where you have gone,
my darling, taking with you my heart,
for in some way I would make you understand
how our ardor is reciprocated!
Perhaps you are afraid that my thoughts
take no account of your valor
and, not believing that I esteem and admire you,
far from me you weep and sigh.

45

"Ah, brave and valorous Biancadoro,
you have overcome not only so many glorious heroes,
but also my heart, which feels no repose
since you hid your lovely figure!
Oh, why have you hidden so quickly from me?

What was your hurry to leave us?
It is a sign that the lover is not very ardent,
when from his lady he can stay absent.

46

"O gods, for which of my foul and wicked errors
do you send this punishment to me,
that I am distressed for one whom I have not seen?
And that I feel in my heart such hard pains?
Cease thinking of him,[4] for whom I sorrow so much.
Perhaps he will never again return to Athens;
I weep and sigh in pain and woe,
and perhaps I will never see him again.

47

"But this is not promised by the warm affection
and the sensitive manner with which he writes me.
They show that to such an extent he's subject to me
that he is mine wherever he is, wherever he lives.
Perhaps for some worthy concern
he has deprived my eyes of the sight of him.
Perhaps he left us reluctantly,
and he will return again one day when heaven wills."

48

These and other reasonable conjectures the beautiful girl
considers privately, and is comforted a little.
Then she marvels at herself,
how she made room for vain thoughts,
and her cheek turns now pale, now vermilion,
as if she is assailed in turn by ice and fire.
The ice of fear makes her bloodless,
but shame and love kindle her blood.

4. "Lassa costui": an alternate translation is "He has left."

49

While thus she thinks and reasons to herself
and, wakeful, sighs and weeps in vain,
and in the carbuncle's light love spurs her
to take that writing in hand a thousand times,
a sudden noise stuns the room.
It seems to come from the garden not far away.
She hears swords resound and people shout,
so timidly she rises and goes to the balcony.

50

By then the moon had gone westward,
and the whole garden is tenebrous and shadowed.
The girl comes into the dark air,
and infinite fear fills her heart.
But shortly she no longer hears anything,
and the clamor and the shouting clear away,
so that without knowing what it was
she returns pensively to bed.

51

The cause of that clamor which the beautiful
girl heard in the garden was this:
Floridoro was lying among the flowers, as I
said, with that thought which infested his heart.
In thinking of his new amorous
desire his soul was now joyous, now sad.
Meanwhile he hears one who speaks, and one who answers
with a low murmur among those fronds.

52

One says, "What happier state
than ours could anyone imagine?
What man would be more delighted and blessed than I
if I can make the beautiful lady mine?
Her sweet visage, benign and pleasant,

promises me sweetness and courtesy.
Her gentle air, her fair serene brow
give me hope, favor, grace, and counsel."[5]

53

"Ah, my lord," that other answers him,
"let your highness watch well where he goes.
Ladies are kind and loving,
and show themselves very agreeable to people;
but when one asks them for those things
which in the giving cause them disgrace,
each woman is so contrary and so inimical
that one loses in an instant all one's toil.

54

"I shall never believe that so lofty a maiden
would be content to stain her honor.
Rather I fear that as you climb to her,
when she sees you or at least hears you,
pitiless and rebellious she will raise her voice so
as to draw the not yet somnolent
household to that shout; and in attempting to bring her to us,
you might remain there forever yourself.

55

"With that reverence and that respect
which the servant must have for his lord,

5. Acreonte's boastful behavior—as well as his thorough misreading of women's facial expressions—makes him similar not only to the equally conceited Rodomonte, but also to the optimist Sacripante in the *Furioso*, who is sure that Angelica will welcome his sexual advances: "I shall pluck the morning rose which I might lose were I to delay. Full well I know that there is nothing that a woman finds so delectable and pleasing, even when she pretends to resent it and will sometimes burst into tears. I shall not be put off by any repulse or show of anger, but shall carry into effect what I propose" (*Orlando furioso* 1.58). Angelica is saved from rape by another woman, Bradamante, arriving right there and then to put a stop to Sacripante's fantasized "gentle assault." In *Floridoro* the case against force is first made by Acreonte's own brother, who correctly tells him that no "maiden would be content to stain her honor" (11.53–54), and then by Floridoro, who indignantly addresses the arrogant Persian as "wicked thief, rapacious thief" (11.59).

I warn you of the perilous consequences
that could result from it, and I do my duty."
"I well know, brother, that honest affection,"
that first one replies, "makes you fear.
But now I am astounded
that you have so little daring, so lowly a heart.

56

"Do not doubt, such an outing will not be in vain,
for of her love I am more than sure.
Yet if destiny is so boorish
that it reserves death for me inside that wall,
then against the wicked killer arm your hand.
I entreat you, I command you, and I implore you,
take for your great brother a worthy vengeance,
if in you just piety and valor reign."

57

He promises, so in accord they go
to gather the flower of lovely girls.
They attach to a two-pointed pole
a cloth ladder which they brought,
and the wicked pair study well how to carry out
their scheme before Phoebus brings the day.
Perhaps they would even have succeeded,
except that Floridoro was too nearby.

58

Next to the wall, right at that balcony
where good Floridoro descended not long before,
they have planted and fixed the wood on the ground.
One approaches where he expects to climb.
The other holds the rope and the trunk upright
for his companion to climb to the top;
he goes with the disgraceful and wicked intention
of stealing away the beautiful Celsidea.

59

When good Floridoro hears the outrage
which the bold knight plans to commit,
and recognizes the danger and understands
what might follow if he allows it and keeps silent,
immediately he takes sword in hand
and shouts, "Ah, wicked thief, rapacious thief,
you are utterly foolish and blind if you believe
you can commit this ignominy against the royal blood of Greece."

60

One of those two is Persia's lord,
and the other a brother of his called Marcane;
anger and astonishment fill their haughty minds
at the insulting and unusual words.
At the sudden horrendous and fierce voice,
both of them leave off from their work.
Floridoro, daring as usual,
rushes upon them without any more words.

61

Although he is unarmored in the faint light
which the stars give him from the highest heaven,
he presumes to battle and to win.
He injures the king of Persia's skin,
and already he makes a river of his blood flow down
the rich golden armor, shining and beautiful;
and because on his arm the blow landed,
he made his sword fall, which he had taken in hand.

62

Ferocious Marcane, who sees his brother
assailed by he doesn't know whom,
strikes a blow at Floridoro's head,
for he comes furiously toward him.

But Floridoro foresees his thought,
and opposes his sword to the wicked blow,
so that when he strikes the sword with his own,
he breaks it in two as if it were made of wood.

63

The point with a bounce comes to strike
the king of Persia, and blinds him in one eye.
Floridoro does not delay to loose a blow
at fierce Marcane, who has it in for him.
Meanwhile the king takes up his sword,
and goes behind the valorous Greek;
with all the anguish he feels,
he delivers a terrible and mighty blow.

64

He planned to cut off his head, and would have
followed through without a doubt on the wicked thought,
except for his brother. Marcane was stunned
by that fierce and horrendous blow;
between the faint light and having lost
his wits and all his good judgment,
just at that moment he mistakes his brother
for Floridoro, when he turns to the boy.

65

With that broken sword in mid-forehead
he strikes him so that he splits him to the chin,
and so the unhappy King Acreonte
by the hand of his brother remains lifeless.
Believing he has truly avenged the shame,
Marcane says to Floridoro with delight,
"Truly I said, lord, that the time and the place
do not make the game too safe for us.

66

"A small fire is dead and a far greater one
could be stirred up from these walls.
Let's get away from here, by God, my lord!
Another time we'll have better luck."
Floridoro, who understands the knight's
great error (that he tries to safeguard
his brother's life, which he has taken from him),
without speaking, listens to him with great pity.

67

He thinks surely he's lost his mind,
not knowing the king is lifeless.
Indeed he knew Acreonte had his shield on his breast,
and was covered with still more armor,
while he himself has no helmet on his head
nor other protection, his sword excepted.
But since he sees him submerged in so much error,
behind him wordlessly he treads.

68

Shortly they reach a narrow door
which opens onto the main street.
Because it is frail and ancient,
for going in and out it's easy and handy.
Pure dawn, more beautiful and lovelier
than ever, has already appeared at the window
when Marcane returns to himself,
and perceives that Floridoro wears no armor.

69

At first he marvels
that the king is not decked with arms.
Then fixing better on him his eyes,
he perceives a face so beautiful and so refined
that, as his intellect sharpens,

he understands the situation and is bewildered;
and the more he turns it through his mind,
he nearly dies from the grief he feels.

70

Because it seems to him that Floridoro
was the cause of so evil a deed
(since, threatening, he had assailed them,
and with his sword had charged against them),
as a cruel tiger or a ferocious bull
employs its strong paw or its hard horn,
just so against Floridoro he wields his sword
to give vent to his onerous pain.

71

"Ah," said Floridoro, "you don't recall
what your still-living brother told you,
when to your words he turned a deaf ear,
hoping his plan might succeed:
that if he happened, owing to his greedy
will, to come to death,
you, pitiful and strong, would not rest until
you dealt death to his killer.

72

"Therefore if you were that very one
who took his wretched life,
it would be truly right for you to kill yourself near him,
so that his shade might be placated.
You shouldn't blame me for the evil outcome,
since your madness caused it.
Yet if you desire to do battle with me,
here I am, even without plate and mail.

73

"Don't hope that because I am alone and unarmored
I will take fright at so base a deed.

The whole world could not frighten me,
nor could the whole world give you courage.
But indeed I hope that soon I can arm myself
with your arms of black and silver.
If I did not earlier make you aware of your error,
it was for pity of you, not for fear."

74

Marcane is so fired with rage
that he neither believes nor wishes to believe he tells the truth.
In two hands he takes his sword
to deliver him a fierce and horrendous blow.
Now while Floridoro defends himself,
behold, there suddenly arrives a knight
who challenges Marcane and threatens him,
and sets a shield at Floridoro's neck.

75

When craven Marcane knows
that against two he cannot contend,
he leaves off the battle immediately,
and entrusts to flight his defense.
The knight who just like a dog
had come after the scent of that venture,
once impious Marcane was driven away,
promptly let Floridoro recognize him.

76

Wise Celidante, who cared
for Floridoro as for a son,
learning that the proud youth
was placed in very great peril,
guided his Filardo to that path
to help him. He gave him advice,
and he gave him the shield to give to him,
so from wicked Marcane he might defend himself.

77

He removed his helm, thus making it clear and plain
that he was his faithful friend,
who had sought him all night in vain
until he found him face to face with an enemy.
As if they had been separated a year or more,
they gave each other such a warm welcome that I cannot tell you.
They went to rest, for by now it was day,
and people were awake and going about.

78

With day come, the king of Persia was
found dead of a malicious assassination.
At once someone made Cleardo aware
of this; he went in person to the garden.
Everyone was sorry at the deed when it was known,
but far more the kings of the barbarian domains.
Each one complained of Cleardo, and he heard of it,
and in his mind a just furor flared up.

79

He grieved more that he was found near
the wall where his daughter dwelled,
for perhaps some malign person intended to impute
to her the cause of such an event.
When she heard of the momentous outrage,
she regretted it greatly and greatly mourned;
not because she felt love for the king of Persia,
but for the great jealousy she had for her honor.

80

The just king whom all Greece honored
made clear his faith in her innocence,
although without a doubt the place and the hour
made everyone speak and believe in their own fashion.
Meanwhile the dead man was carried outside,

just as King Cleardo ordered.
Publicly he was brought into the square,
and all the people ran to the spectacle.

81

Cleardo observed and examined everyone
from his court, and called now one, now another,
to deliver pain and punishment
to the malefactor if he found any clue.
At that very moment Marcane appeared in dark
armor on a large, blackish horse.
Once he was in his dead brother's presence,
he spoke thus to the Cecropian people:

82

"You, O king, who gaze at my great, dead brother,
and you, malicious and uncivil Achaean people,
since by you he has been wrongly killed,
since in the Achaean field he remains lifeless,
know that one day for so great a wrong
I intend to avenge myself—I, Marcane;
and Persia, whence your arms will be driven,
will gaze at you all once you are snuffed out." [6]

83

At the end of his speech he pricked his destrier,
and jumped out from the circle he had around him.
He did not cease from spurring until he reached the port,
and he boarded a ship that same day.
Cleardo remained, his soul afflicted
with anger and sorrow at such a disgrace.
However, since he was prudent and discreet,
he kept his face steady and his expression merry.

---

6. Marcane's vow to avenge his brother's death echoes Achilles' similar promise after Patroklos's death in *Iliad* 24.718–81.

84

He commanded that into a rich sepulcher
his servants lay down the lifeless king,
and they quickly took care
that his will was carried out;
they bore him outside the city walls.
The king ordered that with him be buried
every memory of the matter; and whoever spoke
more of it, he would consider a rebel.

85

The other foreign lords and knights,
who the day before had been celebrating,
and who today, loving the king of the Persians,
accompanied him with dark and gloomy pomp,
cursed the impious and villainous hands
that had offended so honored a personage.
Sated with the pleasures of the Greek realm,
to go to their homelands they planned.

86

These were the prince of Egypt,
who was called Miricelso by name,
and Brandilatte, whose indomitable valor
made the Syrians crown his brow.
The proud African swore he would distress
Cleardo and tame his forces;
to help Marcane he vowed,
since his brother died by treachery.

87

The king of Tartary did likewise,
little satisfied with King Cleardo.
He threatened he would make him sorry
and draw his heart from his breast,
for he had secretly been the cause

that so noble a king was killed and undone.
That much more he regretted his death,
because Acreonte was the brother of his wife.

88

Lofty Cleardo, whom neither heaven nor earth
could terrify much nor even a little,
disdained secretly and publicly such a war,
which threatened Greece with iron and fire.
Despite all that, he did not fail to secure his land
against the great need, at the right time and place.
But of him I no longer tell, now that Silano awaits
me on the isle of Circetta.

89

I said of him that, having found
by chance a paradise in that hidden cell,
he had seated himself at table with Clarido,
in the company of the beautiful young woman.
There amid music, song, games, and laughter,
he satisfied his hearing, his taste, and his speech.
Yet despite all that, he was eager
to be able to quit that dwelling.

90

I don't know, lords, if it has slipped your mind
for what reason Silano departed
from ancient Alba, though he was transferred
by the weather to the island of Ulysses.[7]
It was love that took him from his own site,
for the beauty which transfixed his heart.
The fame of beautiful Celsidea
had moved him to take this course.

7. Legend has it that Aeneas's son, Ascanius, founded the city of Alba Longa in Italy and that later it was the birthplace of Romulus and Remus.

91

But Fortune, the enemy of our desires,
against his will took him to Ithaca,
where he found the modest virgin
who led both of them to the delightful banquet.
Repeating it all would be tiresome,
nor did anything happen that must be recalled.
It is enough that I have returned to the enclosed place
where I left him at play with the damsel.

92

Circetta seemed at that youthful age
that is most disposed to Love's arrow,
and she had a merry and beautiful face,
an aspect most worthy and regal.
The eloquence of her discourse
proved equal to her father's;
her speech was so sweet and so pleasant
that in her age she had few peers in the world.[8]

93

But with all the grace and beauty
which heaven so generously gave her,
the knight Silano esteemed her little,
for by another fire his desires were kindled.
Yet he did not want to deny her that sweetness
which comes from a courteous youthful glance.
He admired her, he regarded her fondly, and cleverly
he showed her always some amorous sign.

94

The young woman was cheered in her private thoughts,
but outwardly she pretended not to notice at all

8. Although usually women's talkative ways have been satirized in literature, here Circetta is
described as having inherited the best trait of her father, Ulysses, an eloquence that makes her
appear intelligent and empathetic.

that so charming and noble a knight
was transfixed and pierced by love of her.
Ah, false love, how often you hide
the truth and show an ardent and fervid heart!
You make one person love, and no one ever believes him;
another man pretends, and the lady trusts him.

9 5

Once they had finished the grand and splendid repast,
which was lengthy, the prince of Italy
and his companion did not long delay,
but returned to gaze again at the room.
There, without a craftsman's wage,
the noble people of whom I told you before
had been sculpted beyond our ability
in hard and very clear diamond.

9 6

The Latin king's astounded offspring
could not get enough of contemplating them.
He would swear this figure reasons and speaks,
and that other is silent and listens to the words.
But who will lend me the lofty knowledge
the incomparable daughter of the sun[9]
possessed to portray them, so that I might narrate part
of it to you today in such lowly pages?

9 7

And so that I might express the greatness and the honors,
which took place later in a future century,
of an illustrious young lady whose splendors
were foreseen by the great sorceress?
And with what agonies, with what pains
must a birth so perfect and so mature
emerge at the height of the horrible war,
which made human blood flow over the earth?

9. See canto 8.14 and note.

98

You, holy Cynthius,[10] whose blond hair
is crowned by the chaste and evergreen laurel,
you who looked over that ancient Rome
which formerly overcame the Tartar, the Turk, and the Moor,
and which had so rich a load of trophies,
of honored triumphs and of treasure—
you know well that to tell of all that would be a base endeavor,
in comparison with a better one that I've undertaken.

99

Therefore reveal to my intellect the lofty excellences
of so lovely and lofty a topic,
where all the boldest minds falter.
Open the passage to a rarer and more worthy style,
since in the next canto I shall explain
the most perfect miracle of the world,
provided it is agreeable to my bountiful homeland
that I give out the origin of her great merits.[11]

---

10. Apollo.

11. Venice was commonly personified as a female figure, as Fonte is about to do extensively in canto 12. See Malpezzi-Price, *Moderata Fonte*, chap. 4 (85–98).

CANTO 12

ARGUMENT

*Circetta narrates to the Latin knights
the illustrious and rare exploits of VENICE,
how she had to place her divine foundations
(as she then did) in the sea.
Of the triumphs on land and at sea,
of a thousand honors, of a thousand clear victories
Circetta makes them aware, and in the enchanted wall
she shows them her every future deed.*

1

Who ever experienced so lucky a fate
in our day or in the ancient age,
from Iberian shores to the Caucasian mountain passes,
or from the burning regions to the humid ones,
that he might draw out life from death,
and extract treasure from poverty,
peace from war, great pleasure from grief,
and from infinite hearts a single will?

2

Fortunate city, you alone had heaven
generous and courteous at your birth.[1]

---

1. In the following octaves Fonte reviews the history of Venice from its origins to her own day. Her account adheres at least outwardly to what modern historians call "the myth of Venice," a

With such privileges you adorned the veil,
that the world forgot the past offenses.
Rather, it was forced (if I do not conceal the truth)
to bless the bloody exploits
of the most dreadful Attila, who put Italy
to fire and the sword in every corner.[2]

3

He destroyed all the others, and made a single
city rise from the scattered relics.
By her sad Italy is consoled,
and the burnt lands and city walls are content.
She steals life from others' death;
from others' poverty, splendid, she appears.
This with all that awaits her,
Circetta wanted to report to the knights.

4

As I said, the knights had approached
with the eloquent young woman near
the pictures of the future people's
long stories with their diverse mottoes.
But what they meant in the end
the knights could not by themselves discern;
nor by reading the captions and the writings
could they interpret those figures.

---

version of history promoted for centuries by the Venetians themselves and believed by many
outsiders as well. This myth emphasizes, among other things, the republican liberty of the city
and its citizens and Venice's destiny to triumph and remain sovereign forever. As for Fonte's
knowledge of Venice in history, she had her uncle Doglioni's book—and library—at hand.
Still, the lengthy historical reconstruction that Fonte puts together constitutes the first sus-
tained effort by an Italian woman writer to construct (and politicize) history. It equals in am-
bitiousness, uniqueness, and breadth what Fonte will do in the "Second Day" of *Worth of Women*
when she uses the scientific tradition to carve a place for women in the hierarchy of nature. For
more on the "Second Day," see Cox's introduction, 10–12.

2. Attila united the Huns and in 452 invaded Italy. He captured and destroyed many cities
north of the Po River, until famine and disease forced his withdrawal.

5

Four pictures on each wall were depicted
between one window and the next. On one side,
in the first picture there appeared gathered
an infinite army of men bearing weapons.
Bathed and stained with human blood,
they seemed to destroy the most beautiful and admired
place in the world. (Alas, what a malign star!)
Above was written BEAUTIFUL ITALY.

6

They were intent on that horrendous conflict
they saw issue from those armed people,
praising the subject matter together with the art
with which it was so vividly engraved,
when the beautiful lady approached that place
as well. To show herself agreeable
to her Silano in all she promised him,
she set out to narrate the story in this way:

7

"It was my mother's principal intention,
when she fashioned such beautiful portraits,
to make known to us from her founding
the bountiful successes of an illustrious city.
She showed her risky origin
and the glory of her progresses,
since in her will flower a lady in time
who will be the honor of her sex and of her time.

8

"Foreseeing the lofty and subtle mind
of this stately and glorious lady,
how she will wear so clear a garment
of excellent habits and of every noble act,
that she will be an unwavering column of virtue

such that no other woman will match her,
so much love my mother conceived for her,
that to her glory she made so wondrous a work.

9

"Even more gladly she described this,
since she will have for a husband (happy fate)
a noble hero who from my father Ulysses
will descend, wiser and stronger than he.
Her fair name (which she predicted to me),
so worthy a lord's dear consort,
is BIANCA, who makes every other seem dark and dull;[3]
and he will be FRANCESCO, Grand Duke of Tuscany.

10

"Now gaze at that haughty and cruel king
who holds the great scourge in place of a sword.
Against him neither mail nor shield will avail
for wretched Italy not to fall.
Attila he will be named, devoid of pity,
who will inundate every region with blood;
he will destroy in a thousand infamous incidents
the soaring towers and the honored temples.

11

"See the flower of the illustrious families,
who must abandon their dear homeland
to live, if they can, longer lustrums,
and they will be fortunate and wise to flee.
Behold how ready and industrious they are
to turn their backs on the ruler of Lemnos,
although with faces tinged with fear
they gaze still at the faraway beloved city walls.[4]

3. Here Fonte is playing on the literal meaning of Bianca, white.
4. For lustrums, see above, canto 1.2n. The reference to Lemnos here is puzzling; Fonte might
be portraying the Venetians' psychological and political separation from the Byzantine Em-

12

"So before the city built by Antenor
with the noble Trojan relics
is by the Huns burned and destroyed,
along with the lands near and far,
the nobility of the wretched Italian
people will be reduced
to living among the most deserted rocks
with their possessions, with their wives.[5]

13

"Seeing the coastline is safe
for their treasures, for their remaining offspring,
they will give origin to the divine city
which will then fill the sun with wonder.
O fortunate Italic ruin,
which will raise so superb a stronghold,
which will cause the birth in the world
of so stupendous and so joyous a monster.[6]

14

"Although earlier in the Latian meadows
there will flower a rare plant with noble roots,
which the boys the she-wolf nourished

pire. The myth of Venice tends to minimize the fact that the city belonged originally to the empire and gained independence gradually in later centuries. See Frederic C. Lane, *Venice: A Maritime Republic* (Baltimore: Johns Hopkins University Press, 1973), 4–5; and Elisabeth Crouzet-Pavan, *Venice Triumphant: The Horizons of a Myth*, trans. Lydia G. Cochrane (Baltimore: Johns Hopkins University Press, 2002), 6–7. Here Fonte implies an earlier and more decisive break. The "beloved city walls" are probably those of Padua (New Troy), whose territory belonged to the Serenissima. The fortified walls of Padua, eleven kilometers long, were a masterpiece of early modern civic defense and saved the Venetian republic after the loss at Agnadello in 1509.

5. A survivor of the destruction of Troy, Antenor led a group of refugees to northern Italy. They renamed their disembarkation point New Troy (later the city of Padua).

6. According to legend, Venice was formally established in 421. Fonte uses the Italian word *mostro*, derived from Latin, which at that time could mean "monster," but also "prodigy" or "divine sign."

will plant there with suitable auspices,[7]
it will not, however, have the fates so benign
as this great seed, and the heavens so friendly.
This city will open fronds rich and beautiful
that will adorn her just as the stars adorn the sky.

1 5

"Though that city up till now boasts
that the head of the future faith
must reside there (that holy faith
in which at present no one hopes, no one believes),
no less is this famous plant honored
and esteemed for the sea, and is not at all second to Rome,
since a thousand times she will defend
Rome, with the Pope and the Christian Church.

1 6

"This immortal republic will adore
not Mars, not Jove, not a thousand other
pagan gods who now have everywhere
in the world sacrifices, altars, and torches,
but only one God, predicted in part
by the most prudent Sybils.
They said he must come to draw out from error the world
which now lies blind and shadowy to the depths.[8]

1 7

"After this grand and miraculous event
takes place on earth,

---

7. According to legend, a she-wolf suckled the twins Romulus and Remus, who founded Rome in the region of Latium in 753 BCE.

8. The Sybil of Cumae was an ancient Roman priestess of Apollo. These verses conflate two passages of Virgil. In the *Aeneid* the Sybil prophesies the future of Rome and guides Aeneas in the underworld. The "Fourth Eclogue" predicts the coming of a marvelous boy who will renew the world, a passage which caused medieval thinkers to see Virgil as a prophet of Christ. See Domenico Comparetti, *Vergil in the Middle Ages*, trans. E. F. M. Benecke (Princeton: Princeton University Press, 1997), 99.

the aforesaid war will begin
in fifty years added to four hundred.
And so at that time, for the glory of the earth,
they will found in the liquid element
the bountiful city; to this happy state
eternal liberty is promised by fate.

18

"It's true that in Radagaisus's arrival earlier
with Gepids and Goths in Italy lies
the origin of habitation in this bay, before
fright sends the peoples here.
Alaric another time oppresses
every heart so (this will be after a while)
that for fear they exchange the agreeable paternal
land with this sea, with this shore.⁹

19

"See how she grows little by little,
almost like a naive, noble, and kind girl.
It seems heaven, earth, sea, and fire
favor her smiling April,
for her foundations have a place in the waves
miraculously, beyond every customary style.
Heaven covers her, and earth supports her
no less than the sea which encircles and encloses her.

20

"Nor these alone—in addition, cheerful and pleasant
Fortune will smile on her origins.

9. The Goths started attacking the Roman Empire in the third century. In 405 the army of the Gothic king Radagaisus laid waste northern Italy until the Goths were destroyed the following year. The Gepids were a Germanic people who eventually settled in Dacia; they also formed part of Attila's army. See J. B. Bury, *The Invasion of Europe by the Barbarians* (New York: Norton, 1967). Alaric (c. 370–410), king of the Visigoths, invaded Italy in 401 and looted Rome in 410. The population of the lagoons increased dramatically and became permanent during the Lombard invasions of the sixth to seventh centuries. See Alvise Zorzi, *La Repubblica del Leone. Storia di Venezia* (Milan: Bompiani, 2001); and Bury, *Invasion of Europe*.

While in other places people will have
fate contrary to their desire, and somber,
she will grow larger quietly,
without dispute and without any war.
She will acquire great strength and advantage
before anyone thinks to do her an outrage.

21

"Never was so beautiful and so graceful a form
seen here in the world or above in the supernal sky
as in her. She will always follow
virtue's footsteps in her divine government,
such that, because of her, vice must sleep—
rather, die and descend to hell.
Happy therefore, and blessed five times
and six any man who is to be born in her.

22

"And happier and more blessed the one
who, with affection lending him boldness,
will paint with a charming and beautiful style,
not her beauty, but his desire.
Since there will never be so divine a brush
that it could even color her mantle,
he must at least have such a name
for generous affection that he will always be known for it.[10]

23

"So that you might see represented
the true example of so worthy a noble figure,
behold her here, not by superb walls
encircled, but by the sea—rather, founded in it.
The caption there up above is the writing
where VENICE, her fair name, is impressed.

10. The most famous Venetian painters of Fonte's period were Giorgione (c. 1478–1510), Titian (1488/90–1576), and Tintoretto (1518–94).

If there were space it would continue:
'Whom Europe and all the world owe.'"

24

So saying she points out to them a superb city
founded in the midst of the sea,
which possesses such majesty, such glory,
that she seems divinely constructed.
Then in the form of an immature maiden,
in the third picture studiously she is engraved;
in the fashion of an excellent and divine queen,
she sits and holds in her hand the precious olive.

25

From one of the sides a little blonde girl
reverently holds out to her a crown,
and, mirroring herself in her, joyfully
with another she crowns herself.
Over there a rosy young woman
gives her a branch of felicitous palm;
one of green laurel from the other side
a boy adorned with rich clothing gives her.

26

Another handsome boy also on that side
has between his lips a sonorous trumpet;
it seems that so much he plays and he plays so much
that the whole universe resounds.
The damsel who was instructed in the enchantment
said, "She who in the fashion of a dove
bears the glorious and sacred olive
is beautiful Venice's simulacrum.

27

'The noble girl who admires her
and wants to adorn her with a rich crown

is called Glory. This one who gazes
more fixedly at her than the eagle at the sun[11]
and, while turning her eyes to her fair visage,
gives her the palm, with which she honors and venerates her,
is named Victory. She will be truly worthy
of one and the other glorious insignia.

2 8

'That charming boy who offers her
the laurel endowed with immortal merit
is divine Triumph, who appears
adorned with such superb and rich mantles.
The other, who on the contrary does not tolerate
wearing a cloth, shows his winged back,
and gives breath to the keen instrument,
is known by all as Fame."

2 9

Having said, in her opinion, enough,
Circetta to another space was turning,
when Silano asked with great insistence
what a Lion was meant to signify.[12]
"It signifies her extreme power,"
she said. "And the Unicorn?" he added.
And she to him, "Her chastity, I believe,
it is meant to indicate." Then she continued:

3 0

"Turn your thoughts to this last part,
to so fair a union of glorious heroes.
Some will follow Pallas, and some Mars;[13]

11. According to the bestiary tradition, the eagle restores its exceptionally acute eyesight by gazing at the sun and casts out any of its chicks which turn away from the sun. See T. H. White, *The Book of Beasts, being a Translation from a Latin Bestiary of the Twelfth Century* (New York: Dover, 1984), 105–7.

12. The Venetians adopted Saint Mark's symbol of the lion when they made him their patron saint.

13. Pallas Athena is the goddess of wisdom, and Mars the god of war.

I speak of those who will be her princes.
If I were to tell you all their names,
I fear my speech would bore you,
though some of them I will name
as I relate her exploits.

3 1

"These singular minds will flourish,
as you will hear, from age to age.
With deeds admirable and divine
they will conserve their homeland in liberty.
While enlarging their borders outside,
they will maintain justice in the city,
having instituted from time to time
orders, laws, magistrates, and rites.

3 2

"Although in the famous Vatican
varied will be the opinions of the various senators,
for the common good, comfort, and repose
they will concur in the lofty consistories.
Nevertheless that one alone will be victorious
(not through authority, not through favors)
who by the sacred and most just Senate
will be tested like gold with a touchstone.[14]

3 3

"Of such bright and glorious squads
of fathers, sons, and princes of this city,
that man will not be a son, prince, or father,
nor will he wear so rich a horn on his head,
who will not show with manifest proof

14. Here "Vatican" refers to the government of Venice. Through the years Venice became more
and more an oligarchy. In choosing the doge, the government was constantly alert to avoid the
predominance of any one person or family, and it furthermore gradually weakened the doge's
power. A touchstone (flinty jasper), in combination with nitric acid, can reveal the percentage
of gold or silver in a metal.

that he is worthy of such a daughter and mother,
by having his merits in proportion
with the lofty seat of that great Lion.[15]

3 4

"Here one can see how he will be elected,
first by four and then by forty-one,
and in what fashion each one spends
his pure affection and his free will.
Of eighty-six is here an elect band,
for the one succeeds the other, and the other the one.
That they are so many I know without counting,
from Paulo Lucio to Nicolò da Ponte.[16]

3 5

"Their successors my mother would have
sculpted as well, but I excuse her.
The picture was full and more would not fit there;
thus she could not carry out her design."
Still discoursing in this manner,
they found themselves at the end of the fourth image.
Then the lady, who wanted to please them,
ushered them to the second wall.

3 6

"Now that we have seen," she said, "the strange foundations
of an eternal, divine, noble city,
it is right that in this part I lay out
her lofty feats at a more mature age.

---

15. The doge's cap was called the *corno* (horn). Doges were elected after long service to Venice.

16. The electoral reform of 1178 established that the Great Council would select four of their own members, who would nominate an electoral team of forty people, who would elect the doge. In 1229 a forty-first person was added to avoid tie votes. In 1268 the process was made even more complicated, all in an attempt to avoid collusion. See Zorzi, *La Repubblica del Leone*, 132–34. According to legend, Paoluccio Anafesto was elected the first doge in 697. Nicolò da Ponte was doge when *Floridoro* was published in 1581.

Here we see the Venetians
removing their togas and girding on swords,
becoming on land and at sea so strong
that they will be the terror of the proudest ports.

37

"But because I am trying to be as brief
as I can, so that talking does not bring you tedium,
and because in the first years she will not
do a deed worthy of your ears,
I will begin from the time when the first doge
receives the esteemed insignia.
I have all the more reason because Circe too, having sculpted
from these onward, left the beginning hidden,

38

"when in the immature time of her age
the still divided and small islets,
which will later become so proud a domain,
by tribunes will be administered and ruled.[17]
This period will last until
six hundred years plus ninety-seven after the incarnation of the Word,
and twenty-five less than three hundred
from her memorable birth.

39

"Now turn your gaze to these people
who together speak and form a friendship and a league,
and one and the other Lombard prince
who with the first doge agree and league themselves.
Behold a later time, when the standard

17. The myth holds that in 466 the various island communities agreed to a loose associa-
tion, with a system of self-government through tribunes elected by each community. These
tribunes were really district officials of the Byzantine Empire. Through these first centuries
Venice gradually moved away from Byzantine rule, though the empire remained of primary
commercial importance to Venice. Although at first Venice served as a protector of the empire,
relations later soured to the point of military conflicts between the two states.

under another doge she unfurls to their harm
and, at the Supreme Pontiff's insistence,
makes them depart from Ravenna and change their abode.[18]

40

"Then Venice will end her principality,
with the hope of having better fortune;
she will create a new magistrate
under whom I see no accomplishment at all.
But shortly after, with the care of the state
seeming more suitable to princes,
she returns to the doge, and at the time when Obelerio
holds dominion at sea she overcomes Pepin.[19]

41

"Under the Participatii (for in Rialto
one after the other obtains the first honors),
she overcomes Friuli. From the Moorish assault
she goes here to defend the Sicilian sands.
Then with Gradenico obtaining the high
seat, she holds Narenta in a rough war.
Here against the Saracens she unfurls her banner,
and carries away a worthy victory.[20]

18. Legend has it that the first Doge, Paoluccio Anafesto, soon made a treaty with the Lombard king Liutprand. In later centuries the Lombards became associated with the French, who during a war between France and Pope Julius II captured and sacked Ravenna in 1512. The French forces were so weakened by the battle that the pope's allies, including the Venetian army, were able to drive them out of Italy. See Norwich, *History of Venice*; and Zorzi, *La Repubblica del Leone*.

19. In 737 the Venetians abolished the office of the doge in favor of a *maestro dei militi*, but the interregnum between doges lasted only until 742. Pepin, king of the Franks and Holy Roman Emperor, attempted to occupy Venice in 810, at the invitation of the treacherous doge Obelerio degli Antenori. The Venetian people, however, put up fierce resistance until fevers forced Pepin to withdraw his army. See Norwich, *History of Venice*, 19–22.

20. In 810 the Venetians made the island of Rialto their capital. The following year Agnello Participazio, who had led the resistance to Pepin, became the first doge in his family. In 864 Doge Orso Participazio wrested control of the Friuli region from the hostile patriarch of Aquileia. In 827 the Saracens took Sicily from the Byzantine Empire. In c. 840 the Byzantines appealed to Venice for help against them, and Doge Pietro Tradonico led the Venetian fleet to total defeat in the attempt. He campaigned more successfully against the pirates who were

42

"Here Comacchio is taken; the Narentans
are those there whose turn it is to go under.
That is Piero Tribun, at whose hands
the Hungarians' army will be broken.
No less is the defeated emperor Berengar
brought to fear the Venetians.
Those Istrian places are taken by the ones
who will then help Bari against the Moor.[21]

43

"Orseolo, who will be the second of that
name, will make Dalmatia stay within bounds.
The other is his son, and he must truly be
a youth wise and of mature intelligence,
since he is considered by the king of Hungary
worthy of his daughter's hand.
See here how he regains Grado,
while he holds his homeland's highest rank.[22]

---

based around the Narenta River in Dalmatia and preyed on Venetian shipping. See Norwich, *History of Venice,* 23–35.

21. Comacchio was an important Lombard city that competed commercially with Venice; Doge Pietro II Candiano sacked it in 933. See Crouzet-Pavan, *Venice Triumphant,* 58–60. Venice struggled repeatedly against the Narenta River pirates; Doge Pietro I Candiano died in battle against them (in 887), and Doge Pietro III Candiano (r. 942–59) led two expeditions against them, without decisive success. See Lane, *Venice,* 24. Doge Pietro Tribuno decisively defeated the invading Magyars in 898. In c. 962 the Holy Roman Emperor Otto defeated Berengar II, king of Italy, in response to Pope John XII's appeal for help. The Istrian peninsula is located on the northern coast of Dalmatia, a region which included parts of modern Croatia and Bosnia-Herzegovina. For more see the following note. Doge Pietro II Orseolo lifted the Saracen siege of Bari in 1002. See Norwich, *History of Venice,* 36–59.

22. In the year 1000 Doge Pietro II Orseolo aided cities in Dalmatia that had asked for help against the encroachments of the Slavic pirates. He assumed the title *dux Dalmatiae,* though Dalmatian cities disputed Venetian lordship through the years, as can be seen from Fonte's repeated mentions of Zara (modern Zadar). Soon after Otto Orseolo became doge in 1008, he married the daughter of King Stephen of Hungary. Patriarch Poppo of Aquileia claimed the city of Grado, whose patriarch was Otto's brother. The brothers took refuge in Istria in 1022–23, then returned to resume their thrones once they gained popular support. See Norwich, *History of Venice,* 52–62; and Filippo De Vivo, "Historical Justifications of Venetian Power in the Adriatic," *Journal of the History of Ideas* 64.2 (2003): 159–76.

4 4

"See Contarini, a vigorous man,
rebuild Grado just taken from the patriarch,
and bring back under the Venetian standard
Zara which had rebelled to Corvatin.
See then in Apulia Guiscard
defeated by him who turns his people to flight,
and Venice's fame exalted so
that every coast, every shore will be full of it.[23]

4 5

"Therefore the Greek emperor for a wife
gives his successor his sister.
Over here Faletro subjects to his will
the cities of Dalmatia and its castles.
Behold, Michael releases the fleet
and sends his son with it to Asia;
near Rhodes he will come to blows,
and twenty-two galleys he will take from the Pisans.[24]

23. In 1043 Doge Domenico Contarini relieved Grado from Patriarch Poppo of Aquileia's second invasion. See Norwich, *History of Venice*, 66. He also returned the Dalmatian city of Zara to Venetian control; historical accounts disagree as to whether it had rebelled under his or the prior dogeship, and to Croatian or to Hungarian control. See Vitaliano Brunelli, *Storia della città di Zara dai tempi più remoti sino al 1409* (Trieste: LINT, 1974), 279–81. Unable to identify Corvatin, I have taken him to be an adversary of Venice; this verse, "Zara che s'era al Corvatin rivolta," could also mean that Zara had rebelled against Corvatin, if he were a Venetian official. Doge Contarini's memorial tablet states that he defeated the Normans in Apulia, an event which never occurred. His successor, however, Domenico Selvo, came to the aid of the Byzantine Empire during the Norman invasion; the Venetian fleet won a decisive victory at Durazzo in 1081. See Norwich, *History of Venice*, 67–70; and Zorzi, *La Repubblica del Leone*, 64–67.

24. Elected in 1071, Doge Domenico Selvo soon afterward married Theodora Ducas, sister of the Byzantine emperor Michael VII. The reign (1084–96) of Doge Vitale Falier (Faledro) was uneventful; perhaps Fonte is referring to Doge Ordelafo Falier's (r. 1102–18) acquisition of the title of *dux Croatiae*. See Crouzet-Pavan, *Venice Triumphant*, 61. In 1099 Doge Vitale Michiel sent his son Giovanni, in command of the Venetian fleet, in support of the First Crusade. On the way, Giovanni answered a Byzantine appeal for help against the Pisans who had opportunistically attacked a Byzantine city; he defeated the Pisan fleet at Rhodes. See Norwich, *History of Venice*, 69–78.

46

"He will be victor with a fame both eternal and bright,
at Smyrna, and at Brindisi in Apulia.
Behold another Faletro who prepares
the fleet to go away into Syria.
Behold, he returns to obedience Zara,
which gave itself to Coloman, king of Hungary.
With Paduan blood he will then make
the earth red to his honor near the Bebe.[25]

47

"In the second square, in response to the just entreaties
sent by the Pope, behold the sails unfurl,
and liberate Jaffa besieged
by the unjust Turks. Another Michael
here takes Tyre and puts the infidels
with his forces in dire straits,
giving the city to the patriarch
of the city which will be called holy.[26]

48

"With Rhodes and Mytilene having revolted
against their devotion to his fair realm,
with Andros, Samos, and Chios, with many others
he will show himself worthy of so great an empire.
This is his son-in-law later who has taken arms

25. In the early twelfth century Venice fought the Normans in the lower Adriatic, where Brindisi is located. In 1109 Doge Ordelafo Falier sent a fleet to Palestine in support of the First Crusade. He recaptured Dalmatian cities taken over by King Coloman of Hungary, but he died in battle when the Hungarians attempted to retake Zara in 1118. See Norwich, *History of Venice*, 83–86. The fortified tower of Bebe in Chioggia, a town at the southern end of the Venetian lagoon, was the site of numerous battles before its destruction in 1380; the forces of Padua and Treviso attacked Chioggia in 1214.

26. In 1119 Pope Calixtus II asked Doge Domenico Michiel for further help for the crusaders. The Muslim enemy had left Jaffa before the Venetians arrived in 1123, but they were instrumental in the siege and capture of Tyre, bringing it under the sway of the Christian king of Jerusalem. See Norwich, *History of Venice*, 87–90.

against the Pisans and disrupts their plan.
He brings Fano under the great Lion,
and overcomes the Paduans and puts them to flight.[27]

49

"Behold, he gives succor to Manuel
against Roger (at that time lord of Apulia),
regains Corcyra, and scourges
Sicily with his great valor.
See Moresin, who succeeds him,
suppress the furor of the wicked corsairs,
and having waged war against Pola and Parenzo,
he makes them tributaries of his land.[28]

50

"Under this one will come the Anconitans,
who have already become friends of the dominion in a league.
Not only they but the king of the Sicilians
with Venice makes peace and unites.
Behold the third Michael, who bends
the Pisans, old enemies, to become friends.
The Thracian wall here he ruins and shatters;
there he knocks down Ragusa's every fortress.[29]

27. During his voyages to and from the crusade, Doge Michiel seized these five Byzantine islands (Mytilene is a town on Lesbos) for a few years, until the emperor restored Venetian trading privileges. His son-in-law, Pietro Polani, succeeded him. The Pisans were commercial rivals of Venice. In 1141 the city of Fano appealed for help against the threats of its neighbors and became a subject ally of Venice. Two years later the Paduans diverted the course of the Brenta River, upsetting the ecological balance and endangering Venice's existence; Venice defeated them quickly. See Norwich, *History of Venice*, 90–94.

28. When the Norman king Roger II of Sicily, who also ruled most of southern Italy, attacked the Byzantines, Emperor Manuel Comnenus enlisted Venice's help in retaking Corcyra (modern Corfu); Doge Polani died before the fleet sailed in 1148. His successor was Domenico Morosini (r. 1148–56). See Norwich, *History of Venice*, 92–98. Venice repeatedly conquered and lost the Istrian cities of Pola and Parenzo.

29. This was in fact a period of conflict between Venice and its commercial rival Ancona. See David Abulafia, "Ancona, Byzantium and the Adriatic, 1155–1173," *Papers of the British School at Rome* 52 (1984): 195–216. Relations were more friendly with Sicily: Doge Domenico Morosini made peace with Sicily in 1148; Venice and Sicily were both members of the Greater Lombard League opposing Frederick Barbarossa in 1167 under Doge Vitale II Michiel, who was the

51

"This naval battle, where one sees
the waves horribly red with blood,
where the too-reckless Eagle gives way
to the great Lion which has overcome and struck it,
will take place between the Venetians and the heir
of the impious Frederick Barbarossa
(who will drive away from Rome the just Pope),
and by him his son Augustus will be taken.[30]

52

"Behold the great Ziani with the victorious ranks
returns, and leads Otto with him.
The holy father, happy at his success,
embraces him here as one can see.
Behold, he has placed a gold ring on his finger
with which he gives him the right to possess
the rule of the sea, and he wants from then onward
that it be subject to his successors.[31]

53

"This is the emperor then who descends
where the great vicar reigns secure,

third doge from this family; and in 1175 Doge Sebastiano Ziani renewed an earlier treaty with
Sicily. See Norwich, *History of Venice*, 98–111. The historical references in the last two verses
remain elusive.

30. Holy Roman Emperor Frederick I Barbarossa (r. 1152–90) supported an antipope and in
1167 drove Pope Alexander III out of Rome. According to legend, Alexander took refuge in
Venice. The Venetians then successfully defended the pope in a naval battle against forces led
by Barbarossa's son, Otto, who was captured. The eagle was the imperial symbol, and "Augus-
tus" refers to Barbarossa's position as emperor. Modern historians accept a different version of
the story: the pope and the emperor agreed on Venice as a neutral place to meet, and there was
no battle. See Norwich, *History of Venice*, 101–16.

31. According to legend, the Venetian fleet had been led by Doge Sebastiano Ziani. The grate-
ful pope greeted the triumphant galleys upon their return to Venice and then gave the doge,
among other gifts, a gold ring, which symbolized Venice's dominion over the sea. Each year
thereafter, on Ascension Day, the doge would throw a gold ring into the sea, symbolizing Ven-
ice's marriage with the sea. This was probably a modification of a preexisting Ascension Day
ritual which celebrated Venetian maritime power. See Crouzet-Pavan, *Venice Triumphant*, 47–49.

because paternal love kindles his heart
to follow the victorious banner.
He so humbles himself before him
that to kiss the holy foot he does not disdain,
and Alexander then pushes down and presses
his proud head, so he sighs and trembles.[32]

5 4

"In the third space here, gaze at how many
sails again on the high seas are unfurled
by the Catholic Lion in the Levant,
sent to regain Jerusalem.
Taken by them is Ptolemais, and so many
of Saladin's people are broken and shattered.
Here, having retaken Pola and Zara,
they make the people of Trieste pay them tribute.[33]

5 5

"See the city of Constantine
taken by them, and the Dictaean island,
and with the Peloponnese they reduce to their dominion
every rock bathed by Aegean waves—
not only those, but as many as the sea has near
Crete, and likewise the island of Euboea.[34]

32. The negotiations between Barbarossa and his enemies in Italy, including Pope Alexander III, took place in Venice in 1177. During the ceremony of reconciliation Barbarossa prostrated himself before the pope and kissed his feet. Legend has it that Alexander placed his foot on the emperor's neck. See Norwich, *History of Venice,* 111–15; and Thomas Madden, "Venice's Hostage Crisis: Diplomatic Efforts to Secure Peace with Byzantium between 1171 and 1184," in *Medieval and Renaissance Venice,* ed. Ellen Kittell and Thomas Madden (Urbana: University of Illinois Press, 1999), 96–108.

33. Jerusalem, along with most of the Holy Land, fell to the Saracens led by Saladin in 1187. In response, the Third Crusade sailed two years later. After a two-year siege, the crusaders recaptured Acre (Ptolemais); after the battle, nearly three thousand Saracen prisoners were massacred. The last two verses refer to the prelude to the Fourth Crusade, which Doge Enrico Dandolo maneuvered against Constantinople rather than Muslim lands. On the way, the fleet made military demonstrations from Trieste to Pola to keep them obedient. Then, in partial payment of their debt for Venetian shipping, the crusaders recaptured Zara for Venice in 1202; Zara had been under Hungarian rule for over a decade. See Norwich, *History of Venice,* 122–30; and Brunelli, *Storia della città di Zara,* 366–71.

34. The crusaders took Constantinople in 1203, and in the division of spoils Venice received many territories of strategic use to its maritime power. See Norwich, *History of Venice,* 134–41;

Here the Paduans again and the Genoese
are defeated by them, and many other countries.[35]

56

"Behold, under Tiepolo Candia is succored,
at that time by pirates molested.
Behold, to lift from it a grave siege
the fleet has sailed all the way to Constantinople.[36]
Behold Fortune who places her wheel in doubt;
now she has stopped it under the great Lion,
which achieves a thousand and more victories, peaces, and truces
time after time, and a thousand honors.

57

"Behold, at Saint Gregory's prayers,
against Apulia these galleys will go
(you must recognize them as well as I,
by the Lion depicted in the flags).
These, which are as great in number,
go against Frederick on the coasts
of Genoa, which is consoled by them,
recovering Zara for Venice, and Pola.[37]

---

and more generally Jonathan Phillips, *The Fourth Crusade and the Sack of Constantinople* (London: Pimlico, 2005); Donald Queller, *The Fourth Crusade: The Conquest of Constantinople, 1201–1204* (Philadelphia: University of Pennsylvania Press, 1977); and Giorgio Ravegnani, "I dogi di Venezia e la corte di Bisanzio," in *L'eredità greca e l'ellenismo veneziano*, ed. Gino Benzoni (Florence: Olschki, 2002), 23–51. Shortly after the Crusade, to obtain clear title, Venice bought the island of Crete, wrested it from a Genoese pirate, and colonized it. See Lane, *Venice*, 43; and Crouzet-Pavan, *Venice Triumphant*, 67.

35. In 1214 Venice defended Chioggia against an attack by Padua and Treviso.

36. Doge Giacomo Tiepolo (r. 1229–49) had previously been Venice's governor of Crete, where Candia was the major city. See Norwich, *History of Venice*, 150. When the Greeks retook Constantinople in 1261, they struck during the absence of the Venetian fleet; afterward it rescued survivors. See Lane, *Venice*, 75. Perhaps Fonte is referring instead to the Turkish siege of Constantinople in 1397, when Venice sent three ships to help the emperor.

37. In this period the power struggles between the pope and the Holy Roman Emperor continued. Pope Gregory IX's appeal in 1239 for aid against Frederick II resulted in an alliance between the fierce commercial rivals Venice, Genoa, and Pisa and a brief expedition against Apulia. See Norwich, *History of Venice*, 154. In 1241 Frederick ordered a naval attack on Genoa, which defended itself without help from Venice. See Steven A. Epstein, *Genoa and the Genoese, 958–1528* (Chapel Hill: University of North Carolina Press, 1996), 124–26. Frederick

58

"Gaze at another much greater enterprise
against Ezzelino, at that time Padua's tyrant.
The cruelty Attila will use will be less
than his furor, less grave the harm,
because the former will show rage and furor
against enemies and will cause them to suffer,
but the latter from his own people with infinite
pain will take honor, gold, and life.

59

"However, you see here where I point and show you,
that, by the great Pontiff admonished,
Moresin is dispatched by the Senate
to take from the world so nefarious a monster.
See him at last, wounded by an arrow,
send his spirit to Pluto's cloister;
and Padua, released from so heavy a burden,
draws breath again under its protector Saint Mark.[38]

60

"Gaze finally at the Genoese,
still being pursued by the Lion.
See defeated those of Fano and Felsina,
and the Istrians returned to submission.
By the Lion a few months later Pera
is taken and undone; with many armed ships

---

attempted to enlist some of Venice's subjects, including Pola. In 1242 Zara rebelled again, possibly at the emperor's encouragement; the following year Venice retook the city. See Brunelli, *Storia della città di Zara*, 401–3.

38. Ezzelino da Romano (1194–1259) was a loyal supporter of Emperor Frederick II. He captured Padua (1237), as well as other cities in northern Italy. He was notorious for cruelty; for instance, after his enemies took Padua in 1256, he executed his Paduan soldiers who reportedly numbered in the thousands. Pope Innocent IV excommunicated him in 1254, and the following year Pope Alexander IV called for a crusade against him. Venice contributed warships to this league. Ezzelino was captured in battle and died from his wounds. For a historical overview of this century in Padua, see Benjamin Kohl, *Padua under the Carrara, 1318–1405* (Baltimore: Johns Hopkins University Press, 1998).

he assails the Greeks, and takes with much gold
fifteen thousand and more prisoners from them.[39]

6 1

"See, here the Lion will make himself lord
of Spalato, Trogir, and Sibenik.
He defends Antenor's walls
from the lord of Verona, the Lion's enemy.
Behold, he sends to the Pope an ambassador
to oppose the Turk, his ancient rival.
The king of Bohemia, brought into a league,
with the princes of Italy he unites and binds.[40]

6 2

"Behold in the end, after many quarrels
between the Veronese and the Venetian dominion,
he will acquire Castel Baldo and Treviso,
and will make peace with Mastino."[41]
Thus the lady who revealed those maternal
vestiges, and had a lofty and divine spirit,
narrated to the warriors the fateful prophecy
of a sacred immortal republic.

---

39. Venice and Genoa were bitter commercial rivals for centuries and fought repeatedly. During the famine of 1268, the mainland cities refused supplies to Venice; the Venetians' economic retaliation led to an inconclusive war with Bologna (ancient Felsina). In 1280 Istria revolted against Venice and was retaken. Pera was an important Genoese commercial base established in 1267 as a suburb of Constantinople; in 1296 the Venetians attacked and damaged it. In 1302 they raided Constantinople again and took over an island housing Greek refugees who had fled the Turks; the emperor paid them off when they threatened to kill or enslave their prisoners. After making peace with Genoa in 1299, Venice raided Byzantine lands for plunder.

40. At the end of the thirteenth century the Dalmatian cities of Spalato (Split), Trogir, and Sibenik were under Hungarian rule; tradition has it that they put themselves under Venetian protection to escape the disorderly conditions of Hungarian succession struggles. For Antenor, see above, canto 12.12n. In 1329 Can Grande della Scala, despot of Verona, took Treviso from Venice, but died three days later. In 1342 Venice joined a league organized by the pope for a crusade against the Turks, but the league soon fell apart. In 1354 Venice formed a league against Milan with other threatened states and persuaded the Holy Roman Emperor Charles IV, king of Bohemia, to serve as its titular head. See also below, canto 12.66n.

41. Mastino della Scala, ruler of Verona, threatened to cut off Venice's supplies. Venice found numerous allies in Mastino's enemies. The peace treaty of 1339 restored Treviso to Venice.

63

She had explained the second wall's
important and weighty maneuvers,
from which one saw that Venice embraces
a universal enterprise with all the world.
Most times she had clear sailing,
nor can she ever be sent to the depths by anyone,
favors which neither the Assyrians nor the Romans
nor the Africans had, nor the Persians nor the Spartans.

64

Having perceived that magnanimous Silano
was not sated or tired of listening,
she took each of them by the hand,
and toward the west she turned her lovely form.
She said, "Of the Venetian empire
I have said nothing compared with what I have yet to say.
Of this beautiful land I have said little,
with respect to what remains in this place."

65

The knights, eager to hear the rest,
directed according to her speech their minds and eyes,
for they did not hope ever at any time
to hear a greater miracle than this.
She with a joyful and gracious gesture
found accents even more charming and gay,
for she knew all the events
that were impressed in the adamantine wall.

66

"Gaze at the great Pontiff Clement,
who then will be united with Venice,
to the detriment of the wild beast of the Orient,
and Bohemia's king on another side,

to make the duke of Milan sorrowful.
Behold, against Genoa the Senate
sends many ships in that same year,
and justly does it outrage and harm.[42]

67

"See next the lofty king who restrains
the island of Cupid's mother;
he comes to see that famous coast
which will gain so glorious a reputation.
Therefore, full of feasting and cheer
we see the people, and the sea, and the shore.
They accept with delighted and benign heart
the duke of Austria and the noble Cyprian king.[43]

68

"Behold, when good Cornelio rules Crete,
it rebels and then returns within bounds.
Contarino quiets Trieste
under the favor of his powerful reign;
and with the surrendered Antenorea humbled and quiet,
it makes a pact with the famous and worthy Lion.
Clodia, which has turned its thoughts to others,
returns as well under the same rule.[44]

42. The forces of Pope Clement VI, Venice, Genoa, and others seized Smyrna from the Turks
in 1344. Venice and Spain won so decisive a victory over Genoa in the naval battle of La Lojera
in 1353 that Genoa then submitted to Giovanni Visconti, leading to the creation of the league
against Milan. See also above, canto 12.61n.

43. Duke Rudolf of Austria visited Venice in 1361. Cyprus's King Peter of Lusignan visited
the city in 1362 and again in 1364. These illustrious guests were received with splendid
hospitality.

44. Crete rebelled against Venetian rule in the 1360s, during the dogeship of Lorenzo Celsi;
guerrilla activity ended only in 1366 under the subsequent doge, Marco Corner. Trieste's in-
surrection in 1369 was quickly put down under the reign of Andrea Contarini. Antenorea is
another name for Padua, which came under Venetian rule after the fall of its Carrara rulers. See
below, cantos 12.69n and 12.71n. Clodia was the ancient name of Chioggia, a town on one
of the Venetian islands. In 1379 it was seized by the combined forces of Genoa, Padua, and
Hungary; it was retaken the following year.

69

"Contemplate the just prince Venier,
who has a son punished for his evil deeds.
To harm the unjust Carrarese
who still despises the Lion's claw,
he unites Ferrara to the robust animal,
and Milan too, and makes the Carrarese lower his brow.
Here they make peace; and that one there
is the duke of Austria who returns to Venice.[45]

70

"And not only he but the lordly grandson
of the king of France descends and comes away from Paris.
He kindles hearts with infinite bliss,
while Mars's great quarrels are extinguished.
For this reason, admirable and stupendous celebrations
are held in honor of the golden fleur-de-lis,
as can be seen finally
and expressly in this first picture.[46]

71

"Over here we see that Vicenza gives itself
with Feltre, with Belluno, and with Bassano
to the great dominion, which cuts short the steps
of the Veronese lord and the Paduan,

---

45. Antonio Venier (r. 1382–1400) refused his son early release from a brief prison sentence, which led to his death there from illness. The lords of Padua, Francesco da Carrara and later his son Francesco Novello, were at first untrustworthy allies and later open enemies of Venice in conflicts from the 1350s until Francesco Novello's death in a Venetian prison in 1405. Padua allied with Genoa during its unsuccessful war with Venice, 1377–80; Ferrara was Venice's ally (the robust animal is the lion). In 1381, during the peace negotiations after this Fourth Genoese War, Venice gave Treviso to the duke of Austria so the Carrara would not have it. Padua's expansion was stopped by Milan and Venice in 1388. During these years Venice and Padua made peace several times.

46. This octave seems to refer to the visit of King Henry III of France in 1574. However, Henry came to Venice not from Paris, but from Poland; see below, canto 13.29n.

so she will acquire Verona and Padua
which against her will hold hands with Genoa.[47]
Then lands from Hungary we see
returned in Cividale to her faith.[48]

72

"Behold, with Foscari holding the banner,
the Florentine with this country united,
so that the Visconti might come to repent;
and at last he chooses the course of making peace.
With that pact to the Venetians he consigns
Ravenna and Brescia.[49] There to the famous shore
Frederick II comes,
after he gets himself crowned by the Pope.[50]

73

"Here Venice sends against Francesco
Sforza, duke of Milan through his wife,
the flags unfurled in the cool wind
(they still bear the generous beast).

47. After the death of Duke Gian Galeazzo Visconti of Milan in 1402, Francesco Novello Carrara attempted to take Vicenza, which preferred to offer itself to Venice. The duchess of Milan offered Verona as well in exchange for Venetian aid. After the fall of the Carrara dynasty, Padua, Feltre, Belluno, and Bassano came under Venetian control. Under Carrara rule, Padua had been an ally of Genoa in the Fourth Genoese War against Venice, concluded in 1380. Doge Michele Steno (r. 1400–13) received Verona and Padua into the republic.

48. After ceding Dalmatia to Hungary in the peace treaty of 1358, Venetian diplomats strove to regain influence there. In 1409 a pretender to the Hungarian throne sold Venice his rights to Dalmatia, as well as the cities he controlled there (including Zara, which thereafter remained under Venetian rule until the end of the republic in 1797). "Julian Forum" is Cividale (original name Forum Julii, the ancient capital of the region of Friuli); King Sigismund of Hungary sent two expeditions to dispute the renewed Venetian rule of Dalmatia, until a Venetian victory in Friuli in 1412 led to a five-year truce. "Her faith" must refer to loyalty to Venice itself, since both Dalmatia and Hungary had been Christian for centuries.

49. Francesco Foscari was elected doge in 1423. He joined a league with Florence against Filippo Maria Visconti of Milan. The treaty of 1426 gave Brescia to Venice, and Ravenna devolved to it in 1441.

50. Pope Honorius III crowned Frederick II Holy Roman Emperor in 1220; he visited Venice in 1233. See also above, canto 12.57 and note.

Next she comes to an agreement with the Turkish empire.[51]
Then under the Malipiera banner
you see here peace with abundance
united, as in their own home.[52]

7 4

"But shortly afterward, with the Moor already having assumed
the highest rank, another dispute arises
between the ferocious Lion and the golden serpents,
which here at Trieste will yet provide things to do.
Here he sends into the Morea against them
by land the Malatesta; and there by sea
brave Giustinian looses the fleet,
and gives Sparta to the Venetian standard.[53]

7 5

"Behold, in his duchy the good Ercole da Este
by them will be established.
And behold the king of Persia, united with them
to lower the serpentine crests.
Then follows the lofty and welcome acquisition,
which at that time those famous heads will make,

51. The soldier of fortune Francesco Sforza married Filippo Maria Visconti's daughter, Bianca, and claimed Milan after his father-in-law died in 1447. However, he was not present at the time, and Milanese citizens instituted the Ambrosian Republic, with which Venice allied itself. The generous beast is Venice's lion symbol. Sforza took Milan in 1450. Sultan Mehmet II the Conqueror succeeded to the Ottoman throne in 1451; Venice renewed with him a preexisting treaty of trade and friendship and made a new treaty with him after he took Constantinople in 1453. For more on the spread and power of the Ottoman Empire at the time, see Metin Kunt and Christine Woodhead, eds., *Süleyman the Magnificent and His Age: The Ottoman Empire in the Early Modern World* (London: Longman, 1995).

52. Venice enjoyed a brief period of calm under the rule of Doge Pasquale Malipiero (1457–62).

53. The Turks made numerous raids into Dalmatia, Istria, and the Venetian mainland in the second half of the fifteenth century, and in 1566 a Turkish fleet sailed to Fiume and Trieste. In the mid-1460s Venice conquered most of the Morea (the Peloponnese, where Sparta is located) from the Turks. Throughout the fifteenth century several members of the Malatesta family served Venice as mercenary soldiers; a Gismondo Malatesta led the land forces, and Orsatto Giustiniano commanded the fleet. See also Michael Mallett, "Venice and Its Condottieri, 1404–54," in *Renaissance Venice*, ed. J. R. Hale (Totowa, NJ: Rowman and Littlefield, 1973), 121–45.

of the sweet and beautiful island nest
of the goddess of the Graces and of Cupid.[54]

7 6

"This other space shows that Marcello
will hold that high and superhuman seat.
Under him they will pain and scourge
the Ottoman, as I see described.
Behold here the victory, behold the band
by whom the Mohammedans will be worsted.
See how, proud and triumphant,
he returns from Scodra to these sacred shores.[55]

7 7

"Discern how under Vendramin Croia
from the impious hands is saved in Albania.
Here that successor who tires of such war
makes peace with the lord of Turkey.
He acquires Corinth, then annoys Ferrara.
Here against King Ferrando he sends troops into the field—[56]
Ferrando, king of the pleasing walls
which were the siren's sepulcher.[57]

54. In 1476 Venice supported Duke Ercole d'Este of Ferrara against a usurper. The Ottomans ("the serpentine crests") warred alternately against Christians and Persia in the sixteenth century; at one point Venice and Persia were allied. In 1489, after decades of political maneuvers, Venice formally annexed Cyprus, in classical times the principal seat of the worship of Aphrodite. On the extent of the Ottoman Empire, see Donald Pitcher, *A Historical Geography of the Ottoman Empire from Earliest Times to the End of the Sixteenth Century* (Leiden: E. J. Brill, 1972).

55. Under the reign of Nicolò Marcello (1473–74), the Venetians celebrated a victory against the Turks, namely, the failure of the siege of Scutari (ancient Scodra, modern Shkodër) in Albania. However, Venice ceded Scutari to the Turks in 1479.

56. Andrea Vendramin was Doge (1476–78) when the Albanian fortress of Croia fell to the Turks. (The original text refers to "Troia" or Troy, but that city was located in modern Turkey.) His successor, Giovanni Mocenigo (r.1478–85), made peace with the Turks in 1479 and war against Ferrara from 1481 to 1484. He sent a naval expedition which consolidated Venetian rule of Dalmatia and Corinth. When in 1480 the Turks took Otranto in southern Italy, Venice was accused of complicity with them for the sake of revenge against King Ferdinand of Naples.

57. According to legend, Naples rose on the site of the tomb of the siren Parthenope, whose body washed ashore there; after Orpheus's song outdid the sirens, most of them were changed into rocks, but Parthenope instead threw herself into the sea.

78

"This one (Barbarico, who succeeds
his good brother) wages war on Sigismund
of Austria for the mines from which emerges
the fiercest metal now known in the world.[58]
Under him the king of France extracts his foot
from Italy, and by them he is broken and placed in the depths.
With him driven away, Cremona
surrenders and gives itself with other lands to the great Lion.[59]

79

"In the other picture is manifest and plain
the memorable league of Cambrai.
See here the Roman emperor,
in league with the kings of France and Spain.
The Ferrarese will not stay distant;
with the duke of Mantua he too joins the league,
so that the empire defended only by God
might be forever oppressed and despised.[60]

80

"But the force and power
shown by all Europe together
will not be able to crush her hope

58. Iron (the fiercest metal) was vital to Venice, especially for the Arsenal's construction of ships. See Philippe Braunstein, "Le commerce du fer à Venise au XVe siècle," *Studi Veneziani* 8 (1966): 267–302. Doge Agostino Barbarigo (r.1486–1501) succeeded his brother Marco and successfully waged the War of Rovereto to retake this town (located in the vicinity of Alpine iron mines) from Archduke Sigismund, who had briefly seized it in 1487.

59. Charles VIII of France invaded Italy in 1494 and retreated the following year. In the course of his retreat he fought the battle of Fornovo against the forces of the Holy League (Venice, the pope, Milan, and others). Charles lost his baggage train and proceeded on his withdrawal from Italy, but his casualties were far lighter than those of the league's forces; nevertheless the league members called it a great victory. In 1499 Venice received Cremona and nearby territories through its alliance with France against Milan.

60. The goal of the League of Cambrai, signed in 1508, was to divide up the Venetian Empire among the league's members, namely, Pope Julius II, the Holy Roman Empire, France, Spain, Ferrara, and Mantua.

in the high and supreme graces,
through which so great a defense yet remains to her
that she can protect herself until others no longer press her.
She rends the union, she scorns the furors,
and returns more than ever to her previous honors.[61]

8 1

"See how in a brief time and easily
she regains the lost lands.
For many years then happily
she blocks the road to hateful wars,
such that by her is long closed
Janus's temple, and there is no one who unlocks it.
There will be many doges of whom I shall not tell
until Venier, friend of every goodness.[62]

8 2

"This honored prince will conserve
the peace of the happy shores.
In his time every vice lies extinguished,
every virtue flowers, every good reigns,
such that the fame his merit creates
induces the high queen of Poland to visit.
On account of his happy and glorious reputation,
behold her come down to the fortunate shore.[63]

61. At first Venice lost most of its territories on the mainland; then it retook some important cities. After Venice submitted to the pope in 1510, the league members turned against each other.

62. In 1516 the signatories of the League of Cambrai restored to Venice most of the lands they had seized from it. There followed a relatively peaceful period for Venice, which devoted its diplomatic efforts toward avoiding war. It was Roman custom to open the gates of the temple of Janus in time of war and close them during peacetime. Sebastiano Venier was doge from 1577 to 1578. See also the notes to canto 13.6–30.

63. During Sebastiano Venier's dogeship the queen of Poland was Anna Jagiellon (1523–96), daughter of Sigismund I and his Italian wife, Bona Sforza (1494–1557). Bona is said to have stayed in the castle at Stigliano, a small town in the Veneto, in 1555.

83

"Then no other figure is seen,
for she is the last one; so I leave her.
To recount another of the future city's
deeds, I pass to the other side.
Of this fortunate, high adventure
I would say much, except that each of you
must already be too exhausted from hearing me;
so with brevity I intend to complete the task.

84

"But before I begin with new verses
and narrate the illustrious and glorious feat,
I want to rest from my fatigue,
and draw you with me, sirs, to repose."
With this she stepped away from the sacred marbles,
nor do I know if this was welcome to them, or annoying.
It is enough; either willingly or against their desire,
they obeyed the courteous young woman.

85

She drew them back to a window
which overlooked the western countryside.
There a zephyr wafted a freshness, an odor
to restore every troubled mind.
Meanwhile Silano saw sweets and delicate wine
brought in goblets of shining gold
by Circetta's astute damsels,
who until then had been seen no more.

86

So they began to refresh themselves,
while conversing of the aforesaid things.
The warriors came up with more questions,
all of which she explained wisely.

But while they take recreation,
it is right that I too rest somewhat,
and recoup the forces of my intellect,
which has to narrate so important a matter.

CANTO 13

ARGUMENT

*The two warriors continue to contemplate
the story incised in the diamond pictures.
In Armenia two others go with Gracisa
where Risamante besieges Artemita.[1]
To them the standard-bearer relates in detail
the cause of the fierce battle. Biondaura's lofty sister
captures the warrior lover; he believes
she is Biondaura when he sees her.*

1

A judicious craftsman sometimes
girds with a rich and precious frieze
a lowly stone so that it pleases and rises in value,
thanks to the enamel work with which he adorns and colors it.
Just so with excellent worth shines
a garment, if a learned hand dyes and gilds it;
in itself it is rough and lowly,
but the embroidery makes it beautiful and noble.

2

I with such beautiful threads adorn and weave
my cloth, which in itself has a rough texture,
that it can indeed seem beautiful; and it can stand near
any other of gold and silver,

368   1. Artemita was a city on the south coast of Lake Van, in modern Turkey.

while I gather in it every clear and vivid
ornament of my beautiful homeland,
and all her proud and beautiful glories,
whose fame ascends beyond the stars.

3

With her lofty exploits, with her splendor,
I make this work of mine lovely and magnificent.
As among beautiful gems the first honor
is held by the pearl, and as among flowers the rose,
as gold among metals has most worth,
similarly excellent and glorious over every other,
and completely fortunate, is the victory
which took place in the salty Ambracia bay.[2]

4

Of this Circetta wanted to discourse,
when to catch her breath she turned her steps;
and the knights to the aforesaid window
she brought with her, intending to refresh them.
But once they had made their way back where they were lured
by the interrupted story, she loosened her lips.
Extending her white and beautiful hand,
she showed the examples, and then spoke:

5

"Gaze at how many people are gathered there,
who appear to deal with important matters together.
It is the Senate of the Venetians, which hears

---

2. In the following octaves Fonte describes the famous naval battle of Lepanto, where the combined Christian fleet won a dramatic victory over the Turks, who for centuries had seemed an unstoppable threat. The ancient city of Ambracia was located to the north of the site of the battle of Lepanto (modern Naupaktos, in Greece). This is probably a reference to the naval battle of Actium, a city near Ambracia, where the future Roman emperor Augustus's forces defeated Antony and Cleopatra in 31 BCE. For a historical overview of the battle of Lepanto, see Jack Beeching, *The Galleys at Lepanto* (New York: Scribner, 1983); and Hugh Bicheno, *Crescent and Cross: The Battle of Lepanto, 1571* (London: Cassell, 2003).

many threats and fears none.
This man who seems to speak, and everyone listens
to him (for to all the case is important and pressing),
is Mocenico, a worthy prince
with high eloquence and profound intelligence.[3]

6

"Afterward appears the Roman see,
and Philip of Spain brings to bear
his forces in favor of the Christian faith.
With those fathers in the end he makes an agreement and a league;
and against the strong king who does not believe in it
they conclude here the fortunate league.
Now behold over here, gone out from the ports
the Christians' fleets united together.[4]

7

"A cruel war, born of a certain incident
between the Turkish lord and the Venetians,
will in time be the cause of putting to sea
so superb and valorous a fleet.
Now over here appears against the Lion,
against the Cross and the well-born Eagle,
General Pertaù, who advances
with his mighty Turkish navy.[5]

3. In 1570 the Ottomans demanded that Venice yield Cyprus to them. Alvise Mocenigo was the leader of the war party which prevailed upon the Senate to reject the ultimatum. Shortly thereafter he was elected doge.

4. In 1571, under the dogeship of Alvise I Mocenigo, Venice formed a league with Pope Pius V and Philip II of Spain against the powerful Ottoman Turks, who had been encroaching on Christian lands for centuries and who had been ruled from 1566 by Selim II. The combined fleets sailed in August of that year. Sebastiano Venier was the Venetian general, and Don John of Austria, Philip's half brother, was in overall command.

5. The Holy League in 1571 agreed on the primary goal of recovering Cyprus (and the Holy Land). The league's fleet learned of Cyprus's fall to the Turks, after a year of fighting, shortly before they came to battle on October 7. The Turks were based in Lepanto; their admiral was Ali Pasha, and his second-in-command was Pertau (or Pertev) Pasha.

8

"Here and there the people prepare themselves,
having perceived the opposing arms are near,
and they pray to their God devoutly
to grant the victory to their side.
Highest hope entices to battle
those men, in order to capture and conduct to ultimate ruin
a rich and mighty realm;
homeland and religion hasten these others.

9

"On the lucky, pleasant, and pretty morning
the sun with new rays will stick his blond head
out of the sea, perhaps a presage
that the Christians' fate will be propitious.
Already the Adriatic men, and those from near the Tagus,
and those of Latium plow forward through the waves.[6]
The gods, the fish, and the shores are intent,
and the sky, the earth, and all the elements.

1 0

"In this third space is next distinct
the approach of the opposing ranks.
Epirus is on that side, here is Corinth,
here the Morea; but they cannot be seen.
This is the Ambracia bay stained with blood
that will make the coasts vermilion,
and this is the very sea (if the prophecy shows me
the truth) which encircles our Ithaca.[7]

6. Here Fonte refers to the major areas involved in the league: the Adriatic Sea, at the top of which Venice is located; the Tagus River, flowing through central Spain; and Latium, the region of Italy where Rome is situated.

7.   Epirus is on the west coast of northern Greece; the Morea is the Peloponnese, or southern Greece. Lepanto is located between them, at the opening of the Gulf of Patras. Corinth is at the eastern end of this gulf. The ancient city of Ambracia was north of Lepanto. Ithaca is directly west of the Gulf of Patras.

11

"Here and there waving in the air go
the various banners with varied fortune.
These are the Turks' banners which on the cloth
bear painted a crescent moon.
These which the Pope musters to the lofty enterprise
will bring the keys with the miter.
Venice has her Lion on the flag;
the Spanish prince has the proud Eagle.

12

"A little farther over there, gaze at the fierce assault;
see how they confront each other.
The artillery sends on high the fog
of black smoke, and the sky resounds and groans.
Birds fall on the liquefied glaze.
At the fierce sound every cavern shakes.
The cannonballs open the sea with such a roar
that up to the sky leap the salty waves.

13

"That horrendous din and that profound
noise which cannot be discerned here,
that carrying away of half the ships to the bottom,
and into the mouths of sea monsters delivering living men,
that ruin never before seen in the world,
that confusion of the dead among the living—
what pen or style will be so excellent
as to describe and portray it fully?[8]

8. This detailed retelling of the battle of Lepanto—certainly the most traumatic event of
Fonte's generation together with the plague that decimated Venice's population a few years
later—must constitute, chronologically speaking, the first account by a woman writer of a na-
val battle. Although the practical results following the victory at Lepanto soon proved ephem-
eral, the boost in morale among Venetians—reflected in a celebratory resurgence of the myth
of Venice—was enormous. Fonte did not have to look far to get detailed factual information
on the subject, since her own uncle was busy writing about it. See Doglioni, *Historia venetiana*.
She also briefly refers to this epic battle in *The Worth of Women*: "'What a happy event!' cried the
Queen. 'A victory worthy of perpetual remembrance! And our Doge's name, too, deserves to be

14

"Now that the fury has ceased, and the hostile cries,
and the lightning weapons' grave damage,
see them board together the remains,
and most of the galleys that are still whole.
Behold one man quicker than the other to wield
the fierce swords, and the blows they give each other.
So close they are to each other that it's pointless
to use harquebuses and other distance weapons.

15

"Each man against those of the beleaguered galley
fights both here and there, and cuts and pierces.
Behold Venier, the Venetian fleet's
commander, with sword in hand on the prow;
he has smashed the opposing galley
with that valor which I will always remember.
One can say with truth that such
prowess as he possesses is far more than a mortal man's.

16

"See that an enemy arrow bloodies his knee
with a pitiless wound,
nor with all that does he want to rest,
nor withdraw his daring person;
but more than ever valorous and bold
he risks for others his own life.
He turns courageously his breast and his brow,
nor does any mortal peril affright him.

---

echoed throughout the whole world and down through the ages'" (200). On the myth of Ven-
ice, see James Grubb, "When Myths Lose Power: Four Decades of Venetian Historiography,"
Journal of Modern History 58 (1986): 43–94; see also Crouzet-Pavan, *Venice Triumphant*. See also
above canto 12, 1n. The idea that the Venetian Empire was generous and benevolent in its aim,
a concept that Fonte espouses like most of her contemporaries—that is, an empire "inspired by
the high and noble ideals of tranquility, neutrality, and peace"—has been hard to rebut. The
words just quoted come in fact from an early twentieth-century historian, Roberto Cessi, in
Storia della Repubblica di Venezia (Florence: Giunti Martello, 1981), 356.

17

"Behold, here is where that brave
John of Austria works to accomplish great feats.
He strikes the enemy's galley on the side;
he smashes and shatters it and takes its captain.
He adorns himself with immortal glory, and also
to his own side gives victory,
while a hundred other ships are oppressed and defeated
by Christians, and their opponents extinguished.[9]

18

"The faithful raise in unity
the beloved name of victory to the sky;
and at that horrible shout they hear,
ice runs through the Ottomans' bones.
Behold them finally all routed,
prey to the defenders of the Gospels.
The wretches cannot flee, since the waves,
while the flames burn their ships, encircle them.

19

"More than one man believes he'll save himself from the heat,
throws himself half burned into the sea, and appears there a little while;
but in a brief time the sea so outmatches him
that in fire he drowns, and burns still in the sea.
That captain who sees of his Turks
part burn alive and part drown,
with sixty galleys escapes from there.[10]
The others remain submerged, burned, and captive.

20

"More than one ship sinks in pieces to the depths,
with its wretched crowd assembled.

9. The flagships of Don John and Ali Pasha met directly, and in fierce fighting Ali Pasha was killed. The Turks lost over two hundred ships, and approximately thirty thousand people were killed; Christian losses were much lighter.

10. The left wing of the Turkish fleet escaped largely intact.

Some grasp pieces of wood so that from the waves
their dear lives might be saved,
but shortly on the same lifeline
by a cruel blow their hands are cut off.
Arrows or wooden beams kill others;
the sword drives others to where the flames crackle.

21

"See in the end, after many, many
fires, killings, agonies, and robberies,
the soldiers of Christ gathered there,
with their eyes to heaven and their knees bent.
Some with tears of joy bathing
their faces, with hands raised to heaven,
give together to God such thanks as
can be given by mortal men.

22

"In this last space one understands
the extreme joy with which Venice is carried away
when she hears the hoped-for news
of victory expressed by a man named Giustinian.[11]
Such immense pleasure seizes every heart,
it seems the people are beside themselves.
So great a throng closes around the messenger
that they do not let his foot touch the earth.

23

"See them embrace together,
weeping with bliss in the streets,
now that the dear homeland no longer fears
the strongest lord of pagan lands.
For the bountiful and supreme graces granted them,
they praise in the temples the son of Mary.

11. Eleven days after the battle, Giuffredo Giustinian arrived in Venice with the news. This victory was the first break in the gloom of Venice's losing struggle against the Turks since before the fall of Constantinople in 1453; consequently the celebrations were extraordinary.

In the whole city, delightedly and devoutly,
some render thanks to God, others fulfill vows.

24

"The doors are opened to prisoners in such great
delight that hearts cannot contain it.
Everyone for the proud and holy victory
shows his pleasure with clear outward signs.
The divine poet celebrates and sings
with sweet style the illustrious victors;
and since Helicon is in the hands of barbarians,
here the Muses sing and Apollo plays.[12]

25

"Rich gems and most precious gold
with lovely spectacle appear outdoors.
Others reveal silk and golden clothes
with a prominence never seen before.[13]
On the days when such a good befalls them,
although it is not a holiday, they do not work;
everyone spends such days in games, in music, in songs,
as if they were bacchanals or holy days.

26

"But what am I saying? Not only human beings
are filled with bliss at the news they've heard,
but the sky, the earth, and all the elements
feel infinite joy at so great a good.
The cold, icy months of mist
return the earth to green and colorful,
for the sun with a bright and temperate ray
makes in winter appear April and May.

---

12. The gates of the Venetian debtors' prison were opened in an act of spontaneous amnesty. Mount Helicon in Greece was the home of the Muses and their leader, Apollo; Greece was under Turkish rule at this time.

13. In times of war, famine, or disease, sumptuary laws restricted any outward display of wealth or any dressing for merriment.

27

"It will render far more marvelous
such a novelty, that in others' borders
the season will be, as usual, rainy,
and the gardens empty of fruits and flowers.
The delicate rose will bloom,
the lilies, violets, and jasmines,
only in Venice; they will adorn
only the fortunate terrain around her.

28

"Behold Venier who, bright and triumphant,
with such favor as I would not know how to express,
returns to his dear homeland proud of so many
spoils worthy of his valor, and trophies.
The nobility of so many demigods
comes toward him on these sacred shores.
At his arrival everyone shouts and calls him
Savior of his fair homeland.

29

"Not long after his beloved return
makes the city doubly happy,
see this honored young man
who descends from Poland to the Adriatic shores.
He is the successor of France, who comes
called by that crown which awaits him.
At his arrival Venice is so delighted
that her bliss and happiness surpass every limit.[14]

14. King Henry III of France visited Venice in 1574. At the death of his elder brother he abandoned the crown of Poland, which he had gained a few months before, and he stopped in Venice on his way back to Paris. Venetians treated him with lavish hospitality. The poet courtesan Veronica Franco had the good luck of spending time with him one night, and she used the encounter first to gain some practical professional benefits and then to compose two sonnets, which appear, together with a dedicatory letter to the king, in her *Lettere familiari a diversi*. See Rosenthal, *Honest Courtesan*, 104.

30

"See at last, upon heaven's assumption
of Mocenico, that man of immortal memory,
with how much applause great Venier has reached
the grandest rank, the highest glory.
But shortly after (with his mortal body worn away),
the bright spirit of so great a victory,
accompanied by angels, returns to God;
and NICOLÒ DA PONTE succeeds him.[15]

31

"So worthy is this prince, I discern
that immense is the honor owed him.
He will be his people's source of pride, and their government,
with that wisdom which would be long to tell.
If anyone could make such a man eternal,
he would be blessed, for he would have great good fortune,
since, under the favor of so great a banner,
in him peace and abundance reign.

32

"Under so bright and glorious a doge,
behold BIANCA most illustrious CAPPELLA,
for whose sake Circe gave to the light
the highest honors of this beautiful country.
See that she shines and glows so much
with intelligence and beauty, that a friendly star
gives her (so I increase her glory far more)
as wife to the most serene FRANCESCO.[16]

---

15. At the death of Alvise I Mocenigo in 1577, Sebastiano Venier, the Venetian hero of Lepanto, was unanimously elected doge. He died the following year, in his eighties. Nicolò da Ponte ruled from 1578 to 1585.

16. On Bianca Capello and Francesco I de' Medici, see also cantos 1.4–5 and 3.59–68. See also the prefatory sonnets.

33

"She will be esteemed before she comes,
when she lives, and after death as well;
nor do I believe her glory will ever be extinguished
by time, which in the end devours everything.
Since she will be worthy of so great a homeland,
for her lineage and also for herself, as I said now,
where is the surprise if by the Tuscan grand duke
she will be elected among a thousand as beloved wife?

34

"At the welcome, felicitous news
of these splendid and regal nuptials,
so much cheer and happiness Venice feels
that she will give very great signs of it.
Noble Florence finds herself so
delighted, enclosing in herself two such personages,
that no other city outdoes her,
either in our age or in theirs."

35

With this and much else that she said in honor
of so great a lady and so magnificent a duke,
the girl puts an end to her speech,
for Phoebus's light is already descending into the sea.
Yet Silano, who has fixed in his mind
exploits so fair, still proceeds
to gaze now at this side, now at that,
remembering the past discourse.

36

They had stayed there more than enough,
when the young men at the urging of Circetta
at last leave off contemplating the room,
because dinner is in order and awaits them.

Silano with a most delighted expression
follows wherever the young woman wants,
nor does he cease to gaze at her; and to seem more faithful
he pretends to be on his guard against Clarido.

3 7

The virgin to herself praises and thanks
the blind love which makes her blind as well.
With chaste pity, she is never sated
with gazing back at that knight whom she adores.
It seems to her that in gazing at her he has such grace,
and shows her his heart outside through his eyes,
that she considers, for the love which she infers from it,
it would be very uncivil if she did not reciprocate.

3 8

With these varied and diverse opinions
the lady and the knights spend the dinner hour;
then each of them turns his steps
where the lady leads them to repose.
But they sleep not at all until in the sky
the pure and serene dawn disperses the night,
since the girl is wounded and tormented by love,
and the knights by trepidation at the prospect of the battle.

3 9

This concern weighs no less on the damsel,
who fears Silano has not such great
prowess as to win the honor of that endeavor,
so it would then be necessary to change him into a plant.
When each man at so great a conflict
ends up the loser, she perforce enchants him.
Although she sorrows quite a bit at such a deed,
she is constrained to will what she does not want.

40

She thinks and thinks again, never closing her eyelids,
about what might be the best path and the best way
to save Silano from that peril,
without changing him into a deaf, green trunk.
At last, resolved on it as the best plan,
she intends to deceive the enchantment with this trick:
she plans to make him invisible, and wants him to go
all the way to the fateful temple without employing his sword.

41

She knows what the enchantment is like and what sort it is,
and that the knight who intends to try it,
provided he is not drawn outside the gates,
fate in no way hurts.
However, if he goes, and the spirits with which the horrible
pass defends itself do not notice him,
she thinks she'll ensure his form to her Silano,
with no fear of an adverse outcome.

42

With the light, the sun, and the day returned,
the knights rise from bed.
The damsel makes her return to them,
and in the accustomed style they greet each other,
but to them she does not make clear and plain
what she has thought about their situation.
They prepare to try the enchantment;
but of others now I shall tell you somewhat.

43

I want us to leave these people; and do not be regretful
at leaving them in such a state for a time,
for later we will come again one day to find them,
and perhaps we will take them from here in time.
Now it is appropriate for me to speak of the two warriors

who, in their eagerness, despaired that ever the time
would come when they would reach that Armenian city
where Biondaura was suffering an atrocious war.

44

They rode with Gracisa very swiftly
(from Europe into Asia they have already passed),
and they saw many cities, many peoples,
varied in custom and varied in language.
They reached in the end the so famous Euphrates,
which through Armenia stretches its course.
Although nowadays there are two Armenias,
formerly by one they understood both.[17]

45

In every place, whether cities or castles
of that realm, wherever they lifted up their brows,
the knights and the damsel saw
flutter the banners of the white lily.
Risamante had already taken everything
from her sister Biondaura's clutches,
and for her all those lands were held
which she had subdued in those wars.

46

So much did they drive forward their destriers
on the shortest, the most traveled way,
that the lady and the knights reached
the threatened walls of Artemita.
An abundant army of bold people
occupied all the paths.
Everywhere were tents and pavilions
which housed knights and foot soldiers.

17. After the Seljuk Turks conquered the independent Armenian kingdoms, refugees founded
the kingdom of Lesser Armenia in Cilicia in 1082. From 1375 Lesser Armenia was controlled
by the Mamluks; the Mongols ruled the inland Armenia from the mid-thirteenth century until
the early fifteenth century. From the beginning of the sixteenth century, the Ottoman Turks
and Persia (Iran) struggled over Armenia; the Ottomans eventually conquered it.

47

That day the townspeople met with no
assault at all, from what could be seen.
They perceived no fighting,
as there had been every day before.
Once they arrived in the camp, the foreign warriors
and Gracisa, who had veiled herself,
saw a great duel in progress
between two warriors in the middle of a stockade.

48

The Artemitans, who had climbed onto the city walls,
contemplated sadly the cruel battle.
The armies outside on the plain
waited to see which of the two was more powerful.
Up high sat the judges who were in charge,
seeing that justice was equal for both parties.
Meanwhile the two who were engaged in horrendous combat
withdrew to the side to rest.

49

Each one was sweaty and bloody.
Of their destriers, one lay on the ground lifeless;
the other with chomping rendered the bit frothy
(the one with a green and white harness).
One warrior did not show need
of repose, and stood with boldness;
the other leaned over deep in thought,
like a man who in his enterprise had little hope.

50

The pair of warriors who had come
with Gracisa approached a standard-bearer.
They asked him in a kindly manner
who were the one and the other knight,
and they beseeched him to tell them the truth
about why they held the fierce fight.

On them the standard-bearer fixed his eyes
and, having stared at them somewhat, said this:

51

"That knight on the eastern side,
who bears on a green shield the white lily,
is our queen Risamante;
in the world there is no knight braver.
The other who to his own detriment came against her,
with the white dove on his left side,
is Babylonia's King Cloridabello,
who for Biondaura undertakes so great a duel.

52

"Biondaura previously did not want to share
with her sister, our queen,
this realm. She set herself to despise
this woman, who was far away and wandering
because a sorcerer previously took her
from the house of the king her father when she was a baby.
He, considering the girl dead,
came to death and left her nothing.

53

"Risamante by the sorcerer was raised
to every trial and military art,
in a castle founded in the sea;
but no one knows where, for it cannot be seen.
From there (once he had informed her
thoroughly about her status) he made her pass
onto the mainland and go in search of adventure,
provided with a horse and armor.

54

"Risamante (after she set out
at liberty) requested from Biondaura her share;

but the sister to her rightful desire,
to her just petition, did not condescend.
So Risamante, angered, united
many people and came against her country,
and has taken it all from her hand with ignominy,
except this city which we surround.

55

"She gathered from diverse troops
the people whom you see united,
and composed so great an army
in a very short time; and hear how:
the sorcerer carried her requests to those
who had offered her their support in this dispute,
and in only one night with his arts
he guided all the people here to these parts.[18]

56

"So sudden was our coming,
so quiet, so quick beyond every judgment,
that we found Armenia unprepared,
and we took it right away upon our arrival.
Biondaura, who had found out the news,
gathered many highly esteemed people,
who joined close battle with us;
and all her supporters remained defeated.

57

"Now the wretched girl has taken refuge
with her few trusted people in this city.
Because they find it poorly furnished
with victuals and munitions for war,

18. The figure of the wizard Celidante is not fully fleshed in *Floridoro*, unfortunately, but we
know that he always helps women in distress. We saw him in canto 1 aiding the queen of Dacia
to escape rape; then he told Nicobaldo that his imprisoned wife would be rescued in due time
by a knight with a most precious ring (Risamante). Now he creates an entire army in Armenia
out of nowhere.

she has placed, for herself and for Artemita
and for all the possessions enclosed there,
the litigation in the hand of King Cloridabello,
either to save herself or to fall with him.

58

"This prince already burned from the renown
of the rare beauty of this woman.
Both for his own virtue and because he loves her,
he came not long ago to defend her.
The pact between one and the other lady
is that if the king sends his soul to the Stygian criminals
or is taken, Biondaura loses the city,
and to the hand of her sister it falls.

59

"But if by chance Risamante is the one
who commits an error, and the king remains the winner,
then if living she must reinvest her sister
with that whole realm instantly,
and she must lift the fell battle,
making all the people go elsewhere.
In this way, to avoid deaths and ruin
for many people, they concurred in the end."

60

But the standard-bearer had not yet finished
saying this when the glorious woman warrior,
with the pause by now too bothersome to her,
returned boldly to the fierce battle.
Cloridabello was not less quick than she,
and he delivered a blow at the proud maiden;
it was somewhat imprecise, for if he had caught
her fully he would have cleft her right shoulder.

61

Yet he cut in such a manner that his shining
weapon made vivid blood issue forth.
At the great blow Risamante's face turned
more vermilion than the rose in the morning,
and her wrath was such that she became
almost senseless and furious.
This was because, though she was indeed all stained with blood,
not yet with her own was she spotted and dirtied.

62

Driven by great furor she throws away her shield,
and, having taken her sword in both hands,
she designs to take on his head the vengeance
more suitable for the hand which had offended her.
Cloridabello raises his shield in a hurry
when he sees the blow falling, for his own defense.
The proud blow cuts in two parts the shield,
and into his head penetrates the cruel sword.

63

The stunned king falls and irrigates
with a flowing vermilion brook the green plain.
The woman warrior, who has a soft and humane heart,
seeing she has the better of that quarrel,
runs to him, and with a pitiful hand
she hurriedly frees his head from the bloody helm;
and she demonstrates to everyone her victory
in his deadly pale face, from which she gains triumph and glory.[19]

19. Although Risamante reacts to Cloridabello's blood with fury, she does not kill her opponent, in sharp contrast to Ruggiero in the *Furioso*, who promises to spare Rodomonte (46.137) and yet wounds him mortally soon after: "so two or three times he raised his arm to its full height and plunged the dagger to the hilt" (46.140). Similarly Aeneas, "aflame with rage," plunges his sword into Turnus's chest (*Aeneid* 12.1268–71). For more on the topic, see the Volume Editor's Introduction.

64

The air which the king took, once deprived of his helm,
kept in him some spirit of life;
so he came to, and showed he was alive,
but captured by the hand of the daring maiden.
Biondaura was pouring out a tearful stream
in the meantime, having heard the news
from some of her people who on the field had discerned
her king captured, and herself landed in a bad fix.

65

To Risamante the judges gave
the palm, and they adorned her with laurel fronds.
She removed her helmet and showed clearly
her beautiful visage and her blonde hair.
But when the kingly prisoner, who felt bitter
grief for Biondaura and was all confused,
gazed at this one so similar to her,
he thought she was his beautiful lady.

66

"Is this not," he said, "the beloved face
that Love's hand stamped in my heart?
Are these not the beautiful eyes that caught me
with a sweet snare and placed me in sweet error?
Indeed I am not so blind nor so foolish
as not to recognize the one who has taken my heart.
By my goddess then I was conquered,
and I remain the prisoner of her beautiful visage.

67

"It is no wonder if she defeated me,
since earlier she had captured and bound me;
for no other than she ever seized me
so tightly, nor could place me in such a state.
But along with the beauty with which she fascinated me,

I did not believe such estimable valor
reigned in her, nor do I know for what reason
she wanted to contend with me.

68

"Happy deceit, if she wanted to deceive me,
perhaps to show me her prowess.
Blessed be the wounds and the blood she took from me,
when with her gaze she gives me health.
The only things that oppress me (nor did anything else ever grieve me
so much) are those blows she received
from me, the dreadful and wicked blows
which through too much ignorance I gave her."

69

So said that unhappy lover.
He certainly did not believe he had been captured,
since it seemed to him Risamante
was the beautiful lady for whom his heart burned,
not knowing that so similar
the young woman who had contended with him
was to Biondaura, that everyone mistook
the one for the other, and did not discern the truth.

70

With great pity the glorious woman warrior
had that king taken to the regal pavilion
and doctored (for he was severely wounded),
treating him like a king, not like a prisoner.
At this moment, out from the city in ranks
came the most honored and noble people.
What happened next elsewhere I'll sing,
for now of Celsidea I want to tell you somewhat.

APPENDIX

This appendix contains the following parts of the text of *Floridoro* in Italian: cantos 1–2 (complete), 4.1–5, 8.1–34, 11.50–77, and 13.36–70.

Cantos 1–2 set up the story, give the background of Risamante's quest, introduce Celsidea, show how good Fonte is in setting up an epic battle, initiate the story of Silano and Clarido, and offer two story lines that are easy to follow independently of the main text.

Excerpts from canto 4 are a feminist manifesto.

Excerpts from canto 8 rewrite the Circe story through the daughter Circetta and return to the story of Silano and Clarido.

Excepts from canto 11 provide a glimpse of Floridoro acting manly in an episode that is very important to women writers (how to think through the possibility of rape); these verses also reintroduce Celsidea.

Excerpts from canto 13 give the reader a sense of where the Circetta story goes and conclude the Risamante/Biondaura story.

NOTE ON THE ITALIAN TEXT

The transcription of *Floridoro* in Italian comes from the 1995 edition of Valeria Finucci's *Tredici canti del Floridoro*. This was based on a printed copy of 1581 in the Special Collection Library of Duke University, where the printer's corrections appear at times directly in the text. For the missing part of the *Argomento* of canto 1 in that edition, a Yale University Library microfilm was used.

The 1995 *Floridoro* edition was conceived as a conservative transcription, and therefore changes were made mostly to enhance reading or to correct printer's mistakes. Thus, the overabundant punctuation that marks early modern texts in Italian was reduced; some unnecessary parentheses were eliminated; words were corrected when spelled differently within the text and were also transcribed in their entirety when shortened; accents and apostrophes were modernized; prepositions were tied (*de le* became for example *delle*); and the *h* at the beginning of words was eliminated (i.e., *huomini* became *uomini*). Also capitalization now follows standard modern practice; the letters *u* and *v* are distinguished; and accents have been standardized according to current usage. For a more precise list of changes, see the "Nota al testo" accompanying that edition (xlv–xlvi).

As in all early modern Italian chivalric and epic romances, Fonte uses the *ottava rim* in *Floridoro*, which is formed of eight hendecasyllabic lines, rhymed ABABABCC. This rhyming not only lends itself to lengthy narratives but was also quite easy to versify and modify—unlike, say, Dante's *terza rima.*

Valeria Finucci

CANTO PRIMO

Argomento

Giunto Macandro alle cecropie mura
Abbatte tutti i cavallier di corte.
Segue il destrier dentro una selva oscura
Lungi il Sican delle palladie porte.
Gli narra una donzella l'avventura
Della ghirlanda e di Parmin la sorte.
Macandro in gran terror pon tutta Atene,
Alfin un cavallier contra gli viene.

1

Scegli d'ornati e ben composti accenti
Il più bel fior, leggiadra Musa, e canta
Li spogliati trofei, gli incendi spenti
Dal tempo, ond'ancor Marte e Amor si vanta.
Di' le battaglie rie, le fiamme ardenti
Ch'uscir dall'arme e dalla face santa,
Allor che 'l fero dio gli altari avea
E Ciprigna adorata era per dea.

2

Canta l'inclite imprese e i dolci affetti
De' cavallieri e delle donne illustri,

Fa' che di quelle man, di questi petti,
Viva il pregio e la gioia, eterni lustri;
E agguaglia lo stil con quei concetti
Ch'escon de' pensier miei vaghi e industri,
Mentre al raggio purissimo e divino
D'un'alma coppia il rude ingegno affino.

3

Frattanto ella, che luce e scorta sia
Della nobil da noi fatica presa,
Favorirà per così lunga via
Quel bel desir di c'ho la mente accesa;
Altrimenti quest'opera saria
Oscura troppo e mal guidata impresa,
Né sperarei senza il suo lume grato
Di pervenirne al fin sì desiato.

4

FRANCESCO Serenissimo, splendore
Del fortunato Imperio di Toscana,
Voi che quel sete senza il cui favore
Ogni fatica mia reputo vana,
Degnisi il vostro generoso core
Per l'alma virtù via più ch'umana
Talor rivolger del mio basso ingegno
Gli incolti versi, che cantando vegno.

5

E voi BIANCA Illustrissima, ch'insieme
Di casto unita e maritale affetto
Lieta regnate, e grazie alte e supreme
Spargete in ogni cor vostro soggetto,
Voi che sete non meno appoggio e speme
Di quei pensier che m'infiammaro il petto,
Non sdegnate accettar questo umil dono,
Poi che fra tanti anch'io serva vi sono.

6

Nel più vago fiorir di quel ben nato
Secol famoso, in quella età novella
Ch'in Atene piovea propizio il fato
Quante può grazie dar benigna stella,
Superbo in lei sen gìa del regno ornato
E d'ogni alma virtù pregiata e bella
Un re, non men prudente che gagliardo,
Giusto e uman, che si nomò Cleardo.

7

Con felice imeneo, lieto e giocondo
Sciolti avea i voti al protettor Cupido,
E la stirpe real del re Alismondo
Tolta al Sicano e tratta al greco lido,
Di cui produsse una fanciulla al mondo
Ch'ebbe sopra le belle il pregio e 'l grido,
E fu dotata d'eccellente ingegno,
Che in bel corpo non regna animo indegno.

8

Erano i graziosi almi sembianti
Di costei, che fu detta Celsidea,
E i suoi costumi sì leggiadri e santi
Che parea non mortal donna ma dea,
Tal che sua fama a tutte l'altre inanti
Pel mondo gìa né d'altro si dicea,
E mentre ogn'uom di lei parla e favella,
Ogn'altra perde il titol d'esser bella.

9

Soleva il re per suo contento il giorno
Farsi seder questa fanciulla a lato
Con la regina e più donzelle intorno,
Ch'eran le più gentil del greco stato.
Or accade che stando in sala un giorno
Co' greci eroi nel modo c'ho narrato,

Comparve in mezzo un gran gigante e fiero,
A cui rivolse ognun gli occhi e 'l pensiero.

10

Costui del regno armenio era partito
Ove gran tempo avea servita invano
Una giovene bella da marito,
Che di quel regno avea lo scettro in mano.
De' cui begli occhi avendo il cor ferito,
Venuto era per lei presso che insano,
E stimando più ch'altro esserle grato
Si tenea sopra ogn'amator beato.

11

Non che l'amasse la gentil donzella,
Ch'era amante per lei disconcio troppo,
Ma perché lite avea con la sorella
E temea ognor di qualche strano intoppo,
Con lieta vista e con dolce favella
Lo tenea stretto all'amoroso groppo,
E l'avea un tempo in corte intertenuto,
Perché al bisogno suo le desse aiuto.

12

Or mentre egli in Armenia alla gran corte
Beato serve e altier di tanta dama,
Ode quanto gran biasmo il grido apporte
Di questa greca a lei ch'egli tanto ama,
E gli accende una rabbia in cor sì forte
Che (se potesse) uccideria la fama,
Pur, quando altro non può, disegna almeno
Sfogar nel regno acheo tanto veleno.

13

S'arma e prende licenza da colei
Di cui nel core impresso ha il viso adorno,
E com'io dissi inanzi al re d'Achei

Si trasferì nella gran sala un giorno.
Tosto ch'ei giunse, agli occhi iniqui e rei
S'appresentò quella beltà che scorno
Al sol facea, nonché ad ogni altra bella,
Della real, illustre verginella.

14

All'estrema bellezza, in cui le ciglia
Non osò di fermar l'uom crudo e fiero,
Conobbe lei per quell'eccelsa figlia
Ch'erede esser dovea del greco impero.
E ne prese tra sé gran maraviglia
Che la sua dea mirando nel pensiero
Non gli parve sì vaga e bella quanto
Era costei, benché l'amasse tanto.

15

Con tutto ciò, per non esser venuto
Indarno e per l'amor ch'a lei portava,
E per aver materia onde veduto
Fusse il valor ch'ei tanto in sé stimava,
Non volse rimaner tacendo muto,
E voltatosi al re ch'attento stava,
Disse con alta e con superba voce
Ch'ognuno intese il suo parlar feroce:

16

—Perchè troppo s'estende il pregio e 'l grido
Ch'alla figliuola tua tal rende onore,
E per colmar di gloria il parthio lido
E all'Armenia donar luce e splendore,
Io Macandro, ch'in Parthia ho 'l proprio nido
E son di tanto imperio alto signore,
Son venuto a provar con l'arme in mano
Com'il grido è dal ver troppo lontano.

17

E dico e vuo' provar nei tuoi terreni
Con chi fra i guerrier tuoi più in pregio sale
Che la bella Biondaura, ch'agli Armeni
Comanda e al valor mio (ch'assai più vale),
Di chiaro viso e d'occhi almi e sereni
Vince tua figlia, e non ha in terra uguale.
Dico c'ha sì bel viso e sì giocondo
Che costei passa, e non ha par nel mondo.

18

La prova con la lancia e con la spada
Sia per tre giorni, e di chi resta a piede
(Questo patto fra noi voglio che vada)
Lo scudo sia del vincitor mercede;
E per ch'altro disturbo non accada
Tu m'assicurerai sulla tua fede
Che 'l patto osserveranno i guerrier tuoi,
Senza ch'altro romor nasca tra noi.

19

Io me n'andrò (se 'l tuo parer l'approva)
Fuor della terra al grand'olivo accanto,
E ivi aspetterò chi venga in prova
Contra di me che di provar mi vanto,
Che la regina mia sol si ritrova
I cui begli occhi e 'l cui viso santo
Non pur non cede alla bellezza altrui,
Ma non è volto uman simile a lui.—

20

Parve a ciascun superba e arrogante
La sua proposta e ne diè segno in vista.
Ma tu, bella fanciulla, che sembiante,
Che cor fu il tuo per così strana vista?
Il re, che vede che quel fier gigante

La bella figlia sua turba e contrista,
Le dice: —Figlia mia, sia il pensier vostro
Di trovar chi difenda il pregio nostro.

21

Io, quanto a me, sulla mia fé prometto
Al cavalier che non gli sia mancato,
E poi che 'l vostro almo e leggiadro aspetto
Sparge un grido sì chiaro e sì lodato
Non troverete un cavallier perfetto
Che vi difenda il pregio che vi è dato?
Vada pur il guerrier, ch'avrà ben cura
Di difendervi alcun, state sicura.—

22

Notò Macandro altier che la richiesta
Non pose in lui terror molto né poco,
E si partì con un crollar di testa
Quasi sprezzando ognun ch'era in quel loco.
Partito l'empio in corte altro non resta
Da ragionar che del futuro gioco,
Che tanto aggrada lor quanto dispiace
La gran superbia del gigante audace.

23

Erano alcuni dì per gran ventura
Ch'era in Atene Apollideo venuto,
Cui lo scettro devea di quelle mura
Che fondò della cetra il suono arguto;
E 'l re di Sparta, e quel di età matura
Griante così forte e così astuto.
Eravi anco Aliforte di Tessaglia,
Che brama esser il primo alla battaglia.

24

Non vede il franco re d'Arcadia l'ora
Che 'l fier Macandro alla battaglia sfide,

E gode di trovarsi ivi a quell'ora;
Il medesimo pensier fa Polinide.
Costui venne del regno ove Etna ogn'ora,
Sospirando Tipheo, s'accende e stride,
Nipote era del re per la consorte,
E venne dianzi a visitar la corte.

25

Io vuo' dir che suo padre era fratello
Della regina, moglie di Cleardo,
Che fur del re Alismondo e questo e quello
Figli, qual fu a dì suoi tanto gagliardo.
Poi morto lui, fu fatto re novello
Il suo figliuol che si nomò Brancardo,
Padre di Polinide, c'ho narrato,
E di tutta Sicilia incoronato.

26

Quel dì tutto e la sera i cavallieri
Ch'uscir devean contra il gigante strano
Spesero in governar l'arme e i destrieri
Per non cader sì facilmente al piano;
E ben ch'ognun d'esser vincente speri
(Se la ragion dà la vittoria in mano),
Non però vol mancar di porsi a mente
Ogni aviso più pronto e diligente.

27

A pena l'alba in oriente apparse
Per far l'antiqua scorta al novo giorno,
Che d'alto suon tutta la terra sparse
Del gran Macandro il formidabil corno.
Subito in piazza Apollideo comparse
E rispose al gigante ingiuria e scorno.
Intanto il popol vano di natura
Corse in gran fretta ad occupar le mura.

28

Il principe teban licenza tolse
Prima dal re poi dalla regia figlia,
Né senza il suo consentimento volse
Torcer un dito al suo destrier la briglia.
Indi ver le gran porte il freno volse
Con pochi che 'l seguir di sua famiglia,
E il re con la figliuola e la mogliere
Anch'ei venne sul muro per vedere.

29

Le cecropie donzelle e preghi e voti
Fanno alla casta e bellicosa dea,
Perché 'l lor cavallier l'arcion non voti
E mantenga l'onor di Celsidea;
E ei, pregando che d'effetto voti
Non vadino i pensier ch'in mente avea,
Lei mira nel passar, ch'in mezzo splende
Di cento belle, e 'l cor gli instiga e accende.

30

Erane occulto il cavaliero amante
Da che mirò le belle luci sole,
E dentro si struggea qual cera inante
Rapido foco o neve esposta al sole.
Ma nol rendeva Amor così arrogante
Che osasse a isguardi aggiunger le parole,
Tacito egli adorava il divo aspetto
Ch'era sol refrigerio all'arso petto.

31

All'aprir della porta e all'uscir fuore
Con molto ardir che fè l'altiero Ismeno,
Brillò nel volto e giubilò nel core
Il gigante di gaudio e d'amor pieno.
E certo di restarne vincitore
E d'antepor al greco il pregio armeno,

Si move anch'ei, ma pria che gli risponda
Rivolge il guardo alla palladia fronda.

3 2

Appeso a un ramo avea del sacro olivo
Un'effigie di donna alma e gentile,
D'un aspetto sì nobile e sì divo
Che raro alcun se gli trovò simile.
A questo che parea non finto, vivo,
Sì lo ritrasse un diligente stile,
Inchinossi l'altier divoto e fido
E roppe insieme il ciel con questo grido:

3 3

—Ben che degn'io non sia d'un favor tale,
O dell'Armenia e del mio cor regina,
Ch'essendo un cavallier vile e mortale
Esaltar cerchi una beltà divina,
Pur accetta il voler pronto e leale
Che sol la tua grandezza adora e inchina,
E degna ch'io per te vinca or gli Achei
Che poi voglio anco in ciel vincer gli dèi.—

3 4

Con questo allentò il freno e punse il fianco
Al suo destrier che per lo prato corse;
L'Agenoreo guerrier non fece manco
Che dritto verso lui la briglia torse,
E andollo a colpir sì ardito e franco
Che maraviglia ai circostanti porse;
Nell'incontrar per colpa del cavallo
Pose la lancia il fier gigante in fallo.

3 5

Non fé così il teban che proprio giunse
Il fier Macandro a mezzo dello scudo,
Ma doppio e ben ferrato indarno il punse

Quantunque fosse il colpo acerbo e crudo.
E perchè troppa forza al braccio aggiunse,
Fracassò l'asta infino al ferro nudo,
Né si piegò il gigante né si mosse
Come una torre innanzi al vento fosse.

36

Dall'impeto i cavalli trasportati
Con poco lor disconcio oltra passaro,
E poi ch'un pezzo andar, furon voltati
Dai cavallier ch'incontra si tornaro.
Macandro bestemmiò le stelle e i fati
Quando conobbe il suo difetto chiaro,
E l'assaltò una furia di maniera
Ch'Aletto è più placabile e Megera.

37

Già tratto il brando onde più genti estinse,
Il buon tebano innanzi si facea,
Quando il gigante addosso se gli spinse
E con quella gran colera ch'avea
Prese col braccio orrendo e in guisa strinse
L'elmetto del campion di Celsidea,
E se 'l tirò con tanta forza al petto
Che fu a cadere il cavallier costretto.

38

Vide a questo ciascun che forza estrema
Avea il gigante e non minor destrezza,
E 'l re (non che perciò s'affligga o tema)
Ben si maravigliò di sua fierezza.
Le donne argive a cui speranza e tema
Combattea 'l cor c'han fama di bellezza,
Molto si contristar che 'l guerrier greco
Fusse caduto e la lor gloria seco.

39

Ma ben maggior fu la vergogna e l'ira
Ch'Apollideo di questo caso prese,
Onde col brando la battaglia dira
Volea seguir per vendicar l'offese;
Se non che 'l re, ch'a questo avea la mira,
Tosto un messo mandò che gliel contese
E insieme gli ordinò secondo il patto
Che 'l vincitor lasciasse satisfatto.

40

Lo scudo, ove la figlia di Peneo
Si vedea ornar d'un novo arbor la terra,
Lascia dunque al gigante Apollideo
E torna vergognoso nella terra;
E nell'entrar del giovene cadmeo
Uscì Aliforte alla seconda guerra,
Che di tanti color vestir gli piace
Ch'aver suol l'arco annunciator di pace.

41

Era questo garzon molto gagliardo
Ma di natura vano e arrogante,
Onde vantossi innanzi al re Cleardo
Di riportar lo scudo del gigante.
Venne sì com'io dissi né più tardo
Di lui fu l'avversario a farsi inante,
Corsero il campo e presero la volta
Con l'aste basse e con la briglia sciolta.

42

Colse Macandro il guerrier di Tessaglia
Pur allo scudo, e fé sì picciol botta
Che senza aprirli pur piastra né maglia
Volò al ciel l'asta in mille tronchi rotta;
Né più felice uscir della battaglia

Lo vide il re della palladia frotta
Del buon teban, quando nell'elmo urtollo
Macandro sì che dell'arcion gettollo.

43

Non fu sì tosto in terra che risorse
Il cavalliero e rimontò in arcione,
E 'l proprio scudo all'avversario porse
Con la gemmata insegna del pavone,
Indi ver la cittade il freno torse
E mal contento uscì della tenzone.
Intanto di giostrar tolse l'assunto
Un altro cavallier ch'era già in punto.

44

Di Sparta era costui signor ch'io dico,
Dell'Amphionio re figliol minore,
Sì liberal, sì di virtute amico,
Che Sparta se lo elesse per signore.
Venne egli incontra al vincitor nemico
Per emendar del suo fratel l'errore;
Porta ben nello scudo anch'ei l'alloro
Ma sopra l'elmo ha una corona d'oro.

45

Non ebbe il buon Algier (così nomosse)
Del frate Apollideo più destra sorte,
Ch'all'incontro il terren verde percosse
Restando in sella il suo avversario forte.
Griante dopo lui ratto si mosse,
Il più prudente cavallier di corte,
E Macandro sfidò sdegnoso e fiero
Ch'era del quarto onor lieto e altero.

46

Quel ch'ad ogn'altro cavallier successe
Col fier Macandro anco a Griante avvenne,

Ch'all'incontro il terren col tergo presse
E 'l re de Parthi in sella si sostenne.
Risorto il cavallier lo scudo cesse
E ripreso il cavallo indietro venne.
Intanto il re d'Arcadia, Elion detto,
Contra Macandro espose il franco petto.

47

Ha nello scudo una pantera pinta
Con arme bigie e sopraveste tale,
Così il destriero avea la spoglia tinta
Però di color vero e naturale.
Macandro intento ad acquistar la quinta
Gloria, com'abbia messo al destrier ale,
Venne a colpirlo con tal furia in fronte
Che'l pose a terra e v'avria posto un monte.

48

In questo Polinide, che nepote
Era del greco re per la mogliera,
Mont'a cavallo, e 'l fren gli allenta e scuote,
E Macandro incontrò che già mosso era.
Ma dell'arcion piegar pur non lo puote,
Anzi cadde egli ancor con gli altri in schiera,
E diè a Macandro il verde scudo in mano,
Ove pinto una spica era di grano.

49

Gli dà lo scudo e dietro il suo destriero
Va per pigliarlo e rimontarvi sopra,
Ma 'l caval corre via tanto leggiero
Che d'acquistarlo era diffficil l'opra;
Non cessa di seguirlo il cavalliero
Alfin che non si celi e non si copra,
Corre il cavallo e tal vantaggio acquista
Ch'esce in breve ora al suo signor di vista.

50

Polinide pur va dietro la pesta
Finchè cacciossi in mezzo un bosco folto,
E or per quella strada ora per questa
Cercollo assai, perché l'amava molto.
Una vaga donzella alfin l'arresta,
La qual gli venne incontra a freno sciolto,
E tenendo il destrier che più non gisse
Sciolse la lingua, e tai parole disse:

51

—Dimmi per sorte, o cavalliero, avresti
Visto un guerrier d'aspetto ardito e franco
Quindi passar con belle e ricche vesti
Di cui l'insegna in verde è un giglio bianco?—
Rispose il buon Tinacrio: —Non han questi
Occhi miei tal guerriero mai veduto anco.
Che nome è 'l suo?—Nol so—disse la dama—
Sol lo conosco all'abito e per fama.

52

Ho bisogno di lui perché mi cavi
D'un gran martire che nel mio petto ha stanza,
Poi ch'egli vince tutti i casi gravi,
Tanto è maggior la sua d'ogni possanza.
Ben narrereiti i miei tormenti pravi
E quel dolor, ch'ogni dolor avanza,
Se non c'ho troppa fretta di trovare
Quel gentil cavallier che non ha pare.

53

Io lo vado cercando in ogni banda,
Ma sempre al desir mio contrario il fato
In loco a lui lontan mi gira e manda;
Pur ho per spia che qui d'intorno è stato.
Forse al Castel sarà della Ghirlanda,
Dove concorre ogni guerrier pregiato

Alla ventura apparsa di novello
Nel paese di Dacia in quel castello.—

54

—Deh (disse Polinide alla donzella),
Narrami questa impresa in cortesia,
Dimmi come sia strana e come bella,
Di che periglio e di che gloria sia,
Perch'io disegno di venir a quella
E sarà forse la vittoria mia.—
Quando la donna la preghiera intese
Subitamente del destrier discese.

55

E disse: —S'hai di venir meco brama,
Monta in arcion che verrò dietro in groppa,
E come udii, ti narrerò per fama
L'alta avventura ove più d'un s'intoppa.—
Il cavallier, che di trovarsi brama
A quella impresa avventurosa troppa,
Accetta il proferir della donzella,
Prende la briglia, e salta nella sella.

56

In groppa la donzella se gli mise,
Poi verso Dacia presero il sentiero,
E cavalcando, come ella promise,
Così narrar comincia al cavalliero:
—La regina di Dacia, a cui conquise
Lo sposo già destin crudel e fiero,
Come a lui piacque erede si rimase
Nelle regali sue splendide case.

57

E avendo quel cor che già tempo ebbe
La casta Dido inverso il suo consorte
(Come aver ogni vedova dovrebbe)

Che non aperse a van desir le porte,
La fede marital ch'al suo re debbe
Pensò di mantener fino alla morte,
E poi ch'avea perduto il suo signore
Di viver senza sposo e senza amore.

58

Or per sciagura un cavallier un giorno
In quella corte venne a dar di petto,
E di costei mirando il viso adorno
(Ch'era ancor fresca e di leggiadro aspetto),
In guisa n'arse che la notte e 'l giorno
Traea caldi sospir dall'arso petto.
Duca di Transilvania il giovene era,
Bello di viso e di real maniera.

59

D'altro già mai non pensa, altro non brama,
Altro non cerca il giovene infelice
Che d'ottener la desiata dama
Che sola far lo può lieto e felice.
D'arrischiar vita, facultade e fama
Per ogni via che lice o che non lice
Non si cura egli, pur ch'abbia il suo intento,
Ch'avutol sia poi di morir contento.

60

In corte era un garzon che 'l re allevato
Sin da fanciul d'ignobil schiatta avea,
E era alla regina il più fidato,
Il più caro di molti che tenea.
Pensa poter costui rendere ingrato
Con danari, e proporli ogni opra rea
Il duca, e 'l trova e come meglio puote
Prova la mente sua con queste note:

61

"Tu sai Parmin (così nomar l'udia)
Che mentre stato in questa corte io sono,
Io servitù da te, tu cortesia
Da me n'avesti e più d'un ricco dono,
E parmi che tra noi contratta sia
Già sì grande amicizia che non sono
Così grandi servigi ov'io vedessi
D'apportarti piacer, ch'io non facessi.

62

E così credo ancor che dal tuo canto,
S'io ti scoprissi un certo mio bisogno,
Tu faresti prontissimo altrettanto
Ad essequir quel ch'io bramo e agogno,
E porresti ad effetto il desir tanto,
Che senza il tuo favor reputo un sogno,
E se in questo mio affar sarai discreto,
Tu ricco e io sarò contento e lieto."

63

Parmin, ch'avea già fatto esperienza
Ch'egli era un ricco e liberal signore,
Gli disse: "Ormai dovresti conoscenza
Aver del mio ver te concetto amore;
Narrami questa tua nova occorrenza,
Fa ch'io sappia quel c'hai chiuso nel core,
Che non son cose al mondo così grandi
Ch'io non facessi a un sol de tuoi comandi."

64

Rispose il cavallier: "Poscia che veggio
Che sei sì pronto e di servirmi hai brama,
Sappi che molti dì son ch'io vaneggio
Per la beltà d'una leggiadra dama,
E ogni giorno andrò di mal in peggio
S'io non ottengo lei che 'l mio cor brama;

Se non mi dai, Parmin, presto soccorso
Io son al fin già di mia vita corso."

65

"Dimmi qual è costei (Parmin gli disse),
Né dubitar, ch'io non la vinci e dome."
"È la regina che 'l mio cor trafisse,"
Rispose Amandrian (così avea nome).
"In lei le voglie mie son ferme e fisse,
Ne' suoi begli occhi e nell'aurate chiome.
Io te l'ho detto, ora che l'odi e sai,
Non mi mancar poi che promesso m'hai."

66

Parmin rimase attonito e confuso,
Della promessa sua molto pentito,
Ma il cavallier ch'era in tal pratiche uso
Tosto un ricco rubin gli pose in dito.
Disse tra sé Parmin: "S'io me ne scuso,
S'io lascio di accettar questo partito,
Quando mai più di farmi ricco il tempo
Verrà, s'io non mi faccio or che n'ho tempo?"

67

Fece animo, e gli disse: "Amandriano,
Grande è la tua richiesta e assai mi doglio
Che vogli ch'io ti tenga in cosa mano
Troppo nefanda, il che mai far non soglio;
Pur perché 'l detto mio non resti vano
E per tua gentilezza oprar mi voglio;
Dimmi pur tu ciò che ti par che faccia,
Che 'l tutto son per far pur ch'io ti piaccia."

68

Il cavallier, ch'innanzi avea pensato
Come ingannar potesse la regina,

Rese Parmin benissimo informato
Del modo onde gabbarla ei si destina.
Lascia Parmino il duca innamorato
E verso la real stanza cammina,
E trova con bel modo occasione
Che la regina il manda a Belgirone.

69

Belgiron di tre leghe era lontano,
Da diporto un castel vago e adorno;
Qui (secondo insegnolli Amandriano)
Fa quella notte il rio Parmin soggiorno;
Poi, quando spunta il sol dall'oceano,
Fa in molta fretta alla città ritorno,
Va alla regina, e voler farla accorta
Mostra d'un caso a suo parer ch'importa.

70

La regina l'ascolta volentieri
(Ch'ognun d'udir da novo ha gran diletto)
E fa le damigelle e i camerieri
A un cenno sol partir dal suo cospetto.
Narra Parmin: "Signora, io fui pur ieri
A Belgiron come m'avete detto,
Dove essequito il vostro alto comando
Per lo cortil men vo iersera errando.

71

Mentre soletto al fresco erro e passeggio
E miro il prato verde e 'l ciel sereno,
Moversi il suolo a me propinquo veggio,
Come una talpe sia sotto il terreno.
Mi fermo e guardo, e nel guardar m'aveggio
Che s'alza il prato e fa gravido il seno,
Né molto sta che dal terren produtto
Vien un felice e mostruoso frutto.

72

Io vidi con questi occhi, e a pena loro
Posso anco prestar fede e pur fu vero,
Con bianco pelo e picciol corno d'oro
Uscirmi incontro un bel giuvenco altiero.
Fioria sotto il suo piè sì bel tesoro
Di chiare gemme che abbagliar mi fero.
Dico ogni fior ch'egli calcando venne,
Di perla o di rubin la forma ottenne.

73

Confuso di sì strana maraviglia
Io non so allor quel che mi debba fare;
Sul principio un desir m'afferra e piglia
D'empir le man di quelle pietre rare;
Ma novello pensier poi mi consiglia
Ch'io provi il bel giovenco di acquistare,
Che non invidio all'eritree maremme
S'acquisto il tor che fa fiorir le gemme.

74

Stendo la man per afferrargli un corno,
Ma quel si scuote e al mio desir non cede,
E io lo vo pur circondando intorno
E affatico invan la mano e 'l piede.
Alfin nel primo mio pensier ritorno
Di farmi almen di quel tesoro erede,
Mi chino e apro la man, ma quel non meno
Sotto la palma mia sgombra il terreno.

75

Poi che quello ottener non posso e vaglio,
Ritorno al toro e quel s'arretra e fugge,
Or con quello or con questo io mi travaglio
E dolor e desir l'alma mi strugge.
Il toro alfin veggendo il mio travaglio
Si volge a me, né come toro mugge,

Ma com'uom ch'intelletto abbia e loquela
Il fin di questo error m'apre e rivela.

76

"Non è fatto per te, Parmin (mi dice),
La strana e felicissima avventura,
Né 'l mio tesor toccare ad alcun lice
E d'acquistarmi indarno altri procura;
Sol la regina tua può gir felice
Del ben di cui il maggior non fé natura,
La ricca preda a lei sola si deve,
Per un disturbo rio ch'aver de' in breve.

77

Sappi ch'in breve un re forte e possente
Le ha da far guerra e porla in gran tristezza,
Perché con l'or le mancherà la gente
E sarà in gran necessità e strettezza;
E però un savio mago suo parente
Pose nel piede mio questa ricchezza,
Avendo l'empio suo caso previsto
Perch'al bisogno ella ne fesse acquisto.

78

Or che 'l tempo è venuto, io m'ho scoperto
A te che sei fra tutti i suoi più fido,
Però diman la trova e falle aperto
Il ben che dentro a me chiudo e annido.
Dille che venga sola e sia coperto
Il suo venir, né alcun ne senta il grido;
Giunga di notte e fuor che te non sia
Altri che venga a farle compagnia.

79

Prenderammi ella, e sia vittoriosa
Sol per virtù dei preziosi sassi."
Così dicendo entro la tana ascosa

Insieme ritirò le pietre e i passi.
Allor s'aggiunse in un la terra erbosa
E io restai in pensier con gli occhi bassi,
Né tutta notte mai potei dormire,
Tanto avea di condurmi a voi desire."

80

La semplice regina, che gran fede
Avea in Parmin per lunga esperienza,
Tutto quel ch'ei le dice ascolta e crede,
Quando men gli devea prestar credenza;
E molto più da credere le diede
Perch'era il ver ch'un zio d'alta scienza
Ella ebbe già nell'arte di Medea,
Che l'avventura fatta aver potea.

81

Subito entra in pensier che re sia quello
Che le ha da muover guerra, e come e quando;
E già più d'un discorso iniquo e fello
La dubbia mente sua vien conturbando.
Già come a lei vicin fosse il drappello
De nemici, si pensa ir preparando:
È donna, il caso è grave che la preme
E breve il tempo, ond'ha ragion se teme.

82

Gli è ver ch'assai le dà speme e conforto
Quel che le ha detto il suo fedel Parmino,
Che felice giovenco da lui scorto
Può trarla d'ogni crudo, empio destino.
Onde non crede mai che resti morto
Il giorno per poter porsi in camino,
Non vede l'ora mai che giunga sera
Per gir a Belgiron con l'aria nera.

83

La notte era lunghetta e la via corta
Sì che spera di far presta tornata,
Né farà l'alba al sol l'usata scorta
Ch'ella nel letto suo sia ritornata.
Come la notte in ciel le stelle apporta
E ch'al suo loco è tutta la brigata,
Parmin due corridori in punto pone
E aspetta che dorman le persone.

84

Ma vince il sonno ogn'alma e sparge a pena
Del suo liquor lo smemorato oblio,
E Morfeo rappresenta in varia scena
Più d'un caso a mortali o buono o rio,
Che la regina fuor di casa mena
D'acquistar l'avventura alto desio,
E l'infido Parmin, di cui si fida
Ella, va seco e le è compagno e guida.

85

Sopra buoni destrier spronaro tanto
Ch'in men d'un'ora giunsero al castello.
Dentro vegghiava Amandrian da un canto,
Ch'a un certo segno aprir devea il portello.
Stava ad udir; Parmin fa il segno intanto,
Né stette il duca a dimandar chi è quello,
Ma chetamene aperse e senza luce
E la regina dentro si conduce.

86

Parmin l'incauta donna al buio tira
Dentro un ostel dove non è persona,
E ecco Amandrian ch'arde e sospira
Vien per sforzar la bella sua persona;
Ma la cosa non va com'ei desira,

Che spesso avvien quel ch'in proverbio suona,
Che per pena riman del suo peccato
L'ingannator a piè dell'ingannato.

87

Amandrian si crede nelle braccia
La bella donna aver ch'ama e desia,
Ma in quella vece una persona abbraccia
Che non gli par che la regina sia,
La qual così lo stringe e sì lo impaccia
Che più tenaglia stringer non potria,
Né val che si dibatta e si dimene
Che preso alfin e via portato viene.

88

Il medesimo fu fatto a Parmino;
La regina rimase al buio sola;
Più di un ohimè sentì dirsi vicino
Che tutta la spaventa e disconsola.
Parmin non sente più; chiama Parmino,
E non s'ode rispondere parola,
Non vede tor, non vede cosa alcuna,
E comincia a temer di sua fortuna.

89

Né sapendo che farsi, afflitta e muta,
Senza punto dormir, con molto affanno
Stette; finché l'aurora in ciel venuta
Scoprì l'aurato suo lucido panno.
Come desto ogni uccello il dì saluta
E rende il bel matin più verde l'anno,
La donna innanzi a sé stupenda e nova
Una superba macchina ritrova.

90

In forma di piramide è composta
E risplende e traspar come un cristallo.

Nell'alta cima una ghirlanda è posta
Di rossi fiori assai più che corallo.
La donna sbigottita se le accosta
E vede in penitenza del suo fallo
Dentro Parmino e 'l transilvanio duce,
Che 'l muro al guardo suo chiaro traluce.

91

La regina conosce ognun di loro
Ma il fatto ancor discernere ben non puote;
E ecco nella pietra in lettere d'oro
Vede uniti i caratteri e le note
Che le scoprir la finzion del toro
E le fer tutte quelle fraudi note.
Lesse poi che Parmino, e 'l duca esterno,
Della pregion non uscirà in eterno.

92

S'un cavallier non viene d'ingegno tale,
Di tal valor, che quell'incanto opprima
E spogli la piramide fatale
Della ghirlanda posta in su la cima.
"Quando (era scritto) alcun pur metta l'ale
E voli ad acquistar la spoglia opima,
Se re sia quel ch'avrà sì ricco pegno
Non sia cacciato mai del proprio regno.

93

Ma se sarà privato cavalliero
Quel ch'avrà la ghirlanda in sua balia,
Sarà col tempo assunto a qualche impero
Né sia cacciato mai di signoria.
E se a donna o donzella il cerchio altero
Venirà nelle man, sicura sia
Che la sua castità le sia guardata
Contra ogni mente disleale e ingrata.

94

E per ch'abbia ciascun conoscimento
Di chi quest'opra fé tanto importante.
Sappi che ti guardò da tradimento,
Nobil regina, il vecchio Celidante."
La regina, compreso il fiero intento
Del servo avaro e dell'audace amante,
Scopertasi alla gente del castello
Lor fé palese il caso iniquo e fello.

95

Sparsesi il grido, onde più d'un provato
S'ha poi per acquistar tanta corona.
Un gran martello d'or quivi è attaccato,
Con cui si batte il marmo che risuona.
Allor s'apre una porta, ond'esce armato
Un re che sembra al volto e alla persona
Il re di Dacia, che fu già diletto
Sposo della regina ch'io t'ho detto.

96

Il qual combatte con sì gran possanza,
Che vince ogni guerrier gagliardo e forte,
E lo caccia per forza in quella stanza
Donde egli è uscito e poi serra le porte,
E se non è chiamato a nova danza
Da novo suon non esce nella corte.—
Così la donna cavalcando parla
Al cavallier, che stava ad ascoltarla.

97

Ma non son di costor per dirvi tanto
Ch'io non pensi tornar nel greco regno
Dove il gigante avea la palma e 'l vanto
Tolto di man a ogni guerrier più degno.
Dissi d'Algier, ch'in Sparta ha 'l regio manto,

Gli ha lo scudo e 'l teban lasciato in pegno,
Elion, Aliforte, e quel prudente
Griante, e Polinide finalmente.

98

Oltra questi Macandro al pian distese
Molti altri e acquistò palma novella,
E gli scudi da lor ch'in premio prese
Consacrò tutti a quella immagin bella
Quando il re, non scorgendo in sue difese
Altri in quel punto apparecchiarsi in sella,
Verso il palagio suo fece ritorno
Ch'era già il sol propinquo al mezzogiorno.

99

Macandro vincitor lieto rimase
A mirar la sua dea, felice amante,
Il cui fervente amor lo persuase
A mostrar qui le sue prodezze tante.
Tornò tutta la gente alle sue case
Con replicar le forze del gigante,
E le donzelle avean tutte dolore
D'aver perduto il lor sì grato onore.

100

Ma Celsidea più ch'altri si sconforta
Che sia la gloria sua sì presto spenta,
Benché la sua modestia non comporta
Che se ne mostri afflitta e malcontenta.
Quel giorno e l'altro uscir fuor della porta
Contra il gigante uom non ardisce e tenta,
Nel terzo vi comparve un cavalliero
Di cui narrar nell'altro canto spero.

CANTO SECONDO

Argomento

Uccide il rio gigante il guerrier strano
E dà di sé notizia al re Cleardo.
Bandisce il re una giostra. Il buon Silano
Dal mar patisce assalto aspro e gagliardo.
D'Egitto in Tracia si conduce il nano.
A lui promette il principe Risardo
La donna liberar dolente e bella.
E ei dà lor de casi suoi novella.

1

Non deve alcun di sé presumer tanto
Che fuor di sé ciascun abbia in dispregio,
Benché sia ricco e onorato quanto
Possa esser uom di sangue illustre e regio.
Se ben avesse indosso il regio manto
E risplendesse di un valor egregio
E fusse ogni saper di Febo in lui,
Non dee per lodar sé dar biasmo altrui.

2

Ogni persona deve esser umile
E benigna mostrarsi e d'amor piena,
Che l'umiltà lega ogni cor gentile
Con dolce e soavissima catena.
La superbia all'incontro è rozza e vile
E in danno proprio i suoi seguaci sfrena,
E Niobe e Penteo e altri fé perire
Sul colmo dell'orgoglio e dell'ardire.

3

Quando più credono esser sulla ruota
E goder di fortuna i beni incerti
Questi, ch'ella a sua posta aggira e ruota,
Lor fa provar mille travagli certi,
E gli getta nel fondo, e lor fa nota
Qual pena era spettante ai lor demerti,

Come del re Macandro udir potrete
Voi che per legger queste carte sete.

4

Lasciai che 'l terzo dì, quando inchinava
Il sol lo sparso crin tepido e giallo
E che doglioso il re con gli altri stava
Per non veder ch'altri venisser in ballo,
Un cavallier ch'alla ventura andava,
Ornato riccamente egli e 'l cavallo,
Nella città fu per ventura entrato
Dove il successo udì ch'io ho narrato.

5

Il cavallier parea gagliardo e franco
Alla presenza, e sopra ogn'altro ardito.
Era sua insegna in verde scudo un bianco
Giglio, era verde e candido il vestito.
A pena entrò che gli fur cento al fianco
Che gli fero accoglienza e grato invito;
Altri porta al gran re di lui le nove,
Altri a lui narra il caso e 'l cor gli move.

6

Onde subitamente al re venuto,
Com'uom cortese e d'animoso core
S'offerse innanzi al termine statuto
Mostrar contra il gigante il suo valore.
Il re, che non sperava altronde aiuto,
Creder si può che l'accettò di core.
Tutto il popolo allora ai merli corse,
E maraviglia al fier Macandro porse.

7

Il cavallier, per ch'era tarda l'ora
Del dì prefisso al termine narrato,

Con licenza del re ritornò fuora
Ben a destrier, di nobili arme ornato.
Gran cosa da notar fu vista allora,
Che tosto ch'egli uscì cascò sul prato
L'effigie che dai rami alta pendea,
Che tanto il gran Macandro in pregio avea.

8

Quanto al gigante il caso increbbe e spiacque
Di veder la sua dea premer la terra,
Tanta a' Greci nel cor letizia nacque.
Che 'l tennero a buon fin di quella guerra.
Il cavalliero a cui l'augurio piacque
Sfida Macandro e al corso si disserra.
Macandro pien di rabbia anch'ei si stese,
E così l'un ver l'altro il corso prese.

9

Lo strano cavallier, ch'era del gioco
Mastro, a incontrar l'empio Macandro venne
Sotto lo scudo, e dar si fece loco
Che l'usbergo il gran colpo non sostenne.
L'asta in più schegge al ciel volò del foco,
Ma la piaga nel fianco il ferro tenne,
Donde in gran copia il sangue fuor si spinse
E 'l puro acciar di rosso fregio tinse.

1 0

Come d'alta montagna interna fonte
Esce con furia, e ruinosa scende
Con torta via per la sassosa fronte,
E largo il fiume al pian conduce e rende,
Così dal vivo e animato monte
Come Macandro par, si sparge e stende
Con larga il sangue e furiosa vena
E fa un lago apparir sopra l'arena.

11

Dall'empio fu nell'elmo il guerrier colto,
Ma nol passò, ch'era di tempra eletta;
Si spezzò l'asta e 'l cavallier fu molto
A trovarsi vicin sopra l'erbetta;
Pur si ritenne e 'l fren presto raccolto
(Ch'era caduto), il destrier punse in fretta,
Ch'al gravissimo incontro in terra posto
Le groppe avea, ma rilevassi tosto.

12

Del colpo felicissimo che dato
Al fier gigante il cavalliero avea,
Si rallegrò ciascun del greco stato
E se ne rise il re con Celsidea.
Il fier Macandro intanto era tornato
Che della piaga molto si dolea,
Pur, credendo esser stato vincitore,
Temprava alquanto il grave suo dolore.

13

Ma quando incontra il cavallier si vede
Col ferro in mano e che la sella preme,
Così gran rabbia il cor gl'ingombra e fiede
Che 'l tempestoso mar tanto non freme.
Tosto del brando anch'ei la man provede
E va sopra il guerrier che nulla teme,
E lo gravò di sì pesanti some
Ch'a tutti i Greci fé arricciar le chiome.

14

Sì forte lo percosse a mezza fronte
Che gli tolse ogni senso, e avrebbe reso
L'alma smarrita al regno di Acheronte,
Se l'elmo fin non lo tenea difeso.
Smarrite quelle forze invitte e pronte,
Per lo prato il destrier correa disteso;

Macandro irato il tempo allor non perde,
E sel pone a seguir per l'erba verde.

15

Ma come altera e ben fondata pianta
In cui gran vento ogni sua forza impiega,
Che non però dal piè la svelle o schianta
Ma gli alti rami alquanto inchina e piega,
Cessato quel furor con altrettanta
Forza la chioma al ciel dirizza e spiega,
Così il guerrier, dal colpo che gli porse
Macandro e 'l fé piegar, tosto risorse.

16

Con quell'estrema furia che si puote
Pensar ch'ira e dolor nel cor gli ha posta,
Il caval gira poi che si riscuote
E al nemico suo la spada accosta,
E sulla spalla destra ove 'l percuote
Gli rende con gran forza la risposta;
Ciò che tocca apre, e sulla coscia scende
E arme, e carne, e ogni riparo fende.

17

Macandro ancora il colpo all'elmo segna
Del cavallier con tutto il suo potere,
Alza ei lo scudo, e sulla vaga insegna
Del giglio il brando impetuoso fere.
Ben crede il cavallier ch'in Parthia regna
Farlo in due pezzi al pian morto cadere,
Taglia lo scudo e taglia anco il cimiero,
Ma resse l'elmo al colpo orrendo e fiero.

18

Stordito dal gran colpo il campion greco
Tutto alla groppa del destrier si stende,

E sì l'aspra percossa il rende cieco
Che s'è ben notte o giorno ei non comprende;
Il feroce Macandro ch'usar seco
Alcuna cortesia già non intende,
Gli afferra il manco braccio, e ha certa fede
Di trarlo in terra, e averne il pregio crede.

19

Ma nel tirar che fece in sé rivenne
Il cavallier più che mai fosse ardito,
E rilevato, in sella si mantenne,
Onde Macandro prese altro partito
E tentò di venir (ma non l'ottenne)
Seco alle braccia, e gli ne fece invito,
Ma l'esperto guerrier col brando in mano
Quanto era lungo il tiene a sé lontano.

20

Macandro disdegnoso che conosce
Ch'alcun de suoi pensier non avea effetto,
Poi che 'l guerrier tien strette ambe le cosce
E non lascia accostar petto con petto,
Per dargli (se esser può) l'estreme angosce
E mandargli lo spirito al stigio tetto,
Ripiglia il brando, e drizza il colpo crudo
In loco tal che nol difende scudo.

21

Sulla sinistra spalla un gran fendente
Che sparato l'avria fin sulla sella
Gli segna, ma 'l guerrier subitamente
Schiva d'un salto la percossa fella,
E poi caccia la spada aspra e pungente
Sopra la coscia all'alma empia e ribella,
Passa la punta ria tra 'l ventre e 'l fianco
Due palmi, e 'l fa venir di vita manco.

22

Di quattro piaghe sanguinoso cade
Il parthio re, ma pria che giunga a morte,
Sì come ancor amore lo persuade,
Dice che non gli duol della sua sorte,
Ma che per esaltar quella beltade
Ch'egli amò sì non fusse ancor più forte,
E sol gli incresce e dà pena infinita
Poi che per lei servir non ha più vita.

23

Già tutto il fatto avea dalla muraglia
Scorto Cleardo e tutta insieme Atene,
Però che da vicin fu la battaglia
Fatta, e ciascun potea mirarla bene.
Onde, come a quel re la Parca taglia
Lo stame e 'l mira spento in sull'arene,
Scende dal muro e corre ogni persona
E 'l vincitor di lode orna e corona.

24

Avea nel fodro il brando egli tornato
E ne veniva a passo tardo e lento,
E giunto alle gran porte ove il re grato
Stava, lasciò la sella in un momento.
Il re lieto l'abbraccia, e 'l vole a lato
Di sé, l'esalta e loda il suo ardimento,
Ma la sua cortesia più loda molto
Che dalle spalle gli ha quel tedio tolto.

25

Il guerrier che gentile era e cortese,
Grazie rendendo al re la lingua sciolse,
E l'onor tutto alla sua figlia rese,
Tutta la lode a lei conceder volse.
Lo prega il re ch'ormai voglia palese
Scoprir la faccia, ond'ei l'elmo si tolse

E mostrò che 'l guerrier sì forte in sella
Era una gentilissima donzella.

26

Si tolse l'elmo e discoprì le bionde
Chiome dell'or più terse e luminose,
E due stelle apparir tanto gioconde
Che per invidia il sol nel mar s'ascose,
Movean le guancie fresche e rubiconde
Invidia ai gigli e alle purpuree rose,
La man, che disarmata anco tenea,
La neve di candor vincer parea.

27

Com'ella a tutti il bel viso scoperse,
Che tutti in lei tenean fiso lo sguardo,
Parve a ciascun colei per cui converse
Macandro il piè nel regno di Cleardo,
Quella a cui il miser già li scudi offerse
Prima che morte in lui scoccasse il dardo,
E si maravigliar non men di questo
Che del valor che vider manifesto.

28

Come chi fosse alla presenza quando
Tiensi donna talor lo specchio inante,
E ora il viso natural mirando
Venisse, ora in quel vetro il suo sembiante,
Non saprebbe ogni parte esaminando
Qual cosa fusse in lor dissimigliante,
Così parve costei del re de' Parthi
L'amata in tutte assimigliar le parti.

29

Volse che si portasse ivi il ritratto
Il re, ch'ancor giacea sopra il terreno,
E il pinto e il ver parve ad un modo fatto

Quando propinqui fur né più né meno.
Il re la prega a dir perch'avea tratto
Di vita un che 'l suo onor chiaro e sereno
Rendea, ch'altra non fu che sì splendesse,
E la cortese figlia il tutto espresse.

30

Perché sappiate il ver, questa donzella
Per cui morto Macandro in terra giacque,
Che Risamante per nome s'appella,
Con la bella Biondaura a un parto nacque.
Figlie del re d'Armenia e questa e quella,
Pari in tutto fra lor come al ciel piacque,
Eccetto ch'una è molle e delicata
E l'altra va come guerriero armata.

31

Al nascer di costei, perché le stelle
La inclinavano ad opre alte e leggiadre,
Celidante gran mago, allor ch'imbelle
E fanciulla era ancor, rubolla al padre,
Tal che dolente il re di tai novelle,
Poi che la moglie sua non fu più madre,
Lasciò morendo a quella che rimase
L'eredità delle sue regie case.

32

Per questo non rimase Celidante
Con diligenza e con paterno amore
D'allevar la fanciulla Risamante,
Di cui previsto avea l'arte e 'l valore,
Tal ch'ella poscia a tutti gli altri inante
Andò nell'arme e n'ebbe eterno onore.
Stette gran tempo seco ella celata
Dentro una rocca in mezzo il mar fondata.

3 3

Ma poi ch'errò diece sette anni il sole
Per lo cerchio ond'apporta il caldo e 'l gelo,
Il buon mago avvertì la regia prole
Dell'onorato suo paterno stelo.
Ond'ella fé con umili parole
Alla sorella dir che poi che 'l cielo
Le fé nascer d'un padre e tanto eguali
Nel dominar doveano anco esser tali.

3 4

Volea inferir che l'accettasse in parte,
Come volea ragion, del patrio impero,
Ma la sorella simulò con arte
Benché da molti avesse inteso il vero;
E così fé risponderli da parte
Di lei che non avria sì di leggiero
Pensato, non che mai creduto, ch'ella
Esser potesse a lei carnal sorella.

3 5

Ch'una che n'ebbe il fato in man condusse
D'un ladro che la uccise di sua mano;
Ma quando ben colei che 'l ciel produsse
Seco fosse ella, e ciò le fosse piano,
Non pretendea che sua di ragion fusse
La metà di quel regno ch'avea in mano,
Poi che morendo il re la regia soma
Lascia a lei sola e l'altra pur non noma.

3 6

Per questa aspra risposta Risamante
Sdegnossi contra lei di giusto sdegno,
E valorosa e d'animo prestante
Armata ogni città cerca, ogni regno,
E giova a questo e a quel perché le tante

Sue cortesie dian opra al suo disegno,
Fa beneficio a questo e a quel signore,
Perché al bisogno suo le dia favore.

37

Il caso raccontò l'alta guerriera
Al re Cleardo, e del gigante aggiunse
Che per la sua sorella venuto era,
La cui bellezza il cor gli accese e punse.
Il re, ch'udì tutta l'istoria vera,
Poi che la donna in suo favor consunse
L'empio gigante, a lei grato s'offerse
E d'aiutarla in tutto si proferse.

38

Risamante al buon re grazia ne rese,
E perch'ormai vincea la notte il giorno,
Il re con gli altri nell'arcion ascese
E al palagio suo fece ritorno.
Ma la regina e Celsidea cortese
A Risamante fur subito intorno,
E in una stanza l'arme li spogliaro,
E di femminile l'abito l'ornaro.

39

Lascio di dir la festa e l'allegrezza
Con l'onor che fu fatto alla donzella,
Che come donna avea tanta bellezza
Quanto valor come guerrier in sella.
Già Celsidea così l'ama e apprezza
Che quella notte vol passar con ella,
E così giro insieme a riposarse
Sin che la fresca aurora in cielo apparse.

40

Come l'altro matin le sveglia e desta,
Le belle donne si levar di letto,

L'una si cinse la feminea vesta,
L'altra il solito acciar fuorché l'elmetto.
Ma Celsidea n'uscì dogliosa e mesta
Che la guerriera ha del partir già detto,
Ed il re supplicò che lei pregasse
Che per tre giorni ancor seco restasse.

41

E così a' preghi lor si fu restata
Altri tre dì, poi quindi accommiatosse
Con general dolor, tanto era grata,
Così ad amarla ogni persona mosse.
Costei passò d'Europa in Asia armata
E tanto andò ch'a un bel giardin trovosse,
Ma vuo' lasciarla qui perché in Atene
Rimaner con Cleardo or mi conviene.

42

Il qual, per allegrezza dell'avuta
Vittoria contra il barbaresco ardire,
La più solenne giostra che veduta
Si fusse ancor fé in publico bandire,
Di cui la fama con la tromba arguta
Fa in ogni parte la novella udire,
E presta occasion felice al mondo
Di veder la nipote d'Alismondo.

43

Vi fece il re della Soria passaggio,
E 'l re di Persia, e un suo fratello forte,
Si pose anco il re d'Africa in viaggio,
E mille altri lasciar la propria corte.
Sol per veder l'achivo almo legnaggio
Si move ognun ver le palladie porte,
Venir ciascuno al lito acheo disegna
Sol per veder quella fanciulla degna.

44

Ode anco Italia il fortunato grido,
Onde Cecropia al ciel suoi pregi estolle,
Tal che Silano col fedel Clarido
Lascia del Lazio anch'ei l'altero colle,
Silano, unico principe del lido
Saturnio, anch'ei si crede all'onda molle,
E per due dì propizio ebbe al suo intento
L'aria chiara, il mar queto, e in poppa il vento.

45

Per due giorni e due notti al legno arrise
Fortuna sì che più nocchier non chiede,
Ma 'l seguente matin sua speme uccise
Che 'l ciel, il vento e 'l mar si rupper fede.
Levossi un vento allor ch'in aria mise
L'oscure nebbie, el sol più non si vede,
Di spessi lampi il ciel rifulge intorno,
El vento, e l'aria el mar minaccia scorno.

46

L'onda tumida cresce a poco a poco
E ad Aquilon contrasta e al ciel ribelle,
E l'acqua sbalza alla sfera del foco
Che par che voglia in sen chiuder le stelle.
Giove al fulmineo stral fa cangiar loco
E le torri percuote e i tronchi svelle,
E 'l cielo, e 'l vento, e 'l mar fanno tal guerra
Ch'abissa il vento, il mar, l'aria, e la terra.

47

Il misero nocchier pallido e smorto,
Ancor che sia di gran terror confuso,
Di far non resta industrioso e accorto
Ciò che conviensi al navigabil uso.
Comanda a questo e a quel, ma 'l vento a torto
Ne porta il grido e ne riman deluso,

Ch'alcun de naviganti non l'intende,
Ma pur ciascuno al proprio officio attende.

48

Grida il mesto nocchier che sia disciolta
Quella fune che tien la maggior vela,
Che spera pur che 'l tempo abbi a dar volta,
Ma non può far sentir la sua querela.
Il mar superbo intanto aggira e volta
La nave che si strazia e si querela,
Né pur del morto gli ha parte levato,
Ma nel vivo anco l'acqua ha penetrato.

49

Ben si tenner perduti i naviganti
Scorto l'onda nemica entrar nel legno,
E con gridi amarissimi e con pianti
Chieser mercede al sommo eterno regno.
Solo non perde il cor fra tanti e tanti
Né sa un minimo usar di viltà segno,
Silano invitto e 'l suo fedel consorte,
C'hanno il cor saldo, el volto ardito e forte.

50

De' naviganti alcun corre a gran fretta
Le fissure a turar dov'entra il mare,
Altri col cavo legno in mar rigetta
L'onde che prima entrar salse e amare.
Ecco intanto repente una saetta
Dalla celeste man sul pin scoccare,
Che l'arbor spezza e 'l timon arde, e seco
Manda il miser nocchier nel mondo cieco.

51

Questo fu ben lo stral crudo e funesto
Ch'uccise un solo e passò a tutti il core,
Ch'a tutti è ormai ben chiaro e manifesto

Non esser scampo a quel mortal furore.
Fu dunque con Silan Clarido presto
Quel partito a pigliar che fu il migliore,
Ricorsero al battel ch'era vicino
Per iscampar l'orgoglio empio marino.

52

Volean molti seguir l'esempio loro,
Ma questi lo vietar col brando nudo,
E dal legno si sciolsero e da loro,
Che restar preda al mar vorace e crudo.
Non san se son vicino all'Indo o al Moro
Che fan le nubi al dì riparo e scudo,
Gli è ver che 'l lampo apria sovente il velo,
Né li mostrava altro che 'l mar e 'l cielo.

53

Come poi si trovasse in miglior stato
Col buon Clarido il giovane Silano,
E come al lido poi fusse salvato
Dalla furia del mar crudo e insano,
In altra parte vi sarà contato
Ch'ora un poco lo stil volgo lontano,
E lascio questi in sì dubbiosa sorte
Per gir in Tracia alla superba corte.

54

È una città posta all'estremo lido
Che da Bitinia il Bosforo disgiunge,
Quinci il mar d'Helle appar fra Sesto e Abido,
Quindi le rive Eusin percote e punge;
Bisanzio è detta, il cui superbo grido
Dal basso centro al ciel superno giunge,
E l'occaso non v'ha né l'oriente
La più feroce e bellicosa gente.

55

Era gran tempo in lei stato Agricorno
Imperador del gran popolo di Marte,
Del cui valor giva la fama intorno
Dando soggetto alle più dotte carte.
Avea un figliuol d'ogni virtute adorno,
D'ogn'alma dote e d'ogni nobil arte,
Ch'in tutte l'opre eccelse, alme e leggiadre
Fu raro al mondo e fu maggior del padre.

56

Oltra questo garzon, che fu Risardo
Nomato, egli ebbe ancora una donzella,
Che come quel cortese era e gagliardo
Così fu questa al par d'ogn'altra bella.
Fu detta Ersina, e l'amoroso dardo
Non facea ancor per lei piaga novella,
Non era stata ancor nell'altrui petto
Cagion di gaudio o di contrario effetto.

57

Questo perché sì saggia era e modesta,
E di sì ornati e nobili costumi,
Che la sua gran beltà non manifesta
E tiene ascosi i due leggiadri lumi,
Perché, essendo non men che bella onesta,
Non vol ch'alcun si strazi e si consumi,
Non vol ch'alcun per lei senta cordoglio
Che s'ha ben molle il viso, ha 'l cor di scoglio.

58

Or mentre sta l'imperador felice
Di questa altera vergine e del figlio,
E seco in sala è un dì l'imperatrice
Con grave aspetto e con sereno ciglio,
E la Tracia d'eroi schiera vittrice
Con tutto il regio suo maggior consiglio,

Appar tra que signori un picciol nano,
Con un ricco vestir leggiadro e strano.

59

Di sì rara bellezza è 'l nano adorno,
Che me' Cupido alcun pittor non finge,
Di tutti il guardo a sé tira d'intorno
Quel bel color che 'l viso orna e dipinge.
Mesto e umil s'inchina ad Agricorno
Il nano, e agli altri, e ognun di pietà cinge;
Si sforza di parlar, ma nella gola
Il suo dolor gli chiude la parola.

60

Alfin tanto il desio gli infiamma il petto
Che rompe del dolor l'aspra catena,
E apre il varco al suo dolente affetto
Malgrado del suo mal, della sua pena,
E spiega il suo mestissimo concetto
Che di sospiri e lagrime incatena,
E fa ch'ogn'alma di pietà sfavilla
Mentre le belle lagrime distilla.

61

—Sperando in voi trovar giusta pietade,
Alto e supremo imperador de Traci,
Ho cercato (dicea) queste contrade
Lasciando i campi egizi empi e fallaci,
Per salvar una angelica beltade
Dalle tiranne man crude e rapaci,
Ch'avendo ucciso il re Galbo d'Egitto
Dan colpa alla nipote del delitto.

62

Sono ormai venti giorni che fu morto
E non si sa da chi per certa prova,

E accusan la giovane del torto
Dove ogni fede, ogni bontà si trova;
E perché Miricelso, il figlio accorto,
Altrove il suo valor dimostra e prova,
Ha preso ardir la setta empia e pergiura
D'impregionar la dolce, alma figura.

63

Per usurpar quel regno all'innocente
L'hanno posta in pregion crudel e fera,
Che più stretto e più prossimo parente
Al defunto signor di lei non era.
Tutta Alessandria è per suo amor dolente,
E per quel che si dice, invan si spera
Sua libertà, perché sentenziat'hanno
Che stia così rinchiusa in fin dell'anno.

64

Nel qual tempo la giovane infelice
Ha da trovar campion che la difenda
Da un cavallier che la calunnia e dice
Che contra ognun che sua difesa prenda
Vol provar ch'ella iniqua e traditrice
Fu cagione a quel re di morte orrenda,
E sosterrà per tutto l'anno intero
Ch'ella diede opra a sì crudel pensiero.

65

Ahi, che se cavallier non viene intanto
A provar ch'innocente è Raggidora
(Così ha nome la donna ch'amo tanto)
Giungerà senza colpa all'ultim'ora.—
Mancò la voce a questo, e crebbe il pianto
Al bel nano, che s'ange, e lagna, e plora.
Quando pervenne a quel pietoso punto
Per forza pose alle parole punto.

66

L'eccelso imperador ch'in alto siede,
E de principi intorno ha una corona,
Veggendo che 'l dolor sì 'l nano fiede
Che 'l fià che brama al suo parlar non dona,
Se ben soccorso e aiuto non li chiede
Sa ben ch'ad altro fin ei non ragiona.
Però dà gli occhi a suoi presso e lontano,
E quai debba mandar pensa col nano.

67

Tutti i traci guerrier giovani e forti
Erano accinti a così santa impresa,
E bramavan veder degli altrui torti
La bella Raggidora esser difesa,
Ma perché tutti allor s'erano accorti
Che più l'alma n'avea Risardo intesa,
Alcun non fu che 'l suo pensier mostrasse
Né che prima di lui parlar osasse.

68

Risardo in piè levato, con licenza
Del padre, disse al nano: —Or datti pace,
Che ti prometto e giuro alla presenza
Del mio signor, de tutto il popol trace,
Di liberar costei da tal sentenza
S'è (come dici) ingiusta, empia, e mendace,
E di farle acquistar quel regno ancora.—
E s'andò a por in punto allora allora.

69

Di tal promessa il nano consolato
Asciuga da begli occhi il tristo umore.
E 'l re, mentre si rende il figlio ornato
Di terso acciar ministro al suo valore,
E ch'al grande armiraglio ordine è dato
Che 'l legno apparecchiar faccia megliore,

Vol ch'all'imperatrice esprima il nano
Più particolarmente il caso strano.

70

E dica la cagion perch'ei sol viene
A procurar per lei sì caldo aiuto,
Che di tanti che 'l muro egizio tiene
Alcun (fuor che lui sol) non è venuto.
Potrebbe essere spia forse d'Atene
(Disse fra sé l'imperador astuto),
E vien con questa fraude e questo inganno
Per saper qui come le cose vanno.

71

Era gran lite allor fra 'l tracio regno
Per cagion de confini e 'l greco nata,
E di questo romor, di questo sdegno
N'era forse cagion la Tracia ingrata.
Or questo re, c'ha in mente empio disegno
Di destrugger (se può) la greca armata,
Pensa che 'l re Cleardo dal suo canto
Brami di far a lui danno altrettanto.

72

Tratto in disparte accanto alla regina
Per volontà del re fu il nano assiso,
Che con la voce angelica e divina
Con via più lieto e grazioso viso
Incominciò: —La vaga e pellegrina
Fama avea dato all'oriente aviso,
Tal ch'era in ogni lingua, in ogni stilo
La bellissima vergine del Nilo.

73

Pervenne il suon altier di lido in lido
Là ove son re nel regno de' Pigmei,
E sì m'accende il cor con questo grido

Ch'ogn'altro e me in oblio posi per lei,
Tal che lasciando il regno amico e fido
Soletto in Alessandria mi rendei,
Quivi me le diè in dono Amor protervo
E me le dedicò perpetuo servo.

74

Gionto trovai che troppo era lontana
La fama al ver, che quanto n'avea inteso
Una relazion fu scarsa e vana
Rispetto a quel c'ho poi visto e compreso.
Non narro la bellezza sopraumana
Ch'è degli omeri miei troppo gran peso,
Basta che ovunque il sol dispiega i rai
Maggior beltà non vide in terra mai.

75

Io che l'amava e pace non potea
Con questo amor trovar longi né presso,
Se non quando il bel viso alla mia dea
Veder m'era dal ciel talor concesso,
Per mitigar la fiamma che m'ardea
Non mi curo mandar lettera o messo,
Ma cangio in rozze e vil le regie spoglie
E fo sì che per servo ella m'accoglie.

76

Poi che non mi trovo atto a esercitarme
Nell'opre illustri e a dimostrar valore,
E col favor della virtù dell'arme
Acquistarmi di lei l'altero amore,
In altra guisa penso d'aiutarme
E d'un tal ben di farme possessore.
Mi fingo umil di stato e faccio ch'ella
Fra suoi mi accetta e per servo m'appella.

77

Uomo non era alcun di me più desto
Nel servir lei di tanti che tenia,
Era negli occhi e nel parlar modesto,
Sempre con gran prontezza la servia.
Tolse ella tanto in grazia ogni mio gesto,
La servitù, la diligenza mia,
Ch'a me sol comandava, e dir solea
Ch'alcun meglio di me non l'intendea.

78

Ella nelle mie man tenea fidato
Le sue più care cose, oro e argento,
Ogni vestir più ricco e più pregiato,
Le gemme, le ghirlande, ogni ornamento;
Io cura avea del suo regale e ornato,
Com'a lei conveniasi, appartamento.
E sì crebbe il mio amor a poco a poco
Che 'l cor era poca esca a tanto foco.

79

Con tutto ciò giammai non presi ardire
D'appalesarmi a lei, che sempre alcuna
Donzella meco la solea servire,
Al mio ingordo pensier troppo importuna.
Alfin un dì propizia al mio desire
Tra le man mi si pose la fortuna,
Un dì ch'ella il bel crin tendeva al sole
Senza la compagnia ch'esser vi suole.

80

Com'io mi trovo solo in sua presenza
E che d'appalesarmi fo pensiero,
Il rispetto ch'avea, la riverenza,
Il timor de turbarle il cor sincero,
E ch'irata mi scacci e dia licenza
Trattandomi da sciocco e da leggiero,

M'avea di tanto affanno il cor ristretto
Ch'io fui per uscir fuor dell'intelletto.

81

Mentre le belle chiome ella apre e stende
A un balcon per cui fa il sol passaggio,
E in tal modo le scuote, acconcia, e tende
Che fa ch'ogni crin gode il solar raggio,
E col dentato e schietto avorio attende
Quanto son longhe a far spesso viaggio,
Getto un sospir sì caldo all'improvviso
Che fa ch'ella i begli occhi alza al mio viso.

82

Non però mi fa motto, e indarno stimo
Che cerchi quel ch'a lei sì poco tocca,
Onde mesto il secondo aggiungo al primo
E fo che 'l terzo ancor più caldo scocca.
Veggendo ella che 'l mal mio non esprimo
Pur alfin per saperlo apre la bocca,
E la cagion mi chiede dolcemente
Che mi fa sospirar sì caldamente.

83

Io non rispondo a questa sua dimanda
Ma gli occhi abbasso e di sospir più abbondo,
Onde ella ancor mi replica e dimanda
E io sto pur tacendo e non rispondo.
Alfin come patrona mi comanda
Che le palesi il mal che dentro ascondo,
Di me si maraviglia e n'ha dispetto
Che scoprir non le voglia il mio concetto.

84

Come sì accesa e avida la veggio
D'intender quel ch'a lei discoprir voglio,

La fo giurar che quel che dir le deggio
Non le darà né sdegno né cordoglio.
E se ben troppo ardito erro e vaneggio,
Non perderò quel ben ch'ottener soglio,
Anzi ch'avrà di me qualche pietade
Risguardo avendo alla mia verde etate.

85

Ella ch'avria pensato ogn'altra cosa
Mi giura e mi promette largamente,
E io con faccia mesta e vergognosa
Il mio stato real narro umilmente.
Poi le discopro la fiamma amorosa
Che per la sua beltà m'arde la mente,
Con la sommission ch'a me s'aspetta
E col modo miglior ch'amor mi detta.

86

Parve che nel principio si turbasse
E la vergogna il volto le dipinse,
Non però ch'a miei danni l'incitasse
Quella gran novità che 'l cor le strinse;
Si tacque un poco pria come pensasse
E per risponder poi la lingua scinse,
Ma in quel punto s'udir le regie genti
Empire il ciel di gridi e di lamenti.

87

Per intender la causa di quel pianto,
Con la chioma sugli omeri negletta
La donzella si move, e io ch'a canto
Me gli spronava amor corro in gran fretta.
Vol saper la cagion d'un romor tanto
Per provederli in quanto a lei s'aspetta,
E alla stanza del re prima s'invia
Ove il grido e 'l maggior tumulto udia.

88

Di questa in quella camera la porta
Il dubbio piè dov'ode il mesto accento,
Tanto ch'arriva alla funesta porta
E fra donne e donzelle entra ben cento;
Come dà l'occhio dentro riman morta,
Che vede il re suo zio di vita spento
Giacer fra 'l popol mesto e lagrimoso,
Di più di venti piaghe sanguinoso.

89

Ella riman sì sconsolata allora
Che si lascia cader co' crini inconti
Sopra 'l freddo cadavero, e uscir fuora
Fa da begl'occhi suoi due caldi fonti.
Mentre costei si strugge, e piange, e plora
La stanza empir duchi, marchesi, e conti,
Ch'avendo inteso il doloroso avviso
Cercavan di saper chi l'avea ucciso.

90

Tra questi cavallieri era un Lideo
Che già d'Eubea in quelle parti venne;
Era valente e spesso combatteo
Coi più famosi, e sempre il pregio ottenne;
Costui gionto fra gli altri al caso reo,
Visto il re morto, un mal giudizio fenne,
La cagion non so dir ch'a questo il mosse,
Basta che giudicò che così fosse.

91

Disse e creder fé a tutti che nissuno
Pensato non avria non che operato
Che restasse di vita il re digiuno,
Che non sperasse ereditar lo stato;
E non essendo in quel reame alcuno
Che possi per tal causa aver peccato

(Che Miricelso estinto era per fama),
La colpa attribuiva a quella dama.

92

Parla con lingua libera e superba
E la sua autorità fede gli dona;
Mostra che 'l gran dolor che nel cor serba
Quel che dir non vorria fa che ragiona.
Dice che giusta merita e acerba
Morte, e tanto ogni petto instiga e sprona
Che molti che maligno hanno il pensiero
Dicon che parla mal, ma dice il vero.

93

Tutti hanno di regnar l'animo ingordo
E credon, o di creder mostra fanno;
I baron più nobili d'accordo
Son con Lideo che mostra ansia e affanno;
Secondo il suo consiglio e 'l suo ricordo,
Senza aver chi lo vieti, ordine danno
Che sia posta in pregion la donna mia,
Come del fatto ella colpevol sia.

94

Fur seco presi ancor paggi e donzelle,
Che vinti da minaccie e da promesse
Confessaro alle menti inique e felle
Ch'un tanto error per sua cagion successe.
Non essendo in contrario chi favelle,
Dunque per tema il vero al falso cesse,
E la innocente allor fu presa e vinta
Della malignità crudele e finta.

95

Vid'io la bella man candida e pura
Ristretta (ahimè) da crudo laccio indegno,
E vidi in carcer posta infame e scura

Colei, che poco il mondo è d'aver degno.
Sepolta l'innocente creatura,
S'hanno tra lor diviso il suo bel regno;
E il popol solo è quel, la plebe è quella,
Che piange l'infelice damigella.

96

Or poi che la natura ingiusta e avara
Non mi diè forza all'animo conforme
Per poter liberar donna sì rara,
Che mi sforzò d'amor seguitar l'orme,
Ricorro a questa patria illustre e chiara
Dove giustizia, ove virtù non dorme,
E prego che vi piaccia aiuto darmi
Contra li egizi rei con le vostre armi.—

97

Così contò l'innamorato nano
Della donzella misera il successo,
E intanto per punir l'Egitto insano
Il buon Risardo in ordine fu messo.
Ma poi che egli ha finito il caso strano
Di raccontar come li fu commesso,
Vo' qui finir questo mio canto anch'io
Poscia di lor dirò ciò che seguio.

EXCERPTS FROM CANTO QUARTO

1

Le donne in ogni età fur da natura
Di gran giudizio e d'animo dotate,
Né men atte a mostrar con studio e cura
Senno e valor degli uomini son nate;
E perché se comune è la figura,
Se non son le sostanze variate,
S'hanno simile un cibo e un parlar, denno
Differente aver poi l'ardire e 'l senno?

2

Sempre s'è visto e vede (pur ch'alcuna
Donna v'abbia voluto il pensier porre)
Nella milizia riuscir più d'una,
E 'l pregio e 'l grido a molti uomini torre;
E così nelle lettere e in ciascuna
Impresa che l'uom pratica e discorre
Le donne sì buon frutto han fatto e fanno,
Che gli uomini a invidiar punto non hanno.

3

E benché di sì degno e sì famoso
Grado di lor non sia numero molto,
Gli è perché ad atto eroico e virtuoso
Non hanno il cor per più rispetti volto,
L'oro che sta nelle miniere ascoso
Non manca d'esser or, benché sepolto,
E quando è tratto e se ne fa lavoro
E' così ricco e bel come l'altro oro.

4

Se quando nasce una figliola il padre
La ponesse col figlio a un'opra eguale,
Non saria nelle imprese alte e leggiadre
Al frate inferior né disuguale,
O la ponesse in fra l'armate squadre
Seco o a imparar qualche arte liberale,
Ma perché in altri affar viene allevata
Per l'educazion poco è stimata.

5

Se la milizia il mago a Risamante
Non proponea né disponeale il core,
Non avria di sua man condotto tante
Inclite imprese alfin col suo valore.
Dissi che questa giovene prestante

Fu dal cortese e liberal signore
Condotta in una loggia a disarmarsi,
Ove dovea la cena apparecchiarsi.

EXCERPTS FROM CANTO OTTAVO

1

Circe già in virtù d'erbe e di parole,
Con alto studio oggi a nissuno espresso,
Poté oscurar l'illustre faccia al sole,
Girar i poli e fermar Cinzia spesso,
E far fiorir le rose e le viole
Quando più il campo è dalla neve oppresso,
Seccar i prati e tornar l'aria nera
Sul più bel verdeggiar di primavera.

2

Ch'ella potesse far contra i statuti
Di natura sì degne opre ammirandi
Mi maraviglio sì, poi che veduti
Oggi non son miracoli sì grandi.
Ma che cangiasse in animal bruti
Gli uomini a sue parole, a suoi comandi,
Mi par sì lieve ch'io stupisco invero
Ch'ella degnasse in ciò porre il pensiero.

3

Poco mi par che fesse ella cangiando
Gli umani corpi in orsi, in lupi, in tori,
Quando alla nostra età gli uomini errando
Di lor medesmi son trasformatori;
E con tal facilità girsi mutando
Gli veggio senza oprar versi o liquori,
Che poco stima in ciò fo di quell'arte
Poi che 'l secol di noi n'ha tanta parte.

4

Ciascun dell'esser proprio è sì buon mago,
Che non ne seppe tanto ella in quel tempo
Quando spese in cangiar la nostra imago
Tant'erbe, tanto studio, e tanto tempo,
E d'uscir di sé stesso è così vago
Che di tornarvi poi non trova il tempo;
Di tutti no, ma ben del più ragiono,
A cui piace parer quel che non sono.

5

Io vi direi come di lupo ingordo
Spesso pigli sembianza or questo or quello,
Altri dell'animal fangoso e lordo,
Altri di stolido orso iniquo e fello.
Ma d'esser aspettata io mi ricordo
Dalla donna del monte [Circetta], a cui sì bello
Parve il giovin latin, che sol desire
Ha di piacergli, onde comincia a dire:

6

—Quel cavallier che già molt'anni visse,
La cui virtù non ebbe pari al mondo,
Qual nelle greche e nelle frigie risse
Mostrò divin saper, valor profondo,
Quel sì prudente e valoroso Ulisse
Che più d'ogni altro ardito era e facondo,
Fu signor di quest'isola che detta
Itaca fu, si chiama or di Circetta.

7

Pria ch'avesse in quel tempo acceso e arso
Il superbo Ilion la greca face,
Fra i più degni di Grecia eroi comparso
Ulisse in ragionar pronto e vivace,
Contra il forte uom ver sé di pietà scarso,
Quel sì famoso e furibondo Aiace,

Ottenne con parole alte e ornate
Del fortissimo Acheo l'arme onorate.

8

E poi ch'al regio campo alto spartano
Rese placato il miser Filotette,
Che nello scoglio irato di Vulcano
Tenea d'Alcide l'arco e le saette,
Senza cui il re de' Greci attendea invano
Sul muro frigio l'ultime vendette,
Si pose a ritentar l'ondoso sdegno
Ver questa patria sua, ver questo regno,

9

Sì come quel che tanto era bramoso
Di riveder la sua progenie bella,
E la casta moglier fida al suo sposo
Ch'a lui sol pensa e sol di lui favella.
Ma 'l gran rettor del mar gonfio e sdegnoso
Gli mosse irato asprissima procella,
Come a fautor della corona achea
E distruttor della grandezza idea.

1 0

L'odio ch'egli ha d'appalesar si affretta
Per vendicare il suo superbo muro,
E mentre irato aspira alla vendetta
E pensa darlo al regno inferno e scuro,
Il vento lo trasporta a una isoletta
Dove sopra uno scoglio infame e duro
Dormir trova il Ciclope in cima il monte,
E l'occhio invola alla terribil fronte.

1 1

Poi spiega i lini e l'isola abbandona
Per fuggir Polifemo infame ed empio;

Va al re de' venti, e così ben ragiona
Col dolce stile, onde non ebbe essempio,
Che Eolo tutti gli prende e gli li dona
Acciò fuggisse il minacciato scempio;
Ma tutto invan, che più d'un servo infido
Del don lo priva e dell'amato lido.

1 2

Sciolser gli avari il vento empio e leggero
E 'l mar rinnovò in mar l'empia tempesta,
L'armata si disperde, e 'l duca altiero
Errando va col legno che gli resta.
Alfine il tempo ingiurioso e fiero
Lo trae di Circe all'inclita foresta,
Circe la bella e virtuosa fata
Si mostrò a Ulisse e a suoi compagni grata.

1 3

E taccia pur chi dice ingiustamente
Che trasformasse i suoi consorti in fiere,
Che mai non fé, se non sforzatamente,
A chi la volse offender dispiacere.
Venne alla fata il cavallier prudente
E ricevé da lei gioia e piacere,
E dell'uno e dell'altra io fui concetta,
E del nome di lei nacqui Circetta.

1 4

Il possente guerrier genitor mio
Ulisse fu, mia madre quella diva
Che figlia fu del luminoso dio
Che l'ombre scaccia e 'l giorno spento aviva.
Data che m'ebbe in luce, al suo desio
Dimostrò Ulisse aver la mente schiva,
E con l'astuzie ond'era esperto e dotto
Un dì se l'involò senza far motto.

1 5

Diè i remi all'acque e con più destro fato
Egli e li amici sui quivi arrivaro,
E dal tempo d'efigie trasformato
Fu conosciuto a pena il signor caro.
Circe s'accorge esser il duca amato
Partito e sparge un rio di pianto amaro,
E seguìto l'avria, ma le 'l contese
La propria sua virtù ch'Ulisse apprese.

1 6

Perché mentre egli in grazie ebbe mia madre
E che gli piacque il bel saturnio colle,
E che d'una figliola si fé padre,
Tutta l'arte di Circe ritender volle.
Ella ch'alle maniere ostar leggiadre
Non può con vari versi e varie ampolle,
Fece all'amante ogni scienza espressa
E per gradir altrui nocque a se stessa.

1 7

Or poi che d'impedir non fu possente
Circe che 'l padre mio non si partisse,
Che l'istess'arte in ch'era ella eccellente
Favor prestava al fuggitivo Ulisse,
Chiuse il dolor nell'affannata mente
E aspettò che 'l cavallier morisse,
Per far sopra quest'isola vendetta
Che la vista di lui l'avea interdetta.

1 8

Fatto il debito rogo usato e pio
Del popol di dolor colmo e di pieta,
E 'l cener mortal del padre mio
Chiuso nell'urna sacra consueta,
Circe per donar loco al suo desio,
Poscia ch'alcun non glie 'l disturba o vieta,

Qui si conduce, e i carmi alti e fatali
Invisibil la rendono a mortali.

19

Copre ella ogni città di nebbia oscura,
Fa leoni apparir, tigri e serpenti,
E furon quei che guardan quelle mura
Che voi meco passar foste contenti.
Quella ferocità c'han per natura
Lor raddoppiava il suon de maghi accenti,
Tal ch'il tosco, la branca, il dente, e 'l corno
Disolar le città tutte d'intorno.

20

E poi che fu d'esercitar ben sazia
Quella gran crudeltà nata d'amore
(Che mentre intorno all'isola si spazia
Non scorge illeso alcun dal suo furore),
Chiede al verso opportun favor e grazia
Per lo nome eternar del suo signore,
Vol che d'Ulisse il pregio al mondo viva
E sia la fama sua splendida e viva.

21

E sforza il vento col suo forte incanto
A penetrar nel centro della terra,
E lì schiude le vie per ogni canto
Sì ch'invan per uscir s'aggira e erra;
Ma il desio natural lo spinge tanto
Che move con gran furia al terren guerra,
S'alza e gonfia il terren vinto e sforzato
Come un pallon s'alcun gli dona il fiato.

22

Cede la terra al vento e forma il monte,
Il monte che ci serra intorno e sopra;
Circe allor con parole accorte e pronte

In sì raro artificio il senno adopra.
Nel giogo altier, nell'elevata fronte
Fece da poi via più mirabil opra,
Un tempio fé, ch'ovunque splende e gira
Più bella cosa il sol di lui non mira.

23

Gli archi, le basi, i capitelli e 'l tetto
Comparte con egual proporzione,
Senza maestro aver, senza architetto,
Con la virtù del magico sermone;
Quando ella il suo lavor vide perfetto
Con l'aiuto dell'orco e di Plutone,
Nella maggior città discende sola
E le reliquie pie d'Ulisse invola.

24

Oltra 'l cener ch'al sacro mausoleo
Dell'ingrato amator ritrova e toglie,
Vi trova ancor del figlio di Peleo
Le gloriose e trionfanti spoglie,
Quell'arme a cui Vulcan la tempra feo,
Appese e sparte, ispicca ella e raccoglie
E le trasporta in questo albergo fido,
Come in più degno e glorioso nido.

25

A tutte queste imprese io fui presente,
Che non aveva mia madre altro conforto
Che d'in me contemplar naturalmente
Quel bel ch'era in Ulisse estinto e morto.
Non però vol far dotta la mia mente
Com'altrui far si possa oltraggio e torto,
M'insegna il ben ch'uscir può da quell'arte
E asconde il mal nelle possenti carte.

26

Come piacque all'inique e dure stelle
Termina allor la genitrice mia
Che dell'uman commercio empia e ribelle
(Da me poi detto) in questo scoglio io stia.
E meco pose ancor le tre donzelle
Che servitù mi fanno e compagnia,
E fé l'incanto a tutto 'l mondo oscuro,
Che 'l secolo durar dovea futuro.

27

E statuì che 'l tempo non potesse
Della mia giovanezza aver trofeo,
E che di quella età mi mantenesse
Ch'ella mi pose in questo incanto reo;
E ben si può veder quanto valesse
Il suo saper ch'invan l'opra non feo,
Quando da indi in qua tanti anni sono
Corsi, e pur fresca e giovanetta sono.

28

E manco ancor di quei (che mentre visse
Il padre mio se gli mostrar contrari),
Circe (che lor più lunga etade ascrisse,
Di quel c'hanno ordinato i cieli avari)
Pose gli eredi a guardar qui d'Ulisse
L'arme, fin ch'un guerrier di virtù pari
A lui di questo carcer venga a trarmi,
E sia signor dell'isola e dell'armi.

29

E come venne a lei l'amato duca
Non per sua volontà ma per ventura,
Così non vol ch'alcun la fama induca
A tentar l'immanissima avventura,
Ma che fortuna a caso lo conduca
A provar s'ha sorte amica o dura,

Né vol che possa alcun nel tempio entrare,
Che non sia in arte a Ulisse e in valor pare.

30

E quando audace alcun di poco merto
Nelle mura infernal d'entrar si sforza,
Così punito vien che 'l tempo incerto
Vive dell'età sua sotto altra scorza.
Pur dianzi il fatto voi vedeste aperto,
Farmi vedeste alla natura forza:
Quel guerrier fu da voi pur dianzi visto
Perder la carne e far del legno acquisto.

31

Or s'a voi cavallier par esser tali,
Se vi dà il cor d'entrar per quella porta
Quando i contrasti avrete empi e mortali
Passati, e 'l gran terror ch'ella vi apporta,
Dalle lastre ricchissime fatali
Vedrete cosa uscir ch'assai più importa,
Colosso e Tantalon ciascun estremo
Che vendetta vorran di Polifemo.

32

Ma ponghiam che 'l feroce empio gigante
Resti da voi mirabilmente ucciso,
Chi vi difenderà dal gran Theante
Che vi moverà assalto all'improvviso?
Dal capo è inviolabile alle piante,
Né può da ferro alcun restar conquiso,
Fatato ha come 'l padre il carnal panno
E brama vendicar d'Aiace il danno.—

33

Il ragionar che fé la giovanetta
Pose in un gran pensier l'alme latine;
Il desio dell'onor ben ambi alletta

A tentar quelle imprese alte e divine,
Ma 'l timor del castigo che s'aspetta
A chi non giunge al desiato fine,
Che vien costretto in arbore a cangiarsi,
Fa ch'in dubbio si stan né san che farsi.

34

Ma l'astuto Silan, che dal periglio
Si cerca trar con arte e con ingegno,
Gira spesso ver lei cortese il ciglio
E le mostra d'amor questo e quel segno,
Che senza aver da lei grazia e consiglio
Giunger non spera al destinato segno,
Non si tien senza il suo favor bastante
D'una impresa trattar tanto importante.

EXCERPTS FROM CANTO UNDICESIMO

50

Era all'occaso in quel gita la luna
E tutto era il giardin tenebre e ombra,
La fanciulla [Celsidea] si pone all'aria bruna
E paura infinita il cor le ingombra.
Ma in breve più non sente cosa alcuna
E lo strepito e 'l grido intorno sgombra,
Talché senza saper ciò che si fosse
Tutta pensosa in letto ritornosse.

51

La cagion di quel strepito ch'udio
La bella figlia nel giardin fu questa:
Giaceva Floridor tra i fior, com'io
Dissi, con quel pensier che 'l cor gl'infesta,
E del novo amoroso suo desio
Pensando or l'alma aveva gioiosa or mesta,
Intanto ode chi parla e chi risponde
Con basso mormorio tra quelle fronde.

52

Uno dicea: —Qual più felice stato
Del nostro imaginarsi alcun potria?
Qual uomo sia più di me lieto e beato
S'io posso far la bella donna mia?
Il dolce viso suo benigno e grato
Mi promette dolcezza e cortesia,
L'aria soave, el bel sereno ciglio
Mi dà speme, favor, grazia, e consiglio.—

53

—Deh, signor mio (quell'altro gli rispose),
Guardi ben vostra altezza ove si pone.
Le donne son gentili e amorose
E si mostran ben grate alle persone,
Ma quando lor si chieggion quelle cose
Che 'l donarle d'infamia è lor cagione,
Ciascuna è sì contraria e sì nimica
Che si perde in un punto ogni fatica.

54

Né credo mai che tanto alta donzella
Di macchiar l'onor suo fusse contenta,
Anzi temo io come saliate a quella,
Sì che vi veggia o almeno ch'ella vi senta,
Alzerà sì la voce empia e ribella,
Che la famiglia ancor non sonnolenta
Trarrà a quel grido, e per menarla a noi
Ne potreste restar per sempre voi.

55

Con quella riverenza e quel rispetto
Che deve il servo al suo signor avere,
Io v'avertisco il periglioso effetto
Che può seguirne e faccio il mio dovere.—
—Ben conosco, fratel, ch'onesto affetto
(Quel primo replicò) ti fa temere,

Ma fin ad or di te prendo stupore
Ch'abbi sì poco ardir, sì basso core.

5 6

Non dubitar, non fia tal gita invano
Ch'io son dell'amor suo più che sicuro,
Pur se sarà il destin tanto villano
Che mi serbi la morte entro a quel muro,
Che contra il rio sicario armi la mano,
Ti prego, ti comando, e ti scongiuro
Fa del tuo gran fratel vendetta degna
S'in te giusta pietà, se valor regna.—

5 7

Promette quei, così d'accordo vanno
Per corre il fior delle fanciulle adorne,
E una scala di lin ch'arrecat'hanno
Attaccano a una pertica bicorne,
E ben studia finir l'ordito inganno
La coppia rea prima che Febo aggiorne,
Che forse li sarebbe anco successo
Se non che Floridor troppo ebbe appresso.

5 8

Accanto al muro, a quel balcon diritto
Dov'il buon Floridor scese pur prima,
In terra il legno avean piantato e fitto
E l'un s'accosta ove montar fa stima,
L'altro tenea la fune el fusto ritto
Mentre salisse il suo compagno in cima,
E se ne va con mente infame e rea
Per involar la bella Celsidea.

5 9

Quando il buon Floridor l'oltraggio intende
Che di far pensa il cavalliero audace,
E che conosce il danno e che comprende

Che seguir ne potria se soffre e tace,
Subitamente in man la spada prende
E grida: —Ahi, rio ladron, ladron rapace
Ben sei, se credi in tutto e stolto e cieco
Far questo scorno al regio sangue greco.—

60

Gli due, che l'un di Persia il signor era
E l'altro un suo fratel detto Marcane,
Empir d'ira e stupor la mente altiera
Alle parole ingiuriose e strane,
E all'improvvisa voce orrenda e fiera
E questo e quel dall'opra si rimane,
Che Floridoro ardito come suole
Lor sopravien senza più dir parole.

61

E benché sia senz'arme al poco lume
Che gli rendea dal sommo ciel le stelle,
Di far battaglia e vincer gli presume
E al re di Persia intacca della pelle,
E già scorrer gli fa di sangue un fiume
Per le ricche armi d'or lucenti e belle,
E perché sopra il braccio il colpo è sceso
Gli fé il brando cader ch'avea in man preso.

62

Il feroce Marcan, ch'assalir vede
Il suo fratel da chi non sa chi sia,
Un colpo a Floridor sul capo diede
Che furioso incontra gli venia,
Ma Floridor che 'l suo pensier prevede
Oppone il brando alla percossa ria,
Sì che quando col suo l'altro percosse
Lo spezzò in due come di legno fosse.

63

E la punta di balzo venne a corre
Il re di Persia e 'l fé d'un occhio cieco.
Floridor non s'indugia un colpo a sciorre
Sopra il fiero Marcan che la vol seco.
Intanto il re va la sua spada a torre
E va di dietro al valoroso greco,
E con tutta l'angoscia che ne sente
Mena un colpo terribile e possente.

64

Pensò troncargli il collo, e ben seguito
Saria senza alcun dubbio il rio pensiero,
Se non che 'l suo fratel, ch'era stordito
Dal colpo ch'avea avuto orrendo e fiero,
Tra ch'era poco lume e avea smarrito
La conoscenza, il buon giudizio intiero,
Proprio in quel punto in fallo il fratel colse
Per Floridor, ch'egli al garzon si volse.

65

Con quella spada rotta a mezza fronte
Lo fere sì che 'l parte infino al mento,
E così l'infelice re Acreonte
Per man del suo fratel rimane spento.
Credendo aver ben vendicate l'onte,
Dice Marcano a Floridoro contento:
—Dissi ben io, signor, che 'l tempo e 'l loco
Non fan per noi troppo sicuro gioco.

66

Un picciol foco è morto e un via maggiore
Suscitar ne potria da queste mura,
Levianci via di qua, per Dio, signore,
Ch'un'altra volta avrem miglior ventura.—
Floridor, che comprende il grande errore
Del cavallier, che cerca a far sicura

Al fratel quella vita che gli ha tolta,
Senza parlar con gran pietà l'ascolta.

67

Ben pensa che sia fuor dell'intelletto
Non conoscendo il re di vita fuora,
Che pur sapea ch'avea lo scudo al petto
E dell'altre arme era coperto ancora,
E che egli in testa non vi tien elmetto
Né altro schermo ha dalla spada in fuora.
Ma poi ch'in tanto error sommerso il vede
Dietro gli move taciturno il piede.

68

Giunsero in breve ad una porta angusta
Che rispondea sulla strada maestra,
La qual fu (perché frale era e vetusta)
All'entrar e all'uscir facile e destra.
Era già più che mai bella e venusta
La candida alba apparsa alla fenestra,
Quando Marcan nell'esser suo tornato
Scorse che Floridor non era armato.

69

A prima giunta prese maraviglia
Come non fosse d'arme il re guarnito,
E poi meglio afisando in lui le ciglia
Scorse un volto sì bello e sì polito
Che mentre l'intelletto rassottiglia
Comprende il caso e ne divien smarrito,
E più che va volgendo per la mente,
Sta per morir tanto dolor ne sente.

70

E perché gli parea che Floridoro
Era stato cagion di sì mal opra,

Che minacciando avea assaliti loro
E con la spada era lor corso sopra,
Qual cruda tigre o qual feroce toro
La forte branca o 'l duro corno adopra,
Tal sopra Floridor la spada mena
Per isfogar la sua gravosa pena.

71

—Ah, disse Floridor, non ti ricorda
Ciò che vivendo il tuo fratel ti disse,
Quando a tuoi detti fé l'orecchia sorda
Sperando ch'ad effetto il pensier gisse,
Che s'avenia per colpa dell'ingorda
Sua volontà ch'a morte ne venisse,
Non cessaresti che pietoso e forte
All'uccisor di lui daresti morte.

72

Dunque se stato sei tu quell'istesso
Che la misera vita gli hai levata,
Ben dritto sia se te gli uccidi appresso
Acciò che l'ombra sua resti placata,
Né dar la colpa a me del rio successo
Che la vostra pazzia cagion n'è stata.
Pur quando brami aver meco battaglia
Eccomi, ancor che senza piastra e maglia.

73

Non sperar perch'io sia solo e senz'arme
Che di sì vile impresa abbia spavento,
Non potria tutto 'l mondo spaventarme
Né tutto 'l mondo a te dare ardimento.
Ma spero ben che potrò tosto armarme
Di queste tue che son nere e d'argento,
E se non ti fei pria noto il tuo errore
Fu per pietà di te non per timore.—

74

Era tanto Marcan di rabbia acceso
Che non gli par né vol che dica il vero,
E avea a due mani il brando preso
Per menargli d'un colpo orrendo e fiero.
Or mentre Floridor si tien difeso,
Ecco lor sopragiunge un cavalliero
Che disfidò Marcane e minacciollo,
E a Floridor pose uno scudo al collo.

75

Quando conosce il timido Marcane
Che contra due non potrà far contesa,
Dalla battaglia subito rimane
E crede nel fuggir la sua difesa.
Il cavallier ch'era sì come il cane
Dietro all'odor venuto a quella impresa,
Poscia che fu l'empio Marcan discosto
A Floridor si dié a conoscer tosto.

76

Il savio Celidante, che pensiero
Avea di Floridor come di figlio,
Avendo aviso che 'l garzon altiero
Posto era in un grandissimo periglio,
Guidò Filardo suo per quel sentiero
A dargli aiuto e gliene diè consiglio,
E lo scudo gli diè perché gliel desse,
Acciò dal rio Marcan si difendesse.

77

Si trasse l'emo e gli fé chiaro e piano
Così ch'egli era il suo fedele amico,
Che tutta notte il va cercando invano,
Sin che trovollo a fronte col nemico.
Come un anno sian stati o più lontano

Quella festa si fer ch'io non vi dico,
E s'andaro a posar ch'era ormai giorno
E la gente veggiava e andava attorno.

EXCERPTS FROM CANTO TREDICESIMO

36

Poi ch'ivi stati fur più ch'abbastanza
I gioveni ai conforti di Circetta,
Lasciaro alfin di contemplar la stanza
Perché la cena è in ordine e gli aspetta.
Silano con lietissima sembianza
Segue dovunque vol la giovanetta,
Né cessa di mirarla, e per più fido
Parer finge guardarsi da Clarido.

37

La vergine tra sé loda e ringrazia
Il cieco amor che lei fa cieca ancora,
E con casta pietà mai non si sazia
Di rimirar quel cavallier ch'adora.
Le par che nel mirarla abbia tal grazia
E sì le mostri il cor per gli occhi fuora,
Che stima per l'amor che ne comprende
Gran villania se 'l cambio non gli rende.

38

Con queste opinion varie e diverse
Passò la donna e i cavallier la cena,
E poi ciascun di loro il piè converse
Dove la donna a riposar gli mena.
Ma non dormiron mai, ch'in ciel disperse
La notte l'alba candida e serena
Poi che la figlia amor fere e travaglia
E il dubbio i cavallier della battaglia.

39

Né manco questo alla donzella pesa,
Che teme che Silan non sia di tanta
Virtù ch'abbia l'onor di quella impresa,
Onde convenga poi cangiarlo in pianta.
Quando ciascun che di sì gran contesa
Resta perdente ella per forza incanta,
E se ben di tal opra assai si duole,
È costretta voler quel che non vole.

40

Pensa e ripensa, e mai non chiude il ciglio,
Qual sia la migliore strada e 'l miglior modo
Perché salvi Silan da quel periglio
Senza cangiarlo in tronco verde e sodo.
Alfin risolta per miglior consiglio
Vol l'incanto ingannar con questo frodo:
Pensa invisibil farlo e vol che vada
Sin al tempio fatal senza oprar spada.

41

Sa come sia l'incanto e di che sorte,
Che 'l cavallier, che di provarlo intende,
Pur che tratto non sia fuor delle porte
Il fato in alcun modo non l'offende,
Però se va, né di lui sieno accorte
L'alme ond'il passo orribil si difende,
Pensa senza temer di caso strano
Assicurar la forma al suo Silano.

42

Ritornata la luce, il sole e 'l giorno
I cavallier di letto si levaro,
E la donzella a lor fece ritorno
E con l'usato stil si salutaro;
Ma lor di quanto ella pensato intorno
Ai casi lor non fa palese e chiaro.

Quei si dispongon di provar l'incanto,
Ma d'altro or son per ragionarvi alquanto.

43

Io vo' che lasciam questi, e di lasciarli
Non vi rincresca in tale stato un tempo,
Che poi verremo un giorno anco a trovarli
E li trarrem di qui forse col tempo.
Or de li due guerrier dritto è ch'io parli
Che non credean che mai venisse il tempo
D'arrivar in Armenia a quella terra
Ove patia Biondaura atroce guerra.

44

Cavalcan con Gracisa a gran giornate
(Fatto d'Europa in Asia già passaggio),
E veggion più città, più genti nate,
Varie d'usanza e varie di linguaggio.
Giunser nel fine al sì famoso Eufrate,
Che per l'Armenia stende il suo viaggio,
Benché oggidì l'Armenie sono due,
Ma già per una intesero ambedue.

45

In ogni loco, o sian città o castella
Di quel reame, ovunque ergono il ciglio
Veggiono i cavallieri e la donzella
L'insegne sventolar del bianco giglio;
Che 'l tutto Risamante alla sorella
Biondaura avea già tratto dell'artiglio,
E si tenean per lei tutte le terre
Ch'ella avea debellate in quelle guerre.

46

Tanto spinsero inanzi i lor destrieri
Per la più breve via, per la più trita,
Che giunsero la donna e i cavalieri

Al minacciato muro d'Artemita.
Da copioso esercito i sentieri
Tutti occupati son di gente ardita,
Per tutto son trabacche e padiglioni
Che cavallieri alloggiano e pedoni.

47

Quel giorno non aveano i terrazzani
Assalto alcun per quanto si vedea,
Non si scorgeva alcun menar le mani,
Come ogni giorno inanzi si facea.
Giunti che furo in campo i guerrier strani
Con Gracisa, ch'un velo posto s'avea,
Videro un gran duello incominciato
Tra duo guerrieri in mezzo uno steccato.

48

Gli Artemitani ascesi in su le mura
Mesti contemplan la crudel battaglia,
Gli eserciti di fuori alla pianura
Stanno a mirar qual di lor due più vaglia.
Siedono in alto i giudici c'han cura
Della giustizia che le parti agguaglia,
Intanto i due che fan l'orrendo marte,
A riposar si traggono in disparte.

49

Era ciascun sudato e sanguinoso;
De' lor destrier, l'un giace in terra spento,
L'altro rodendo il fren rendea spumoso,
Che di verde e di bianco ha 'l guarnimento;
Ma l'un guerrier non mostra di riposo
Aver bisogno e sta con ardimento,
L'altro stassi appoggiato in gran pensieri
Com'uom che di sua impresa poco speri.

50

La coppia de' guerrier che venuta era
Con Gracisa accostossi ad un alfiero,
E dimandolli con gentil maniera
Chi fosse l'uno e l'altro cavalliero,
E perché si facea la pugna fiera
Lo supplicò che lor dicesse il vero.
L'alfier sopra costor le luci fisse
E, miratoli alquanto, così disse:

51

—Quel cavallier dal lato di levante
Ch'in verde scudo arreca il giglio bianco
È la nostra regina Risamante,
Che non ha 'l mondo un cavallier più franco.
L'altro, che mal per lui le venne innante,
Con la bianca colomba al lato manco,
Di Babilonia è il re Cloridabello,
Che per Biondaura fa sì gran duello.

52

Biondaura già partecipar non volse
Con la sorella sua di noi regina
Questo reame, e a sprezzar si volse
Costei, ch'era lontana e peregrina,
Perché di casa un mago già la tolse
Dal re suo genitor sendo bambina,
Il qual, morta stimando la fanciulla,
A morte venne e non le lasciò nulla.

53

Risamante dal mago fu allevata
In ogni prova e arte militare
Dentro una rocca ch'è nel mar fondata,
Ma dove non si sa che non appare.
Quindi (poi che benissimo informata
L'ebbe dell'esser suo) la fé passare

In terra ferma e gire alla ventura
Provvista di cavallo e d'armatura.

54

Risamante a Biondaura (poi ch'uscìo
In libertà) la parte sua richiese,
Ma la sorella al suo retto desio,
Al giusto dimandar non condiscese;
Talché sdegnata Risamante unio
Gran gente e venne sopra il suo paese,
E 'l tutto le ha di man tolto con scorno
Fuor che questa città cui siamo intorno.

55

Ella raccolse da diverse bande
Le genti che vedete insieme unite,
E compose uno esercito sì grande
In brevissimo spazio, e il modo udite:
Il mago a quei portò le sue dimande
Che se le avean proferto in questa lite,
E solo in una notte con sue arti
Guidò tutte le genti in queste parti.

56

Fu d'improvviso sì nostra venuta,
Tacita sì, sì presta oltra ogni stima,
Che trovammo l'Armenia sproveduta
E la pigliammo in sù la giunta prima.
Biondaura che la nova ebbe saputa
Raccolse molta gente e di gran stima,
Ch'alla battaglia s'appicciò con noi,
E sconfitti rimaser tutti i suoi.

57

Or la misera figlia è rifuggita
Con pochi suoi fidati in questa terra,

E perché mal si trova esser fornita
Di vettovaglie e munizion da guerra,
Ha posto di sé stessa e d'Artemita
E di tutto l'aver che in lei si serra
La causa in man del re Cloridabello,
O per salvarsi o per cader con ello.

58

Questo principe acceso già per fama
Della rara bellezza di costei
E per propria virtute e perché l'ama,
Venne pur dianzi in difension di lei.
Il patto è tal fra l'una e l'altra dama
Che se 'l re manda l'alma ai stigi rei
O riman preso, perde la cittade
Biondaura e in man della sorella cade.

59

Ma se per caso Risamante è quella
Che faccia fallo e 'l re resti vincente,
Vivendo reinvestir de' la sorella
Di tutto quel reame incontinente,
E de' rimover la battaglia fella
Facendo altrove gir tutta la gente;
Così per ischivar morti e ruine
Di genti assai son convenute alfine.—

60

Ma non avea finito di dir questo
Anco l'alfier che l'inclita guerriera,
Sendole ormai 'l posar troppo molesto,
Ritornò ardita alla battaglia fiera.
Cloridabel non fu di lei men presto
E menò un colpo alla donzella altiera,
Ma scarso alquanto fu, che se cogliea
A pien la spalla destra le fendea.

61

Pur tagliò di maniera ch'uscir fenne
Il sangue vivo l'arme luminosa;
Risamante al gran colpo in viso venne
Vermiglia più che in sul mattin la rosa,
E fu lo sdegno tal che ne divenne
Poco men che insensata e furiosa,
Perché se tinta è ben di sangue tutta
Non era ancor del suo macchiata e brutta.

62

Spinta da gran furor lo scudo getta,
E con ambe le man la spada presa,
Disegna far sul capo la vendetta
Più debita alla man che l'avea offesa.
Cloridabello alza lo scudo in fretta,
Visto il colpo calar, per sua difesa,
Taglia in due parti il colpo altier lo scudo
E penetra nel capo il brando crudo.

63

Il re stordito cade e 'l verde piano
D'un corrente ruscel vermiglio irriga;
La guerriera, c'ha 'l cor molle e umano,
Vistosi il meglio aver di quella briga
Gli corre sopra, e con pietosa mano
Dell'elmo sanguinoso il capo sbriga,
E dimostra a ciascun la sua vittoria
Nel volto smorto, ond'ha trionfo e gloria.

64

L'aer che prese il re dell'elmo privo
Qualche spirito in lui serbò di vita,
Onde rivenne e dimostrossi vivo,
Ma preso in man della donzella ardita.
Spargeva intanto un lagrimoso rivo
Biondaura, avendo la novella udita

Da alcuni suoi, ch'avean nel campo scorto
Il suo re preso e lei giunta a mal porto.

65

A Risamante i giudici donaro
La palma e l'adornar di lauree fronde,
Si tolse ella l'elmetto e mostrò chiaro
Il suo bel viso e le sue chiome bionde.
Ma come il re prigion, che sente amaro
Duol per Biondaura e dentro si confonde,
Costei mirò tanto simile ad ella,
Pensò che fusse la sua donna bella.

66

—Non è questo (dicea) l'amato volto
Che mi stampò nel cor la man d'Amore?
Non son questi i begli occhi, che m'han colto
Al dolce laccio e posto in dolce errore?
Io non son già sì cieco né sì stolto
Che non conosca chi m'ha tolto il core.
Dunque della mia dea restai conquiso,
E rimango prigion del suo bel viso.

67

Maraviglia non è s'ella mi vinse
Poi che prima m'avea preso e legato,
Ché altri che costei mai non mi strinse
Tanto, né potea pormi in tale stato.
Ma presso la bellezza onde m'avinse
Non credea che valor tanto pregiato
Regnasse in lei, né so per qual cagione
Abbia voluto far meco tenzone.

68

Felice inganno, se ingannar mi volse
Per mostrar forse a me la sua virtute,
Beate piaghe e 'l sangue che mi tolse

Quando col guardo suo mi dà salute.
M'aggreva sol (né d'altro unqua mi dolse
Tanto) delle percosse ricevute
Da lei per me, dei colpi iniqui e rei
Che per troppa ignoranza io diedi a lei.—

69

Così dicea quell'infelice amante,
E certo non credea di restar preso
Parendoli che fusse Risamante
La bella donna ond'avea 'l petto acceso,
Per non saper che tanto simigliante
La giovene che seco avea conteso
Era a Biondaura, che ciascun prendea
L'una per l'altra e 'l ver non discernea.

70

Con gran pietà fé l'inclita guerriera
Quel re condur nel regio padiglione
E medicar, che forte piagato era,
Trattandolo da re non da prigione.
In questo uscir della cittade in schiera
Le più onorate e nobili persone.
Quel che poi ne successe altrove io canto,
Ch'ora di Celsidea vuo' dirvi alquanto.

SERIES EDITORS'
BIBLIOGRAPHY

PRIMARY SOURCES\

Alberti, Leon Battista (1404–72). *The Family in Renaissance Florence.* Translated by Renée Neu Watkins. Columbia: University of South Carolina Press, 1969.

Arenal, Electa and Stacey Schlau, eds. *Untold Sisters: Hispanic Nuns in Their Own Works.* Translated by Amanda Powell. Albuquerque: University of New Mexico Press, 1989.

Astell, Mary (1666–1731). *The First English Feminist: Reflections on Marriage and Other Writings.* Edited and introduction by Bridget Hill. New York: St. Martin's Press, 1986.

Atherton, Margaret, ed. *Women Philosophers of the Early Modern Period.* Indianapolis, IN: Hackett, 1994.

Aughterson, Kate, ed. *Renaissance Woman: Constructions of Femininity in England: A Source Book.* London: Routledge, 1995.

Barbaro, Francesco (1390–1454). *On Wifely Duties* (preface and book 2). Translated by Benjamin Kohl in Kohl and R. G. Witt, eds., *The Earthly Republic.* Philadelphia: University of Pennsylvania Press, 1978, 179–228.

Behn, Aphra. *The Works of Aphra Behn.* 7 vols. Edited by Janet Todd. Columbus: Ohio State University Press, 1992–96.

Boccaccio, Giovanni (1313–75). *Famous Women.* Edited and translated by Virginia Brown. The I Tatti Renaissance Library. Cambridge, MA: Harvard University Press, 2001.

———. *Corbaccio or the Labyrinth of Love.* Translated by Anthony K. Cassell. 2nd rev. ed. Binghamton, NY: Medieval and Renaissance Texts and Studies, 1993.

Brown, Sylvia. *Women's Writing in Stuart England: The Mother's Legacies of Dorothy Leigh, Elizabeth Joscelin and Elizabeth Richardson.* Thrupp, Stroud, Gloucestershire: Sutton, 1999.

Bruni, Leonardo (1370–1444). "On the Study of Literature (1405) to Lady Battista Malatesta of Moltefeltro." In *The Humanism of Leonardo Bruni: Selected Texts.* Translated and introduction by Gordon Griffiths, James Hankins, and David Thompson. Binghamton, NY: Medieval and Renaissance Studies and Texts, 1987, 240–51.

Castiglione, Baldassare (1478–1529). *The Book of the Courtier.* Translated by George Bull. New York: Penguin, 1967. *The Book of the Courtier.* Edited by Daniel Javitch. New York: W. W. Norton, 2002.

Christine de Pizan (1365–1431). *The Book of the City of Ladies.* Translated by Earl Jeffrey Richards. Foreword by Marina Warner. New York: Persea, 1982.

———. *The Treasure of the City of Ladies.* Translated by Sarah Lawson. New York: Viking Penguin, 1985. Also translated and introduction by Charity Cannon Willard. Edited and introduction by Madeleine P. Cosman. New York: Persea, 1989.

Clarke, Danielle, ed. *Isabella Whitney, Mary Sidney and Aemilia Lanyer: Renaissance Women Poets.* New York: Penguin, 2000.

Crawford, Patricia, and Laura Gowing, eds. *Women's Worlds in Seventeenth-Century England: A Source Book.* London: Routledge, 2000.

Daybell, James, ed. *Early Modern Women's Letter Writing, 1450–1700.* Houndmills, England:: Palgrave, 2001.

Elizabeth I: Collected Works. Edited by Leah S. Marcus, Janel Mueller, and Mary Beth Rose. Chicago: University of Chicago Press, 2000.

Elyot, Thomas (1490–1546). *Defence of Good Women: The Feminist Controversy of the Renaissance.* Facsimile Reproductions. Edited by Diane Bornstein. New York: Delmar, 1980.

Erasmus, Desiderius (1467–1536). *Erasmus on Women.* Edited by Erika Rummel. Toronto: University of Toronto Press, 1996.

Female and Male Voices in Early Modern England: An Anthology of Renaissance Writing. Edited by Betty S. Travitsky and Anne Lake Prescott. New York: Columbia University Press, 2000.

Ferguson, Moira, ed. *First Feminists: British Women Writers 1578–1799.* Bloomington: Indiana University Press, 1985.

Galilei, Maria Celeste. *Sister Maria Celeste's Letters to Her Father, Galileo.* Edited by and Translated by Rinaldina Russell. Lincoln, NE: Writers Club Press of Universe. com, 2000. Also published as *To Father: The Letters of Sister Maria Celeste to Galileo, 1623–1633.* Translated by Dava Sobel. London: Fourth Estate, 2001.

Gethner, Perry, ed. *The Lunatic Lover and Other Plays by French Women of the 17th and 18th Centuries.* Portsmouth, NH: Heinemann, 1994.

Glückel of Hameln (1646–1724). *The Memoirs of Glückel of Hameln.* Translated by Marvin Lowenthal. New introduction by Robert Rosen. New York: Schocken Books, 1977.

Henderson, Katherine Usher, and Barbara F. McManus, eds. *Half Humankind: Contexts and Texts of the Controversy about Women in England, 1540–1640.* Urbana: Illinois University Press, 1985.

Hoby, Margaret. *The Private Life of an Elizabethan Lady: The Diary of Lady Margaret Hoby 1599–1605.* Thrupp, Stroud, Gloucestershire: Sutton, 1998.

Humanist Educational Treatises. Edited and translated by Craig W. Kallendorf. The I Tatti Renaissance Library. Cambridge, MA: Harvard University Press, 2002.

Joscelin, Elizabeth. *The Mothers Legacy to Her Unborn Childe.* Edited by Jean leDrew Metcalfe. Toronto: University of Toronto Press, 2000.

Kaminsky, Amy Katz, ed. *Water Lilies, Flores del agua: An Anthology of Spanish Women Writers from the Fifteenth Through the Nineteenth Century.* Minneapolis: University of Minnesota Press, 1996.

Kempe, Margery (1373–1439). *The Book of Margery Kempe.* Translated by and edited by Lynn Staley. A Norton Critical Edition. New York: W. W. Norton, 2001.

King, Margaret L., and Albert Rabil, Jr., eds. *Her Immaculate Hand: Selected Works by and about the Women Humanists of Quattrocento Italy.* Binghamton, NY: Medieval and Renaissance Texts and Studies, 1983; second revised paperback edition, 1991.

Klein, Joan Larsen, ed. *Daughters, Wives, and Widows: Writings by Men about Women and Marriage in England, 1500–1640.* Urbana: University of Illinois Press, 1992.

Knox, John (1505–72). *The Political Writings of John Knox: The First Blast of the Trumpet against the Monstrous Regiment of Women and Other Selected Works.* Edited by Marvin A. Breslow. Washington, DC: Folger Shakespeare Library, 1985.

Kors, Alan C., and Edward Peters, eds. *Witchcraft in Europe, 400–1700: A Documentary History.* Philadelphia: University of Pennsylvania Press, 2000.

Krämer, Heinrich, and Jacob Sprenger. *Malleus Maleficarum* (ca. 1487). Translated by Montague Summers. London: Pushkin Press, 1928. Reprint, New York: Dover, 1971.

Larsen, Anne R., and Colette H. Winn, eds. *Writings by Pre-Revolutionary French Women: From Marie de France to Elizabeth Vigée-Le Brun.* New York: Garland, 2000.

de Lorris, William, and Jean de Meun. *The Romance of the Rose.* Translated by Charles Dahlbert. Princeton, NJ: Princeton University Press, 1971. Reprint, University Press of New England, 1983.

Marguerite d'Angoulême, Queen of Navarre (1492–1549). *The Heptameron.* Translated by P. A. Chilton. New York: Viking Penguin, 1984.

Mary of Agreda. *The Divine Life of the Most Holy Virgin.* Abridgment of *The Mystical City of God.* Abridged by Fr. Bonaventure Amedeo de Caesarea, M.C. Translated from the French by Abbé Joseph A. Boullan. Rockford, IL: Tan Books, 1997.

Myers, Kathleen A., and Amanda Powell, eds. *A Wild Country Out in the Garden: The Spiritual Journals of a Colonial Mexican Nun.* Bloomington: Indiana University Press, 1999.

Russell, Rinaldina, ed. *Sister Maria Celeste's Letters to Her Father, Galileo.* San Jose: Writers Club Press, 2000.

Teresa of Avila, Saint (1515–82). *The Life of Saint Teresa of Avila by Herself.* Translated by J. M. Cohen. New York: Viking Penguin, 1957.

Weyer, Johann (1515–88). *Witches, Devils, and Doctors in the Renaissance: Johann Weyer, De praestigiis daemonum.* Edited by George Mora with Benjamin G. Kohl, Erik Midelfort, and Helen Bacon. Translated by John Shea. Binghamton, NY: Medieval and Renaissance Texts and Studies, 1991.

Wilson, Katharina M., ed. *Medieval Women Writers.* Athens: University of Georgia Press, 1984.

———, ed. *Women Writers of the Renaissance and Reformation.* Athens: University of Georgia Press, 1987.

Wilson, Katharina M., and Frank J. Warnke, eds. *Women Writers of the Seventeenth Century.* Athens: University of Georgia Press, 1989.

Wollstonecraft, Mary. *A Vindication of the Rights of Men and a Vindication of the Rights of Women.* Edited by Sylvana Tomaselli. Cambridge: Cambridge University Press, 1995. Also *The Vindications of the Rights of Men, The Rights of Women.* Edited by D. L. Macdonald and Kathleen Scherf. Peterborough, Ontario, Canada: Broadview Press, 1997.

Women Critics 1660–1820: An Anthology. Edited by the Folger Collective on Early Women Critics. Bloomington: Indiana University Press, 1995.

Women Writers in English, 1350–1850. 15 vols. published through 1999 (projected 30-volume series suspended). Oxford University Press.

Wroth, Lady Mary. *The Countess of Montgomery's Urania.* 2 parts. Edited by Josephine A. Roberts. Tempe, AZ: MRTS, 1995, 1999.

———. *Lady Mary Wroth's "Love's Victory": The Penshurst Manuscript.* Edited by Michael G. Brennan. London: The Roxburghe Club, 1988.

———. *The Poems of Lady Mary Wroth.* Edited by Josephine A. Roberts. Baton Rouge: Louisiana State University Press, 1983.

de Zayas, Maria. *The Disenchantments of Love.* Translated by H. Patsy Boyer. Albany: State University of New York Press, 1997.

———. *The Enchantments of Love: Amorous and Exemplary Novels.* Translated by H. Patsy Boyer. Berkeley and Los Angeles: University of California Press, 1990.

SECONDARY SOURCES

Ahlgren, Gillian. *Teresa of Avila and the Politics of Sanctity.* Ithaca, NY: Cornell University Press, 1996.

Akkerman, Tjitske, and Siep Sturman, eds. *Feminist Thought in European History, 1400–2000.* London: Routledge, 1997.

Allen, Sister Prudence, R.S.M. *The Concept of Woman: The Aristotelian Revolution, 750 B.C. – A.D. 1250.* Grand Rapids, MI: William B. Eerdmans, 1997.

———. *The Concept of Woman.* Vol. 2, *The Early Humanist Reformation, 1250–1500.* Grand Rapids, MI: William B. Eerdmans, 2002.

Andreadis, Harriette. *Sappho in Early Modern England: Female Same-Sex Literary Erotics 1550–1714.* Chicago: University of Chicago Press, 2001.

Armon, Shifra. *Picking Wedlock: Women and the Courtship Novel in Spain.* New York: Rowman & Littlefield Publishers, Inc., 2002.

Backer, Anne Liot Backer. *Precious Women.* New York: Basic Books, 1974.

Ballaster, Ros. *Seductive Forms.* New York: Oxford University Press, 1992.

Barash, Carol. *English Women's Poetry, 1649–1714: Politics, Community, and Linguistic Authority.* New York: Oxford University Press, 1996.

Battigelli, Anna. *Margaret Cavendish and the Exiles of the Mind.* Lexington, KY: University of Kentucky Press, 1998.

Beasley, Faith. *Revising Memory: Women's Fiction and Memoirs in Seventeenth-Century France.* New Brunswick: Rutgers University Press, 1990.

Beilin, Elaine V. *Redeeming Eve: Women Writers of the English Renaissance.* Princeton, NJ: Princeton University Press, 1987.

Benson, Pamela Joseph. *The Invention of Renaissance Woman: The Challenge of Female Independence in the Literature and Thought of Italy and England.* University Park, PA: Pennsylvania State University Press, 1992.

Benson, Pamela Joseph, and Victoria Kirkham, eds. *Strong Voices, Weak History? Medieval and Renaissance Women in their Literary Canons: England, France, Italy.* Ann Arbor: University of Michigan Press, 2003.

Bilinkoff, Jodi. *The Avila of Saint Teresa: Religious Reform in a Sixteenth-Century City.* Ithaca: Cornell University Press, 1989.

Bissell, R. Ward. *Artemisia Gentileschi and the Authority of Art.* University Park: Pennsylvania State University Press, 2000.

Blain, Virginia, Isobel Grundy, AND Patricia Clements, eds. *The Feminist Companion to Literature in English: Women Writers from the Middle Ages to the Present.* New Haven, CT: Yale University Press, 1990.

Bloch, R. Howard. *Medieval Misogyny and the Invention of Western Romantic Love.* Chicago: University of Chicago Press, 1991.

Bornstein, Daniel and Roberto Rusconi, eds. *Women and Religion in Medieval and Renaissance Italy.* Translated by Margery J. Schneider. Chicago: University of Chicago Press, 1996.

Brant, Clare, and Diane Purkiss, eds. *Women, Texts and Histories, 1575–1760.* London: Routledge, 1992.

Briggs, Robin. *Witches and Neighbours: The Social and Cultural Context of European Witchcraft.* New York: HarperCollins, 1995; Viking Penguin, 1996.

Brink, Jean R., ed. *Female Scholars: A Tradition of Learned Women before 1800.* Montréal: Eden Press Women's Publications, 1980.

Broude, Norma, and Mary D. Garrard, eds. *The Expanding Discourse: Feminism and Art History.* New York: HarperCollins, 1992.

Brown, Judith C. *Immodest Acts: The Life of a Lesbian Nun in Renaissance Italy.* New York: Oxford University Press, 1986.

Brown, Judith C. , and Robert C. Davis, eds. *Gender and Society in Renaissance Italy.* London: Addison Wesley Longman, 1998.

Bynum, Carolyn Walker. *Fragmentation and Redemption: Essays on Gender and the Human Body in Medieval Religion.* New York: Zone Books, 1992.

———. *Holy Feast and Holy Fast: The Religious Significance of Food to Medieval Women.* Berkeley: University of California Press, 1987.

Cambridge Guide to Women's Writing in English. Edited by Lorna Sage. Cambridge: University Press, 1999.

Cavanagh, Sheila T. *Cherished Torment: The Emotional Geography of Lady Mary Wroth's Urania.* Pittsburgh: Duquesne University Press, 2001.

Cerasano, S. P. and Marion Wynne-Davies, eds. *Readings in Renaissance Women's Drama: Criticism, History, and Performance 1594–1998.* London: Routledge, 1998.

Cervigni, Dino S., ed. *Women Mystic Writers. Annali d'Italianistica* 13 (1995) (entire issue).

Cervigni, Dino S., and Rebecca West, eds. *Women's Voices in Italian Literature. Annali d'Italianistica* 7 (1989) (entire issue).

Charlton, Kenneth. *Women, Religion and Education in Early Modern England.* London: Routledge, 1999.

Chojnacka, Monica. *Working Women in Early Modern Venice.* Baltimore: Johns Hopkins University Press, 2001.

Chojnacki, Stanley. *Women and Men in Renaissance Venice: Twelve Essays on Patrician Society.* Baltimore: Johns Hopkins University Press, 2000.

Cholakian, Patricia Francis. *Rape and Writing in the "Heptameron" of Marguerite de Navarre.* Carbondale: Southern Illinois University Press, 1991.

———. *Women and the Politics of Self-Representation in Seventeenth-Century France.* Newark: University of Delaware Press, 2000.

Christine de Pizan: A Casebook. Edited by Barbara K. Altmann and Deborah L. McGrady. New York: Routledge, 2003.

Clogan, Paul Maruice, ed. *Medievali et Humanistica: Literacy and the Lay Reader.* Lanham, MD: Rowman & Littlefield, 2000.

Clubb, Louise George (1989). *Italian Drama in Shakespeare's Time.* New Haven, CT: Yale University Press.

Conley, John J., S.J. *The Suspicion of Virtue: Women Philosophers in Neoclassical France.* Ithaca, NY: Cornell University Press, 2002.

Crabb, Ann. *The Strozzi of Florence: Widowhood and Family Solidarity in the Renaissance.* Ann Arbor: University of Michigan Press, 2000.

Cruz, Anne J., and Mary Elizabeth Perry, eds. *Culture and Control in Counter-Reformation Spain.* Minneapolis: University of Minnesota Press, 1992.

Davis, Natalie Zemon. *Society and Culture in Early Modern France.* Stanford: Stanford University Press, 1975. Especially chapters 3 and 5.

———. *Women on the Margins: Three Seventeenth-Century Lives.* Cambridge, MA: Harvard University Press, 1995.

DeJean, Joan. *Ancients Against Moderns: Culture Wars and the Making of a Fin de Siècle.* Chicago: University of Chicago Press, 1997.

———. *Fictions of Sappho, 1546–1937.* Chicago: University of Chicago Press, 1989.

———. *The Reinvention of Obscenity: Sex, Lies, and Tabloids in Early Modern France.* Chicago: University of Chicago Press, 2002.

———. *Tender Geographies: Women and the Origins of the Novel in France.* New York: Columbia University Press, 1991.

Dictionary of Russian Women Writers. Edited by Marina Ledkovsky, Charlotte Rosenthal, and Mary Zirin. Westport, CT: Greenwood Press, 1994.

Dixon, Laurinda S. *Perilous Chastity: Women and Illness in Pre-Enlightenment Art and Medicine.* Ithaca: Cornell Universitiy Press, 1995.

Dolan, Frances, E. *Whores of Babylon: Catholicism, Gender and Seventeenth-Century Print Culture.* Ithaca: Cornell University Press, 1999.

Donovan, Josephine. *Women and the Rise of the Novel, 1405–1726.* New York: St. Martin's Press, 1999.

De Erauso, Catalina. *Lieutenant Nun: Memoir of a Basque Transvestite in the New World.* Translated by Michele Ttepto and Gabriel Stepto; foreword by Marjorie Garber. Boston: Beacon Press, 1995.

Encyclopedia of Continental Women Writers. 2 vols. Edited by Katharina Wilson. New York: Garland, 1991.

Erdmann, Axel. *My Gracious Silence: Women in the Mirror of Sixteenth-Century Printing in Western Europe.* Luzern: Gilhofer and Rauschberg, 1999.

Erickson, Amy Louise. *Women and Property in Early Modern England.* London: Routledge, 1993.

Ezell, Margaret J. M. *The Patriarch's Wife: Literary Evidence and the History of the Family.* Chapel Hill: University of North Carolina Press, 1987.

———. *Social Authorship and the Advent of Print.* Baltimore: Johns Hopkins University Press, 1999.

———. *Writing Women's Literary History.* Baltimore: Johns Hopkins University Press, 1993.

Farrell, Michèle Longino. *Performing Motherhood: The Sévigné Correspondence.* Hanover, NH: University Press of New England, 1991.

The Feminist Companion to Literature in English: Women Writers from the Middle Ages to the Present. Edited by Virginia Blain, Isobel Grundy, and Patricia Clements. New Haven, CT: Yale University Press, 1990.

The Feminist Encyclopedia of German Literature. Edited by Friederike Eigler and Susanne Kord. Westport, CT: Greenwood Press, 1997.

Feminist Encyclopedia of Italian Literature. Edited by Rinaldina Russell. Westport, CT: Greenwood Press, 1997.

Ferguson, Margaret W. *Dido's Daughters: Literacy, Gender, and Empire in Early Modern England and France.* Chicago: University of Chicago Press, 2003.

Ferguson, Margaret W., Maureen Quilligan, and Nancy J. Vickers, eds. *Rewriting the Renaissance: The Discourses of Sexual Difference in Early Modern Europe.* Chicago: University of Chicago Press, 1987.

Ferraro, Joanne M. *Marriage Wars in Late Renaissance Venice.* Oxford: Oxford University Press, 2001.

Fletcher, Anthony. *Gender, Sex and Subordination in England 1500–1800.* New Haven, CT: Yale University Press, 1995.

French Women Writers: A Bio-Bibliographical Source Book. Edited by Eva Martin Sartori and Dorothy Wynne Zimmerman. Westport, CT: Greenwood Press, 1991.

Frye, Susan and Karen Robertson, eds. *Maids and Mistresses, Cousins and Queens: Women's Alliances in Early Modern England.* Oxford: Oxford University Press, 1999.

Gallagher, Catherine. *Nobody's Story: The Vanishing Acts of Women Writers in the Marketplace, 1670–1820.* Berkeley: University of California Press, 1994.

Garrard, Mary D. *Artemisia Gentileschi: The Image of the Female Hero in Italian Baroque Art.* Princeton, NJ: Princeton University Press, 1989.

Gelbart, Nina Rattner. *The King's Midwife: A History and Mystery of Madame du Coudray.* Berkeley: University of California Press, 1998.

Glenn, Cheryl. *Rhetoric Retold: Regendering the Tradition from Antiquity through the Renaissance.* Carbondale: Southern Illinois University Press, 1997.

Goffen, Rona. *Titian's Women.* New Haven, CT: Yale University Press, 1997.

Goldberg, Jonathan. *Desiring Women Writing: English Renaissance Examples.* Stanford: Stanford University Press, 1997.

Goldsmith, Elizabeth C. *Exclusive Conversations: The Art of Interaction in Seventeenth-Century France.* Philadelphia: University of Pennsylvania Press, 1988.

———, ed. *Writing the Female Voice.* Boston: Northeastern University Press, 1989.

Goldsmith, Elizabeth C., and Dena Goodman, eds. *Going Public: Women and Publishing in Early Modern France.* Ithaca: Cornell University Press, 1995.

Grafton, Anthony, and Lisa Jardine. *From Humanism to the Humanities: Education and the Liberal Arts in Fifteenth-and Sixteenth-Century Europe.* London: Duckworth, 1986.

Greer, Margaret Rich. *Maria de Zayas Tells Baroque Tales of Love and the Cruelty of Men.* University Park: Pennsylvania State University Press, 2000.

Hackett, Helen. *Women and Romance Fiction in the English Renaissance.* Cambridge: Cambridge University Press, 2000.

Hall, Kim F. *Things of Darkness: Economies of Race and Gender in Early Modern England.* Ithaca, NY: Cornell University Press, 1995.

Hampton, Timothy. *Literature and the Nation in the Sixteenth Century: Inventing Renaissance France.* Ithaca, NY: Cornell University Press, 2001.

Hannay, Margaret, ed. *Silent But for the Word.* Kent, OH: Kent State University Press, 1985.

Hardwick, Julie. *The Practice of Patriarchy: Gender and the Politics of Household Authority in Early Modern France.* University Park: Pennsylvania State University Press, 1998.

Harris, Barbara J. *English Aristocratic Women, 1450–1550: Marriage and Family, Property and Careers.* New York: Oxford University Press, 2002.

Harth, Erica. *Ideology and Culture in Seventeenth-Century France.* Ithaca: Cornell University Press, 1983.

———. *Cartesian Women: Versions and Subversions of Rational Discourse in the Old Regime.* Ithaca: Cornell University Press, 1992.

Harvey, Elizabeth D. *Ventriloquized Voices: Feminist Theory and English Renaissance Texts.* London: Routledge, 1992.

Haselkorn, Anne M., and Betty Travitsky, eds. *The Renaissance Englishwoman in Print: Counterbalancing the Canon.* Amherst: University of Massachusetts Press, 1990.

Herlihy, David. "Did Women Have a Renaissance? A Reconsideration." *Medievalia et Humanistica,* NS 13 (1985): 1–22.

Hill, Bridget. *The Republican Virago: The Life and Times of Catharine Macaulay, Historian.* New York: Oxford University Press, 1992.

A History of Central European Women's Writing. Edited by Celia Hawkesworth. New York: Palgrave Press, 2001.

A History of Women in the West.

    Volume 1: *From Ancient Goddesses to Christian Saints.* Edited by Pauline Schmitt Pantel. Cambridge, MA: Harvard University Press, 1992.

    Volume 2: *Silences of the Middle Ages.* Edited by Christiane Klapisch-Zuber. Cambridge, MA: Harvard University Press, 1992.

    Volume 3: *Renaissance and Enlightenment Paradoxes.* Edited by Natalie Zemon Davis and Arlette Farge. Cambridge, MA: Harvard University Press, 1993.

A History of Women Philosophers. Edited by Mary Ellen Waithe. 3 vols. Dordrecht: Martinus Nijhoff, 1987.

A History of Women's Writing in France. Edited by Sonya Stephens. Cambridge: Cambridge University Press, 2000.

A History of Women's Writing in Germany, Austria and Switzerland. Edited by Jo Catling. Cambridge: Cambridge University Press, 2000.

A History of Women's Writing in Italy. Edited by Letizia Panizza and Sharon Wood. Cambridge: University Press, 2000.

A History of Women's Writing in Russia. Edited by Alele Marie Barker and Jehanne M. Gheith. Cambridge: Cambridge University Press, 2002.

Hobby, Elaine. *Virtue of Necessity: English Women's Writing 1646–1688.* London: Virago Press, 1988.

Horowitz, Maryanne Cline. "Aristotle and Women." *Journal of the History of Biology* 9 (1976): 183–213.

Howell, Martha. *The Marriage Exchange: Property, Social Place, and Gender in Cities of the Low Countries, 1300–1550.* Chicago: University of Chicago Press, 1998.

Hufton, Olwen H. *The Prospect Before Her: A History of Women in Western Europe, 1: 1500–1800.* New York: HarperCollins, 1996.

Hull, Suzanne W. *Chaste, Silent, and Obedient: English Books for Women, 1475–1640*. San Marino, CA: The Huntington Library, 1982.

Hunt, Lynn, ed. *The Invention of Pornography: Obscenity and the Origins of Modernity, 1500–1800*. New York: Zone Books, 1996.

Hutner, Heidi, ed. *Rereading Aphra Behn: History, Theory, and Criticism*. Charlottesville: University Press of Virginia, 1993.

Hutson, Lorna, ed. *Feminism and Renaissance Studies*. New York: Oxford University Press, 1999.

Italian Women Writers: A Bio-Bibliographical Sourcebook. Edited by Rinaldina Russell. Westport, CT: Greenwood Press, 1994.

Jaffe, Irma B., with Gernando Colombardo. *Shining Eyes, Cruel Fortune: The Lives and Loves of Italian Renaissance Women Poets*. New York: Fordham University Press, 2002.

James, Susan E. *Kateryn Parr: The Making of a Queen*. Aldershot: Ashgate, 1999.

Jankowski, Theodora A. *Women in Power in the Early Modern Drama*. Urbana: University of Illinois Press, 1992.

Jansen, Katherine Ludwig. *The Making of the Magdalen: Preaching and Popular Devotion in the Later Middle Ages*. Princeton, NJ: Princeton University Press, 2000.

Jed, Stephanie H. *Chaste Thinking: The Rape of Lucretia and the Birth of Humanism*. Bloomington: Indiana University Press, 1989.

Jordan, Constance. *Renaissance Feminism: Literary Texts and Political Models*. Ithaca: Cornell University Press, 1990.

Kagan, Richard L. *Lucrecia's Dreams: Politics and Prophecy in Sixteenth-Century Spain*. Berkeley: University of California Press, 1990.

Kehler, Dorothea and Laurel Amtower, eds. *The Single Woman in Medieval and Early Modern England: Her Life and Representation*. Tempe, AZ: MRTS, 2002.

Kelly, Joan. "Did Women Have a Renaissance?" In her *Women, History, and Theory*. Chicago: University of Chicago Press, 1984. Also in Renate Bridenthal, Claudia Koonz, and Susan M. Stuard, eds., *Becoming Visible: Women in European History*. 3rd ed. Boston: Houghton Mifflin, 1998.

———. "Early Feminist Theory and the *Querelle des Femmes*." In *Women, History, and Theory*.

Kelso, Ruth. *Doctrine for the Lady of the Renaissance*. Foreword by Katharine M. Rogers. Urbana: University of Illinois Press, 1956, 1978.

King, Catherine E. *Renaissance Women Patrons: Wives and Widows in Italy, c. 1300–1550*. Manchester: Manchester University Press (distributed in the U.S. by St. Martin's Press), 1998.

King, Margaret L. *Women of the Renaissance*. Foreword by Catharine R. Stimpson. Chicago: University of Chicago Press, 1991.

Krontiris, Tina. *Oppositional Voices: Women as Writers and Translators of Literature in the English Renaissance*. London: Routledge, 1992.

Kuehn, Thomas. *Law, Family, and Women: Toward a Legal Anthropology of Renaissance Italy*. Chicago: University of Chicago Press, 1991.

Kunze, Bonnelyn Young. *Margaret Fell and the Rise of Quakerism*. Stanford: Stanford University Press, 1994.

Labalme, Patricia A., ed. *Beyond Their Sex: Learned Women of the European Past*. New York: New York University Press, 1980.

Laqueur, Thomas. *Making Sex: Body and Gender from the Greeks to Freud.* Cambridge, MA: Harvard University Press, 1990.

Larsen, Anne R. and Colette H. Winn, eds. *Renaissance Women Writers: French Texts/American Contexts.* Detroit, MI: Wayne State University Press, 1994.

Lerner, Gerda. *The Creation of Patriarchy* and *Creation of Feminist Consciousness, 1000–1870.* 2 vols. New York: Oxford University Press, 1986, 1994.

Levin, Carole, and Jeanie Watson, eds. *Ambiguous Realities: Women in the Middle Ages and Renaissance.* Detroit: Wayne State University Press, 1987.

Levin, Carole, et al. *Extraordinary Women of the Medieval and Renaissance World: A Biographical Dictionary.* Westport, CT: Greenwood Press, 2000.

Lewalsky, Barbara Kiefer. *Writing Women in Jacobean England.* Cambridge, MA: Harvard University Press, 1993.

Lewis, Jayne Elizabeth. *Mary Queen of Scots: Romance and Nation.* London: Routledge, 1998.

Lindsey, Karen. *Divorced Beheaded Survived: A Feminist Reinterpretation of the Wives of Henry VIII.* Reading, MA: Addison-Wesley, 1995.

Lochrie, Karma. *Margery Kempe and Translations of the Flesh.* Philadelphia: University of Pennsylvania Press, 1992.

Lougee, Carolyn C. *Le Paradis des Femmes: Women, Salons, and Social Stratification in Seventeenth-Century France.* Princeton, NJ: Princeton University Press, 1976.

Love, Harold. *The Culture and Commerce of Texts: Scribal Publication in Seventeenth-Century England.* Amherst: University of Massachusetts Press, 1993.

MacCarthy, Bridget G. *The Female Pen: Women Writers and Novelists, 1621–1818.* Preface by Janet Todd. New York: New York University Press, 1994. Originally published 1946–47 by Cork University Press.

Maclean, Ian. *Woman Triumphant: Feminism in French Literature, 1610–1652.* Oxford: Clarendon Press, 1977.

———. *The Renaissance Notion of Woman: A Study of the Fortunes of Scholasticism and Medical Science in European Intellectual Life.* Cambridge: Cambridge University Press, 1980.

MacNeil, Anne. *Music and Women of the Commedia dell'Arte in the Late Sixteenth Century.* New York: Oxford University Press, 2003.

Maggi, Armando. *Uttering the Word: The Mystical Performances of Maria Maddalena de' Pazzi, a Renaissance Visionary.* Albany: State University of New York Press, 1998.

Marshall, Sherrin. *Women in Reformation and Counter-Reformation Europe: Public and Private Worlds.* Bloomington: Indiana University Press, 1989.

Masten, Jeffrey. *Textual Intercourse: Collaboration, Authorship, and Sexualities in Renaissance Drama.* Cambridge: Cambridge University Press, 1997.

Matter, E. Ann, and John Coakley, eds. *Creative Women in Medieval and Early Modern Italy.* Philadelphia: University of Pennsylvania Press, 1994. (Sequel to the Monson collection, below.)

McLeod, Glenda. *Virtue and Venom: Catalogs of Women from Antiquity to the Renaissance.* Ann Arbor: University of Michigan Press, 1991.

Medwick, Cathleen. *Teresa of Avila: The Progress of a Soul.* New York: Knopf, 2000.

Meek, Christine, ed. *Women in Renaissance and Early Modern Europe.* Dublin-Portland: Four Courts Press, 2000.

Mendelson, Sara and Patricia Crawford. *Women in Early Modern England, 1550–1720.* Oxford: Clarendon Press, 1998.

Merchant, Carolyn. *The Death of Nature: Women, Ecology, and the Scientific Revolution.* New York: HarperCollins, 1980.

Merrim, Stephanie. *Early Modern Women's Writing and Sor Juana Inés de la Cruz.* Nashville, TN: Vanderbilt University Press, 1999.

Messbarger, Rebecca. *The Century of Women: The Representations of Women in Eighteenth-Century Italian Public Discourse.* Toronto: University of Toronto Press, 2002.

Miller, Nancy K. *The Heroine's Text: Readings in the French and English Novel, 1722–1782.* New York: Columbia University Press, 1980.

Miller, Naomi J. *Changing the Subject: Mary Wroth and Figurations of Gender in Early Modern England.* Lexington: University Press of Kentucky, 1996.

Miller, Naomi J., and Gary Waller, eds. *Reading Mary Wroth: Representing Alternatives in Early Modern England.* Knoxville: University of Tennessee Press, 1991.

Monson, Craig A., ed. *The Crannied Wall: Women, Religion, and the Arts in Early Modern Europe.* Ann Arbor: University of Michigan Press, 1992.

Musacchio, Jacqueline Marie. *The Art and Ritual of Childbirth in Renaissance Italy.* New Haven, CT: Yale University Press, 1999.

Newman, Barbara. *God and the Goddesses: Vision, Poetry, and Belief in the Middle Ages.* Philadelphia: University of Pennsylvania Press, 2003.

Newman, Karen. *Fashioning Femininity and English Renaissance Drama.* Chicago: University of Chicago Press, 1991.

Okin, Susan Moller. *Women in Western Political Thought.* Princeton, NJ: Princeton University Press, 1979.

Ozment, Steven. *The Bürgermeister's Daughter: Scandal in a Sixteenth-Century German Town.* New York: St. Martin's Press, 1995.

Pacheco, Anita, ed. *Early [English] Women Writers: 1600–1720.* New York: Longman, 1998.

Pagels, Elaine. *Adam, Eve, and the Serpent.* New York: HarperCollins, 1988.

Panizza, Letizia, ed. *Women in Italian Renaissance Culture and Society.* Oxford: European Humanities Research Centre, 2000.

Parker, Patricia. *Literary Fat Ladies: Rhetoric, Gender, and Property.* London: Methuen, 1987.

Pernoud, Regine, and Marie-Veronique Clin. *Joan of Arc: Her Story.* Revised and translated by Jeremy DuQuesnay Adams. New York: St. Martin's Press, 1998 (French original, 1986).

Perry, Mary Elizabeth. *Crime and Society in Early Modern Seville.* Hanover, NH: University Press of New England, 1980.

———. *Gender and Disorder in Early Modern Seville.* Princeton, NJ: Princeton University Press, 1990.

Perry, Ruth. *The Celebrated Mary Astell: An Early English Feminist.* Chicago: University of Chicago Press, 1986.

Petroff, Elizabeth Alvilda, ed. *Medieval Women's Visionary Literature.* New York: Oxford University Press, 1986.

Rabil, Albert. *Laura Cereta: Quattrocento Humanist.* Binghamton, NY: MRTS, 1981.

Ranft, Patricia. *Women in Western Intellectual Culture, 600–1500.* New York: Palgrave, 2002.

Rapley, Elizabeth. *A Social History of the Cloister: Daily Life in the Teaching Monasteries of the Old Regime.* Montreal: McGill-Queen's University Press, 2001.

Raven, James, Helen Small, and Naomi Tadmor, eds. *The Practice and Representation of Reading in England.* Cambridge: University Press, 1996.

Reardon, Colleen. *Holy Concord within Sacred Walls: Nuns and Music in Siena, 1575–1700.* Oxford: Oxford University Press, 2001.

Reiss, Sheryl E., and David G. Wilkins, ed. *Beyond Isabella: Secular Women Patrons of Art in Renaissance Italy.* Kirksville, MO: Truman State University Press, 2001.

Rheubottom, David. *Age, Marriage, and Politics in Fifteenth-Century Ragusa.* Oxford: Oxford University Press, 2000.

Richardson, Brian. *Printing, Writers and Readers in Renaissance Italy.* Cambridge: University Press, 1999.

Riddle, John M. *Contraception and Abortion from the Ancient World to the Renaissance.* Cambridge, MA: Harvard University Press, 1992.

———. *Eve's Herbs: A History of Contraception and Abortion in the West.* Cambridge, MA: Harvard University Press, 1997.

Rose, Mary Beth. *The Expense of Spirit: Love and Sexuality in English Renaissance Drama.* Ithaca, NY: Cornell University Press, 1988.

———. *Gender and Heroism in Early Modern English Literature.* Chicago: University of Chicago Press, 2002.

———, ed. *Women in the Middle Ages and the Renaissance: Literary and Historical Perspectives.* Syracuse: Syracuse University Press, 1986.

Rosenthal, Margaret F. *The Honest Courtesan: Veronica Franco, Citizen and Writer in Sixteenth-Century Venice.* Foreword by Catharine R. Stimpson. Chicago: University of Chicago Press, 1992.

Sackville-West, Vita. *Daughter of France: The Life of La Grande Mademoiselle.* Garden City, NY: Doubleday, 1959.

Sánchez, Magdalena S. *The Empress, the Queen, and the Nun: Women and Power at the Court of Philip III of Spain.* Baltimore: Johns Hopkins University Press, 1998.

Schiebinger, Londa. *The Mind Has No Sex? Women in the Origins of Modern Science.* Cambridge, MA: Harvard University Press, 1991.

———. *Nature's Body: Gender in the Making of Modern Science.* Boston: Beacon Press, 1993.

Schutte, Anne Jacobson, Thomas Kuehn, and Silvana Seidel Menchi, eds. *Time, Space, and Women's Lives in Early Modern Europe.* Kirksville, MO: Truman State University Press, 2001.

Schofield, Mary Anne, and Cecilia Macheski, eds. *Fetter'd or Free? British Women Novelists, 1670–1815.* Athens: Ohio University Press, 1986.

Shannon, Laurie. *Sovereign Amity: Figures of Friendship in Shakespearean Contexts.* Chicago: University of Chicago Press, 2002.

Shemek, Deanna. *Ladies Errant: Wayward Women and Social Order in Early Modern Italy.* Durham, NC: Duke University Press, 1998.

Smith, Hilda L. *Reason's Disciples: Seventeenth-Century English Feminists.* Urbana: University of Illinois Press, 1982.

———. *Women Writers and the Early Modern British Political Tradition.* Cambridge: Cambridge University Press, 1998.

Sobel, Dava. *Galileo's Daughter: A Historical Memoir of Science, Faith, and Love.* New York: Penguin, 2000.

Sommerville, Margaret R. *Sex and Subjection: Attitudes to Women in Early-Modern Society.* London: Arnold, 1995.

Soufas, Teresa Scott. *Dramas of Distinction: A Study of Plays by Golden Age Women.* Lexington: The University Press of Kentucky, 1997.

Spencer, Jane. *The Rise of the Woman Novelist: From Aphra Behn to Jane Austen.* Oxford: Basil Blackwell, 1986.

Spender, Dale. *Mothers of the Novel: 100 Good Women Writers Before Jane Austen.* London: Routledge, 1986.

Sperling, Jutta Gisela. *Convents and the Body Politic in Late Renaissance Venice.* Foreword by Catharine R. Stimpson. Chicago: University of Chicago Press, 1999.

Steinbrügge, Lieselotte. *The Moral Sex: Woman's Nature in the French Enlightenment.* Translated by Pamela E. Selwyn. New York: Oxford University Press, 1995.

Stocker, Margarita. *Judith, Sexual Warrior: Women and Power in Western Culture.* New Haven, CT: Yale University Press, 1998.

Stretton, Timothy. *Women Waging Law in Elizabethan England.* Cambridge: Cambridge University Press, 1998.

Stuard, Susan M. "The Dominion of Gender: Women's Fortunes in the High Middle Ages." In*Becoming Visible: Women in European History,* edited by Renate Bridenthal, Claudia Koonz, and Susan M. Stuard. 3rd ed. Boston: Houghton Mifflin, 1998.

Summit, Jennifer. *Lost Property: The Woman Writer and English Literary History, 1380–1589.* Chicago: University of Chicago Press, 2000.

Surtz, Ronald E. *The Guitar of God: Gender, Power, and Authority in the Visionary World of Mother Juana de la Cruz (1481–1534).* Philadelphia: University of Pennsylvania Press, 1991.

———. *Writing Women in Late Medieval and Early Modern Spain: The Mothers of Saint Teresa of Avila.* Philadelphia: University of Pennsylvania Press, 1995.

Teague, Frances. *Bathsua Makin, Woman of Learning.* Lewisburg, PA: Bucknell University Press, 1999.

Tinagli, Paola. *Women in Italian Renaissance Art: Gender, Representation, Identity.* Manchester: Manchester University Press, 1997.

Todd, Janet. *The Secret Life of Aphra Behn.* London: Pandora, 2000.

———. *The Sign of Angelica: Women, Writing and Fiction, 1660–1800.* New York: Columbia University Press, 1989.

Valenze, Deborah. *The First Industrial Woman.* New York: Oxford University Press, 1995.

Van Dijk, Susan, Lia van Gemert, and Sheila Ottway, eds. *Writing the History of Women's Writing: Toward an International Approach.* Proceedings of the Colloquium, Amsterdam, 9–11 September. Amsterdam: Royal Netherlands Academy of Arts and Sciences, 2001.

Vickery, Amanda. *The Gentleman's Daughter: Women's Lives in Georgian England.* New Haven, CT: Yale University Press, 1998.

Vollendorf, Lisa, ed. *Recovering Spain's Feminist Tradition.* New York: MLA, 2001.

Walker, Claire. *Gender and Politics in Early Modern Europe: English Convents in France and the Low Countries.* New York: Palgrave, 2003.

Wall, Wendy. *The Imprint of Gender: Authorship and Publication in the English Renaissance.* Ithaca, NY: Cornell University Press, 1993.

Walsh, William T. *St. Teresa of Avila: A Biography.* Rockford, IL: TAN, 1987.

Warner, Marina. *Alone of All Her Sex: The Myth and Cult of the Virgin Mary.* New York: Knopf, 1976.

Warnicke, Retha M. *The Marrying of Anne of Cleves: Royal Protocol in Tudor England.* Cambridge: Cambridge University Press, 2000.

Watt, Diane. *Secretaries of God: Women Prophets in Late Medieval and Early Modern England.* Cambridge: D. S. Brewer, 1997.

Weber, Alison. *Teresa of Avila and the Rhetoric of Femininity.* Princeton, NJ: Princeton University Press, 1990.

Welles, Marcia L. *Persephone's Girdle: Narratives of Rape in Seventeenth-Century Spanish Literature.* Nashville: Vanderbilt University Press, 2000.

Whitehead, Barbara J., ed. *Women's Education in Early Modern Europe: A History, 1500–1800.* New York: Garland, 1999.

Wiesner, Merry E. *Women and Gender in Early Modern Europe.* Cambridge: Cambridge University Press, 1993.

———. *Working Women in Renaissance Germany.* New Brunswick, NJ: Rutgers University Press, 1986.

Willard, Charity Cannon. *Christine de Pizan: Her Life and Works.* New York: Persea Books, 1984.

Winn, Colette and Donna Kuizenga, eds. *Women Writers in Pre-Revolutionary France.* New York: Garland, 1997.

Woodbridge, Linda. *Women and the English Renaissance: Literature and the Nature of Womankind, 1540–1620.* Urbana: University of Illinois Press, 1984.

Woods, Susanne. *Lanyer: A Renaissance Woman Poet.* New York: Oxford University Press, 1999.

Woods, Susanne, and Margaret P. Hannay, eds. *Teaching Tudor and Stuart Women Writers.* New York: MLA, 2000.

INDEX